Bṛhad Bhāgavatāmṛta
Canto I

Finding the Essence of the Supreme Lord's Mercy

With Dig-darśinī Commentary

By
Śrīla Sanātana Gosvāmī

Translated into English by
HH Bhanu Swami

Readers interested in the subject matter of this book are invited by the publishers to correspond at the following address:

His Holiness Bhanu Swami
ISKCON
Hare Krishna Land (off ECR),
Bhaktivedanta Swami Road,
Akkarai,
Sholinganallur,
Chennai- 600 119.

For any feedback or queries please contact the below email id.
Email: bhanuswamibooks@gmail.com
Web: www.bhanuswami.org

First paperback edition: July 2019
ISBN: 978-10-9642-294-5

Published by: Tattva Cintāmaṇi Publishing

Book cover picture: V.V.Sapar
Book cover design: Mohinī Mādhavī Devī Dāsī

Dedication

This book is dedicated to

His Divine Grace A.C. Bhaktivedānta Svāmī Prabhupāda
Founder-Ācārya of International Society for Krishna Consciousness

who inspired the world to take up the path of bhakti.

FOREWORD

This volume answers the question "Who receives the greatest mercy of Kṛṣna?" The answer is illustrated through a story. Nārada visits various persons in this planet and higher planets in order to find the answer, and each person indicates some devotee who has received greater mercy. The end of the quest indicates the conclusion of Gauḍīya philosophy and Caitanya Mahāprabhu's teachings.

TABLE OF CONTENTS

Chapter One

Bhauma: On the Earth

TEXT 1

jayati nija-padābja-prema-dānāvatīrṇo
vividha-madhurimābdhiḥ ko 'pi kaiśora-gandhiḥ
gata-parama-daśāntaṁ yasya caitanya-rūpād
anubhava-padam āptaṁ prema gopīṣu nityam

All glories to the Lord who descended to bestow prema for his own lotus feet. He is an ocean of various sweetnesses, and has the fragrance of indescribable youth. In his form as Śrī Caitanya he has attained the highest limits of transcendental experience of the love eternally residing in the gopīs.

I offer respects to Bhakti-devī, who fulfils all human goals, who bestows bliss superior to Brahman realization, who frees one from material objects, whose greater shelter is the lotus feet of Rādhā-Ramaṇa, and whose actions are performed with great prema which is similar to that of the people of Vraja.

I offer respects to Caitanya Mahāprabhu who relishes the name of Kṛṣṇa, and whom I serve with devotion by taking shelter of his lotus feet.

I write this commentary called Dig-darśinī in order to show partially the intended meaning of the verses.

In this work, bhakti for the Lord, which gives dharma, artha, kāma and mokṣa is described; but it gives much more happiness than the realization of Brahman. This bhakti should be directed to the lotus feet of Kṛṣṇa, and with the most intense, unmotivated prema, like that of the people of Vraja. It will later be shown that those persons with such bhakti attain constant, unrestricted pastimes with Kṛṣṇa in Goloka above Vaikuṇṭha. All this will be explained in detail in the appropriate place later.

The author invokes auspiciousness, as if requesting great mercy, with a description of the excellence of the most dear, astonishing Kṛṣṇa.

The word jayati means "He exists with the highest excellence." Excellence means to attain the highest limit, without restrictions. Even to the most fallen people, he gives bhakti and even prema to his lotus feet. Those lotus feet produce excellence in all hearts by manifesting the sweetness of his extraordinary form, qualities and pastimes.

His identity is then explained with details. He is indescribable (ko' pi). He is an unfathomable, limitless, constant shelter of various types of sweetness concerning his form, qualities, etc.

The sweetness of his form is described. He has a constant contact with kaiśora age. Even when an infant or when a youth, he is always ornamented with kaiśora, since the beauty of his most attractive kaiśora never leaves him.

In Bhāgavatam Kapila says:

apīcya-darśanaṁ śaśvat sarva-loka-namaskṛtam
santaṁ vayasi kaiśore bhṛtyānugraha-kātaram

He is beautiful, and worshipped by all people. He is eternally fifteen years old and eager to bless his servants. SB 3.28.17

"Kṛṣṇa plays in Goloka, situated above Vaikuṇṭha since he is very difficult to attain. The great mercy described in glorification of bhakti is also difficult to attain. Thus, efforts to attain him are useless."

In answer to this, first his compassion is described in order to show sweetness of his qualities. He has appeared on earth in Mathurā from Goloka in order to bestow prema for his lotus feet. Thus his mercy and Kṛṣṇa himself are easy to attain. Though he appeared in order to kill Kaṁsa and others, that is partially his goal. His main goal is to give prema in an extraordinary manner. In Kunti's prayers it is said:

tathā paramahaṁsānāṁ
munīnām amalātmanām
bhakti-yoga-vidhānārthaṁ
kathaṁ paśyema hi striyaḥ

How can we women hope to see you, who have appeared to give bhakti to the omniscient, liberated sages? SB 1.8.20

Śrīdhara Svāmī explains this: "How can we women see you, who have appeared to give bhakti to the ātmārāmas by attracting them with your qualities?"

Thus first this quality of mercy is stated and then his qualities of sweetness are listed. His extraordinary nature is then indicated by mentioning his sweet pastimes in the last half of the verse. He is the object of constant love of the gopīs. This is also the meaning of the ten-syllable mantra. In the description of Goloka the glories of that love will be explained. This prema attained the highest limits (gata-parama-daśāntam). Since he appeared on earth to give that prema, by his mercy others also had that prema. He had prema for them, but the gopīs are glorified as the greatest.

Though those who have prema for Kṛṣṇa become the object of his prema, according to the intensity of their prema, his prema corresponds. But the gopīs are the objects of his eternal pure prema. The great position of these eternal beloveds is naturally manifested.

Is his love constant (nityam) to them? He seems to sometimes show indifference to them. This will become clear in the words of Nārada and others in the glorification of Goloka.

"If they are in that condition, how can one comprehend their prema, since it is beyond the material mind?" That is true, but it can be understood by the power of his avatāra. Because of the avatāra Caitanya Mahāprabhu, that eternal prema is attained as the object of knowledge or experience (anubhava).

The meaning is this. Though Catianya-deva is an avatāra of the Lord, the Lord himself manifests the prema of the gopīs within himself in order to reveal the gopīs' special prema. By the special prema for Kṛṣṇa shown by Caitanya, who manifested this prema constantly, one can understand the gopīs prema for Kṛṣṇa. And all fallen people of the present world can realize directly the Lord's love for the gopīs by the influence of Caitanya Mahāprabhu, the friend of the suffering and low people.

By proving the excellence of the gopīs' love, the supreme excellence of Kṛṣṇa is also proved. This indicates the goal of this work. By describing the objects of the Lord's mercy and ultimately by explaining the greatness of the gopīs, the Lord's (and his intimate devotees') special prema for them is also shown.

By realization through Caitanya's mercy, it is not impossible to describe this. One should not doubt this. With faith, all devotees should hear this work.

TEXT 2

śrī-rādhikā-prabhṛtayo nitarāṁ jayanti
gopyo nitānta-bhagavat-priyatā-prasiddhāḥ
yāsāṁ harau parama-sauhṛda-mādhurīṇāṁ
nirvaktum īṣad api jātu na ko 'pi śaktaḥ

May all the gopīs, headed by Śrī Rādhikā, who are famous as the Lord's dearmost devotees, remain ever excellent. No one even has the power to begin describing the exhalted sweetness of their affection for Kṛṣṇa.

Mercy of the Lord is attained by gaining the mercy of his dearest devotees. The excellence of these devotees is described. Since Rādhā is the greatest devotee, she and others of similar nature are described. May these gopīs remain ever (nitarām) excellent.

Kṛṣṇa sometimes seems to ignore them, from ordinary perspective and thus his excellence is not perfect at all times in all places, from all points of view. But they are not like that. Their excellence is realized at all times in all places by all people. He says to them:

na pāraye 'haṁ niravadya-saṁyujāṁ
sva-sādhu-kṛtyaṁ vibudhāyuṣāpi vaḥ
yā mābhajan durjara-geha-śṛṅkhalāḥ
saṁvṛścya tad vaḥ pratiyātu sādhunā

I am not able to repay my debt for your spotless service, even within a lifetime of Brahmā. Your connection with me is beyond reproach. You have worshiped me, cutting off all domestic ties, which are difficult to break. Therefore, please let your own glorious deeds be your compensation. SB 10.32.22

Because these beloveds had attained the highest, deepest love, they are famous as the shelter of prema. And because they are famous for that, there is no need of proving it. The cause of love is described with great joy and devotion. Not even Kṛṣṇa, what to speak of others, can describe at any time, even a little among the various types of sweetness of their exalted prema (sauhṛdam) for most attractive Kṛṣṇa (harau). This verse shows the special, eternal prema mutually exchanged between Kṛṣṇa and the gopīs.

TEXT 3

sva-dayita-nija-bhāvaṁ yo vibhāvya sva-bhāvāt
su-madhuram avatīrṇo bhakta-rūpeṇa lobhāt
jayati kanaka-dhāmā kṛṣṇa-caitanya-nāmā
harir iha yati-veśaḥ śrī-śacī-sūnur eṣaḥ

Perceiving that the ecstasy of his beloved devotees is sweeter than his own, the Lord, out of greed, advented in the form of his own devotee. All glories to that Lord Hari, who has a golden lustre, who bears the

name Śrī Kṛṣṇa Caitanya, who has the dress of a renunciant in this world, and who is the son of Mother Śacī!

How is it possible to begin describing such exalted love? The answer was already given and in order to obtain his mercy, it is repeated by describing the great excellence of the greatest guru, Caitanya Mahāprabhu, who was the deliverer of the most fallen souls, and who distributed the rasa of bhakti through saṅkīrtana of his name, and who descended as his dearest devotee.

Considering that the extraordinary prema of his dear gopīs was sweeter than his own prema for his devotees (sva-bhāvāt), out of greed for that prema, he appeared as his own devotee on earth in Navadvīpa, Bengal. The Lord, the son of Śacī, remains ever excellent (jayati).

What is his description? He has a complexion like gold (kanaka-dhāmā). In other words, he is Gaura-sundara. The word eṣaḥ (this person, standing here) indicates that he can be directly realized at this very moment. Previously, Kṛṣṇa was not able to describe their love. Now, in the avatāra of his devotee, he made people realize the love of the gopīs. That is the excellence of this avatāra.

nirapekṣaṁ muniṁ śāntaṁ
nirvairaṁ sama-darśanam
anuvrajāmy ahaṁ nityaṁ
pūyeyety aṅghri-reṇubhiḥ

I always follow the footsteps of my pure devotees, who are free from all personal desire, are rapt in thought of my pastimes, are fixed in me, without any feelings of enmity, and are equal to all conditions of the world. Let me be purified by the dust from their feet! SB 11.14.16

This verse from Bhāgavatam shows that Kṛṣṇa considers his devotees greater than himself. This is made clear in the form of Caitanya Mahāprabhu. The word nitarām (always) is suitable for this verse also.

The words bhakta-rūpeṇa can also mean that Caitanya appeared along with Rūpa Gosvāmī, the son of Śrī-Kumāra, in a line of great ācāryas famous in Karnataka. Caitanya had the dress of a sannyāsī. He appeared as a devotee, not as a sannyāsī, but took up the dress of a sannyāsī in order to spread the rasa of bhakti to Kṛṣṇa. Acting as a devotee, he appeared as avatāra to spread everywhere in Kali-yuga prema-bhakti for the Lord, which is most rare.

This is explained by Sārvabhauma Bhaṭṭācārya:

kālān naṣṭaṁ bhakti-yogaṁ nijaṁ
yaḥ prāduṣkartuṁ kṛṣṇa-caitanya-nāmā
āvirbhūtas tasya pādāravinde
gāḍhaṁ gāḍhaṁ līyatāṁ citta-bhṛṅgaḥ

Let the bee of my heart merge deeply into the lotus feet of Kṛṣṇa Caitanya, who appeared in order to reveal bhakti for the Lord, which had disappeared for a long time.

TEXT 4

jayati mathurā-devī śreṣṭhā purīṣu mano-ramā
parama-dayitā kaṁsārāter jani-sthiti-rañjitā
durita-haraṇān mukter bhakter api pratipādanāj
jagati mahitā tat-tat-krīḍā-kathāstu vidūrataḥ

All glories to goddess Mathurā, the best of holy cities, enchanting to the mind, most dear to the enemy of Kaṁsa, and adorned with the Lord's birthplace! Let it remain great in this world, since it destroys misery, produces liberation and bhakti, what to speak of his various pastimes.

The attainment of such bhakti which fulfils all desires should take place in sacred Mathurā, since it is the supreme object of Kṛṣṇa's prema and Kṛṣṇa performs his pastimes continually in that place. With that intention the author praises Mathurā to gain its mercy. Devī means the supreme goddess (śakti of the Lord) or she who continually shines, since by her constant association with the Lord she is free of time, fear, etc.

Mathurā is the best among the seven cities like Kāśī, or among the abodes of the devatās in upper middle and lower realms, and even among abodes of the Lord, since it is most beautiful (manoramā), being ornamented with astonishing glories. Or the city gives delight to the minds (manoramā) of all people by fulfilling all their desires. It is said in Padma Purāṇa:

tri-varga-dā kāmināṁ yā
mumukṣūṇāṁ ca mokṣa-dā
bhaktīcchor bhakti-dā kas tāṁ
mathurāṁ nāśrayed budhaḥ

What intelligent person would not take shelter of Mathurā, which gives artha, dharma and kāma to those desiring those benedictions, which gives liberation to those desiring liberation and which gives bhakti to the person desiring bhakti.

Thus it is very dear (parama-dayitā) to Kṛṣṇa , the enemy of Kaṁsa (kaṁsārāteḥ). This name indicates Kṛṣṇa's great compassion, since by destroying Kaṁsa he freed the people of Mathurā from great suffering.

Mathurā is also the eternal place (sthitiḥ) of Kṛṣṇa's birth (jani).

rājadhānī tataḥ sābhūt
sarva-yādava-bhūbhujām
mathurā bhagavān yatra
nityaṁ sannihito hariḥ

Since that time, the city of Mathurā had been the capital of all the kings of the Yadu dynasty. The city and district of Mathurā are very intimately connected with Kṛṣṇa, for Kṛṣṇa lives there eternally. SB 10.1.28

Mathurā is made beautiful (rañjitā) by being his birth place. The place is worshipped by all in this world because it destroys sins and bestows liberation and bhakti. What to speak of the famous or indescribable pastimes that Kṛṣṇa performed there. Who can describe Mathurā's greatness caused by those pastimes?

The ability to destroy sin is described in the Purāṇas:

anyatra yat kṛtaṁ pāpaṁ
tīrtham āsādya naśyati
tīrthe tu yat kṛtaṁ pāpaṁ
vajra-lepo bhaviṣyati
mathurāyāṁ kṛtaṁ pāpaṁ
mathurāyāṁ vinaśyati
eṣā purī mahā-puṇyā
yatra pāpaṁ na tiṣṭhati

Sins committed outside a tīrtha are destroyed at that tīrtha but sins committed at the tīrtha produce a sin hard to remove. Sins committed at Mathurā are removed at Mathurā. This city is a powerful purifier, in which no sin can remain. Varāha Purāṇa

jñānato 'jñānato vāpi
yat pāpaṁ samuparjitam
su-kṛtaṁ duṣkṛtaṁ vāpi
mathurāyāṁ praṇaśyati

A sin committed knowingly or unknowingly, a sin or even a pious result, is destroyed at Mathurā. Varāha Purāṇa

kāśy-ādi-puryo yadi nāma santi
tāsāṁ tu madhye mathuraiva
dhanyā yā janma-mauñjī-
vrata-mṛtyu-dāhair nṛṇāṁ
caturdhā vidadhāti mokṣam

Though there are many famous cities, Mathurā is the best. Mathurā bestows liberation to men by four means: being born there, accepting the sacred thread there, dying there and being burned there.

anyeṣu puṇya-kṣetreṣu
muktir eva mahā-phalam
muktaiḥ prārthyā harer bhaktir
mathurāyāṁ hi labhyate

The greatest result in other holy places is liberation. But in Mathurā one can attain bhakti to the Lord, which is sought even by liberated souls.

TEXT 5

jayati jayati vṛndāraṇyam etan murāreḥ
priya-tamam ati-sādhu-svānta-vaikuṇṭha-vāsāt
ramayati sa sadā gāḥ pālayan yatra gopīḥ
svarita-madhura-veṇur vardhayan prema rāse

All glories, all glories to this Vṛndāvana forest, most dear to Lord Murāri! It is dearer to him than residing in Vaikuṇṭha or in the hearts of great devotees. There while tending his cows, he gives pleasure to the gopīs and increases their prema in the rāsa dance by sweetly playing his flute.

Within Mathurā is Vrajabhūmi, the place of astonishing, sweet pastimes of the Lord.

vṛndāvanaṁ govardhanaṁ yamunā-pulināni ca
vīkṣyāsīd uttamā prītī rāma-mādhavayor nṛpa

O King Parīkṣit, when Rāma and Kṛṣṇa saw Vṛndāvana, Govardhana and the banks of the River Yamunā, they both enjoyed great pleasure. SB 10.11.36

The three places mentioned are the dearest. Describing their excellence to obtain their mercy, the author first speaks of Vṛndāvana in this verse. Jayati is repeated out of great joy on understanding the greatness of the place. The word etat (this) indicates that the author lives in that place at the time of writing the verse. This Vṛndāvana is most dear to Kṛṣṇa. (murāreḥ). He prefers staying (vāsāt) in Vṛndāvana to residing in the hearts of great devotees or in Vaikuṇṭḥa, though these are also dwelling places of the Lord. Or it is dearer than (vāsāt) these attractive places. This is because it spreads sweet waves of sweet, spontaneous pastimes at all times.

This is not possible in other places. Even if he appears in those places, he does so in a covered manner (by aiśvarya). Nityaṁ sannihito hariḥ: Kṛṣṇa is present eternally in Mathurā. (SB 10.1.28)[1] But he is not covered in Vṛndāvana.

puṇyā bata vraja-bhuvo yad ayaṁ nṛ-liṅga
gūḍhaḥ purāṇa-puruṣo vana-citra-mālyaḥ
gāḥ pālayan saha-balaḥ kvaṇayaṁś ca veṇuṁ
vikrīdayāñcati giritra-ramārcitāṅghriḥ

How pious are the tracts of land in Vraja, for there the oldest person, disguising himself with human traits, wanders about, enacting his many pastimes! Adorned with wonderfully variegated forest garlands, he whose feet are worshiped by Śiva and Lakṣmī vibrates his flute as he tends the cows in the company of Balarāma. SB 10.44.13

Añcati is in the present tense in the Bhāgavatam verse to indicate that he eternally wanders there. The present verse also indicates this. There, while tending the cows, he eternally gives pleasure (ramayati) to the gopīs headed by Rādhā, by giving them great pleasure in the rāsa dance. Or he increases his own prema through the rāsa dance.

He plays the flute, or, using the flute, produces colourful notes which attract the minds of everyone in the universe (svarita-madhura-venuḥ). Though vardhayan indicates a cause[2], increasing prema is actually the main goal. This is accomplished through his flute for herding the cows, and through his giving the gopīs pleasure as their lover (ramayati). Increasing their prema was his main purpose since he appeared on earth to distribute a special rasa of prema. Herding cows and sporting with the gopīs were instruments for that.

---

[1] In Vaikuṇṭha Kṛṣṇa is covered to the extent that his form is different. He is covered in Mathurā and Dvārakā by aiśvarya, though he has a form similar to that of Vṛndāvana.

[2] Increasing prema (cause), he gives enjoyment to the gopīs. But the sentence should actually mean "Playing the flute and giving enjoyment to the gopīs (causes), he increases prema."

TEXT 6

jayati taraṇi-putrī dharma-rāja-svasā yā
kalayati mathurāyāḥ sakhyam atyeti gaṅgām
mura-hara-dayitā tat-pāda-padma-prasūtaṁ
vahati ca makarandaṁ nīra-pūra-cchalena

All glories to Yamunā, the daughter of the sun god and sister of Yamarāja, beloved of Kṛṣṇa - the killer of Mura, who has made friends with Mathurā District and has exceeded the greatness of Gaṅgādevī. On the pretext of being a river, she carries the nectar flowing from Lord Śrī Kṛṣṇa's lotus feet.

He describes Yamunā, which ornaments Vṛndāvana. Yamunā is the daughter of the sun god, and thus illuminates the universe. She is the sister of Yamarāja, and thus protects dharma. She is the greatest tīrtha and bestows all things. She makes friends with Mathurā (sakhyam kalayati) since she flows abundantly in the Mathurā area with attractive movements. She surpasses Gaṅgā, since she has greater glories and power.

gaṅgā śata-guṇā proktā
māthure mama maṇḍale
yamunā viśrutā devi
nātra kāryā vicāraṇā
tasyāḥ śata-guṇā proktā
yatra keśī nipātitaḥ
keśyāḥ śata-guṇā proktā
yatra viśramito hariḥ

O Devī! Yamunā in my Mathurā district is known to have a hundred times more qualities than Gaṅgā. One need not think further about this. The place on the Yamunā where Keśī was killed has a hundred times more qualities, and the place where Kṛṣṇa rested after killing Keśī has a hundred times more qualities than that. Varāha Purāṇa

Why is it so great? Yamunā is dear to Kṛṣṇa (murahara-dayitā). She is the shelter of various pastimes in Gokula, Mathurā and even Dvārakā[3].

Moroever on the pretext of being a river, she carries the special sweet rasa of bhakti arising from Kṛṣṇa's lotus feet. Because of this, by taking

---

[3] Perhaps this refers to Kālindī, Kṛṣṇa's queen in Dvārakā, who is another form of Yamunā. See BB 1.7.113.

shelter of Yamunā, one can immediately destroy unlimited suffering and attain the highest bliss. (Thus it is great).

TEXT 7

govardhano jayati śaila-kulādhirājo
yo gopikābhir udito hari-dāsa-varyaḥ
kṛṣṇena śakra-makha-bhaṅga-kṛtārcito yaḥ
saptāham asya kara-padma-tale 'py avātsīt

All glories to Govardhana, the king of mountains, whom the Lord's dear gopīs called the best servant of Hari, who was worshipped by Lord Kṛṣṇa after disrupting the sacrifice for worship of Indra, and who rested for a week in the Lord's lotus palm.

Govardhana is then glorified. Govardhana is the king of mountains. This means that it is greater than Himalaya, Sumeru and other famous mountains. It is further described. It is called the best among Kṛṣṇa's servants by the gopīs, since by his various services he causes great pleasure to Kṛṣṇa. The gopīs say:

hantāyam adrir abalā hari-dāsa-varyo
yad rāma-kṛṣṇa-caraṇa-sparśa-pramodaḥ
mānaṁ tanoti saha-go-gaṇayos tayor yat
pānīya-sūyavasa-kandara-kandamūlaiḥ

Of all the servants, this Govardhana Hill is the best! O my friends! This hill, blissful with the touch of the feet of Kṛṣṇa and Balarāma, along with their calves, cows and cowherd friends, gives respect with all kinds of necessities—water for drinking, honey, very soft grass, caves, bulbs and roots. SB 10.21.18

Govardhana was worshipped by Kṛṣṇa, thus disrupting the sacrifice meant for Indra. Govardhana was worshipped by Nanda and others with the materials after the annual worship of Indra was given up. Then Govardhana was respected by Kṛṣṇa when he circumambulated the hill. One should see the Tenth Canto for the details. This incident shows that Govardhana was greater than Indra.

Astonishing greatness is then shown: Govardhana remained for seven days in Kṛṣṇa's (asya) hand. The word api indicates that this is a further glory added to the previous statements. Or api means "What more can be said? Govardhana even remained in his lotus hand for seven days."

TEXT 8

jayati jayati kṛṣṇa-prema-bhaktir yad-aṅghriṁ
nikhila-nigama-tattvaṁ gūḍham ājñāya muktiḥ
bhajati śaraṇa-kāmā vaiṣṇavais tyajyamānā
japa-yajana-tapasyā-nyāsa-niṣṭhāṁ vihāya

All glories, all glories to kṛṣṇa-prema-bhakti, whose feet comprise all the confidential truths of the Vedas, knowing which liberation herself has come to worship her. Liberation, abandoned by the Vaiṣṇavas, has now given up her dependence on japa, yajña, tapasya and renunciation and is eager to take shelter of Prema-bhakti.

Now the author describes the excellence of kṛṣṇa-bhakti, a form of eternity, knowledge and bliss, in order to gain her mercy. Bhakti endowed with prema for Kṛṣṇa remains ever excellent (jayati). Liberation takes shelter of one portion of one of bhakti's lotus feet: just taking shelter of bhakti's actions like hearing or chanting once, to a small degree, produces liberation. No other process does this.

What does liberation do? Conclusively discerning the essence of all the Vedic scriptures, while emphatically (vihāya) giving up the position (niṣṭhām) most highly regarded by the followers of the four āśramas, along with japa (brahmacārī) , yajña (gṛhastha), tapasya (vānaprastha) and renunciation (sannyāsī), liberation takes shelter of bhakti's lotus foot.

This means that liberation cannot be attained even if one is fixed in the four āśramas. And if one performs bhakti to Kṛṣṇa, one attains liberation. But the devotees have no regard for liberation (vaiṣṇavaiḥ tyājamānā). Vaiṣṇava here refers to a person who has taken dīkṣā with Viṣṇu mantra. Though liberation approaches them as a servant (offering liberation), they ignore her offer. Tyājamānā is in the present tense. This indicates that they reject liberation in the past, present and future.

For what purpose does liberation take shelter of bhakti? Liberation desires shelter (śaraṇa-kāmā): liberation simply desires to take shelter of bhakti, regarding bhakti as the sole refuge. By not surrendering to bhakti, liberation is destroyed.

The meaning is this. For those who take shelter of Kṛṣṇa, liberation acts as their servant. For persons who desire liberation (without worshipping Kṛṣṇa), liberation does not even glance at them and remains far away. Though others desire liberation they do not attain it. Liberation cannot be attained thought they undertake japa, yajña, tapasya, etc. Such persons do not understand the conclusion of the scriptures.

TEXT 9

jayati jayati nāmānanda-rūpaṁ murārer
viramita-nija-dharma-dhyāna-pūjādi-yatnam
katham api sakṛd āttaṁ mukti-daṁ prāṇināṁ yat
paramam amṛtam ekaṁ jīvanaṁ bhūṣaṇaṁ me

The name of Kṛṣṇa, whose very form is bliss, which destroys the suffering caused by performance of dharma, meditation and worship and other processes, which gives liberation by being chanted once, which gives happiness superior to liberation, which is my life and ornament, remains ever excellent.

In order to attain the mercy of the most excellent chanting of Kṛṣṇa's name, the author describes the name's excellence. The name of Kṛṣṇa, which manifests bliss (ānanda-rūpa), or whose very form is bliss, remains ever excellent (jayati). Repetition of jayati indicates great respect on understanding the special excellence of the Lord's name.

The special nature of the name's excellence is shown. It negates the suffering caused by performance of dharma for persons performing duties in varṇāśrama. For persons who take shelter of bhakti and have no interest in varṇāśrama, it negates the suffering in meditation arising from difficulty in controlling the mind. It negates the suffering for persons performing deity worship, since they have difficulty in collecting pure items. It negates the suffering in the hearing process caused by dependence on finding a good speaker. This is indicated by the word ādi. This is because chanting the name alone yields all results.

aho bata śva-paco 'to garīyān
yaj-jihvāgre vartate nāma tubhyam
tepus tapas te juhuvuḥ sasnur āryā
brahmānūcur nāma gṛṇanti ye te

How astonishing! The outcaste on the tip of whose tongue your name appears becomes the guru! All those who chant your name, becoming most respectable, have completed all austerities, all sacrifices, all bathing and all study of the Vedas. SB 3.33.7

dhyāyan kṛte yajan yajñais
tretāyāṁ dvāpare 'rcayan
yad āpnoti tad āpnoti
kalau saṅkīrtya keśavam

The results attained by meditation in Sayta-yuga, by sacrifices in Tretā-yuga, and by deity worship in Dvāpara-yuga are attained by chanting the name of Kṛṣṇa in Kali-yuga. Viṣṇu Purāṇa

"One may attain artha, dharma and kāma, but liberation is achieved only by qualitied persons. That would also apply to persons who chant the name with faith and bhakti." The name gives liberation to all living beings whoever they may be. This takes place even if the name is chanted (āttam) in nāmābhāsa, with pride and greed, when chanted by persons wandering about exhausted from hunger, or when chanted as a joke.

etāvatālam agha-nirharaṇāya puṁsāṁ
saṅkīrtanaṁ bhagavato guṇa-karma-nāmnām
vikruśya putram aghavān yad ajāmilo 'pi
nārāyaṇeti mriyamāṇa iyāya muktim

The attentive chanting of the names, pastimes and qualities of the Lord destroys the sins of man. But even attentive chanting is not necessary. Sinful Ajāmila, crying out for his son, uttered "Nārāyaṇa" while dying and still attained liberation. SB 6.3.24

madhura-madhuram etan maṅgalaṁ maṅgalānāṁ
sakala-nigama-vallī-sat-phalaṁ cit-svarūpam
sakṛd api parigītaṁ śraddhayā helayā vā
bhṛgu-vara nara-mātraṁ tārayet kṛṣṇa-nāma

The name of Kṛṣṇa is sweeter than the sweetest, the most auspicious of all things auspicious. It is the highest fruit in the tree of all the Vedas, and is composed entirely of pure consciousness. O best of Bhṛgu's dynasty! Heard once with faith or in negligence, it can deliver any human being. Skanda Purāṇa, Prabhāsa-khaṇḍa

Āttam can also mean "even if the name is accepted by any sense." Even if chanted once, it gives liberation.

One can contemplate the syllables of the name in the antaḥkaraṇa or use the external senses. Using the voice and ear, is easily understood. With the eye, one can see the written letters of the name. Using the skin, one can engage the sense of touch by imprinting the syllables of the name on the chest or other limbs or by writing the syllables of the name on paper. Using the hand, one can hold stamps engraved with the syllables of the name.

For me, giving up all interests, the name has one great result. It gives the happiness of Vaikuṇṭha which far surpasses the happiness of liberation (paramam amṛtam), or it gives the greatest sweetness. The word paramam can be repeated with jīvanam and bhūṣaṇam. It is the highest life and the highest ornament. For me it is the only thing. It supplies all wonderful things.

TEXT 10

namaḥ śrī-kṛṣṇa-candrāya
nirupādhi-kṛpā-kṛte
yaḥ śrī-caitanya-rūpo 'bhūt
tanvan prema-rasaṁ kalau

I bow down to Kṛṣṇacandra, the bestower of unconditional mercy who has appeared in Kali-yuga as Śrī Caitanya to distribute the taste of prema.

After invoking auspiciousness, the author, in order to achieve his desired goal, offers respects to the greatest guru, in the form of his worshipable deity, according to the custom of the sampradāya. "I offer respects to Kṛṣṇa, who gives causeless mercy (nirupādhi-kṛpā-kṛte)."

For spreading in Kali-yuga (tanvan) the special sweetness (rasa) of most rare prema to Kṛṣṇa's lotus feet, he appeared as Caitanya Mahāprabhu. Or he appeared as Caitanya Mahāprabhu to distribute rāga (rasa) in prema.

TEXT 11

bhagavad-bhakti-śāstrāṇām
ayaṁ sārasya saṅgrahaḥ
anubhūtasya caitanya-
deve tat-priya-rūpataḥ

This book is the conclusion of the scriptures which teach bhakti to the Lord, a conclusion which was realized under the shelter of Lord Caitanya Mahāprabhu, from his dear devotee Śrī Rūpa.

Now the author speaks about this book. This work is a compilation of the conclusion (or the portion devoid of inferior elements) of scriptures related to bhakti directed to the Lord. By this statement it is understood the author does not show boldness of creating his own work and shows its authoritative nature. It is a compilation, since it sometimes brings together various verses, sometimes various phrases of verses and sometimes various meanings of scriptures in a poetic form.

"How is it possible to make a compilation, since it is difficult to bring together in one place many bhakti scriptures and it is difficult to discern their meanings?" The conclusion or essence was directly realized by internal and external senses (anubhūtasya) in Vāsudeva, the presiding deity of consciousness (caitanya-devasya), through the dearest form, Kṛṣṇa, the threefold bending form playing his flute. This means that by meditation and service to Kṛṣṇa, the conclusions were realized. When Kṛṣṇa, dwelling within and possessing natural causeless mercy, manifests himself by his mercy through meditation and other devotional processes, everything becomes revealed.

Or, the conclusions were realized in Caitanya Mahāprbhu, through that golden form in the dress of a sannyāsī, or through his dear Rūpa Gosvāmī. Since the conclusions were realized by the mercy of the Lord, it was not difficult to compile them.

TEXT 12

śṛṇvantu vaiṣṇavāḥ śāstram
idaṁ bhāgavatāmṛtam
su-gopyaṁ prāha yat premṇā
jaiminir janamejayam

May the Vaiṣṇavas kindly hear this confidential work, Śrī Bhāgavatāmṛta, which teaches the highest spiritual path, and which Jaimini Ṛṣi carefully spoke to King Janamejaya in prema.

The Vaiṣṇavas should hear the scripture (śāstram), which has been compiled (idam). It teaches (śāstram comes from śās: to instruct) the highest spiritual path or inspires a person on the highest path. It is called Bhāgavatāmṛtam since it highest sweet essence of scriptures meant for devotees. It is appropriately named. This will become evident later.

The Vaiṣṇavas should hear. This indicates that others are not qualified. Non-devotees with dried up hearts, not having developed faith, will go to hell on hearing this work while lacking taste. Excluding the non-devotees should be understood to be an act of mercy.

A person who has taken Vaiṣṇava dīkṣā is called a Vaiṣṇava. It is said:

sāṅgaṁ sa-mudraṁ sa-nyāsaṁ sa-ṛṣi-cchanda-daivatam
sa-dīkṣā-vidhi sa-dhyānaṁ sa-yantraṁ dvādaśākṣaram
aṣṭākṣaram athānyaṁ vā ye mantraṁ samupāsate
jñeyās te vaiṣṇavā lokā viṣṇv-arcana-ratāḥ sadā

Persons who chant the twelve-syllable, eight-syllable or other mantra after taking dīkṣā according to the rules, while performing mudras, nyāsas, while reciting the name of sage who revealed the mantra, its meter and deity of the mantra, along with meditation and worship of the yantra are called Vaiṣṇavas.[4] They are always engaged in worshipping the deity. Padma Purāṇa

Among the Vaiṣṇavas are those who relish rasa, who have great greed for the nectar from the lotus feet of Kṛṣṇa. Generally these are the Vaiṣṇavas who will develop great prīti on hearing Bhāgavatāmṛta.

Though engaged in constantly serving the Vaiṣṇavas' lotus feet, he addresses them indirectly in the verse, out of great respect: May the Vaiṣṇavas hear this work. Or the sentence can mean "O Vaiṣṇavas! Hear this work." This is also a formal, respectful address.

The meaning of this work is very secret or confidential. To relate the work to history, it is said the Jaimini, a great sage, spoke (āha) this story to King Janamejaya with great care (pra). Both were well known as great devotees. Jaimini was a teacher of the Sāma Veda, the best among the four Vedas as mentioned in BG 10.22, when speaking of the Lord's vibhūtis. He understood its essence, taught the path of bhakti while propounding karma prominently, and thus ultimately indicating bhagavad-bhakti. He also glorified Jagannātha elequently.

Janamejaya, son of Parīkṣit, was also a great devotee and had a taste for hearing about Viṣṇu and Vaiṣṇavas. Thus it was suitable that Jaimini spoke to him. He spoke with prema (premnā) for the Lord or with prema for the great devotee, his disciple Janamejaya. Or he spoke with great attraction for the path of bhakti (premnā), and not for any other reason, since the teaching was very confidential.

TEXT 13

munīndrāj jaimineḥ śrutvā
bhāratākhyānam adbhutam

---

[4] Before reciting a mantra it is customary to utter the name of the sage who revealed the mantra (Nārada in the case of eighteen-syllable Kṛṣṇa mantra), the meter (gāyatrī), the form of the Lord who is the subject of the mantra (Kṛṣṇa), the bīja of the mantra (klīm), the śakti of the mantra (svāhā), the prakṛti of the mantra (Kṛṣṇa), the adhiṣṭhātṛ-devatā (puruṣa, Kṛṣṇa) and the purpose of uttering the mantra. See Hari-bhakti-vilāsa 5.146

parīkṣin-nandano 'pṛcchat
tat-khilaṁ śravaṇotsukaḥ

Having heard the wonderful Mahābhārata recited by the great sage Jaimini, Janamejaya was still eager to hear more, and so he inquired about the supplement to that epic.

When did this take place? Two verses (13-14) explain this. Having heard the story of the kings in the lineage of Bharata (bhārātkhyānam), or having heard the story of Mahābhārata, which was most astonishing, since he had not heard it before, he became eager to hear its concluding part (khilam).

TEXT 14

śrī-janamejaya uvāca
na vaiśampāyanāt prāpto
brahman yo bhārate rasaḥ
tvatto labdhaḥ sa tac-cheṣaṁ
madhureṇa samāpaya

Janamejaya said: O brāhmaṇa, I never obtained the same relish of Mahābhārata from Vaiśampāyana that I have now obtained by hearing from you. Please complete this recitation with sweet taste.

O brāhmaṇa, Jaimini, direct form of the Vedas! I have heard Bhārata from you. I did not attain such relish in hearing the story of Bhārata from Vaiśampāyana as I have in hearing from you, since you have narrated the work with sweet bhakti for the Lord. Therefore please complete the concluding portion of that Bhārata with sweet taste, just as one concludes a meal with something sweet.

TEXTS 15–17

śrī-jaiminir uvāca
śuka-devopadeśena
nihatāśeṣa-sādhvasam
samyak-prāpta-samastārthaṁ
śrī-kṛṣṇa-prema-samplutam

sannikṛṣṭa-nijābhīṣṭa-
padārohaṇa-kālakam
śrīmat-parīkṣitaṁ mātā
tasyārtā kṛṣṇa-tatparā

virāṭa-tanayaikānte
'pṛcchad etan nṛpottamam
prabodhyānanditā tena
putreṇa sneha-samplutā

Jaimini said: Relieved of all fear by the instructions of Śukadeva, Parīkṣit, obtaining all his amibitions, was immersed in kṛṣṇa-prema. Now, as the time approached for him to ascend to the destination he desired, his mother, Virāṭa's daughter, a surrendered devotee of Kṛṣṇa, approached him in great distress in a solitary place. After Parīkṣit had consoled and pleased her by his greetings, immersed in love for her son, she asked of him as follows.

The conversation between Uttarā and Parīkṣit, favourable to the topic being discussed is now described.

O best of kings, Janamejaya! Uttarā, mother of Parīkṣit and daughter of King Virāṭa, inquired from Parīkṣit. This is described in three verses. First, Parīkṣit is described in half a verse to reveal the speaker's (Parīkṣit's) special glory. Śuka, the son of Vyāsadeva, was worthy of the highest worship. Thus he is called deva. By Śukadeva's instructions, in the form of recitation of Bhāgavatam, Parīkṣit completely destroyed (nihata) unlimited fear (sādhvasam) of Takṣaka and saṁsāra and attained everything—artha, dharma, kāma and mokṣa very easily (samyak prāpta). In other words he became completely submerged in the waves of sweet prema from Kṛṣṇa's lotus feet.

"Śukadeva did not teach him in the city, and Parīkṣit immediately went to Vaikuṇṭha. Where was the opportunity for Uttarā to inquire from him?" The time for Parīkṣit to attain his desired destination was approaching (sannikṛṣta). There was a short period of time after Śukadeva departed and before Parīkṣit attained Vaikuṇṭha. During that time Uttarā asked him and he replied.

She was pained with lamentation (ārtā). She asked because she was most anxious to hear topics about Kṛṣṇa (kṛṣṇa-tat-parā). Because the topics were most confidential, she approached him in a solitary place.

"Being overcome with grief for her son, a great devotee, how could she hear and understand his answer?" She was made to understand and even realize (prabodhya) by her son Parīkṣit that birth and death are all illusory. Thus she became blissful and was completely filled with affection for Kṛṣṇa or her son, the greatest devotee.

TEXT 18

śrī-uttarovāca
yac chukenopadiṣṭaṁ te
vatsa niṣkṛṣya tasya me
sāraṁ prakāśaya kṣipraṁ
kṣīrāmbhodher ivāmṛtam

Uttarā said: My dear son, extracting, like the nectar from the Milk Ocean, the essence of what Śukadeva has taught you, please quickly reveal it to me.

O son! Please reveal to me the essence, the highest teachings, of what was taught to you. Reveal the highest secrets. "Then hear about the rāsa dance in Vṛndāvana." As one crushes sugar cane with a machine and extracts the essence - sugar, after considering with effort by your intelligence and realization the conclusion of all the attractive teachings, speak. A suitable example of extracting nectar from the Milk Ocean is given.

TEXT 19

śrī-jaiminir uvāca
uvāca sādaraṁ rājā
parīkṣin mātṛ-vatsalaḥ
śrutāty-adbhuta-govinda-
kathākhyāna-rasotsukaḥ

Jaimini said: Being affectionate to his mother, King Parīkṣit spoke respectfully, eager to relish recounting the wonderful narrations he had just heard about Lord Govinda.

Parīkṣit was joyful with attraction (rasotsukaḥ) or was inclined to speak about topics of Kṛṣṇa he had heard from Śukadeva. Moreover he had affection for his mother since she had inquired about this. Thus he spoke thoroughly the truth about the Lord, though it was confidential.

TEXT 20

śrī-viṣṇurāta uvāca
mātar yady api kāle 'smiṁś
cikīrṣita-muni-vrataḥ
tathāpy ahaṁ tava praśna-
mādhurī-mukharī-kṛtaḥ

Parīkṣit, Viṣṇurāta, said: O Mother, though at this time one should be silent, nonetheless your delightful question impels me to speak.

"O mother! Though I should be silent at this time, the sweetness of your question has made me desirous of speaking. I will speak Bhagavatāmṛta." This verse is connected with the three following verses.

TEXTS 21–23

guroḥ prasādatas tasya
śrīmato bādarāyaṇeḥ
praṇamya te sa-putrāyāḥ
prāṇa-daṁ prabhum acyutam

tat-kāruṇya-prabhāveṇa
śrīmad-bhāgavatāmṛtam
samuddhṛtaṁ prayatnena
śrīmad-bhāgavatottamaiḥ

munīndra-maṇḍalī-madhye
niścitaṁ mahatāṁ matam
mahā-guhya-mayaṁ samyak
kathayāmy avadhāraya

By the mercy of my spiritual master Śukadeva Gosvāmī, let me offer respects to Lord Acyuta, who gifted life to both you and your son. By the power of Lord's compassion I shall recite Śrīmad-Bhāgavatāmṛta, distilled by best of his pure devotees with great expertise, and approved by the greatest sages, and which is full of confidential truth. Please listen with attention as I faithfully repeat it to you.

Śrīmad-bhāgavatāmṛta means the sweetest essence (amṛta) of the scriptures concerning bhakti (bhāgavata), endowed with all wealth (śrīmat). The work is like the nectar of Milk Ocean, which is the abode of great jewels and treasures endowed with all good qualities. Though Śukadeva taught Parīkṣit Bhāgavatam and not other bhakti scriptures because Bhāgavatam is the essence of all Vedic scriptures, the answer to the request to reveal the essence includes the content of unlimited bhakti scriptures. (Thus it includes all wealth.)

Or śrimat means that this work is most beautiful in the sound of its words and its meaning, since by reciting this work, the nectar of the Bhāgavatam, the supreme Purāṇa, the recitation of all Vedic scriptures is achieved.

Since Bhāgavatam is the ripened fruit of the tree of the Vedas, and full of sweetness (SB 1.1.3) and realized by the devotees, it has no inferior portion. However, persons who have greed for the sweetness of Kṛṣṇa's lotus feet take pleasure in topics related to the rāsa dance and not other topics in the work, just as those who enter bhakti do not desire to hear about jñāna-yoga and impersonal Brahman liberation, and persons desiring liberation do not desire to hear about artha and kāma. Thus the present work is the essence of topics concerning such sweet rasa. For such persons, it is not a fault if they consider other works disgusting.

Though all scriptural stories are ultimately a glorification of the devotees and Kṛṣṇa's lotus feet, this glorification is not clear from the direct meaning. Thus the rasikas are not satisfied with those stories and consider them detestable.

This work was completely extracted (samuddhṛta) by great devotees like Śukadeva and Nārada. It was completely extracted, not partly, as is done when explaining mantras in scriptures (to keep them hidden), or because of agitation with the short period of time remaining. This extraction recalls the example of extracting nectar from the Milk Ocean. It is approved by great devotees (mahatāṁ) like Nārada, Parāśara and Vyāsa.

Please hear what I will speak (avadhāraya). Or with faith, accept it firmly and keep it in your heart.

TEXTS 24–25

ekadā tīrtha-mūrdhanye
prayāge muni-puṅgavāḥ
māghe prātaḥ kṛta-snānāḥ
śrī-mādhava-samīpataḥ

upaviṣṭā mudāviṣṭā
manyamānāḥ kṛtārthatām
kṛṣṇasya dayito 'sīti
ślāghante sma parasparam

Once, during the month of Māgha, at Prayāga, the best of holy places, a group of exalted sages, having taken their bath in the morning, were happily seated before the deity of Mādhava. They were overcome with bliss and felt themselves successful. They praised each other saying, "You are dear to Krsna."

Related events are described. One day at Prayāga the best of sages began praising each other. This is described in two verses. What did they say? "You are the object of Kṛṣṇa's mercy." It was not proper for sages to praise themselves, since they were humble. Thus each one praised another. Prayāge was the king of all the best tīrthas since it was the meeting place of Gaṅgā and Yamunā.

The reason for praising each other is given. The time was Māgha month. By bathing during this month one becomes a devotee of Kṛṣṇa. It is said:

vrata-dāna-tapobhiś ca na tathā prīyate hariḥ
māghe majjana-mātreṇa yathā prīṇāti mādhavaḥ

The Lord is not pleased as much by vratas, charities and austeritiees as he is pleased by a person bathing during Māgha month. Padma Purāṇa.

And they sat near Mādhava, who is the presiding deity of Prayāga. Thus they were blissful and thought themselves fully accomplished (kṛtārthatām).

TEXT 26

mātas tadānīṁ tatraiva
vipra-varyaḥ samāgataḥ
daśāśvamedhike tīrthe
bhagavad-bhakti-tatparaḥ

O mother, at that time an excellent brāhmaṇa arrived at that holy site called Daśāśvamedha-tīrtha. He was fully absorbed in bhakti to the Supreme Lord.

At Prāyaga, at Daśāśvamedha-tirtha, an excellent brāhmaṇa arrived. He is then described: he was absorbed in bhakti.

TEXT 27

sevito 'śeṣa-sampadbhis
tad-deśasyādhikāra-vān
vṛtaḥ parijanair vipra-
bhojanārthaṁ kṛtodyamaḥ

Possessing all assets, he was the leader of that region. His subordinates surrounded him as he prepared to distribute food to the local brāhmaṇas.

TEXT 28

vicitrotkṛṣṭa-vastūni
sa niṣpādya mahā-manāḥ
āvaśyakaṁ samāpyādau
saṁskṛtya mahatīṁ sthalīm

Collecting various valuable items which were necessary, the generous brāhmaṇa then saw to the nitya-kriyas, first by purifying a large area on the ground.

TEXT 29

satvaraṁ catvaraṁ tatra
madhye nirmāya sundaram
upalipya sva-hastena
vitānāny udatānayat

There in the middle he swiftly made a beautiful altar, which he smeared with cow dung with his own hand and covered with a canopy.

The excellent bṛāhmaṇa collected the best items of food, etc., made an altar after levelling the ground, and then spread out canopies high in the air. He performed nitya-kriyas (āvaśyakam). He cleaned a place by scrubbing it and applied cow dung. In that place (tatra) he built the altar.

TEXT 30

śālagrāma-śilā-rūpaṁ
kṛṣṇaṁ svarṇāsane śubhe
niveśya bhaktyā sampūjya
yathā-vidhi mudā bhṛtaḥ

Placing Lord Kṛṣṇa's form as śālagrāma-śilā on an auspicious golden throne, he worshiped the Lord with devotion, joyfully according to the rules.

TEXT 31

bhogāmbarādi-sāmagrīm
arpayitvāgrato hareḥ
svayaṁ nṛtyan gīta-vādyā-
dibhiś cakre mahotsavam

Presenting food, clothes, and other offerings in front of Lord Hari, he made a festival by personally dancing, singing, playing music, and so on.

Worshipping Kṛṣṇa with devotion by offering foot water, arghya and other items according to the rules, he then celebrated a festival. He was filled with bliss (mudā bhṛtaḥ). He then danced before the Lord (hareḥ agrataḥ)

TEXT 32

tato veda-purāṇādi-
vyākhyābhir vāda-kovidān
viprān praṇamya yatino
gṛhiṇo brahma-cāriṇaḥ

Then he offered respects to the brāhmaṇas, who were expert in arguing from the Vedas, Purāṇas, and other texts. He also offered respects to the sannyāsīs, householders, and brahmacārīs.

TEXT 33

vaiṣṇavāṁś ca sadā kṛṣṇa-
kīrtanānanda-lampaṭān
su-bahūn madhurair vākyair
vyavahāraiś ca harṣayan

And he pleased the many Vaiṣṇavas, who are always greedy to enjoy the bliss of glorifying Kṛṣṇa, with sweet words and behavior.

TEXT 34

pāda-śauca-jalaṁ teṣāṁ
dhārayan śirasi svayam
bhagavaty arpitais tadvad
annādibhir apūjayat

After placing on his head the water that had washed their feet, he worshiped those persons with the food and other items that he had offered to the Supreme Lord.

He then worshipped many brāhmaṇas and Vaiṣṇavas as he had worshipped the Lord, by offering food and other articles. This is described in three verses (34-36). He offered respects to brāhmaṇas who were expert at arguing using the Vedas. They would debate with each other on the strength of their learning.

Having described the brāhmaṇas, the speaker describes the Vaiṣṇavas. Among the Vaiṣṇavas there may be brāhmaṇas. Those brāhmaṇas are not distinguished from the Vaiṣṇavas. And there are others who are not brāhmaṇas, but who have taken Vaiṣṇava dīkṣā. And there are also brāhmaṇas who have not taken Vaiṣṇava dīkṣā. Thus it is proper to mention brāhmanas separately from Vaiṣṇavas.

Both groups (vaiṣṇavas and brāhmaṇas) were pleased by sweet words in the form of praise, by sweet treatment in the form of offering respects on the ground, washing their feet, etc. He offered them food offered to the Lord as well as fanned them (ādibhiḥ).

TEXT 35

bhojayitvā tato dīnān
antyajān api sādaram
atoṣayad yathā-nyāyaṁ
śva-śṛgāla-khaga-krimīn

Then he respectfully fed others, including the most fallen outcastes. In suitable ways, he satisfied even the dogs, jackals, birds, and insects.

He fed śūdras who were devoid of bhakti (dīnān) or persons suffering from hunger (dīnān). He satisfied all beings described in suitable ways (yathā-nyāyam).

TEXT 36

evaṁ santarpitāśeṣaḥ
samādiṣṭo 'tha sādhubhiḥ
parivāraiḥ samaṁ śeṣaṁ
sa-harṣaṁ bubhuje 'mṛtam

Thus, having satisfied everyone, and invited by the holy men that brāhmaṇa, along with his family and servants, then enjoyed the nectarean remnants with great delight.

Having satisfied unlimited beings in this way, he took some food along with his family members and servants. That food was like nectar (amṛtam) because it was the remnants of a great sacrifice, because it was very tasty, because it destroyed death (amṛta means deathless), and because it caused great happiness.

TEXT 37

tato 'bhimukham āgatya
kṛṣṇasya racitāñjaliḥ
tasminn evārpayām āsa
sarvaṁ tat-phala-sañcayam

After this, he again went before Lord Kṛṣṇa. And with folded hands he offered to the Lord all the merit he had accumulated.

He came in front of the śālagrāma-śīla of Kṛṣṇa again and offered to him all the results of the actions he had just performed (phala-sañcayam).

TEXT 38

sukhaṁ saṁveśya devaṁ taṁ
sva-gṛhaṁ gantum udyatam
dūrāc chrī-nārado dṛṣṭvo-
tthito muni-samājataḥ

Putting the deity comfortably to rest, he got ready to return home. Nārada, however, who had been watching him at a distance from within the assembly of sages, stood up just then.

Devam refers to the śālagrāma form of the Lord. Tam refers to the best of brāhmaṇas.

TEXTS 39–40

ayam eva mahā-viṣṇoḥ
preyān iti muhur bruvan
dhāvan gatvāntike tasya
viprendrasyedam abravīt

śrī-kṛṣṇa-paramotkṛṣṭa-
kṛpāyā bhājanaṁ janam
loke vikhyāpayan vyaktaṁ
bhagavad-bhakti-lampaṭaḥ

Nārada, again and again announcing, "This person truly is the most dear devotee of Lord Mahā-viṣṇu!" ran up to the chief of brāhmaṇas and declared him the recipient of Lord Kṛṣṇa's highest mercy. Nārada proclaimed this openly to all, beside himself with eagerness for devotional service to Lord Kṛṣṇa.

Nārada repeatedly exclaimed, "This person is very dear to the Lord."

"Why did he say this?" Though he knew this, he spoke clearly because he wanted to announce to the world that some people receive the great mercy of Kṛṣṇa. Janam in the singular to indicate a type. The final intention is to show that Rādhā is the highest recipient of Kṛṣṇa's mercy. He did this because he was attached to drinking the sweetness of various sweet tastes of Kṛṣṇa (bhagavad-bhakti-lampataḥ).

TEXT 41

śrī-nārada uvāca
bhavān viprendra kṛṣṇasya
mahānugraha-bhājanam
yasyedṛśaṁ dhanaṁ dravyam
audāryaṁ vaibhavaṁ tathā

Nārada said: O leader of the brāhmaṇas, you who have received Lord Kṛṣṇa's greatest mercy. After all, you have such wealth, possessions, generosity, and personal opulence.

O best in the brāhmaṇa families! You are the object of Kṛṣṇa's great mercy. That is shown. You have such great wealth, possessions, generosity and followers and paraphernelia (vaibhavaṁ).

TEXT 42

sad-dharmāpādakaṁ tac ca
sarvam eva mahā-mate
dṛṣṭaṁ hi sākṣād asmābhir
asmiṁs tīrtha-vare 'dhunā

O wise one, in this best of holy places we have now personally seen that you are using all these assets exclusively to establish pure religion.

You establish (āpādakam) dharma in the form of bhakti to the Lord. You use everything for that, and for nothing else. You cannot hide this fact. I have seen it.

TEXT 43

vidvad-vareṇa tenokto
nanv idaṁ sa mahā-muniḥ
svāmin kiṁ mayi kṛṣṇasya
kṛpā-lakṣaṇam īkṣitam

That most learned brāhmaṇa then replied to Nārada: O master, what signs of Kṛṣṇa's mercy have you seen in me?

Nārada was spoken to by the learned brāhmaṇa with the following words (idam). He speaks till verse 58. "O Nārada (svamin)! What quality of Kṛṣṇa's mercy did you see in me? You did not see any quality."

TEXT 44

ahaṁ varākaḥ ko nu syāṁ
dātuṁ śaknomi vā kiyat
vaibhavaṁ vartate kiṁ me
bhagavad-bhajanaṁ kutaḥ

Who am I but a most insignificant person? How much charity can I give? What wealth do I have? And how have I ever reciprocated with the Lord in devotional service?

The reason is given. "What type of person was I to attain his mercy. I am not such a person (kaḥ), because I am very insignificant (varākaḥ). How much wealth do I have?"

TEXT 45

kintu dakṣiṇa-deśe yo
mahā-rājo virājate
sa hi kṛṣṇa-kṛpā-pātraṁ
yasya deśe surālayāḥ

But in South India there lives a great king whose kingdom has many temples. He is the true recipient of Kṛṣṇa's mercy.

He was the leader of several kings in the vicinity, and not the king of the whole country. At that time, Yudhiṣṭhira was the ruler of the country (cakravarti). Thus, because he controlled several kings, this king is later addressed as sārvabhauma: ruler of all places. In his state (deśe) there were many temples.

TEXT 46

sarvato bhikṣavo yatra
tairthikābhyāgatādayaḥ
kṛṣṇārpitānnaṁ bhuñjānā
bhramanti sukhinaḥ sadā

Saintly mendicants come to his kingdom from all directions, along with pilgrims and other visitors. They wander happily, sustained by food that has been offered to Kṛṣṇa.

Tairtikā refers to penniless person who travelled to tīrthas to take bath. Abhyagatāḥ refers to others who came unannounced. Ādi refers to others who were hungry. Since the food was offered to Kṛṣṇa, it was pure and sweet.

TEXT 47

rājadhānī-samīpe ca
sac-cid-ānanda-vigrahaḥ
sākṣād ivāste bhagavān
kāruṇyāt sthiratāṁ gataḥ

Near this king's palace is the deity of the Lord, as if directly in his original form of eternity, knowledge, and bliss. He has mercifully assumed a nonmoving appearance.

Sthiratām indicates that the deity was one which generally did not move about from place to place.

TEXT 48

nityaṁ nava-navas tatra
jāyate paramotsavaḥ
pūjā-dravyāṇi ceṣṭāni
nūtanāni prati-kṣaṇam

There, an ever-new festival is always being celebrated. At each moment there are new offerings and worship taking place.

At every moment in the worship new items dear to the people (iṣṭāni) were offered. Or the items appeared newer and newer at every moment.

TEXT 49

viṣṇor niveditais tais tu
sarve tad-deśa-vāsinaḥ
vaideśikāś ca bahavo
bhojyante tena sādaram

The king respectfully feeds all the residents of his kingdom and the many foreign visitors with the food offered to Lord Viṣṇu.

The king fed the local people as well as persons from other places with the food offered to the Lord. First he fed all the people in the towns and villages and then beggers at all the temples. Verse 46 mentioned the people wandered about happily in order to eat. This verse describes the situation at the main temple near the king's city.

TEXTS 50–51

puṇḍarīkākṣa-devasya
tasya darśana-lobhataḥ
mahā-prasāda-rūpānnādy-
upabhoga-sukhāptitaḥ

sādhu-saṅgati-lābhāc ca
nānā-deśāt samāgatāḥ
nivasanti sadā tatra
santo viṣṇu-parāyaṇāḥ

Saintly devotees of Lord Viṣṇu come from various foreign lands to reside permanently in the kingdom. They come because they are eager to see the lotus-eyed deity of the Lord, to relish the food and other enjoyable items offered to the Lord, and to obtain the association of advanced saintly persons.

Because they can easily obtain (sukhāptitaḥ) enjoyable items (upabhoga) and food in the form of mahā-prasāda of the deity (mahāprasāda-rūpānna), or because they felt happiness on attaining enjoyment of the food and other things, saintly persons and particularly devotees, or saintly persons who were devotees, came and resided there.

TEXT 52

deśaś ca deva-viprebhyo
rājñā datto vibhajya saḥ
nopadravo 'sti tad-deśe
ko 'pi śoko 'tha vā bhayam

The king has given away his kingdom to the deities and brāhmaṇas, dividing it among them. There are neither disturbances nor sorrow or fear in his kingdom.

The kingdom (deśaḥ) was divided up by the king and given to the deities and brāhmaṇas.

TEXT 53

akṛṣṭa-pacyā sā bhūmir
vṛṣṭis tatra yathā-sukham
iṣṭāni phala-mūlāni
su-labhāny ambarāṇi ca

In that kingdom, the earth yields crops without being plowed, rain falls just enough for people's comfort, and whatever fruits, vegetables, and clothing one desires are easily obtained.

Without plowing (akṛṣṭa-pacyā) the earth yielded crops. Iṣṭāni means dear, of good quality.

TEXT 54

sva-sva-dharma-kṛtaḥ sarvāḥ
sukhinyaḥ kṛṣṇa-tatparāḥ
prajās tam anuvartante
mahā-rājaṁ yathā sutāḥ

The citizens happily perform their own dharma and are devoted to Lord Kṛṣṇa. They all follow the king as if they were his children.

Out of affection they followed the orders of the king (anuvartante). Or they followed the behavior of the king.

TEXT 55

sa cāgarvaḥ sadā nīca-
yogya-sevābhir acyutam
bhajamāno 'khilān lokān
ramayaty acyuta-priyaḥ

The king is always prideless. Worshiping Lord Acyuta with by performing menial services, he pleases all the people and is dear to Lord Acyuta.

In spite of the elaborate service to the Lord, following dharma, possession of wealth and kingdom, the king was without pride. He performed proper services which were menial, such as cleansing, applying purificatory unguents, offering lamps, etc. Worshipping the Lord with prema he is dear to the Lord (acyuta-priyaḥ).

TEXTS 56–57

tasyāgre vividhair nāma-
gāthā-saṅkīrtanaiḥ svayam
nṛtyan divyāni gītāni
gāyan vādyāni vādayan

bhrātṛ-bhāryā-sutaiḥ pautrair
bhṛtyāmātya-purohitaiḥ
anyaiś ca sva-janaiḥ sākaṁ
prabhuṁ taṁ toṣayet sadā

Performing saṅkīrtana before the Lord's Deity, chanting the Lord's names composed in various attractive arrangements, he dances, sings transcendental songs, and plays instruments along with his brothers, wives, sons, grandsons, servants, ministers, priests, and other associates. He always tries to please the Lord.

His actions are described in two verses. These verses show that his brothers, wives, sons and others were also great devotees.

TEXT 58

te te tasya guṇa-vrātāḥ
kṛṣṇa-bhakty-anuvartinaḥ
saṅkhyātuṁ kati kathyante
jñāyante kati vā mayā

These good qualities follow his devotion to Kṛṣṇa. How many can be spoken of or known in order to count them?

All the good qualities of the king, well known or indescribable (te te), favorable to bhakti (anuvartinaḥ), cannot be described or known.

The meaning is this. "All this qualities I have mentioned indicate that he is the recipient of the Lord's mercy. I am not, since I do not have such qualities." This is true of future discussions with other devotees as well.

Without regard for birth, the qualities show the great mercy of the Lord and thus show the greatness of that devotee. Otherwise it would be inappropriate to say that the king, a kṣatriya was greater than the brāhmaṇa. The Lord will later say that all of them were successful, but there are degrees of mercy and bhakti. That will be explained later.

TEXT 59

śrī-parīkṣid uvāca
tato nṛpa-varaṁ draṣṭuṁ

tad-deśe nārado vrajan
deva-pūjotsavāsaktās
tatra tatraikṣata prajāḥ

Parīkṣit said: Then Nārada went to the kingdom of that best of kings to see him. Wherever Nārada went he found the people absorbed in festive worship of the Lord.

Nārada went to see that king (nṛpa-varam). In various places (tatra tatra) he saw people absorbed in worship of the Lord.

TEXT 60

harṣeṇa vādayan vīṇāṁ
rājadhānīṁ gato 'dhikam
viproktād api sampaśyan
saṅgamyovāca taṁ nṛpam

Nārada arrived at the capital, struming his vīṇā with delight. Seeing more than what the brāhmaṇa had described, he approached the king and spoke.

He experienced (saṁpaśyan) that the worship of this king was even greater that what the brāhmaṇa described about it at Dāśāśvamedha (vipra uktāt).

TEXT 61

śrī-nārada uvāca
tvaṁ śrī-kṛṣṇa-kṛpā-pātraṁ
yasyedṛg rājya-vaibhavam
sal-loka-guṇa-dharmārtha-
jñāna-bhaktibhir anvitam

Nārada said: You are the recipient of Kṛṣṇa's mercy! After all, you have a wealthy kingdom,which has the best citizens, endowed with good qualities, dharma, wealth, jñāna, and bhakti.

The wealthy kingdom (rājya-vaibhavam) was endowed with excellent citizens (sal-loka), since they were engaged in their sva-dharma, which was previously described. The kingdom showed affection for the people and other good qualities (guṇa), since there was propogation of bhakti. There was absence of pride in the citizens. The citizens showed dharma since they gave food to beggars and others, and made offerings to the Lord. Their wealth (artha) was used to obtain articles for worshipping the

Lord. It is implied that they had the best kāma also (desiring to please the Lord). Through study of authorized scriptures, and from absorption in bhakti, they understood that their goal was liberation, etc. (jñāna). They also engaged in serving the Lord (bhakti). Their actions were performed with prema.

TEXT 62

śrī-parīkṣid uvāca
tat tad vistārya kathayann
āśliṣyan bhūpatiṁ muhuḥ
praśaśaṁsa guṇān gāyan
vīṇayā vaiṣṇavottamaḥ

Parīkṣit said: Nārada, the best of Vaiṣṇavas, playing his vīṇā, elaborately described all this, praising the king's good qualities and embraced him again and again.

Nārada described in detail the wealth of the kingdom. He sang about the king's qualities—acts of worshipping the Lord (guṇān). He praised the king, "You are the recipient of Kṛṣṇa's greatest mercy."

TEXT 63

sārvabhaumo muni-varaṁ
sampūjya praśrito 'bravīt
nija-ślāghā-bharāj jāta-
lajjā-namita-mastakaḥ

The king, the ruler of a vast region, with his head bowed down in embarrassment by the weight of hearing his own praise, then worshiped the topmost sage and humbly replied.

The king bowed his head or his head was bowed, out of shame arising from Nārada praising him excessively.

TEXTS 64–65

devarṣe 'lpāyuṣaṁ svalpai-
śvaryam alpa-pradaṁ naram
asvatantraṁ bhayākrāntaṁ
tāpa-traya-niyantritam

kṛṣṇānugraha-vākyasyāpy
ayogyam avicārataḥ

tadīya-karuṇā-pātraṁ
kathaṁ māṁ manyate bhavān

The king said: O Devaṛṣī, I am a human being with a short life span, little opulence, and little to give others. I am not independent. I am attacked by fear and ruled by the threefold miseries of life. I am unworthy of words indicating that Kṛṣṇa bestowsmercy to me. Why do you wrongly consider me an object of his mercy?

"O Nārada! I am a man (naram) with little to give." This is connected with the second verse. "Why do you consider me, a man with little to give (alpa-pradam), dependent on others for executing sva-dharma (asvatantram) the recipient of Kṛṣṇa's mercy without carefully considering the facts? I am unworthy for Kṛṣṇa to say 'I will give you mercy.' (kṛṣṇānugraha-vākya). I have not received that mercy. Or I am not the object of words like 'This person is the object of Kṛṣṇa's mercy.' What is the use of all this wealth? You speak without considering carefully."

TEXT 66

devā eva dayā-pātraṁ
viṣṇor bhagavataḥ kila
pūjyamānā narair nityaṁ
tejo-maya-śarīriṇaḥ

The devatās are certainly the recipients of the Supreme Lord Viṣṇu's mercy. They have effulgent bodies and are always worshipped by us.

The devatās are worshipped by us (naraiḥ).

TEXT 67

niṣpāpāḥ sāttvikā duḥkha-
rahitāḥ sukhinaḥ sadā
svacchandācāra-gatayo
bhaktecchā-vara-dāyakāḥ

They are sinless, situated in goodness, free from distress, and always happy. They act and travel at their will, and grant what their devotees desire.

They act and travel at their will, since they are not dependent on rules like humans, and travel through the sky. According to the desire of those devotees (icchā), they give blessings (vara-dāyakāḥ) to persons who worship them (bhakta).

TEXT 68

yeṣāṁ hi bhogyam amṛtaṁ
mṛtyu-roga-jarādi-hṛt
svecchayopanataṁ kṣut-tṛḍ-
bādhābhāve 'pi tuṣṭi-dam

Their food is amṛta, which removes miseries such as death, disease, and old age. Though they have no hunger or thirst, the devatās enjoy great satisfaction in partaking of this food by their own sweet will.

Amṛta is food for the devatās (yeṣām) and takes away death, disease and old age. The word ādi indiceates fatigue, perspiration and bad smell. "The devatās do not have hunger or thirst. It was said they are always happy (verse 67). Without having hunger or thirst, eating will not give them happiness." Though they do not have hunger or thirst, they happily partake of food.

TEXT 69

vasanti bhagavan svarge
mahā-bhāgya-balena ye
yo nṛbhir bhārate varṣe
sat-puṇyair labhyate kṛtaiḥ

O Nārada, on the strength of their great fortune they live in the Svarga, which humans in Bharata-varṣa attain only by excellect pious acts.

"Nārada (bhagavan)! The devatās (ye) live in Svarga which (yaḥ) is attained by humans in Bharata-varṣa by doing excellent pious acts (sat-puṇya-kṛtaiḥ). The devatās are recipients of the Lord's mercy since they are opposite of humans. Humans have short lives and devatās long lives because of drinking nectar which takes away death. Humans attain great wealth by constant worship while devatās give at their will to those who worship them. Devatās are very independent, actings as they please. Humans are opposite to devatās in many other qualities also." This is explained later also.

TEXT 70

mune viśiṣṭas tatrāpi
teṣām indraḥ purandaraḥ
nigrahe 'nugrahe 'pīśo
vṛṣṭibhir loka-jīvanaḥ

My dear sage, the most distinguished of these devatās is Purandara Indra. He is capable of both cursing and giving benedictions, and he gives the world prosperity by providing rain.

Among the devatās Indra is the Lord's special object of mercy (viśiṣṭaḥ). He has the ability (īśaḥ) to curse (nigrahe) and give benedictions (anugrahe). It was said previously that the devatās give what their worshippers desire. However, Indra, without considering what they desire, can give much more. Thus he is superior to the other devatās. He gives prosperity to the worlds (loka-jīvanaḥ) by giving rain.

TEXT 71

tri-lokīśvaratā yasya
yugānām eka-saptatim
yāśvamedha-śatenāpi
sārvabhaumasya durlabhā

He rules the three planetary systems for seventy-one yuga cycles, a length of sovereignty no mundane king could earn, even by one hundred aśvamedha-yajña.

For seventy-one cycles of the four yugas Indra controls the three planetary systems. That is impossible for me, even if I controlled the whole earth. Even by performing a hundred aśvamedha-yajña (horse sacrifice) it would be difficult since I am under control of my karma and since performing the yajña is difficult, with possibility of mistakes.

TEXT 72

haya uccaiḥśravā yasya
gaja airāvato mahān
kāma-dhug gaur upavanaṁ
nandanaṁ ca virājate

Uccaiḥśravā is his horse, and Airāvata his mighty elephant. His cow is Kāmadhuk, and his garden is the resplendent Nandana.

His horse and elephant are great, having the best qualities, since they arose from churning the Milk Ocean.

TEXT 73

pārijātādayo yatra
vartante kāma-pūrakāḥ

kāma-rūpa-dharāḥ kalpa-
drumāḥ kalpa-latānvitāḥ

In that garden are trees like the pārijāta, which yield whatever one may desire. Those trees, adorned with desire-fulfilling creepers, assume whatever forms one may like.

Yatra means "in that garden."

TEXT 74

yeṣām ekena puṣpeṇa
yathā-kāmaṁ su-sidhyati
vicitra-gīta-vāditra-
nṛtya-veśāśanādikam

Just by one flower from those trees one can fully satisfy one's desires, whether for varities of songs, music, dances, clothing, ornaments, food, or anything else.

By just one flower from the garden one attains astonishing songs, music, dancing, ornaments (veśa), food as well as drinks, beds and seats (ādi). One's desires are fully satisfied.

TEXT 75

āḥ kiṁ vācyaṁ paraṁ tasya
saubhāgyaṁ bhagavān gataḥ
kaniṣṭha-bhrātṛtāṁ yasya
viṣṇur vāmana-rūpa-dhṛk

And, oh, what more can be said of Indra's greatest fortune? Viṣṇu has taken the form of Vāmanadeva and become his younger brother!

Tasya means "of Indra."

TEXT 76

āpadbhyo yam asau rakṣan
harṣayan yena vistṛtām
sākṣāt svī-kurute pūjāṁ
tad vetsi tvam utāparam

Lord Vāmanadeva pleases Indra by protecting him from dangers and personally accepts the elaborate worship Indra offers. But you already know this besides other things.

"Not only does the Lord become Indra's younger brother, but performs actions suitable to that position. Viṣṇu (asau) protects Indra (yam) from dangers and accepts directly the worship performed (vistṛtām) elaborately by Indra. He personally accepts the articles offered. This is a further description of Indra's good fortune. You know about Indra's good fortune (tat). You know other things as well (uta aparam). Since Viṣṇu has become his younger brother, Indra can intimately show his affection for him. Or you know things other than what I have stated (uta aparam). How can I describe them?"

Thus ends the first chapter of Canto One of Śrīla Sanātana Gosvāmī's Bṛhad-b

Chapter Two, entitled “Bhauma: On the Earth.”

Chapter Two

Divya: In Svarga

TEXT 1

śrī-parīkṣid uvāca
praśasya taṁ mahā-rājaṁ
svar-gato munir aikṣata
rājamānaṁ sabhā-madhye
viṣṇuṁ deva-gaṇair vṛtam

Parīkṣit said: After glorifying the great king, Nārada went to Svarga. There in the assembly he saw Lord Viṣṇu in all his brilliance, surrounded by hosts of devatās.

Having gone to Svarga (svaḥ), Nārada saw Viṣṇu in the assembly.

TEXT 2

vicitra-kalpa-druma-puṣpa-mālā-
vilepa-bhūṣā-vasanāmṛtādyaiḥ
samarcitaṁ divyataropacāraiḥ
sukhopaviṣṭaṁ garuḍasya pṛṣṭhe

He was decorated with sandalwood pulp, divine ornaments and clothing, and a garland made of varied flowers from desire trees. Sitting comfortably on Garuḍa's back, he was worshiped with celestial offerings.

Four verses (2-5) describe Viṣṇu. The Lord was being worshipped by sixteen or sixty-four articles (upacāraiḥ). One should see Viṣṇu-bhakti-candrodaya and other scriptures for details of such worship.

TEXT 3

bṛhaspati-prabhṛtibhiḥ
stūyamānaṁ maharṣibhiḥ
lālyamānam adityā tān
harṣayantaṁ priyoktibhiḥ

Bṛhaspati and other great sages praised his glories, and Mother Aditi pampered him. He gave joy to each of them with his affectionate words.

He was pampered by his mother Aditi. He was satisfied with the soft touch of her hand. He gave joy to the devatās and great sages with his affectionate words.

TEXT 4

siddha-vidyādhra-gandharvā-
psarobhir vividhaiḥ stavaiḥ
jaya-śabdair vādya-gīta-
nṛtyaiś ca paritoṣitam

Siddhas, Vidyādharas, Gandharvas, and Apsarās recited prayers. They cried "Jaya!" and sang, danced, and played instruments, all for his pleasure.

He was pleased with prayers offered by Siddhas and others. The Siddhas uttered "Jaya! Jaya!" and the Vidyādharas played instruments, Gandharavas sang and Apsarās danced.

TEXT 5

śakrāyābhayam uccoktyā
daityebhyo dadataṁ dṛḍham
kīrtyārpyamāṇaṁ tāmbūlaṁ
carvantaṁ līlayāhṛtam

In loud voice, the Lord assured Indra that he need not be afraid of the Daityas. Kīrtidevī offered the Lord betel nut, which he gracefully accepted and chewed.

He made Indra free of fear of the demons by his loud statements. "Do not fear the demons. Killing them, I will protect you." While clearly saying this, he had his right lotus hand raised in a special gesture. Kīrti, Viṣṇu's wife offered him betel nut. He took it gracefully with his thumb and forefinger.

Though Nārada's discussion with Indra is the main aim, rather than seeing Viṣṇu, seeing Viṣṇu at the beginning reveals Viṣṇu's special greatness, since Viṣṇu is most prominent among the devatās. Thus this description is given. Of course it also shows Viṣṇu's special mercy to Indra. The same should be understood in the descriptions of Brahmaloka.

TEXT 6

śakraṁ ca tasya māhātmyaṁ
kīrtayantaṁ muhur muhuḥ
svasmin kṛtopakārāṁś ca
varṇayantaṁ mahā-mudā

Repeatedly chanting the Lord's glories, Indra described with great joy how the Lord had helped him in the past.

He also saw Indra, who glorified the Lord, relating how the Lord was affectionate to his devotees. Indra described how the Lord helped him, and how he received power over the three worlds which had been taken by Bali.

TEXT 7

sahasra-nayanair aśru-
dhārā varṣantam āsane
svīye niṣaṇṇaṁ tat-pārśve
rājantaṁ sva-vibhūtibhiḥ

Indra, glorious with this own wealth, sat on his own throne next to the Lord, shedding tears of joy from his thousand eyes.

Indra was showering tears of joy. He was seated on a throne next to Viṣṇu. He was glorious with his own wealth—cāmaras, ornaments and vehicle.

TEXT 8

atha viṣṇuṁ nijāvāse
gacchantam anugamya tam
sabhāyām āgataṁ śakram
āśasyovāca nāradaḥ

As Lord Viṣṇu then proceeded to his own residence, Indra followed him for some distance and then returned to the assembly hall, where Nārada greeted him and began to speak.

Nārada spoke to Indra who was so fortunate (tam), who had returned to the assembly, since it was inappropriate to praise Indra in front of Viṣṇu. Nārada greeted Indra by offering blessings of victory.

TEXT 9

śrī-nārada uvāca
kṛtānukampitas tvaṁ yat
sūrya-candra-yamādayaḥ
tavājñā-kāriṇaḥ sarve
loka-pālāḥ pare kim u

Nārada said: You have surely received the Lord's mercy, because devatās like Sūrya, Candra, and Yama, what to speak of the other rulers of planets, all obey your orders.

Yat means because. Others (pare) indicates Vasus, Maruts and Rudras. "What can one say about these others, who all carry out your orders?"

TEXT 10

munayo 'smādṛśo vaśyāḥ
śrutayas tvāṁ stuvanti hi
jagad-īśatayā yat tvaṁ
dharmādharma-phala-pradaḥ

Sages like me are your subjects, and the Vedas praise you as the lord of the universe, for you bestow the fruits of dharma and adharma.

The śrutis praise your position as Indra since you are the controller of the universe. That is proper, since you give the results of dharma and adharma in the form of heaven or hell.

TEXT 11

aho nārāyaṇo bhrātā
kanīyān yasya sodaraḥ
sad-dharmaṁ mānayan yasya
vidadhāty ādaraṁ sadā

How amazing that Lord Nārāyaṇa is your younger brother, born of the same womb. Honoring the codes of civilized people, he always treats you respectfully.

"What to speak of controlling the universe, you control even what is beyond the material realm. How amazing (aho)! Nārāyaṇa, the lord of all jīvas, is your brother, coming from the same mother, and younger as well. He follows (mānayan) the code of civilized people (sad-dharmam) of respecting his elder brother, by words and giving protection."

TEXT 12

śrī-parīkṣid uvāca
ittham indrasya saubhāgya-
vaibhavaṁ kīrtayan muhuḥ
devarṣir vādayan vīṇāṁ
ślāghamāno nanarta tam

Parīkṣit said: Nārada thus profusely glorified the extreme good fortune of Indra. As he chanted Indra's glories, he played his vīṇā and danced.

Nārada praised Indra (tam), as being the best recipient of the Lord's mercy, according to the descriptions given by the king on earth.

TEXT 13

tato 'bhivādya devarṣim
uvācendraḥ śanair hriyā
bho gāndharva-kalābhijña
kiṁ māṁ upahasann asi

Indra then welcomed Nārada and in a soft voice humbly said: My dear Nārada, expert in singing, why are you making fun of me?

It was not possible for a person who was expert in singing (gandharva-kalābhijñaḥ) to tell lies or make fun of another person. That was Indra's intention in addressing Nārada as "expert in singing."

TEXT 14

asya na svarga-rājyasya
vṛttaṁ vetsi tvam eva kim
kati vārān ito daitya-
bhītyāsmābhir na nirgatam

Are you not familiar with what ruling Svarga means? Don't you know how many times we devatās have had to flee Svarga in fear of the Daityas?

"You may say that this was neither false praise nor a joke. But do you not know? You must know. Not a few times but many times, we have been driven from Svarga (itaḥ) and to live in fear, disguised as austere persons, on earth." By this description he negates the idea that living on Svarga is better than living on earth, since constantly there arises new disturbances. The people of Svaraga were praised as being free in action and in travelling. This is also negated by this verse.

TEXT 15

ācaran balir indratvam
asurān eva sarvataḥ
sūryendv-ādy-adhikāreṣu
nyayuṅkta kratu-bhāga-bhuk

Bali, once even took over as Indra. He appointed demons to all the posts of Sūrya, Candra and other devatās and took for himself my shares of sacrifice.

Nārada said that Sūrya and Candra and other devatās take the orders of Indra. In this verse, Indra refutes that statement. "With obstacles to my and the devatās' control, what is the glory of being rulers of planets? Or what is my glory in giving them orders to follow? Bali enjoyed the sacrifices and we were left suffering from hunger, as if dead." This refutes the statement that the devatās enjoy nectar and are free from hunger and thirst.

TEXT 16

tato nas tāta-mātṛbhyāṁ
tapobhir vitatair dṛḍhaiḥ
toṣito 'py aṁśa-mātreṇa
gato bhrātṛtvam acyutaḥ

Our father and mother then performed many severe austerities, by which they satisfied the Supreme Lord Acyuta, who then appeared as my brother assuming his aṁśa form.

"My father and mother performed severe austerities for a long time, which caused great suffering. Then the Lord appeared as an aṁśa form, not in his complete form." This refutes the stastement that Nārāyaṇ is Indra's brother.

TEXT 17

tathāpy ahatvā tāṣ chatrūn
kevalaṁ nas trapā kṛtā
māyā-yācanayādāya
bale rājyaṁ dadau sa me

And even then, instead of killing those enemies, he only embarrassed us by deceptively begging Bali for the kingdom and returning it to me.

"He caused embarrassment for us devatās by tricky begging. First, he asked for three steps of land when he had the form of a dwarf and then, manifesting a huge form, stepped over the whole universe. Taking the kingdom from Bali, the Lord gave it to me. I can now no longer be happy with attaining the kingdom, since it causes me shame."

TEXT 18

spardhāsūyādi-doṣeṇa
brahma-hatyādi-pāpataḥ
nitya-pāta-bhayenāpi
kiṁ sukhaṁ svarga-vāsinām

We residents of Svarga are tainted with faults like rivalry and jealousy, and get entangled in the reactions of sin for such acts as killing brāhmaṇas, and hence live in constant fear of losing our posts. So what happiness do we truly enjoy?

The brāhmaṇa had stated that the devatās are always worshipped by humans (1.66). That is now refuted. Because the devatās compete with each other, their state of sattva is rejected. Indra is not sinless since he killed Viśvarūpa and Vṛtra, and had to suffer sinful reactions for killing a brāhmaṇa. Since the devatās have fear of falling from Svarga, one should not say that their bodies are effulgent.

ko 'nv arthaḥ sukhayaty enaṁ kāmo vā mṛtyur antike
āghātaṁ nīyamānasya vadhyasyeva na tuṣṭi-daḥ

What object or desire can bring a person happiness? Death standing next to you does not bring satisfaction. Similarly the person being led to the place of execution cannot be satisfied by an offering of sweets. SB 11.10.20

Since the devatās are similar to humans, they should not be worshipped by humans.

TEXT 19

kiṁ ca māṁ praty upendrasya
viddhy upekṣāṁ viśeṣataḥ
sudharmāṁ pārijātaṁ ca
svargān martyaṁ ināya saḥ

And furthermore you must know that my brother Lord Upendra intentionally disregarded me by taking the the Sudharmā hall and the pārijāta flower to earth.

"Among the devatās Indra is the greatest object of mercy." He refutes that in this verse. "Since the inhabitnats of Svarga are subject to fear and faults, I am considered insignificant. The Lord ignores me. You have understood that by my words. Understand that Viṣṇu has particularly been indiffierent to me. He took the Sudharma hall and the Pārijāta flower to earth (martyam). That is not proper since earth is subject to death." Since Upendra ignored Indra, Nārada's words concerning the Lord's mercy to Indra is refuted. The Lord has done this many times. Whatever seems to be the Lord's mercy is actually insignificant. Other later statements should also be understood as refutations of Nārada's praise of Indra. As with previous devotees, Indra should not be considered so great.

Since devotees naturally feel sorrow from being unsatisfied with their own bhakti, their words should not be taken seriously. One should accept both types: devotees who do not object when others describe them as objects of the Lord's mercy, and devotees who reject themselves as objects of mercy. The rejection may arise because of sorrow at not attaining enough mercy, because of considering oneself insignicant, or because of expressing anger in affection. For fear of lengthening the work, no more is explained about this.

TEXT 20

gopālaiḥ kriyamāṇāṁ me
nyahan pūjāṁ cirantanīm
akhaṇḍaṁ khāṇḍavākhyaṁ me
priyaṁ dāhitavān vanam

He destroyed the worship the cowherds had been offering me for a long time, and he burned down the vast Khāṇḍava forest, dear to me.

"He completely destroyed (nyahan) the worship performed by the cowherds headed by Nanda for a long time. He started worship of Govardhana using the ingredients of worship (meant for me). Through Arjuna he burned the thick Khāṇḍava forest, dear to me." Arjuna was Indra's own son.

TEXT 21

trai-lokya-grāsa-kṛd-vṛtra-
vadhārthaṁ prārthitaḥ purā
audāsīnyaṁ bhajaṁs tatra
prerayām āsa māṁ param

On begging the Lord to kill Vṛtra, who was devouring the three worlds, the Lord responded indifferently, merely sending me on his behalf.

This incident happened previously. In comparison, actions like taking the Sudharma hall happened recently. "He sent me only (param) to kill Vṛtra, and did not personally go. He only assisted."

TEXT 22

utsādya mām avajñāya
madīyām amarāvatīm
sarvopari sva-bhavanaṁ
racayām āsa nūtanam

Disregarding me, he destroyed my capital, Amarāvatī, and built a new residence, above Brahmaloka, for Himself.

"Breaking my city Amarāvtī, he built his new residence above Brahmaloka (sarvopari)." This Vaikuṇṭha is called Ramā-priya and exists within the universe. It is ever new (nūtanam) since it is a spiritual place of eternity, knowledge and bliss within the material world. This is described in Hari-vaṁśa in relation to stealing the Pārijāta tree:

idaṁ bhaṅktvā madīyaṁ ca
bhavanaṁ viṣṇunā kṛtam
upary upari lokānām
adhikaṁ bhuvanaṁ mune

O sage, Lord Viṣṇu broke my capital city and then built a new planet above all others.

Indra, born in the seventh manvantara says this. In the Eighth Canto it is said:

patnī vikuṇṭhā śubhrasya
vaikuṇṭhaiḥ sura-sattamaiḥ
tayoḥ sva-kalayā jajñe
vaikuṇṭho bhagavān svayam

From the combination of Śubhra and his wife named Vikuṇṭhā, there appeared the Supreme Lord, Vaikuṇṭha, along with devatās called the Vaikuṇṭhas, who were his expansions.

vaikuṇṭhaḥ kalpito yena
loko loka-namaskṛtaḥ
ramayā prārthyamānena
devyā tat-priya-kāmyayā

Just to please the goddess of fortune, Vaikuṇṭha, at her request, created another Vaikuṇṭha planet, which is worshiped by everyone. SB 8.5.4-5

This however describes an event that occurred in the fifth manvantara. The contradiction can be resolved by explaining that in different days of Brahmā the events occur in different manvantaras or that the Vaikuṇṭha planet was conceived in the fifth manvantara but was actually created now, in the seventh manvantara.

TEXT 23

ārādhana-balāt pitror
āgrahāc ca purodhasaḥ
pūjāṁ svī-kṛtya naḥ sadyo
yāty adṛśyaṁ nijaṁ padam

He accepts our worship by the power of worship performed by my parents and at the insistence of Bṛhaspati. And then, after accepting our offerings, he at once disappears to his own abode.

"You should understand that the Lord is as inscrutable as a million oceans, but being pained by other's suffering, acts with mercy." "That is true, but if he is pleased, he should personally accept our worship at all times. We can tolerate everything. Let us not consider this point, but we do not even see him constantly." That is explained in seven verses (23-29). "By the power of worship performed by my parents in their previous life and in this life, and because of Bṛhaspati's insistence, the Lord accepts our worship. It was not out of mercy to me." This verse refutes the statement that the Lord directly accepts Indra's worship. "He immediately goes to his abode, which is invisible to us. Or he goes without our seeing it."

TEXTS 24–25

punaḥ satvaram āgatya
svārghya-svī-karaṇād vayam
anugrāhyās tvayety ukto
'smān ādiśati vañcayan

yāvan nāhaṁ samāyāmi
tāvad brahmā śivo 'tha vā
bhavadbhiḥ pūjanīyo 'tra
matto bhinnau na tau yataḥ

Then he suddenly comes back. I tell him, "We are very much obliged to You for accepting our offerings of arghya," but he cheatingly replies, "When I am not here, you may worship Brahmā or Śiva because they are nondifferent from me."

TEXT 26

eka-mūrtis trayo devā
rudra-viṣṇu-pitāmahāḥ
ity-ādi-śāstra-vacanaṁ
bhavadbhir vismṛtaṁ kim u

"According to scriptural statements, 'The one form is the three devatās Rudra, Viṣṇu, and Brahmā.' Have you forgotten?"

"We are fully dedicated to Viṣṇu's lotus feet and have no taste for worshipping anyone else. He knows that. But he tells us to worship others according to the scriptural statement eka-mūrtis trayo devāḥ: the one form is three devatās. That is his cheating (vañcayan)." Following the Lord's words, one sees worship of Śiva in Svarga in the stealing of the Pārijāta tree.

TEXT 27

vāso 'syāniyato 'smābhir
agamyo muni-durlabhaḥ
vaikuṇṭhe dhruva-loke ca
kṣīrābdhau ca kadācana

We cannot determine his abode. It is unapproachable, difficult even for sages to attain. He is sometimes in Vaikuṇṭha, sometimes on Dhruvaloka, and sometimes within the Milk Ocean.

"If what you say is true, you should go to him." Since he is rarely attained by the ātmārāmas, we cannot determine his abode. We cannot approach him. He is sometimes in Vaikuṇṭha, the place called Ramāpriya within the universe, sometimes on Dhruvaloka called Viṣṇupada and sometimes on the Milk Ocean in Svetadvīpa.

TEXT 28

samprati dvārakāyāṁ ca
tatrāpi niyamo 'sti na

kadācit pāṇḍavāgāre
mathurāyāṁ kadācana

And now he is in Dvārakā, but even that is not fixed since sometimes he goes from there to the house of the Pāṇḍavas, and sometimes to Mathurā.

TEXT 29

puryāṁ kadācit tatrāpi
gokule ca vanād vane
itthaṁ tasyāvaloko 'pi
durlabho naḥ kutaḥ kṛpā

He is sometimes in Mathurā and sometimes wandering in Gokula from forest to forest. In this way it is difficult for us to see him. Where is his mercy to us?

"Now he is easily available on earth since he has come as avatāra with a most attractive form." Though he is in Dvārakā on earth, it is not certain that he is always there, for sometimes he is in Dvārakā, sometimes in the Pāṇḍavas' house at Indraprasthā in order to see them. Previously he was in Mathurā, in the city, but before that he was in Gokula in places like Bṛhadvana. From there he went to Vṛndāvana and other places.

Or though he lives in Dvārakā, that is not fixed, since sometimes he goes to the Pāṇḍavas' house and sometimes to Mathurā. It is said in the First Canto:

yarhy ambujākṣāpasasāra bho bhavān
kurūn madhūn vātha suhṛd-didṛkṣayā
tatrābda-koṭi-pratimaḥ kṣaṇo bhaved
raviṁ vinākṣṇor iva nas tavācyuta

O lotus-eyed Lord! When you go to Hastināpura or Vraja to see your friends, one moment becomes like a trillion years for us, who belong to you, and who become like eyes without the sun. SB 1.11.9

Sometimes he is in Mathurā and sometimes in Gokula, and in Gokula he goes from forest to forest. Since this is irregular and very confidential, we cannot approach him. Thus we do not see him to satisfaction. Where is his mercy to us?

TEXT 30

parameṣṭhi-suta-śreṣṭha
kintu sva-pitaraṁ hareḥ
anugraha-padaṁ viddhi
lakṣmī-kānta-suto hi saḥ

But you should know, O best son of Brahmā, that your own father is the true recipient of the Lord's mercy. He is the son of Lord Viṣṇu, the husband of Lakṣmī.

"O best of Brahmā's sons, Nārada!" Though the Kumāras were older, Nārada is considered the best, since he had the greatest bhakti. That was previously explained. "He, your father Brahmā, is the recipient of the Lord's mercy. He is the son of Lakṣmī's husband. Though he arose from Viṣṇu's navel, and not from Lakṣmī's womb, he is still her son also." Thus Brahmā is endowed with unlimited wealth as well.

TEXT 31

yasyaikasmin dine śakrā
mādṛśāḥ syuś caturdaśa
manv-ādi-yuktā yasyāś ca
catur-yuga-sahasrakam

In one day of Brahmā, fourteen Indras like me appear and disappear, along with different sets of Manus and all the devatās. That one day equals one thousand cycles of four yugas.

Besides fourteen Indras and Manus, other devatās, sages, sons of Manus and avatāras (ādi) appear and disappear. It is said:

manvantaraṁ manur devā
manu-putrāḥ sureśvarāḥ
ṛṣayo 'ṁśāvatārāś ca
hareḥ ṣaḍ-vidham ucyate

Manvantaram means the reign of Manu, during which six types of persons carry out specific duties: the ruling Manu, the devatās, the sons of Manu, Indra, the great sages and the incarnations of the Supreme Lord. SB 12.7.15

This happens in a thousand cycles of four yugas.

TEXT 32

niśā ca tāvatītthaṁ yā-
ho-rātrāṇāṁ śata-trayī

ṣaṣṭy-uttarā bhaved varṣaṁ
yasyāyus tac-chataṁ śrutam

Brahmā's night is of the same duration. Three hundred and sixty of such days and nights make one of his years, and his life span is a hundred years.

Double of this duration is Brahmā's day and night. One year of Brahmās is three hundred and sixty of these days. A hundred years is Brahmā's life span. We have heard this (śṛutam) but cannot confirm it, since our life spans are very short.

TEXT 33

lokānāṁ loka-pālānām
api sraṣṭādhikāra-daḥ
pālakaḥ karma-phala-do
rātrau saṁhārakaś ca saḥ

He is the creator of the planets and their rulers, and he gives them positions. He is the protector, the dispenser of the fruits of karma, and the destroyer of the world during his night.

Brahmā gives positions to Indra and the devatās (adhikāra-daḥ). He is the protector and gives results of happiness or suffering according to pious or sinful acts by establishing sacrifices and other methods, and establishing rules for different types of persons. This is all instituted by Brahmā. The first three lines of the verse indicate that Brahmā creates and maintains the universe. At night he becomes the destroyer. Hiraṇyapakśipu says:

kalpānte kāla-sṛṣṭena yo 'ndhena tamasāvṛtam
abhivyanag jagad idaṁ svayañjyotiḥ sva-rociṣā
ātmanā tri-vṛtā cedaṁ sṛjaty avati lumpati
rajaḥ-sattva-tamo-dhāmne parāya mahate namaḥ

I offer respects to the great, supreme, self-effulgent lord, the shelter of rajas, sattva and tamas, who manifests by his effulgence the universe covered with darkness at the end of his day through the influence of time, and who creates, maintains and destroys this universe by accepting the three guṇas. SB 7.3.26-27

TEXT 34

sahasra-śīrṣā yal-loke
sa mahā-puruṣaḥ sphuṭam
bhuñjāno yajña-bhāgaugham
vasaty ānanda-daḥ sadā

The Mahāpuruṣa, the thousand-headed form of the Lord, always resides on Brahmā's planet distinctly, personally accepting the myriad oblations offered to him and thus always giving bliss to his devotees.

On Brahmā's planet the astonishing (saḥ) Supreme Lord with a thousand heads resides very clearly at all times. This Mahāpuruṣa is described in Bhāgavatam:

ādyo 'vatāraḥ puruṣaḥ parasya
kālaḥ svabhāvaḥ sad-asan manaś ca
dravyaṁ vikāro guṇa indriyāṇi
virāṭ svarāṭ sthāsnu cariṣṇu bhūmnaḥ

Mahā-viṣṇu, an expansion of the Lord of Vaikuṇṭha, is time, svabhāva, effect and cause, mahat-tattva, the five gross elements, false ego, the three guṇas, the senses, the universal form, the totality of jīvas, the individual jīvas as non-moving and moving beings. All of these are related to the Supreme Lord. SB 2.6.42

jagṛhe pauruṣaṁ rūpaṁ
bhagavān mahad-ādibhiḥ
sambhūtaṁ ṣoḍaśa-kalam
ādau loka-sisṛkṣayā

First of all, the Supreme Lord accepted the form of the eternal first puruṣa full like the moon for creating the universes from mahā-tattva, etc. and sixteen other elements. SB 1.3.1

The Lord accepted a form mixed (saṁbhūtam) with the eleven senses and five gross elements (śodaśa-kalam) along with mahat-tattva, ahaṅkāra, the five tan-mātras, etc. All the elements, which are causes of the universe, take shelter of that first form of the Lord. He is the superindendent of prakṛti, the origin of the universe made of elements.

yasyāmbhasi śayānasya
yoga-nidrāṁ vitanvataḥ
nābhi-hradāmbujād āsīd
brahmā viśva-sṛjāṁ patiḥ
yasyāvayava-saṁsthānaiḥ
kalpito loka-vistaraḥ

tad vai bhagavato rūpaṁ
viśuddhaṁ sattvam ūrjitam

After Garbhodakaśāyī-viṣṇu lay on the water and went into trance, Brahmā, lord of the universal creation, appeared from the lotus in the water of his navel. The expanse of planets is imagined to be situated at various places on the lotus. This form of the Lord is pure sattva, unmixed with rajas and tamas, and is composed of eternity, knowledge and bliss. SB 1.3.2-3

From the lotus in the navel of the form which lay on the water, Brahmā appeared. The planets are imagined to be situated on the petals and other portions of the lotus (avayava-sanniveśa).

tad vilokya viyad-vyāpi
puṣkaraṁ yad-adhiṣṭhitam
anena lokān prāg-līnān
kalpitāsmīty acintayat

Seeing the lotus on which he was situated spread up to Satyaloka, he thought, "I will create the planets from this lotus, just as they were before destruction." SB 3.10.7

padma-kośaṁ tadāviśya
bhagavat-karma-coditaḥ
ekaṁ vyabhāṅkṣīd urudhā
tridhā bhāvyaṁ dvi-saptadhā

Inspired to do the work by the Lord, Brahmā entered into the whorl of the lotus, and divided it into three divisions and later expanded it into fourteen divisions in order to produce varieties. SB 3.10.8

Though this form of Viṣṇu gives shelter to māyā, it remains uncontaminated (viśuddham). It is in all places situated in brahman by its existence (sattvam).

paśyanty ado rūpam adabhra-cakṣuṣā
sahasra-pādoru-bhujānanādbhutam
sahasra-mūrdha-śravaṇākṣi-nāsikaṁ
sahasra-mauly-ambara-kuṇḍalollasat

With spiritual eyes, the devotees see this amazing form with thousands of legs and arms, thousands of heads, ears, eyes and noses, shining with thousands of crowns, earrings and clothes. SB 1.3.4

etan nānāvatārāṇāṁ
nidhānaṁ bījam avyayam
yasyāṁśāṁśena sṛjyante
deva-tiryaṅ-narādayaḥ

He is the indestructible source of various avatāras. His expansion is Brahmā and Brahmā's expansions are Marīci and others. Through them the Lord creates the devatās, animals and human beings. SB 1.3.5

Though situated in the world as avatāra, this form in nondifferent from Nārāyaṇa, the Lord in Vaikuṇṭha, and has great powers, supervises prakṛti and manifests (nidhānam) various other avatāras. Or when this form created Brahmā, almost all the avatāras also manifested.

Śrīdhara Svāmī explains in relation to SB 2.6.82 that puruṣa stimulates prakṛti. His form with a thousand heads is a līlā-vigraha, and is the first avatāra (ādyo avatāra). In the Eleventh Canto it is said:

bhūtair yadā pañcabhir ātma-sṛṣṭaiḥ
puraṁ virājaṁ viracayya tasmin
svāṁśena viṣṭaḥ puruṣābhidhānam
avāpa nārāyaṇa ādi-devaḥ

When the primeval Nārāyaṇa accepted the form of the puruṣa, he created the universe from the five elements produced from himself and then entered within the universe by his own portion. SB 11.4.3

Making the universe (puraṁ virājam) he entered it for pastimes, not as an enjoyer of the material objects of the unvierse. Pious jīvas are the enjoyers of the universe. He is called the puruṣa.

yat-kāya eṣa bhuvana-traya-sanniveśo
yasyendriyais tanu-bhṛtām ubhayendriyāṇi
jñānaṁ svataḥ śvasanato balam oja īhā
sattvādibhiḥ sthiti-layodbhava ādi-kartā

Within the body of Mahā-viṣṇu reside clusters of millions of universes composed of three planetary systems. By the Lord's senses, the action and knowledge senses of the jīvas arise. From his expansion antaryāmī, the knowledge of the jīvas arises. From his prāṇa the physical and sensual strength and action of the jīvas arise. He is the final cause of creation, maintenance and destruction through the three guṇas. SB 11.4.4

This form is described. In his body (yat-kaye) reside the three worlds. He is the cause of creation, maintenance and destruction through the three guṇas. This describes his actions.

The Third Canto describes how this form also resides on Brahmaloka. He has a thousand heads, eyes and feet. This is a gross form of the Lord, giving shelter to the universe, and is seen in Brahmā's heart by meditation. Engaged in creation Brahmā prayed, "This form should manifest directly and stay here on Brahmaloka." Thus this form remained on Brahmaloka.

Returning to the main text, the form is described as enjoying all the sacrificial offerings (yajña-bhāgaugham). Sacrifices are continually performed, like waves in the ocean. This form gives bliss to all persons present there.

When Kṛṣṇa appears in Mathurā, complete with all avatāras, this form does not remain on Brahmaloka but joins with Kṛṣṇa. However, because of Brahmā's great expanse of time, the time that the form appears on earth with Kṛṣṇa is very little. Thus it is said that the form always resides on Brahmaloka. This should be understood in later cases also.

Of course the words sadā (always) can modify "giving bliss" but the meaning is ultimately the same. (For very short periods of time he may not give bliss).

TEXT 35

itthaṁ yukti-sahasraiḥ sa
śrī-kṛṣṇasya kṛpāspadam
kiṁ vaktavyaṁ kṛpā-pātram
iti kṛṣṇaḥ sa eva hi

I could give you thousands of other reasons why Brahmā is the real recipient of Śrī Kṛṣṇa's mercy. What more needs to be said — he is in fact Kṛṣṇa Himself!

In this way (ittham) Brahmā (saḥ) is the object of Kṛṣṇa's mercy.

TEXT 36

tac chruti-smṛti-vākyebhyaḥ
prasiddhaṁ jñāyate tvayā
anyac ca tasya māhātmyaṁ
tal-lokānām api prabho

You know this, since it is proclaimed in both śruti and smṛti. You must also be familiar, my lord, with other aspects of Brahmā's glories and the glories of the residents of his planet.

"O Nārada (prabho)! It is well known from śruti and smṛti statements that Brahmā is the object of Kṛṣṇa's mercy and is similar to Kṛṣṇa. You also know this. You also know things I have not stated: the glories of the inhabitants of his planet and his establishing the process of bhakti and his devotion to the Lord."

ahaṁ brahmā ca śarvaś ca
jagataḥ kāraṇaṁ param
ātmeśvara upadraṣṭā
svayan-dṛg aviśeṣaṇaḥ

The Lord said: I am the supreme cause of the universe, the Lord of the soul, the witness, and self-revealing. I, Brahmā and Śiva are non-different from each other. SB 4.7.50

ātma-māyāṁ samāviśya
so 'haṁ guṇamayīṁ dvija
sṛjan rakṣan haran viśvaṁ
dadhre saṁjñāṁ kriyocitām

Situated in my energy composed of the guṇas, creating, maintaining and destroying the universe, I take on names according to the activity. SB 4.7.51

trayāṇām eka-bhāvānāṁ
yo na paśyati vai bhidām
sarva-bhūtātmanāṁ brahman
sa śāntim adhigacchati

O Dakṣa! The person who does not see difference between the three of us, the souls of all beings, who have one nature, attains peace. SB 4.7.54

TEXT 37

śrī-parīkṣid uvāca
indrasya vacanaṁ śrutvā
sādhu bhoḥ sādhv iti bruvan
tvarāvān brahmaṇo lokaṁ
bhagavān nārado gataḥ

Parīkṣit said: Hearing these words from Indra, godly Nārada replied, "Well said, sir, well said!" and hastily went to Brahmā's planet.

TEXT 38

yajñānāṁ mahatāṁ tatra
brahmarṣibhir anāratam
bhaktyā vitāyamānānāṁ
praghoṣaṁ dūrato 'śṛṇot

There, on Brahmaloka, Nārada first heard from a distance the sound of the great sacrifices performed unceasingly and with great devotion by the sages.

On Brahmaloka, he heard the sound of great sacrifices being performed extensively by great sages.

TEXT 39

dadarśa ca tatas teṣu
prasannaḥ parameśvaraḥ
mahā-puruṣa-rūpeṇa
jaṭā-maṇḍala-maṇḍitaḥ

Among them he saw the Supreme Lord in his Mahāpuruṣa form, looking very much satisfied, decorated with crowns of matted locks.

TEXT 40

sahasra-mūrdhā bhagavān
yajña-mūrtiḥ śriyā saha
āvirbhūyādadad bhāgān
ānandayati yājakān

Accompanied by his consort the Lord in his thousand-headed form, the personification of sacrifice, had appeared there just to please his performers of sacrifice by accepting their offerings.

After hearing, what did Nārada see? That is described. The description continues till verse 43. Being pleased, the Supreme Lord appearing as the Mahāpuruṣa in the sacrifices, accepted the offerings from the sacrifices and gave bliss to the performers of sacrifice. This is described in two verses (40-41). The presiding deity of the sacrifices, in order to pacify the sacrificers dedicated to the Vedas by giving results to the sacrifice, manifested as the Mahāpuruṣa described in Vedic verses like puruṣa-sūkta.

TEXT 41

padma-yoneḥ praharṣārthaṁ
dravya-jātaṁ niveditam
sahasra-pāṇibhir vaktra-
sahasreṣv arpayann adan

To please Brahmā, the Lord consumed all the items offered to him by placing them into his thousand mouths with his thousand hands.

But he also satisfied the desires of the worshippers by directly eating the offerings. That is explained in two verses (41-42). He threw (arpayan) the offerings into his mouth and also ate them (adan). Or in order to eat the offerings he threw them into his mouth. Or the description indicates that he was not fully satisfied with eating and thus ate a lot.

TEXT 42

dattveṣṭān yajamānebhyo
varān nidrā-gṛhaṁ gataḥ
lakṣmī-saṁvāhyamānāṅghrir
nidrām ādatta līlayā

The Mahāpuruṣa awarded the performers of the sacrifices the benedictions they desired, and went to his sleeping quarters. As Lakṣmī massaged his feet, he accepted sleep.

He gave the benedictions desired by the performance of the sacrifices. While his feet were massaged by Lakṣmī he accepted (ādatta) sleep. Since he went to a bedroom, no one could see him at that time. Accepting the sacrifices and sleeping are two pastimes described by Vaiśampāyana after the killing of Kālanemi.

sa dadarśa makheṣv ājyair ijyamānaṁ maharṣibhiḥ
bhāgaṁ yajñīyam aśnānaṁ svaṁ deham aparaṁ sthitam

He saw the Lord siuated in another form, consuming his share of the oblations of ghee offered in sacrifices by great sages.

sa tatra praviśann eva jaṭā-bhāraṁ samudvahan
sahasra-śiraso bhūtvā śayanāyopacakrame

The thousand-headed Lord, his heads covered with matted locks, entered that room and lay down to sleep.

Sahasra-śirasaḥ is poetic license for sahasra-śirā. Though the Lord manifests himself on Brahmaloka and lives there constantly, Śukadeva at the beginning of the Tenth Canto also describes how Brahmā, along with the devatās, goes to the shore of the Milk Ocean on the instructions of earth deity, where Keśava resides. It should be understood to be a description during a different day of Brahmā, since in Hari-vaṁśa it is also described that the Lord lives on Brahmaloka. Or Brahmā went to see Viṣṇu on the Milk Ocean because the Lord was not visible on Brahmaloka, having entered his bedroom, or because it would not be proper to wake him up.

Or Brahmā may have thought, "If I request the Mahā-puruṣa to appear on earth, he will no longer be present on my planet. Let the Lord on the Milk Ocean go and appear on earth."

TEXT 43

tad-ājñayā ca yajñeṣu
niyujyarṣīn nijātmajān
brahmāṇḍa-kārya-carcārthaṁ
svaṁ dhiṣṇyaṁ vidhir āgataḥ

At the Lord's request, Brahmā then ordered his sons to continue the sacrifices while he went to his own abode to tend to the management of the universe.

Before the Lord went to sleep, he ordered Brahmā to engage his sons in performing the sacrifices, either directly or in their hearts by acting as their antaryāmī. Or the order was the direction of the śrutis, which Brahmā eternally protects. Brahmā went to his own place (dhiṣṇyam).

TEXTS 44–45

pārameṣṭhyāsane tatra
sukhāsīnaṁ nija-prabhoḥ
mahima-śravaṇākhyāna-
paraṁ sāsrāṣṭa-netrakam

vicitra-paramaiśvarya-
sāmagrī-parisevitam
sva-tātaṁ nārado 'bhyetya
praṇamyovāca daṇḍa-vat

As Brahmā sat comfortably on his throne, absorbed in hearing and reciting the glories of his Lord, his eight eyes flowed with tears of bliss. Lord Brahmā was being thoroughly served by the various powers

personified. Nārada came close, offered respects to his father by falling to the ground like a stick, and then spoke.

Similar to his previous conversations, thinking it improper to express his proposal in front of the Lord, he remained at a distance and observed everything. Or even after leaving the Lord, there was still no opportunity to express his intentions. When the opportunity arose, at a convenient place, Nārada spoke to Brahmā. This is described in two verses.

Nārada approached his father, Brahmā, who was sitting on his throne in his own residence and offered respects. Since it is forbidden to offer respects to another person in front of the Lord, previously he did not pay his respects to Brahmā. Or he paid respects previously since it is not a fault to respect the highest guru, but again he offered respects in order to fulfil his intentions. Having offered respects, Nārada spoke.

Brahmā was absorbed in hearing and speaking about (śravaṇākhyāna) the glories of the Lord's qualities such as his affection for his devotees. Thus his eight eyes flowed with tears of bliss. He was thoroughly (pari) served by the assembly of a variety of the highest powers.

TEXT 46

śrī-nārada uvāca
bhavān eva kṛpā-pātraṁ
dhruvaṁ bhagavato hareḥ
prajāpati-patir yo vai
sarva-loka-pitāmahaḥ

Nārada said: You truly are the object of Lord Hari's mercy! After all, you are the master of all masters of the living beings of the universe, the grandfather of all the worlds.

In six and a half verses (46-52) Nārada shows how Brahmā is the object of Kṛṣṇa's mercy. You are famous (vai) as the recipient of mercy and are famous as the master of all masters of the world.

TEXT 47

ekaḥ sṛjati pāty atti
bhuvanāni caturdaśa
brahmāṇḍasyeśvaro nityaṁ
svayam-bhūr yaś ca kathyate

You alone create, maintain, and destroy the fourteen worlds. You eternally rule the universe, and you are known as the self-born.

You destroy (atti) the fourteen worlds. Your rulership is not destroyed at the time of pralaya like that of Indra.

TEXT 48

sabhāyāṁ yasya vidyante
mūrtimanto 'rtha-bodhakāḥ
yac-catur-vaktrato jātāḥ
purāṇa-nigamādayaḥ

In your assembly are present the personified Vedas, Purāṇas, and other scriptures, the revealers of truth, born from your four mouths.

"The scriptures reveal artha, dharma, kāma and mokṣa and the means to attain them (artha-bodhakaḥ). From your four mouths the scriptures arose." This shows that he has a wealth of all knowledge.

TEXT 49

yasya lokaś ca niśchidra-
sva-dharmācāra-niṣṭhayā
madādi-rahitaiḥ sadbhir
labhyate śata-janmabhiḥ

Your world can be attained only by saintly persons who faultlessly perform their svadharma, free from pride and other vices, for a hundred births.

"What to speak of your glories, your place also is most astonishing." This is explained in four verses (49-52). "Your planet is attained by saintly person who are steady in practicing their svadharma perfectly or purely (niścindra), who are free of lust (mada), pride and greed (ādi), for a hundred births." Śiva says to the Pracetas:

sva-dharma-niṣṭhaḥ śata-janmabhiḥ pumān viriñcatām eti

A person who executes his occupational duty properly for one hundred births becomes qualified to occupy the post of Brahmā. SB 4.24.29

TEXT 50

yasyopari na varteta
brahmāṇḍe bhuvanaṁ param

loko nārāyaṇasyāpi
vaikuṇṭhākhyo yad-antare

Within the universe there is no higher planet than yours. Even Lord Nārāyaṇa's Vaikuṇṭha planet is within your planet.

There is nothing higher since your planet is at the top of all planets. "But above my planet, there is Vaikuṇṭha." Vaikuṇṭha is within your planet. It is not separate.

TEXT 51

yasmin nityaṁ vaset sākṣān
mahā-puruṣa-vigrahaḥ
sa padmanābho yajñānāṁ
bhāgān aśnan dadat phalam

There Lord Nārāyaṇa resides eternally in his manifest form as the lotus-naveled Mahāpuruṣa. He eats his shares of sacrifice and gives the sacrificial results.

In that Vaikuṇṭha (within your planet) Nārāyaṇa is seen and resides. By directly enjoying the offerings, he gives results of the sacrifices through benedictions.

TEXT 52

paramānveṣaṇāyāsair
yasyoddeśo 'pi na tvayā
purā prāptaḥ paraṁ dṛṣṭas
tapobhir hṛdi yaḥ kṣaṇam

Although in the remote past you made many attempts and were unable to find him, by performing tapas you finally saw him just for a moment in your heart.

He describes the difficulty in attaining the Lord in order to describe the special mercy of the Lord to Brahmā who attained the unattainable. "The Lord's dwelling place or knowledge of the Lord's existence (uddeśaḥ) could not be attained by you, O great one (parama), he could not be attained by you through your attempts to find him in the ocean by going down the lotus stem." This happened long ago (purā) at the beginning of the kalpa. But at another time, by tapas he was seen for a moment. One may see the Second Canto for more details if so desired. This statement is connected with the previous statement that the Lord exists on that planet constantly (verse 51).

TEXT 53

tat satyam asi kṛṣṇasya
tvam eva nitarāṁ priyaḥ
aho nūnaṁ sa eva tvaṁ
līlā-nānā-vapur-dharaḥ

Therefore you are surely very dear to Kṛṣṇa. Indeed, you are none other than Kṛṣṇa himself assuming various forms for pastimes.

It is true that you are very dear to Kṛṣṇa. Moreover, the Lord and you are one. This is astonishing (aho). Or can this be (aho)? Or this is certain (aho). "The Lord with a thousand heads is sleeping. Many other of his forms exist. I, with four heads, am different from him." You assume those many forms as a pastime.

TEXT 54

śrī-parīkṣid uvāca
itthaṁ māhātmyam udgāyan
vistārya brahmaṇo 'sakṛt
śakra-proktaṁ sva-dṛṣṭaṁ ca
bhaktyāsīt taṁ naman muniḥ

Parīkṣit said: Thus bowing before Brahmā with great devotion again and again, the sage Nārada elaborately sang Brahmā's glories, as he had heard them from Indra and seen them with his own eyes.

He sang the glories of Brahmā that had been spoken by Indra and seen by himself, or he sang the glories of Brahmā that had been spoken by Indra, and that he had understood from scriptures, and now realized directly. He offered respects to Brahmā in devotion without cessation (tam naman āsīt).

TEXT 55

śṛṇvann eva sa tad-vākyaṁ
dāso 'smīti muhur vadan
catur-vaktro 'ṣṭa-karṇānāṁ
pidhāne vyagratāṁ gataḥ

By merely hearing what Nārada said, Brahmā anxiously covered his eight ears and said repeatedly, "I am only a servant."

TEXT 56

aśravya-śravaṇāj jātaṁ
kopaṁ yatnena dhārayan
sva-putraṁ nāradaṁ prāha
sākṣepaṁ catur-ānanaḥ

With some effort, the four-headed Brahmā checked the anger that stirred within him by hearing what should not be heard and rebuked his son Nārada.

Hearing Nārada say, "You are one with the Lord," four headed Brahmā made anxious efforts to cover his eight ears, since he heard what should not be heard. But this was difficult since he would have to cover eight ears with two or four hands.[5] Controlling (dharayan) his anger, he spoke.

TEXT 57

śrī-brahmovāca
ahaṁ na bhagavān kṛṣṇa
iti tvaṁ kiṁ pramāṇataḥ
yuktitaś ca mayābhīkṣṇaṁ
bodhito 'si na bālyataḥ

Brahmā said: I am not the Supreme Lord Kṛṣṇa! On what authority and by what logic do you say this? Haven't I constantly taught you this from childhood?

"From what śruti or smṛti do you say this? Have you not constantly understood the truth from childhood?" Api indicates that he does know. One should see conversation between Brahmā and Nārada in the Second Canto.

TEXT 58

tasya śaktir mahā-māyā
dāsīvekṣā-pathe sthitā
sṛjatīdaṁ jagat pāti
sva-guṇaiḥ saṁharaty api

---

[5] Brahmā is usually depicted with four arms.

His energy Mahā-māyā, standing within his sight like a maidservant, creates, maintains, and destroys this world by her guṇas.

By the three guṇas, māyā creates, maintains, and destroys this universe.

TEXT 59

tasyā eva vayaṁ sarve
'py adhīnā mohitās tayā
tan na kṛṣṇa-kṛpā-leśasy-
āpi pātram avehi mām

All of us are subject to her and bewildered by her. Therefore, do not think me the recipient of even a trace of Kṛṣṇa's mercy.

I, my sons and grandsons (vayam) are subject to māyā and bewildred by her. Thus you speak in this way. Because you being bewildered (tat), you should not think that I am the recipient of Kṛṣṇa's mercy.

TEXTS 60–62

tan-māyayaiva satataṁ
jagato 'haṁ guruḥ prabhuḥ
pitāmahaś ca kṛṣṇasya
nābhi-padma-samudbhavaḥ

tapasvy ārādhakas tasyety-
ādyair guru-madair hataḥ
brahmāṇḍāvaśyakāpāra-
vyāpārāmarśa-vihvalaḥ

bhūta-prāyātma-lokīya-
nāśa-cintā-niyantritaḥ
sarva-grāsi-mahā-kālād
bhīto muktiṁ paraṁ vṛṇe

By the power of his Māyā, I think of myself as the controller, grandfather, and guru of the universe. Proud of my birth from Kṛṣṇa's lotus navel, I think myself a great ascetic, his great worshiper. Overwhelmed by the countless duties of universal management and worrying about the imminent destruction of my planet, I live in fear of the all-devouring end of time. All I want for myself is liberation.

Having shown this, Brahmā now shows characteristics of lack of Kṛṣṇa's mercy. "I am the destroyer (guruḥ—controller), maintainer (prabhu) and creator (pitāmahaḥ). Or I am the teacher (guru) since I promote the

Vedas. I am the master by assigning posts to devatās (prabhu)." Brahmā does not mention destruction, since it would not sound like the Lord's mercy to assign Brahmā something inauspicious. "I am overcome with great pride (guru-madaiḥ). I am confused by having to consider unlimited matters necessary for the universe. I am under the control of thoughts about the imminent (bhūta-praya) end of my planet and in great fear of the great destruction (mahā-kālāt) where everything is annihiliated (sarva-grāsi). Thus I only (param) desire liberation from the sufferings of saṁsāra. Being the master of the inhabitants of the universe is simply a cause of great pride. It is not a sign of the mercy of Kṛṣṇa."

"I am not self-born (verse 47) but arise from the lotus in the Lord's navel (nābhi-padma-samudbhavaḥ). The personal presence of the Vedas in the assembly is not a sign of Kṛṣṇa's mercy because I am bound by its rules in considering how to handle the necessary duties in the universe." The excellence of Brahmaloka is refuted by showing its imminent destruction. Brahmā's long life is refuted by showing fear of the sufferings of saṁsāra.

TEXT 63

tad-arthaṁ bhagavat-pūjāṁ
kārayāmi karomi ca
āvāso jagad-īśasya
tasya vā na kva vidyate

For that purpose, I engage others in worshiping the Lord and also worship him myself. Since he is the Lord of the universe, is there any place where he is not present?

He criticizes Narāda's praise of the place by describing how he worships the Lord. "I worship him to attain liberation, not for the happiness of bhakti." This worship is not a sign of his mercy. Nārada said that Vaikuṇṭha was within Brahmaloka. This is refuted here. He does not have a residence (āvāsaḥ) anywhere. Rather he lives inside and outside of everything since he is the master of the universe (jagad-īśasya).

TEXT 64

veda-pravartanāyāsau
bhāgaṁ gṛhṇāti kevalam
svayaṁ-sampādita-preṣṭha-
yajñasyānugrahāya ca

He accepts offerings from me only to promote the Vedic injunctions and to show special favor to the sacrifices themselves, which are dear to him because he is their original creator.

Brahmā rejects Nārada's claim that the Lord directly accepts the offerings of sacrifice. "He accepts the offerings in order to promote the injunctions of the Vedas to the people and to show mercy to sacrifices or rules of sacrifice, which are dear to him (being his dear form) and which are promoted by him (svayam sampādita) by suppling all paraphernalia, to protect the Vedas. He does not accept the offering out of affection for me at all."

TEXT 65

vicārācārya budhyasva
sa hi bhakty-eka-vallabhaḥ
kṛpāṁ tanoti bhakteṣu
nābhakteṣu kadācana

Just consider this, O ācārya of logic: Only bhakti is dear to him. He shows his mercy only to his devotees, never to nondevotees.

"O ācārya of discernment!" This is joking. Bhakti alone is dear to the Lord. bhaktyā-ham ekayā grāhyaḥ: I can be realized only by devotional service. (SB 11.14.21) He gives mercy to his devotees.

TEXT 66

bhaktir dūre 'stu tasmin me
nāparādhā bhavanti cet
bahu manye tad ātmānaṁ
nāham āgaḥsu rudra-vat

Forget my having any bhakti for him, I would be happy if I do not offend Him. He does not tolerate my offenses as he does Lord Śiva's.

If I do not offend the Lord I consider myself a proper person (bahu manye). "But the Lord not does accept offenses from you." He does not ignore offenses that I commit as he does with Śiva.

TEXT 67

mad-āpta-vara-jāto 'sau
sarva-lokopatāpakaḥ

hiraṇyakaśipur duṣṭo
vaiṣṇava-droha-tatparaḥ

Obtaining benedicitons from me, the wicked Hiraṇyakaśipu became the tormentor of all the worlds, dedicated to violence against Vaiṣṇavas.

Brahmā explains his offenses till verse 77. Four verses (67-70) explain in relation to the killing of Hiraṇyakaśipu how by his words and actions, the Lord did not forgive Brahmā for his offense. By pointing out the reason why Hiraṇyakaśipu should be destoyed, Brahmā shows his offense and thus his disqualification from attaining the mercy of the Lord's lotus feet.

TEXTS 68–69

śrīman-nṛsiṁha-rūpeṇa
prabhuṇā saṁhṛto yadā
tadāhaṁ sa-parivāro
vicitra-stava-pāṭavaiḥ

stuvan sthitvā bhayād dūre
'pāṅga-dṛṣṭyāpi nādṛtaḥ
prahlādasyābhiṣeke tu
vṛtte tasmin prasādataḥ

After the Lord in his form as Nṛsiṁhadeva destroyed Hiraṇyakaśipu, I and my entourage stood fearfully at a distance, trying to praise the Lord with prayers, but he did not honor us even with a sidelong glance. Yet when Prahlāda was coronated king, the Lord at once became pacified.

He did not honor me even with a sidelong glance. This action indicates that the Lord did not tolerate his offense.

TEXT 70

śanair upasṛto 'bhyarṇam
ādiṣṭo 'ham idaṁ ruṣā
maivaṁ varo 'surāṇāṁ te
pradeyaḥ padma-sambhava

Then I gently approached him, and he angrily ordered me, "You should not give such benedictions to demons, O lotus-born!"

This is indicated by the Lord's words as well. "I approached him when he was pleased with Prahlada or because of Prahlāda (tasmin prasādataḥ), by his prayers. Or seeing that he was pleased with Prahlāda I approached. I thought, 'Now that he is happy, he will give me mercy.' Very gently I came near. He ordered this (idam) in anger or, becoming angry, he ordered : 'you should not give benedictions to demons.' He was angry that Hiraṇyakaśipua had committed violence to his devotee Prahlāda." This is stated in the following:

maivaṁ vibho 'surāṇāṁ te
pradeyaḥ padma-sambhava
varaḥ krūra-nisargāṇām
ahīnām amṛtaṁ yathā

O powerful Brahmā born from the lotus! Just as it is dangerous to feed milk to a snake, so it is dangerous to give benedictions to demons, who are by nature cruel. Do not give them such benedictions in the future. SB 7.10.30

"Since you have come from the lotus in my navel (and are therefore my son), I cannot simply overlook your mistake."

TEXT 71

tathāpi rāvaṇādibhyo
duṣṭebhyo 'haṁ varān adām
rāvaṇasya tu yat karma
jihvā kasya gṛṇāti tat

Nonetheless, I still gave benedictions to wicked demons like Rāvaṇa. Whose tongue can even mention the sins Rāvaṇa committed?

Though the Lord forbade me to do such things I still gave benedictions. Whose tongue can mention the sins Rāvaṇa committed, such as stealing Sītā? The wicked acts of Rāvaṇa and Hiraṇyakaśipu were done because of my benedictions. Thus their wicked acts are my offense.

TEXT 72

mayā dattādhikārāṇāṁ
śakrādīnāṁ mahā-madaiḥ
sadā hata-vivekānāṁ
tasminn āgāṁsi saṁsmara

Remember the offenses committed by Indra and other devatās, I appointed, against the Lord. The excessive pride of those devatās constantly perverts their discrimination.

Nārada praised Brahmā for appointing devatās to their posts. Now Brahmā rejects this praise and reveals the offense of Indra, which Indra had not mentioned previously because of his pride. Brahmā , in four verses (72-75),concludes that the offenses of the devatās ultimately are his offenses to the Lord. "Remember the offenses committed by the devatās against the Lord (tasmin). You know about them certainly, but now reflect upon them or investigate them (saṁsmara)."

TEXT 73

vṛṣṭi-yuddhādinendrasya
govardhana-makhādiṣu
nandāharaṇa-bāṇīya-
dhenv-adānādināp-pateḥ

Indra sent rain to retaliate for the Govardhana worship, sometimes fought against the Lord, and committed other offenses. The lord of the waters, Varuṇa, offended the Lord by kidnapping Nanda Mahārāja, by keeping the cows belonging to Bāṇa, and so on.[6]

Offense was caused by Indra sending rain when the people of Vraja worshipped Govardhana (govardhana-makha), and by Indra fighting and using proud words (ādinā) when Kṛṣṇa took the Pārijāta tree (ādiṣu).

Varuṇa committed offense by kidnapping Nanda as he bathed at the end of night on the Dvādaśī tithi. He tied him up and took him to his city. He also did not offer cows belonging to Bāṇa, and used deceptive words in speaking to the Lord.

TEXT 74

yamasya ca tad-ācāryā-
tmaja-durmāraṇādinā
kuverasyāpi duśceṣṭa-
śaṅkhacūḍa-kṛtādinā

Yamarāja allowed inauspicious death of the son of the Lord's teacher. And Kuvera was responsible for the misdeeds of Śaṅkhacūḍa and others.

Yamarāj caused the inauspicious death of Sandīpani's son named Madhumaṅgala through the agency of Pañcajanya. The word ādi

---

[6] After defeating Baṇa, Kṛṣṇa fought with Varuṇa, who had Bāṇa's cows. Kṛṣna defeated him and let him keep the cows.

indicates that Yama also fought with the Lord. This story is found in Viṣṇu Purāṇa.

Kuvera committed offense through the evil action of allowing Śaṅkhacūḍa to steal the gopīs. Ādi indicates that his two sons who became yamalārjuna trees were followers of Kaṁsa according to the Purāṇas, and thus offended the Lord.

TEXT 75

adho loke tu daiteyā
vaiṣṇava-droha-kāriṇaḥ
sarpāś ca sahaja-krodha-
duṣṭāḥ kāliya-bāndhavāḥ

In the lower planetary systems live the Daityas, who always attack Vaiṣṇavas, and also living there are the serpent friends of Kāliya, who by nature are contaminated by anger.

After pointing out the offenses of the main protectors of the directions, Brahmā points out the offenses of the inhabitants of Pātāla. Remembring the offenses commited by Kāliya to the Lord, he shows the great offense of snakes related to Kāliya.

TEXT 76

sampraty api mayā tasya
svayaṁ vatsās tathārbhakāḥ
vṛndāvane pālyamānā
bhojane māyayā hṛtāḥ

And recently by trickery I stole the young friends and calves the Lord was watching after in Vṛndāvana. I took them all away while the boys were having lunch.

Having described how the offenses of others are ultimately Brahmā's offenses, Brahmā shows his own great offense. Tathā means all or boys of such nature. "I stole the calves and boys while they were eating, or sitting there enjoying eating (bhojane)." This indicates the gravity of the offense. Moreover this occurred in Vṛndāvana. And they were being protected by Kṛṣṇa. And he stole them by trickery (māyayā).

TEXT 77

tato vīkṣya mahāścaryaṁ
bhītaḥ stutvā namann api
dhṛṣṭo 'haṁ vañcitas tena
gopa-bālaka-līlayā

I then saw an amazing event and became frightened. Offering prayers and bowing down to the Lord, I thought, "I am so arrogant! But now, in his pastime as a cowherd boy, he has tricked me."

I saw an amazing event: Kṛṣṇa, the shelter of the universe, the form of eternity, knowledge and bliss, had become each of the boys and played with them for one year. I became frightened because of committing a great offense. I have been proud, repeatedly committing offense (dhṛṣṭaḥ), or though having committed a great offense, I now approached him, offered respects and prayed to him. But now I have been tricked or bewildered by the Lord (tena), by the pastime of a cowherd boy, in which he calls and searches for the calves and boys with a lump of rice in his hand. I was not the object of his mercy. One obtains his mercy by satisfying him.

TEXT 78

tasya svābhāvikāsyābja-
prasādekṣaṇa-mātrataḥ
hṛṣṭaḥ svaṁ bahu manye sma
tat-priya-vraja-bhū-gateḥ

Simply by the natural glance of his lotus face, I became joyful. I realized how fortunate I was to have visited the indescribable land of Vraja, which is so dear to the Lord.

"Then how do you live joyfully on your planet?" Joyful simply from seeing the natural brightness of his lotus face, I consider myself successful. Another reason is given: I had gone to his dear land of Vraja, or I had surrendered to the indescribable (tat) land of Vraja dear to the Lord. This suggests the serious offense he had committed by stealing the boys and calves from Vraja. It indicates a reason for his leaving, described in the next verse.

TEXT 79

tatrātmanaś cira-sthityā-
parādhāḥ syur iti trasan

apāsaraṁ kim anyais tan
nijāsaubhāgya-varṇanaiḥ

Fearful of committing more offenses if I stayed there any longer, I then went away. What else need I tell you about my ill fortune?

"Why did Brahmā not stay there?" He feared he would commit offense by staying a long time in Kṛṣṇa's confidential place. "What use is there if I remember my misfortune? All of what you said has been refuted."

TEXT 80

atha brahmāṇḍa-madhye 'smin
tādṛṅ nekṣe kṛpāspadam
viṣṇoḥ kintu mahādeva
eva khyātaḥ sakheti yaḥ

Actually, in this universe I do not see an object of Lord Viṣṇu's mercy equal to Mahādeva Śiva. He is famous as the dear friend of the Lord.

Since everyone in the lower, middle and upper planets have faults, no one in the material universe is the real object of the Lord's mercy. Even though Śiva and others are mentioned later as the objects of the Lord's mercy, and persons like Prahlāda exist within the universe, their abodes are actually beyond the material realm, since their nature is beyond the material realm. They are not considered part of the material world.

Or it is possible to appreciate in one's mind the mercy given to persons similar to oneself, since one can experience that identity. But one cannot appreciate mercy given to dissimilar persons who are much greater than oneself, since one's mind cannot identify with them because they have such difference natures. Or one can judge the good and bad qualities of a similar person, but not the qualities of a very different type of person, just as it is difficult to compare the qualities of a blade of grass and a mountain. Thus in Hari-vaṁśa, Gaṅgā compares her good fortune to that of the ocean, and not to the good fortune of Brahmā, who has much greater good fortune.

Thus, here Brahmā considers Śiva's good fortune to be great than his own, but does not consider Prahlāda, what to speak of the cowherd boys and others. This same consideration should be applied to earlier and later descriptions in the book. Śiva is alone is the object of mercy. The characteristics are mentioned: he is well known (khyātaḥ) as the friend of the Lord. This glorification continues till verse 90.

TEXT 81

yaś ca śrī-kṛṣṇa-pādābja-
rasenonmāditaḥ sadā
avadhīrita-sarvārtha-
paramaiśvarya-bhogakaḥ

He is always intoxicated by the taste of Kṛṣṇa's lotus feet, disregarding the normal goals of life, universal supremacy and facilities for enjoyment.

Śiva disdainfully rejects enjoyment of artha, dharma, kāma and mokṣa as well as being the Supreme Lord (paramaiśvarya). Or he rejects the happiness (kaḥ) of enjoying (bhoga) things greater than artha, dharma, kāma and mokṣa.

TEXT 82

asmādṛśo viṣayiṇo
bhogāsaktān hasann iva
dhustūrārkāsthi-mālā-dhṛg
nagno bhasmānulepanaḥ

Laughing at materialists like me, who are simply addicted to sense enjoyment, he goes around naked, wearing garlands of dhustūra, arka, and bones and smeared all over with ashes.

He seems to laugh at us. "Oh! What significance do Indra and Brahmā have?" He seems to laugh at our attachment to enjoyable items like celestial garlands, ointments, etc. They are causes of suffering since they are destructible. His garland of dhustūra[7] and bones is lowly, but more attractive, since it does not cause suffering even if it is destroyed. The greatest ornament and enjoyment however is the mercy of Kṛṣṇa. Not having such mercy, wearing such lowly garlands is suitable. It is only an external decoration. Or he only seems to mock Brahmā and others since he considers himself like them (without mercy). Why else would he wear such a garland?

TEXT 83

---

[7] Commonly called Datura, this plant has poison seeds and flowers. It is commonly offered to Śiva.

viprakīrṇa-jaṭā-bhāra
unmatta iva ghūrṇate
tathā sva-gopanāśaktaḥ
kṛṣṇa-pādābja-śauca-jām
gaṅgāṁ mūrdhni vahan harṣān
nṛtyaṁś ca layate jagat

His matted locks scattered about, he wanders about like a madman, yet he is unable to conceal his glories. He joyfully carries on his head the Gaṅgā, born from the water that washed Kṛṣṇa's lotus feet. By his dancing, he destroys the universe.

Dancing, he makes the universe tremble.

TEXT 84

kṛṣṇa-prasādāt tenaiva
mādṛśām adhikāriṇām
abhīṣṭārpayituṁ muktis
tasya patnyāpi śakyate

By Kṛṣṇa's grace, Śiva and even his wife are able to award liberation to candidates like me who eagerly want it.

Those who have been given posts, like Indra and Brahma desire liberation. Because of undertaking their various duties, they become disgusted with their positions and pray for liberation. Śiva is able to give them this liberation.

Though Brahmā is an avatāra of the Lord controlling rajoguṇa, he considers himself like others with posts but it should be understood that he says this out of natural humility as an avatāra who promotes bhakti.[8] This should be understood elsewhere also.

TEXT 85

aho sarve 'pi te muktāḥ
śiva-loka-nivāsinaḥ

---

[8] It would appear that even Śiva giving liberation is somewhat of an over-statement made out of Brahmā's humility. *mukti-pradātā sarveṣāṁ viṣṇur eva na saṁśayaḥ*: there is no doubt that Viṣṇu is the deliverer of liberation for everyone. (Hari-vaṁśa) Śiva's powers are bestowed by the Lord.

muktās tat-kṛpayā kṛṣṇa-
bhaktāś ca kati nābhavan

What can be said? Everyone who lives on Śivaloka is liberated. By his mercy, so many persons have become liberated souls and even pure devotees of Kṛṣṇa.

What can be said? Śiva is eternally liberated. His devotees are also eternally liberated. What can be said (aho)? Those who live on his planet are liberated. By his mercy many others attain liberation and bhakti.

TEXT 86

kṛṣṇāc chivasya bhedekṣā
mahā-doṣa-karī matā
āgo bhagavatā svasmin
kṣamyate na śive kṛtam

To consider Śiva as different from Kṛṣṇa is a grave error. The Lord tolerates offenses against himself but not against Śiva.

By saying that Śiva is the object of Viṣṇu's mercy, difference from the Lord is rejected. Thus it is said in Padma Purāṇa:

śivasya śrī-viṣṇor ya iha guṇa-nāmādi sakalaṁ
dhiyā bhinnaṁ paśyet sa khalu hari-nāmāhita-karaḥ

The person who sees difference in the qualities and names of Śiva and Viṣṇu is an enemy of the Lord's name.

The Lord tolerates offenses (āgaḥ) against himself by people, but not against Śiva since he is very dear, being a great avatāra endowed with bhakti-rasa.

TEXTS 87–88

śiva-datta-varonmattāt
tripureśvarato mayāt
tathā vṛkāsurādeś ca
saṅkaṭaṁ paramaṁ gataḥ

śivaḥ samuddhṛto 'nena
harṣitaś ca vaco-'mṛtaiḥ
tad-antaraṅga-sad-bhaktyā
kṛṣṇena vaśa-vartinā

svayam ārādhyate cāsya
māhātmya-bhara-siddhaye

When Maya, the master of Tripura, and other demons, like Vṛkāsura, grew intoxicated with pride by Śiva's benediction and placed him in danger, the Supreme Lord saved him and gladdened him with sweet words. And sometimes, to broadcast Śiva's glories, Kṛṣṇa takes the role of his subordinate and worships him with intimate devotion.

This is shown in four verses (87-90). The benedictions given by Śiva, such as blessing Maya to make a well of nectar at Tripura and blessing Vṛkāsura to have anyone's head to fall off by his touch as well as blessing Rāvaṇa and others with great prowess, caused them to become intoxicated. Śiva experienced great danger: he could not destroy Tripura, he was pursued by Vṛkāsura and experienced Kailāsa being trembled (by Rāvaṇa). Śiva was protected from the dangers by the Lord drinking up the nectar in the well, bewildering Vṛkāsura and killing Rāvaṇa. Since the stories are found in Bhāgavatam and other scriptures, it is not necessary to write here.

Śiva was ashamed because of his offense, but was not scolded with harsh words. He was made joyful by the Lord with sweet words:

muktaṁ giriśam abhyāha
bhagavān puruṣottamaḥ
aho deva mahā-deva
pāpo 'yaṁ svena pāpmanā
hataḥ ko nu mahatsv īśa
jantur vai kṛta-kilbiṣaḥ
kṣemī syāt kim u viśveśe
kṛtāgas ko jagad-gurau

The Supreme Lord then addressed Śiva, who was now out of danger: "Just see, O Mahādeva, my lord, how this wicked man has been killed by his own sinful reactions. What living being can hope for good fortune if he offends exalted saints, what to speak of offending the lord and guru of the universe?" SB 10.88.38-39

Moreover Śiva was worshipped by the Lord as Paraśurāma and others. Why? He does this to show that Śiva is greater than himself (māhāmya-bhara-siddhaye). This shows the Lord's great affection for Śiva.

TEXTS 89–90

tiṣṭhatāpi svayaṁ sākṣāt
kṛṣṇenāmṛta-manthane
prajāpatibhir ārādhya
sa gaurī-prāṇa-vallabhaḥ

samānāyya viṣaṁ ghoraṁ
pāyayitvā vibhūṣitaḥ
mahā-mahima-dhārābhir
abhiṣiktaś ca tat sphuṭam

Although Kṛṣṇa was personally present at the churning of nectar from the Milk Ocean, he and the Prajāpatis chose to worship Śiva, the very life of Gaurī. Lord Śiva collected and drank the terrible poison, which thereafter became his ornament. He was then was glorified with floods of praise and ceremonially bathed in the presence of everyone assembled.

The Lord was personally present. The meaning is this. What fear can exist if the Lord is personally present? Producing a fearful situation and producing the remedy himself, the Lord brought Śiva there in order to broadcast Śiva's glories. Śiva was respected or requested by the Prajāpatis with prayers. By them, he was made to drink the poison, though he was the very life of Gaurī (gaurī-prāṇa-vallabhaḥ). Or the phrase is used in order glorify Gaurī as well.

By drinking the poison, Śiva became decorated with a blue throat. He was clearly bathed by successive (mahimā-dhārābhiḥ) praises of great souls (mahā) such as "This has been done by Śiva, not by the Lord."

TEXT 91

purāṇāny eva gāyanti
dayālutvaṁ harer hare
jñāyate hi tvayāpy etat
paraṁ ca smaryatāṁ mune

The Purāṇas sing of Lord Hari's mercy toward Lord Hara. You surely know all this and more. O contemplative one! You just have to recall this.

The Purāṇas sing of the great affection of the Lord for Śiva (hare). Thus you know everything that was just said, not just what I said. Other than what I have said (paraṁ), you know other facts as well. For instance Śiva gave a benediction to Kṛṣṇa to have an excellent son. O contemplative one! You just have to recollect this in your heart.

TEXT 92

śrī-parīkṣid uvāca
guruṁ praṇamya taṁ gantuṁ
kailāsaṁ girim utsukaḥ
ālakṣyoktaḥ punas tena
sva-putraḥ putra-vatsale

Parīkṣit said: O mother, affectionate to your son! Nārada bowed down to his guru, Brahmā. And when Brahmā noticed his son Nārada eager to set off for Kailāsa, Brahmā then told him something more.

Brahmā is addressed as guru because he was Nārada's father and teacher. Understanding that Nārada was about to go to Kailāsa Mountain, since he was omniscient and had this revealed in his heart, Brahmā spoke to him. Or noticing that Nārada was glancing down from Brahmaloka to Kailāsa in order to go there, Brahmā spoke to his son Nārada. "O mother, affectionate to your son! You show mercy to me with great affection. Brahmā spoke to Nārada with such affection."

TEXT 93

śrī-brahmovāca
kuvereṇa purārādhya
bhaktyā rudro vaśī-kṛtaḥ
brahmāṇḍābhyantare tasya
kailāse 'dhikṛte girau

Brahmā said: Kuvera earned the favor of Śiva by once devotedly worshiping him. From then on, within this universe, Śiva has submitted to Kuvera's authority on Mount Kailāsa, ruling the north-east.

Controlled by Kuvera, Śiva lives within the universe on the Kailāsa, supervising wealth (adhikṛte).

TEXT 94

tad-vidik-pāla-rūpeṇa
tad-yogya-parivārakaḥ
vasaty āviṣkṛta-svalpa-
vaibhavaḥ sann umā-patiḥ

Śiva, the husband of Umā, lives there as the guardian of Kuvera's direction. Accompanied by suitable attendants, he manifests a small fraction of his opulence.

He is surrounded by attendants suitable for his form as protector of the north-east direction of this Kailāsa, not in his form full of all powers. He manifests a small portion of his full powers which are beyond the material realm. He lives with Umā.

TEXT 95

yathā hi kṛṣṇo bhagavān
mādṛśāṁ bhakti-yantritaḥ
mama loke svar-ādau ca
vasaty ucita-līlayā

Just as Lord Kṛṣṇa, controlled by the devotion of servants like me, resides on my planet, and in Svarga and elsewhere, displaying suitable pastimes (Lord Śiva lives in Kailāsa).

An example is given. The Lord is brought under control by persons like me. The plural is used to indicate Kaśyapa and others. He thus lives on my planet, as well as below, on earth, and above, in Maharloka and other planets (ādau). He lives there displaying powers, associates, paraphernalia and pastimes suitable to living on that planet (līlayā). He lives there with objects suitable to his form, performing suitable pastimes with suitable associates and paraphernelia. If you go to Kuvera's Kailāsa on earth, you will not understand the exalted greatness of Śiva compared to mine by seeing his powers there.

TEXT 96

atha vāyu-purāṇasya
matam etad bravīmy aham
śrī-mahādeva-lokas tu
saptāvaraṇato bahiḥ

Now I shall speak the opinion of the Vāyu Purāṇa: The abode of Mahādeva lies outside the seven coverings of the universe.

"Where is Śiva's other abode?" Starting from earth, there are seven coverings on the universe. His abode is outside those coverings.

TEXTS 97–98

nityaḥ sukha-mayaḥ satyo
labhyas tat-sevakottamaiḥ
samāna-mahima-śrīmat-
parivāra-gaṇāvṛtaḥ

mahā-vibhūtimān bhāti
sat-paricchada-maṇḍitaḥ
śrīmat-saṅkarṣaṇaṁ svasmād
abhinnaṁ tatra so 'rcayan

nijeṣṭa-devatātvena
kiṁ vā nātanute 'dbhutam

Eternal and blissful, that abode is absolutely real. It can be attained by the best among Śiva's servants. There Śiva, served by the most excellent paraphernalia, reveals himself in his full splendor, surrounded by companions who have similar power and beauty. He worships Saṅkarṣaṇa, who is nondifferent from himself, as his deity. What wonders does Śiva not display there?

This abode is eternal not temporary like the universe and it is not illusory but reality itself. It is not contaminated by any suffering but rather the very form of full bliss (sukha-mayaḥ). It is attained by the best among Śiva's servants. They are completely fixed in devotion to him.

Or the place is possible to attain by those who do not see difference between Kṛṣṇa and Śiva, and cannot be attained by persons fixed in karma or jñāna. Or the place is attained by worshippers of Śiva, who is non-different from Kṛṣṇa.

He is surrounded by associates who have similar powers and also beauty (śrīmat). Or he is completely surrounded by associates, having equal beauty and equal powers. He has eternal, variegated houses and vehicles, superior to those of Brahmā, or dharma, artha, kāma, mokṣa and bhakti (mahāvibhūti-mān), endowed with the highest wealth. He is decorated with objects like cāmara, umbrella and ornaments (paricchada).

Śiva worships the Lord with a thousand hoods, called Saṅkārṣaṇa, as his deity on that planet. What astonishing power does he not display? He causes great amazement. Why? He worship Saṅkarṣaṇa who is non-different from himself—both are avatāras of Bhagavān. For destruction and for presiding over tamoguṇa, Saṅkarṣaṇa manifests as Rudra. He astonishes everyone because he worships as his Lord someone who is non-different (Saṅkarṣaṇa).

Or does Śiva not cause amazement by his dancing? He astonishes everyone. This is because he shows the greatest bliss from worshipping this non-different form as his deity. In the Fifth Canto of Bhāgavatam it is described the Śiva worships Saṅkarṣaṇa on Ilāvṛta-varṣa.

TEXT 99

tatra gantuṁ bhavāñ chaktaḥ
śrī-śive śuddha-bhaktimān
abhigamya tam āśritya
kṛpāṁ kṛṣṇasya paśyatu

You have the power to go there because you have pure bhakti for Śiva. Therefore go, take shelter of him, and see the real mercy of Kṛṣṇa.

"How is it possible for me to go there?" You have pure bhakti which is non-different from Kṛṣṇa. Bhaktimān indicates his great bhakti or his praiseworthy bhakti. Realize the mercy of Kṛṣṇa in Śiva's characteristics by worshipping Śiva with prayers and respects. The cause and the effect (mercy) are taken as the same (see how Kṛṣṇa is merciful to him by seeing the mercy's effects). Or experience the mercy of Kṛṣṇa.

TEXT 100

śrī-parīkṣid uvāca
ity evaṁ śikṣito mātaḥ
śiva kṛṣṇeti kīrtayan
nāradaḥ śiva-lokaṁ taṁ
prayātaḥ kautukād iva

Parīkṣit said: My dear mother, thus hearing these instructions and chanting "Śiva! Kṛṣṇa!", Nārada left for Śivaloka with great eagerness.

Being instructed to take shelter of Śiva, thinking him non-different from Kṛṣṇa (iti evam), with great astonishment in his heart (kautukāt) by hearing this amazing fact, he went there.

Or he seemed to be surprised (iva) but actually he knew everything. He wandered about in order to announce to people the persons who were objects of Kṛṣṇa's great mercy. He went to Śivaloka as if with great astonishment to see Kṛṣna's amazing mercy.

Thus ends the second chapter of Canto One of Śrīla Sanātana Gosvāmī's Bṛhad-bhāgavatāmṛta, entitled "Divya: In Svarga."

CHAPTER THREE

PRAPAÑCĀTĪTA: BEYOND THE MATERIAL WORLD

TEXTS 1–4

śrī-parīkṣid uvāca
bhagavantaṁ haraṁ tatra
bhāvāviṣṭatayā hareḥ
nṛtyantaṁ kīrtayantaṁ ca
kṛta-saṅkarṣaṇārcanam

bhṛśaṁ nandīśvarādīṁś ca
ślāghamānaṁ nijānugān
prītyā sa-jaya-śabdāni
gīta-vādyāni tanvataḥ

devīṁ comāṁ praśaṁsantaṁ
kara-tālīṣu kovidām
dūrād dṛṣṭvā munir hṛṣṭo
'namad vīṇāṁ ninādayan

paramānugṛhīto 'si
kṛṣṇasyeti muhur muhuḥ
jagau sarvaṁ ca pitroktaṁ
su-svaraṁ samakīrtayat

Parīkṣit said: Entranced in ecstatic love, there Śiva was dancing and loudly singing the glories of Lord Saṅkarṣaṇa having just worshipped him. He was enthusiastically praising his associates like Nandīśvara and others, who played instruments and shouted "Jaya! Jaya!", and he praised goddess Umā, who was expertly clapping her hands. The sight of all this delighted Nārada, who vibrating his vīṇā and nodding his head to show respect, called out several times, "You are the greatest recipient of Kṛṣṇa's mercy!" and in a sweet voice he recounted to Śiva everything just told to him by their father, Lord Brahmā.

In the Third Chapter Śiva explains that Prahlāda and others, in Vaikuṇṭha, are superior to himself.

From far off, on Śivaloka, Nārada saw Śiva dancing and singing, overcome with prema (bhāva), loudly chanting the Lord's name in an attractive voice. He also praised the Lord as in the following:

bhaje bhajenyāraṇa-pāda-paṅkajaṁ
bhagasya kṛtsnasya paraṁ parāyaṇam

bhakteṣv alaṁ bhāvita-bhūta-bhāvanaṁ
bhavāpahaṁ tvā bhava-bhāvam īśvaram

I worship wholeheartedly the Lord with lotus feet, the highest shelter of all six qualities[9], the ornament of the devotees, the object of meditation for Brahmā, the destroyer of material life, who has prema for me, your servant. SB 5.17.18

Nārada offered his respects. The reason for Śiva's prema was that he had just worshipped his deity Saṅkarṣaṇa. Here, the worship is not described in detail as it was previously. Since Śiva is an avatāra of the Lord, he performed worship in order to promote bhakti to the Lord among the people. Though Brahmā is also an avatāra, Śiva is non-different from Viṣṇu to a greater degree than Brahmā. "One should see no difference between them." Later it is said that Vasiṣṭha becomes Brahmā. Sometimes even a jīva can become Brahmā.

sva-dharma-niṣṭhaḥ śata-janmabhiḥ pumān
viriñcatām eti tataḥ paraṁ hi mām
avyākṛtaṁ bhāgavato 'tha vaiṣṇavaṁ
padaṁ yathāhaṁ vibudhāḥ kalātyaye

A person fixed in dharma attains the post of Brahmā after a hundred births, and by more pious acts than that a person attains me, Śiva. But the devotee attains the abode of Vaikuṇṭha beyond the material world after leaving the body. Similarly, I in another form reside there, and the devatās who are qualified go there after destroying their subtle bodies. SB 4.24.27

But it is never said that Śiva is a jīva. Jīvas can become Brahmā, but not Śiva. Since Śiva is a bhaktāvatāra, he is here described as one among all devotees who receive the mercy of the Lord.

Śiva praised his assistants saying "Well done! Well done!" because they were playing instruments and shouting "Jaya!" With affection he praised Umā who was clapping her hands skillfully. All his followers were great devotees, following his example.

Nārada offered respects with his head. It was not possible to lay on the ground since he was absorbed in playing his vīṇā which was necessary when he was dancing. It was proper to sing at this time. What he said is described. He repeated what his father Brahmā had said.

---

[9] *Aiśvarya, yaśa, vīra, śrī, jñāna* and *vairāgya*

TEXTS 5–6

atha śrī-rudra-pādābja-
reṇu-sparśana-kāmyayā
samīpe 'bhyāgataṁ devo
vaiṣṇavaika-priyo munim

ākṛṣyāśliṣya sammattaḥ
śrī-kṛṣṇa-rasa-dhārayā
bhṛśaṁ papraccha kiṁ brūṣe
brahma-putreti sādaram

Then Nārada came closer, desiring to touch the dust of the lotus feet of Śiva, the dear friend of the Vaiṣṇavas. But as the sage came near, Śiva, frenzied by drinking the streams of rasa of kṛṣṇa-prema, pulled Nārada closer, embraced him and asked him respectfully, "O son of Brahmā, what are you saying?"

After dancing, Śiva pulled Nārada close and embraced him. "O Nārada, son of Brahmā! What are you saying?" he repeatedly asked him with respect. Becoming completely frenzied by drinking the streams of rasa of kṛṣṇa-prema, Śiva did not hear the words or could not understand their meaning. Thus he repeatedly asked.

TEXTS 7–8

tataḥ śrī-vaiṣṇava-śreṣṭha-
sambhāṣaṇa-rasāplutam
santyakta-nṛtya-kutukaṁ
mita-priya-janāvṛtam

pārvatī-prāṇa-nāthaṁ taṁ
vṛṣyāṁ vīrāsanena saḥ
āsīnaṁ praṇaman bhaktyā
paṭhan rudra-ṣaḍ-aṅgakam

Absorbed in the taste of conversing with the best of Vaiṣṇavas, Nārada, Śiva then stopped his joyful dancing and sat down. He sat on a straw mat in the vīrāsana posture, and a few of his gentle companions surrounded him. With devotion Nārada bowed down to Śiva, the life of Pārvatī, and chanted the six-syllable Rudra mantra.

Nārada offered respects to Śiva and praised him. Śiva was absorbed in speaking with the best of Vaiṣṇavas, Nārada. He had given up dancing in joy and was surrounded by a few (mita) associates. He was seated on a straw mat in vīrāsana.

ekaṁ pādam athaikasmin vinyased ūru-saṁsthitam
itarasiṁs tatha bāhuṁ vīrāsanam idaṁ smṛtam

One should place one foot upon the other which is situated on the thigh. One arm should be placed on the other. This is called vīrāsana.[10]

Nārada chanted the rudra-ṣad-aṅga mantra from the Vedas.

TEXT 9

jagad-īśatva-māhātmya-
prakāśana-paraiḥ stavaiḥ
astaud vivṛtya tasmiṁś ca
jagau kṛṣṇa-kṛpā-bharam

Nārada then recited prayers revealing Śiva as the lord of the universe and elaborately sang the great mercy bestowed upon Śiva by Lord Kṛṣṇa.

Nārada praised Śiva with verses of praise which revealed Śiva's greatness as the lord of the universe, or which revealed the greatness of Śiva, who is the lord of the universe. He elaborately sang the great mercy of Kṛṣṇa on Śiva (tasmin), according to Brahmāṇḍa Purāṇa.

TEXT 10

karṇau pidhāya rudro 'sau
sa-krodham avadad bhṛśam
sarva-vaiṣṇava-mūrdhanyo
viṣṇu-bhakti-pravartakaḥ

Lord Rudra, the best of Vaiṣṇavas, the promoter of bhakti to Viṣṇu, at once covered his ears and angrily replied.

Śiva is the best of all Vaiṣṇavas. Vaiṣṇavānāṁ maheśvaraḥ: "Of all Vaiṣṇavas, Lord Maheśvara is the greatest." He is the best because he broadcasts bhakti to Viṣṇu. Though he is directly Bhagavān, being an

[10] The *Gheraṇḍa-saṁhitā* has *paścād* instead of *bāhum* in the second line. This is probably more correct. One foot is placed on the thigh and the other foot is placed behind (or below) the other leg. In any case this is different from the commonly known vīrāsana.

avatāra of Viṣṇu, it is suitable to call him "the best Vaiṣṇava" because he promotes bhakti as an avatāra.

TEXT 11

śrī-rudra uvāca
na jātu jagad-īśo 'haṁ
nāpi kṛṣṇa-kṛpāspadam
paraṁ tad-dāsa-dāsānāṁ
sadānugraha-kāmukaḥ

Rudra said: "I am neither the lord of the universe, nor an object of Kṛṣṇa's mercy! I simply hanker for the mercy of the servants of his servants."

I simply (param) desire the mercy of his servants at all times. I do not have their mercy.

TEXT 12

śrī-parīkṣid uvāca
sambhrānto 'tha munir hitvā
kṛṣṇenaikyena tat-stutim
sāparādham ivātmānaṁ
manyamāno 'bravīc chanaiḥ

Parīkṣit said: Shocked at hearing this, Nārada at once stopped praising Śiva as non-different from Kṛṣṇa. Thinking he had acted offensively, he began to speak in a soft voice.

Nārada gave up praising Śiva as non-different (aikyena) from Kṛṣṇa.

TEXT 13

śrī-nārada uvāca
satyam eva bhavān viṣṇor
vaiṣṇavānāṁ ca durgamām
nigūḍhāṁ mahima-śreṇīṁ
vetti vijñāpayaty api

Nārada said: You truly know the confidential, mysterious glories of Lord Viṣṇu and the Vaiṣṇavas. And you also explain those glories.

You known the glories of the Lord which are difficult to understand by others (durgamam), since they are most secret (nigūḍham) and you reveal (vijñāpayati) those glories to the people.

TEXT 14

ato hi vaiṣṇava-śreṣṭhair
iṣyate tvad-anugrahaḥ
kṛṣṇaś ca mahimānaṁ te
prīto vitanute 'dhikam

Therefore, the best Vaiṣṇavas aspire for your mercy. Lord Kṛṣṇa also has great affection for you and extensively spreads your glories.

Kṛṣṇa has more affection for you (adhikam) than for other devotees or than for myself.

TEXT 15

kati vārāṁś ca kṛṣṇena
varā vividha-mūrtibhiḥ
bhaktyā bhavantam ārādhya
gṛhītāḥ kati santi na

How many times has Kṛṣṇa not taken boons from you? How many times has he not worshiped you with devotion in his various incarnations?

Nārada shows how Kṛṣṇa is more affectionate to Śiva. "Did Kṛṣṇa not accept many benedictions from Śiva?" He accepted many boons. One can understand this from the Dāna-dharma section of Vāmana Purāṇa. One can examine the stories of obtaining the Sudarśana cakra and the son Sāmba.

TEXT 16

śrī-parīkṣid uvāca
iti śrutvā tu sahasā
dhairyaṁ kartum aśaknuvan
lajjito drutam utthāya
nāradasya mukhaṁ haraḥ
karābhyāṁ pidadhe dhārṣṭyaṁ
mama tan na vader iti

Parīkṣit said: Unable to remain sober hearing this, and feeling ashamed, Śiva sprang to his feet, and covered Nārada's mouth with both hands, and said, "Don't even mention that rashness of mine!"

He was ashamed when he remembered giving boons to Kṛṣṇa. "You should not speak of my rash behavior." He covered (pidadhe) Nārada's mouth.

TEXT 17

anantaram uvācoccaiḥ
sa-vismayam aho mune
durvitarkya-taraṁ līlā-
vaibhavaṁ dṛśyatāṁ prabhoḥ

Wonder-struck, Śiva loudly said, "Just see the most incomprehensible power of the pastimes of the Lord! O sage!"

See the greatness of the Lord's pastimes, so that the Lord accepts from me benedictions after he performs austerities.

TEXT 18

aho vicitra-gambhīra-
mahimābdhir mad-īśvaraḥ
vividheṣv aparādheṣu
nopekṣeta kṛteṣv api

"Oh, my Lord is steady deep ocean of various great qualities! In spite of the many kinds of offenses I committed against him, he still does not reject me."

My Lord Kṛṣṇa is a steady, uncrossable ocean of unfathomable greatness of great variety or of forms of power since he does not care for my committing a variety of offenses, such as giving benedictions and showing pride in my power. Even now I can continue to promote devotion to him as previously.

TEXT 19

śrī-parīkṣid uvāca
paramānandito dhṛtvā
pādayor upaveśya tam
nāradaḥ parituṣṭāva
kṛṣṇa-bhakti-rasa-plutam

Parīkṣit said: Nārada, extremely pleased, grasped the feet of Śiva, who was completely absorbed in the rasa of kṛṣṇa-bhakti, and made him sit down again, and spoke to appease him.

Nārada grasped Śiva's feet and made him sit down.

TEXT 20

śrī-nārada uvāca
nāparādhāvakāśas te
preyasaḥ kaścid acyute
kadācil loka-dṛṣṭyāpi
jāto nāsmin prakāśate

Nārada said: You are so dear to Lord Acyuta. Is it possible you could ever offend the Lord? Though in the eyes of ordinary people you may seem to have offended the Lord, the Lord never sees them at all.

Actually there is no offense, but in the eyes of people it seems so. Even if sometimes there is offense, the Lord does not take it as offense since Śiva is very dear to him (preyasaḥ).

TEXTS 21–22

sva-bāhu-bala-dṛptasya
sādhūpadrava-kāriṇaḥ
māyā-baddhāniruddhasya
yudhyamānasya cakriṇā

hata-prāyasya bāṇasya
nija-bhaktasya putra-vat
pālitasya tvayā prāṇa-
rakṣārthaṁ śrī-hariḥ stutaḥ

Bāṇa created trouble for saintly persons and was too proud of the strength of his arms. He used mystic powers to arrest Aniruddha and fight against Kṛṣṇa, the wielder of the disc. When you saw that Bāṇa, your devotee, who was like a son, was on the verge of being killed, to protect his life you offered prayers to the Lord.

Three verses (21-23) describe how the Lord does not accept offenses of Śiva. "You praised Kṛṣṇa in order to protect the life of Bāṇa."

TEXT 23

sadyo hitvā ruṣaṁ prīto
dattvā nija-svarūpatām
bhavat-pārṣadatāṁ ninye
taṁ durāpāṁ surair api

At once, Lord Kṛṣṇa put aside his anger and, being pleased, gave Bāṇa a form similar to his and made him one of your associates, a position rarely obtained even by devatās.

Kṛṣṇa made Bāṇa into an associate of Śiva, though he had fought with the Lord, who raised his cakra. The many offenses of Bāṇa are listed in verse 21. Śiva offered prayers on Bāṇa's behalf because Bāṇa was his devotee and was protected by Śiva like a son. Bāṇa attained a form with four arms. This is described by the Lord to Śiva in the Tenth Canto:

catvāro 'sya bhujāḥ śiṣṭā bhaviṣyaty ajarāmaraḥ
pārṣada-mukhyo bhavato na kutaścid-bhayo 'suraḥ

This demon, who still has four arms, will be immune to old age and death, and he will serve as one of your principal attendants. Thus he will have nothing to fear on any account. SB 10.63.49

TEXT 24

bhavāṁś ca vaiṣṇava-drohi-
gārgyādibhyaḥ su-duścaraiḥ
tapobhir bhajamānebhyo
nāvyalīkaṁ varaṁ dade

When Gārgya and other enemies of the Vaiṣṇavas worshiped you by severe penances, the benedictions you gave them were not true.

There is no actual offense (from the Lord's point of view). That was explained. Now it is explained in two verses (24-25) that there was no opportunity for offense. "You did not give perfect boons to Gārgya, as well to Jayadratha and Sudakṣiṇa, who desired to harm the Yādavas and Pāṇdavas, even though they were your devotees."

To Gārgya he gave the boon that Gārgya's son could frighten and arrest the Yadus but not kill them. To Jayadratha, he gave the boon that he could defeat each of the Pāṇdavas only once, and not defeat Arjuna at all. To Sudakṣiṇa he gave the boon of producing a fire that could be used against persons who did not respect brāhmaṇas. One can find the details in Hari-vaṁśa, Viṣṇu Purāṇa and Bhāgavatam.

TEXT 25

citraketu-prabhṛtayo
'dhiyo 'py aṁśāśritā hareḥ
nindakā yady api svasya
tebhyo 'kupyas tathāpi na

Although Citraketu and others like him foolishly dared criticize you, you never became angry at them, because they took shelter of aṁśas of Lord Hari.

It was explained that Śiva does not give perfect benedictions to his followers since they are not Vaiṣṇavas. Now it is explained that Śiva does not disrespect those who hate him, if they are related to Viṣṇu. These devotees take shelter of aṁśas of the Lord such as Śeṣa. They are called aṁśas because they are non-different from the Lord. Though they are not aware of the real nature of Śiva (adhiyaḥ), and thus criticize him, Śiva does not become angry.

TEXT 26

kṛṣṇasya prītaye tasmāc
chraiṣṭhyam apy abhivāñchatā
tad-bhaktataiva cāturya-
viśeṣeṇārthitā tvayā

For the satisfaction of Kṛṣṇa, you once desired to become even greater than he. But actually you prayed to be his devotee, with special cleverness.

"I committed offense to Kṛṣṇa by asking to be superior to him, in order to have special worship."

alabdhvā cātmanaḥ pūjāṁ
samyag ārādhito hariḥ
mayā tasmād api śraiṣṭhyaṁ
vāñchatāhaṅkṛtātmanā

Nor receiving great worship, I worshipped the Lord intently with pride, and with a desire to excel him. Bṛhad-sahasra-nāma-stotra

That is explained in this verse. Śiva made the request to please Kṛṣṇa, since the Lord is not satisfied by a request to be his servant, since Kṛṣṇa is gentle and shy by nature. Actually he prayed to be the servant (bhaktatā) of Kṛṣṇa, with special cleverness. Mad-bhakta-pūjābhyadhikā: more important than worshiping me is worshiping my devotee. (SB

11.19.21) Thus he actually wanted to be the best devotee, not to be superior (to Kṛṣṇa). The Lord uttered this to the dice when he was playing dice with Rukmiṇī.

TEXT 27

ato brahmādi-samprārthya-
mukti-dānādhikāritām
bhavate bhagavatyai ca
durgāyai bhagavān adāt

Therefore the Lord given you and Durgā the power to grant liberation, which Brahmā and many others pray for.

Because you are more attentive to the Vaiṣṇavas than to your followers, the Lord has given you and Durgā the power to grant liberation.

TEXT 28

aho brahmādi-duṣprāpye
aiśvarye saty apīdṛśe
tat sarvaṁ sukham apy ātmyam
anādṛtyāvadhūta-vat

Oh! Though you have power unobtainable by Brahmā and the other devatās, you disregard your personal happiness and live like an avadhūta.

Four verses (28-31) summarize how the Lord gives Śiva the most mercy. "You disregard your powers (tat ātmyam) and all happiness."

TEXT 29

bhāvāviṣṭaḥ sadā viṣṇor
mahonmāda-gṛhīta-vat
ko 'nyaḥ patnyā samaṁ nṛtyed
gaṇair api dig-ambaraḥ

Absorbed in love for Viṣṇu, you appear totally insane. Who else but you, dressed by the directions, would dance with his wife and attendants?

You disregard all happiness because you are absorbed in love of Viṣṇu (bhāvāviṣṭaḥ). The word sadā (always) can be linked to other statements also. You seemed to be possessed like a madman since you ignore the dance movements normally seen in the world.

TEXT 30

dṛṣṭo 'dya bhagavad-bhakti-
lāmpaṭya-mahimādbhutaḥ
tad bhavān eva kṛṣṇasya
nityaṁ parama-vallabhaḥ

Today I have finally seen your amazing intense greed to engage in bhakti to the Lord. No wonder you alone are supremely dear to Kṛṣṇa!

"I have directly realized today your greatness in relishing bhakti to the Lord." This is astonishing to Nārada, since Śiva acts insanely, though he is the master of the greatest yogīs, the crest jewel of ātmārāmas and the husband of Pārvatī.

TEXT 31

āḥ kiṁ vācyānavacchinnā
kṛṣṇasya priyatā tvayi
tvat-prasādena bahavo
'nye 'pi tat-priyatāṁ gatāḥ

What more can I say? Kṛṣṇa's affection for you is uninterrupted. And by your mercy many others have become objects of Kṛṣṇa's prema.

Many others, like the ten Pracetās, have become the objects of Kṛṣṇa's prema (tat-priyatām) by your mercy.

TEXT 32

pārvatyāś ca prasādena
bahavas tat-priyāḥ kṛtāḥ
tattvābhijñā viśeṣeṇa
bhavator iyam eva hi

By Pārvatī's mercy, many others have become dear to Kṛṣṇa. She knows in detail the true nature of you and Kṛṣṇa.

Many others like Janaśarmā[11] have become dear to Kṛṣṇa by Pārvatī's mercy. She knows the excellence of you and Kṛṣṇa (bhavatoḥ).

TEXT 33

---

[11] His story is told in the second part of *Bṛhad-bhāgavatāmṛta*.

kṛṣṇasya bhaginī vaiṣā
sneha-pātraṁ sadāmbikā
ata eva bhavān ātmā-
rāmo 'py etām apekṣate

Pārvatī, Ambikā, is like Kṛṣṇa's own sister, who always receives his affection. That is why you care for her even though fully satisfied in yourself.

Pārvatī is like the sister of Kṛṣṇa because she is non-different from māyā who was present in Yaśodā's womb. The word iva indicates she is not directly the sister (since Kṛṣṇa was born to Devakī). Or she is the object of affection of Kṛṣṇa just like his sister Subhadrā. You enjoy in yourself (ātmārāmaḥ). This can be said since Śiva is the Lord's avatāra. Or you take pleasure in the Lord (ātmārāmaḥ). Even so, you give regard to Ambikā (since she is the object of Kṛṣṇa's affection.)

TEXT 34

vicitra-bhagavan-nāma-
saṅkīrtana-kathotsavaiḥ
sademāṁ ramayan viṣṇu-
jana-saṅga-sukhaṁ bhajet

You give her pleasure by always holding wonderful festivals of nāma-saṅkīrtana and recitation of his pastimes. At those times she experiences joy in the association of Lord Viṣṇu's devotees.

The result is described. He gives her (imam) pleasure by colorful festivals of kīrtana and discussion of pastimes or by festivity caused by kīrtana and discourses. Plural is used to show respect or to indicate the great variety of festivals. "You always attain happiness of festivals of kīrtana from associating with devotees."

TEXT 35

śrī-parīkṣid uvāca
tato maheśvaro mātas
trapāvanamitānanaḥ
nāradaṁ bhagavad-bhaktam
avadad vaiṣṇavāgraṇīḥ

Parīkṣit said: Dear mother, Śiva, embarrassed by hearing this , lowered his face. Then that chief of the Vaiṣṇavas replied to the great devotee Nārada.

Embarrassed by being praised or by thinking it a joke since it was impossible for him to have such qualities, he lowered his head since he was the chief of the Vaiṣṇavas.

TEXT 36

śrī-maheśa uvāca
aho bata mahat kaṣṭaṁ
tyakta-sarvābhimāna he
kvāhaṁ sarvābhimānānāṁ
mūlaṁ kva tādṛśeśvaraḥ

Maheśa said: Oh, how painful this is! O completely prideless Nārada, how can you compare me, the root of all pride, to Kṛṣṇa?

What am I, the root of those who falsely identify themselves as lords of the planets? Or what am I, the root of all jīvas intoxicated with wealth, fame and power, since I am the deity of ahaṅkāra. What is Kṛṣṇa, the lord of all who have rejected false identity? I have no relationship with Kṛṣṇa at all.

TEXT 37

lokeśo jñāna-do jñānī
mukto mukti-prado 'py aham
bhakto bhakti-prado viṣṇor
ity-ādy-ahaṅ-kriyāvṛtaḥ

I consider myself the lord of the universe, the all-knowing giver of knowledge, the liberated bestower of liberation, the devotee who gives viṣṇu-bhakti. I am covered by many false identities.

"As the deity of ahaṅkāra, I also am influenced by ahaṅkāra. I have more false identity than all others. I am covered with false ego (ahaṁkriyā), thinking I am Viṣṇu's devotee and the giver of viṣṇu-bhakti." The word ādi indicates that he also thinks he is dear to the Lord and the greatest object of mercy.

"He who makes others identify falsely has the greatest false identity." Thus, Śiva says that he is not at all the object of Kṛṣṇa's mercy.

TEXT 38

sarva-grāsa-kare ghore
mahā-kāle samāgate
villaje 'śeṣa-saṁhāra-
tāmasa-sva-prayojanāt

When the terrible time of annihilation arrives, I am obliged by the mode of ignorance to destroy the entire cosmos. When I think of this, I feel ashamed.

Moreover, I am ashamed that my necessary duty is the tamasic destruction of unlimited universes. Thinking about this duty, I am ashamed.

TEXT 39

mayi nārada varteta
kṛpā-leśo 'pi ced dhareḥ
tadā kiṁ pārijātoṣā-
haraṇādau mayā raṇaḥ

Dear Nārada, if I had even a drop of the mercy of Lord Hari, why did he fight with me during the stealing of pārijāta, stealing of Uṣā and on other such occasions?

"One cannot infer his mercy to me by examining my activities in my post. Rather one can see he is completely indifferent to me." This is expressed in two verses (39-40). "When Kṛṣṇa stole the pārijāta and when Aniruddha was imprisoned because of stealing Uṣā, why should he fight with me?" He should not.

TEXT 40

māṁ kim ārādhayed dāsaṁ
kim etac cādiśet prabhuḥ
svāgamaiḥ kalpitais tvaṁ ca
janān mad-vimukhān kuru

Why should the Lord worship me, his servant, and why should he order me, "By concocting your own scriptures turn the people away from me"?

"Why should the Lord worship me, his servant?" It is to cause ridicule by the people. Or one can understand that this is a special show of the Lord's internal anger at Śiva. "By acting so modestly in worshipping me, he causes me great sorrow ." This must be the intention when Kṛṣṇa worshipped Śiva in order to obtain an excellent son. His accepting many boons from Śiva is not a sign of giving mercy to Śiva but rather contempt for him. Thus he does not tolerate my offenses. That is the deep meaning.

"Furthermore, why did he order me to make false scriptures? Ordering promotion of bhakti is a sign of mercy and ordering false scriptures is a sign of his indifference to me." Though the Lord ordered this to hide bhakti which should not be given to everyone, and though following the order is perfection for the devotee who prays intensely to the Lord for such service, Śiva felt remorse and could not tolerate it, because of his great bhakti.

TEXT 41

āvayor mukti-dātṛtvaṁ
yad bhavān stauti hṛṣṭa-vat
tac cāti-dāruṇaṁ tasya
bhaktānāṁ śruti-duḥkha-dam

You joyfully praise us both for the power to give liberation. But we consider this power terrible, because the Lord's devotees feel distressed to hear of it.

Giving liberation is actually very cruel, since it is contrary to bhakti. The benediction of giving liberation gives sorrow to the devotees by hearing about it with the ears (śruti) or by simply hearing the phrase.

TEXT 42

tat kṛṣṇa-pārṣada-śreṣṭha
mā māṁ tasya dayāspadam
viddhi kintu kṛpā-sāra-
bhājo vaikuṇṭha-vāsinaḥ

Therefore, O best of Kṛṣṇa's associates, do not consider me a recipient of Kṛṣṇa's mercy. Rather, those who have obtained the essence of his mercy are the residents of Vaikuṇṭha.

Therefore (tat), do not think that I am the object of Kṛṣṇa's mercy. O best of Kṛṣṇa's associates! You, who are superior to me, know everything.

TEXT 43

yaiḥ sarvaṁ tṛṇa-vat tyaktvā
bhaktyārādhya priyaṁ harim
sarvārtha-siddhayo labdhvā-
pāṅga-dṛṣṭyāpi nādṛtāḥ

Having given up everything as worthless straw, and worshiping their dear Hari in pure devotion, they have no respect for the wealth of this world; they will not even glance at those perfections.

In order to show that the residents of Vaikuṇṭha are the highest recipients of Kṛṣṇa's mercy, Śiva glorifies them in six verses (43-48). First he describes their greatness, by showing the excellent sādhana necessary to attain Vaikuṇṭha. They worship the Lord with prema (bhaktyā) because he is dear (priyam). Though artha, dharma, kāma and mokṣa (sarvārtha) as well as siddhis like anima (siddhayaḥ) are achieved by them, or, though a wealth of all objects are achieved by them as secondary results of worship of the Lord, they are not accepted by the devotees as significant (na ādhṛtāḥ) even with a glance from the corner of their eyes.

TEXT 44

tyakta-sarvābhimānā ye
samasta-bhaya-varjitam
vaikuṇṭhaṁ sac-cid-ānandaṁ
guṇātītaṁ padaṁ gatāḥ

Having given up all false identity, they have attained the world beyond the guṇas and devoid of all fear: Vaikuṇṭha, which is sac-cid-ānanda — full of eternity, knowledge, and bliss.

They have been described as greater than materialists, desirers of liberation and liberated souls. Now they are described as greater than Śiva. Those who have attained Vaikuṇṭha, which is not temporary or material, being made of eternity, knowledge and bliss, since it is beyond the guṇas, have given up all false identity. In the conversation between Brahmā and Nārada in Nārada Pañcarātra, we can read, in the Jitaṁ-te-stotra:

lokaṁ vaikuṇṭha-nāmānaṁ
divya-ṣaḍ-guṇa-saṁyutam
avaiṣṇavānām aprāpyaṁ
guṇa-traya-vivarjitam
nitya-siddhaiḥ samākīrṇaḥ
tan-mayaiḥ pañca-kālikaiḥ

sabhā-prāsāda-saṁyuktaṁ
vanaiś copavanaiḥ śubham
vāpī-kūpa-taḍāgaiś ca
vṛkṣa-ṣaṇḍaiḥ su-maṇḍitam
aprākṛtaḥ surair vandyam
ayutārka-sama-prabham

The place called Vaikuṇṭha is beyond the material world, endowed with six qualities[12], devoid of the three material guṇas and not obtainable by non-devotees. It is filled with eternally perfect devotees engaged in the five actions[13]. There are halls and palaces, which are resplendent with attached forests and groves. The place is decorated with wells, ponds and canals and groves of trees. This spiritual place, praised by the devotees, is as effulgent as ten thousand suns. (Nārada-pañcarātra)

In the Brahmāṇḍa Purāṇa it is said:

tam ananta-guṇāvāsaṁ
mahat-tejo durāsadam
apratyakṣaṁ nirupamaṁ
parānandam atīndriyam

That place is endowed with unlimited qualities and great effulgence. It is difficult to understand, invisible to material eyes, incomparable, supremely blissful, and beyond the senses.

tasmai sva-lokaṁ bhagavān sabhājitaḥ
sandarśayām āsa paraṁ na yat-param
vyapeta-saṅkleśa-vimoha-sādhvasaṁ
sva-dṛṣṭavadbhiḥ puruṣair abhiṣṭutam

The Lord, gratified by his worship, showed Brahmā Mahā-vaikuṇṭha, to which nothing is superior, which is free of suffering, confusion and fear of offenses and which is praised by the devatās who constantly see the self. (SB 2.9.9)

---

[12] *Aiśvarya, vīrya, yaśa, śrī, jñāna* and *vairāgya*

[13] These are *pañcarātraika* divisions of time for engagement in service.

1. *abhigamana* (approaching the temple, cleaning the temple, removing used articles and cleaning them, and decorating the temple)
2. *upādāna* (gathering articles like flowers)
3. *yoga* (attaining spiritual identity fit for service)
4. *ijyā* (direct worship of the Lord)
5. *svādhyāya* (praising the Lord through recitation of scripture, hearing, etc.)

pravartate yatra rajas tamas tayoḥ
sattvaṁ ca miśraṁ na ca kāla-vikramaḥ
na yatra māyā kim utāpare harer
anuvratā yatra surāsurārcitāḥ

In Vaikuṇṭha there are no rajas or tamas, and no sattva mixed with rajas and tamas. There is no influence of time. There is no influence of māyā at all, what to speak of its products such as material elements. In Vaikuṇṭha the inhabitants are fully dedicated to the Lord and are worshipable by the devas, asuras and devotees. (SB 2.9.10)

iti sañcintya bhagavān mahā-kāruṇiko hariḥ
darśayām āsa lokaṁ svaṁ gopānāṁ tamasaḥ param

Thus, deeply considering the situation, the all-merciful Supreme Lord revealed to the cowherd men his abode, which is beyond prakṛti. (SB 10.28.14)

satyaṁ jñānam anantaṁ
yad brahma-jyotiḥ sanātanam
yad dhi paśyanti munayo
guṇāpāye samāhitāḥ

Kṛṣṇa revealed the place which was real, cognizant, infinite, eternal, and self effulgent. Sages see that place in trance, when their consciousness is free of the modes of material nature. (SB 10.28.15)

The meaning is this. The supreme planet beyond prakṛti is described in verse 15. Brahman means "all-pervading." It has existence, knowledge and eternity spread everywhere. Or it has existence, knowledge and eternity as its svarūpa (brahma). If the version with yad brahma occurs, yad is in the neuter to modify brahma. Or it is an indeclinable standing for yam.

The ātmārāmas perceive this place with jñāna-cakṣu (eyes of knowledge) but cannot attain it.

TEXT 45

tatra ye sac-cid-ānanda-
dehāḥ parama-vaibhavam
samprāptaṁ sac-cid-ānandaṁ
hari-sārṣṭiṁ ca nābhajan

There the residents have sac-cid-ānanda bodies. And though they have obtained supreme opulence of the Lord and sac-cid-ānanda powers equal to his, yet they do not like to use them.

Though the residents of Vaikuṇṭha have forms, they are eternal and not material. That is indicated in this verse.

dehendriyāsu-hīnānāṁ vaikuṇṭha-pura-vāsinām
deha-sambandha-sambaddham etad ākhyātum arhasi

The inhabitants of Vaikuṇṭha are completely spiritual, having no material body, senses or life airs. Therefore, please tell the story of how they became bound with bodies in this world. SB 7.1.35

They are devoid of material bodies and senses (dehendriyāsu-hīnānām), and thus have forms of eternity, knowledge and bliss. After the forms are glorified, there is a glorification of their external powers. They do not accept with reverence these most excellent (parama) powers (vaibhavam) that they attain easily and completely (samprāptam). Each one possesses the wealth of millions of universes with their coverings. But that wealth or power is full of eternity (sat).That wealth is Brahman, but full of great variety and most sweet, since it is the special śakti of the Lord. Vaikuṇṭha shines with this wealth belonging to its residents. This will be revealed later with logic and proof. The residents do not accept powers equal to the Lords (sārṣṭim).

TEXT 46

harer bhaktyā paraṁ prītā
bhaktān bhaktiṁ ca sarvataḥ
rakṣanto vardhayantaś ca
sañcaranti yadṛcchayā

They are satisfied simply with devotion to the Lord. They travel about at will, protecting and promoting the Lord's devotees and the Lord's devotional service.

The cause of their disinterest in powers is explained. The word sarvataḥ should be applied appropriately to the different statements. Simply (param) satisfied (prītāḥ) with devotion to the Lord in all conditions, they travel about at will.

akiñcanasya dāntasya śāntasya sama-cetasaḥ
mayā santuṣṭa-manasaḥ sarvāḥ sukha-mayā diśaḥ

One who does not desire anything within this world, who has controlled his senses, who has fixed his intelligence on me, who regards heaven and hell equally, and whose mind is completely satisfied in me finds only happiness wherever he goes. SB 11.14.13

Those who are fixed in bhakti, who simply engage in the Lord's service, are satisfied because they naturally attain all perfections. The residents of Vaikuṇṭha protect and increase the devotees and bhakti. They, in all cases (sarvataḥ), protect the devotees from degradation due to carelessness or from material persons and Yama's punishment. They nourish the devotees by preserving the parampara, by bestowing great powers to the devotees and increasing the number of devotees. They protect bhakti from obstacles of attachment to karma and jñāna. They increase bhakti by providing various stimuli (uddīpanas) to the devotees and spreading bhakti everywhere. Thus they wander everywhere at their own will (yadṛcchayā), not under the influence of karma and without obstructions anywhere.

TEXT 47

muktān upahasantīva
vaikuṇṭhe satataṁ prabhum
bhajantaḥ pakṣi-vṛkṣādi-
rūpair vividha-sevayā

Seemingly amused by those who are merely liberated, they are always busy in various services for worshiping the Lord in Vaikuṇṭha, for which they even take on forms like those of birds, trees, etc.

"If Vaikuṇṭha is such a place as described, then how is it said that animals and plants exist there, as if born from tamasic wombs?"

pārāvatānyabhṛta-sārasa-cakravāka-
dātyūha-haṁsa-śuka-tittiri-barhiṇāṁ yaḥ
kolāhalo viramate 'cira-mātram uccair
bhṛṅgādhipe hari-kathām iva gāyamāne

The clamor of the doves, cuckoos, cranes, cakravākas, gallinules, swans, parrots, partridges and peacocks immediately ceases when the king of bees loudly hums, with resemblance to glorification of the Lord. SB 3.15.18

mandāra-kunda-kurabotpala-campakārṇa-
punnāga-nāga-bakulāmbuja-pārijātāḥ

gandhe 'rcite tulasikābharaṇena tasyā
yasmiṁs tapaḥ sumanaso bahu mānayanti

In the forests of Vaikuṇṭha, on smelling the scent of tulasī used in the garlands of the Lord, the mandāra, kunda, kuraba, water lily, campaka, arṇa, punnāga, nāgakeśara, baluka, lotus and pārijāta trees, being of pure mind, give great respect to tulasī for her performance of austerity to achieve that position. SB 3.15.19

The verse gives an explanation. The residents laugh at persons who give up the great happiness of varieties of worship and accept insignificant liberation. They mock those persons who are ignorant the nature of bhakti by showing them that they can even accept lower forms like trees, etc. Actually they only seem to laugh but do not laugh (iva) since they are compassionate to the wretched and are completely immersed in the rasa of bhakti.

Or they only meditate on taking forms of animals and trees, imitating those forms for obtaining bliss in various types of service, so that they can joke with the liberated souls.

TEXT 48

kamalā-lālyamānāṅghri-
kamalaṁ moda-vardhanam
sampaśyanto hariṁ sākṣād
ramante saha tena ye

They always directly see and enjoy with the Lord, who inspires everyone's pleasure and whose lotus feet are tended to by Lakṣmī.

"They see the Lord directly (saṁpaśyantaḥ)." Present tense is used to indicate that they see the Lord without interruption. "They enjoy with the Lord directly. On the other hand, I sometimes see the Lord and sometimes enjoy with him. And that is generally done in meditation only. Thus they are the objects of Kṛṣṇa's mercy more than we are. They are the best recipients of his mercy."

TEXT 49

aho kāruṇya-mahimā
śrī-kṛṣṇasya kuto 'nyataḥ
vaikuṇṭha-loke yo 'jasraṁ
tadīyeṣu ca rājate

Ah, where else can one see the great mercy which Kṛṣṇa showers constantly on the residents of Vaikuṇṭha-loka?

Where else can one see the great mercy that exists in Vaikuṇṭha among its residents? One cannot see it anywhere else.

TEXT 50

yasmin mahā-mudāśrāntaṁ
prabhoḥ saṅkīrtanādibhiḥ
vicitrām antarā bhaktiṁ
nāsty anyat prema-vāhinīm

There nothing exists but bhakti, rendered through saṅkīrtana and in many other forms. It goes on incessantly, with great enthusiasm, spreading the ecstasy of prema.

There is nothing else except various activities of bhakti with saṅkīrtana, songs, dancing and services (ādi) praising their Lord (prabhoḥ), occurring incessantly and with great bliss. Bhakti alone exists there. Or all the activities that take place there are filled with bhakti-rasa, since all those actions without interruption are meant for experiencing prema for the Lord (prema-vāhinīm).

TEXT 51

aho tat-paramānanda-
rasābdher mahimādbhutaḥ
brahmānandas tulāṁ nārhed
yat-kaṇārdhāṁśakena ca

Oh! That supremely great ocean of highest bliss is most indescribable! The bliss of Brahman cannot compare to even a fraction of half a drop of it.

Aho indicates astonishment. The greatness of the ocean of the highest bliss is most indescribable (adbhutaḥ). The reason is given. The bliss of Brahman, the happiness of realizing one's svarūpa, cannot compare to half a drop of that ocean or a very small fraction of it.

TEXT 52

sa vaikuṇṭhas tadīyāś ca
tatratyam akhilaṁ ca yat

tad eva kṛṣṇa-pādābja-
para-premānukampitam

That Vaikuṇṭha world, its residents, and everything there are blessed by the mercy of prema for Kṛṣṇa's lotus feet.

"Vaikuṇṭhā-loka as described (saḥ), all of it (akhilam), unlike me and my place, is graced by Kṛṣṇa's lotus feet, producing the highest prema. Or the place is graced by great prema of his lotus feet." Neuter (yat tat) is used in order to agree with akhilam.

TEXT 53

tādṛk-kāruṇya-pātrāṇāṁ
śrīmad-vaikuṇṭha-vāsinām
matto 'dhika-taras tat-tan-
mahimā kiṁ nu varṇyatām

As recipients of such mercy, the divine residents of Vaikuṇṭha are much glorious than I in many ways. How is it possible for me to describe their glories?

The residents of Vaikuṇṭha are endowed with a wealth of prema (śrīmat), even though they have the wealth available in millions of universes and eternal happiness from that. It is by that prema that they manifest outstanding excellence.

TEXT 54

pāñca-bhautika-dehā ye
martya-loka-nivāsinaḥ
bhagavad-bhakti-rasikā
namasyā mādṛśāṁ sadā

Though living within the material world, in bodies composed of the five elements, persons expert in tasting bhakti to the Lord are always worshipable by persons like me.

"These devotees are worshipable by persons like me. That means they are superior to me." In the Nārāyaṇa-vyūha-stava of the Hayaśīrṣa Pañcarātra it is said:

ye tyakta-loka-dharmārthā
viṣṇu-bhakti-vaśaṁ gatāḥ
bhajanti paramātmānaṁ
tebhyo nityaṁ namo namaḥ

I offer repeated respects to those who have given up dharma and artha, are absorbed in bhakti to Viṣṇu and worship the Supreme Lord.

TEXT 55

śrī-kṛṣṇa-caraṇāmbhojā-
rpitātmāno hi ye kila
tad-eka-prema-lābhāśā-
tyaktārtha-jana-jīvanāḥ

They surrender themselves fully to the lotus feet of Kṛṣṇa. Hoping to obtain exclusive prema for him, they abandon their wealth, their families, and their very lives.

After mentioning the relishers of bhakti, they are further described in four verses (55-58). They desire to attain exclusive prema for Kṛṣṇa's lotus feet. By that desire alone, they give up wealth (artha), sons and family (jana) and even their life (jīvanāḥ).

TEXT 56

aihikāmuṣmikāśeṣa-
sādhya-sādhana-nispṛhāḥ
jāti-varṇāśramācāra
dharmādhīnatva-pāragāḥ

They are not interested in any of the means and ends of success, in this world or the next. They have surpassed dependence on rules that apply according to birth, varṇa, and āśrama.

They are without desire for the unlimited goals of happiness from material objects (sādhya) and methods (sādhana) such as earning money and performing acts of dharma, related to this life and the next. They have surpassed (pāragāḥ) dependence on rules and conduct concerning birth (as a human, etc.), varṇa (such as brāhmaṇa), and āśrama (such as brahmacārī). Dependence would mean that they think they must perform nitya and naimittika duties.

TEXT 57

ṛṇa-trayād anirmuktā
veda-mārgātigā api
hari-bhakti-balāvegād
akutaścid-bhayāḥ sadā

Even if they have not repaid their three debts and are therefore transgressing path of Vedas, by the strenght of their bhakti to Kṛṣṇa they are without fear.

Because they have offered themselves completely to the lotus feet of Kṛṣṇa, though they are not free of the three debts, and have transgressed the path of Vedas by non-performance of their svadharma, they are without fear. Just by birth, one has debts to the devatās, sages, and pitṛs. If one does not perform sacrifices, does not study the Vedas and does not produce sons, one is not free of the debt.

ṛṇais tribhir dvijo jāto devarṣi-pitṝṇāṁ prabho
yajñādhyayana-putrais tāny anistīrya tyajan patet

O Lord, a member of the twice-born classes is born with three kinds of debts—those owed to the devatās, to the sages and to his forefathers. If he leaves his body without first liquidating these debts by performing sacrifice, studying the scriptures and begetting children, he will fall down into a hellish condition. SB 10.84.39

On the authority of the sages, by not following the rules and prohibitions, one should fear punishment from Yamarāja. But the devotees do not have fear, because of the bold strength of bhakti (bala āvegāt). This is also the reason for previous and later statements. Since the devotee is not qualified for karmas, and consequently does not commit sin by non-performance, it is suitable that he has no fear.

tāvat karmāṇi kurvīta
na nirvidyeta yāvatā
mat-kathā-śravaṇādau vā
śraddhā yāvan na jāyate

As long as one is not satiated by fruitive activity and has not awakened his taste for devotional service by śravaṇaṁ kīrtanaṁ viṣṇoḥ, one has to act according to the regulative principles of the Vedic injunctions. SB 11.20.9

sarva-dharmān parityajya mām ekaṁ śaraṇaṁ vraja
ahaṁ tvāṁ sarva-pāpebhyo mokṣayiṣyāmi mā śucaḥ

Giving up all dharmas, just surrender unto Me alone. I will deliver you from all sins. Do not worry. BG 18.66

tyaktvā sva-dharmaṁ caraṇāmbujaṁ harer
bhajann apakvo 'tha patet tato yadi

yatra kva vābhadram abhūd amuṣya kiṁ
ko vārtha āpto 'bhajatāṁ sva-dharmataḥ

If a person having given up his duties in varṇāśrama, begins the worship of the Lord's lotus feet, and happens to deviate or not reach perfection, there is no misfortune for him at all in the future. But what does the person who follows all duties of varṇāśrama but does not worship the Lord gain? SB 1.5.17

TEXT 58

nānyat kim api vāñchanti
tad-bhakti-rasa-lampaṭāḥ
svargāpavarga-narakeṣv
api tulyārtha-darśinaḥ

Greedy to taste the pleasure of bhakti to the Lord, they have no desire for anything else. To them Svarga, liberation, and hell all appear the same.

Their fearless state has been described. Now their indifference is described. They regard sārūpya, sālokya, etc., the enjoyment on Brahmaloka and the happiness of liberation as most detestable since these are obstacles to bhakti or are like the pain of hellish existence. They regard (darśinaḥ) the results or goals (artha) of Svarga, liberation and hell to be the same (tulya). Śiva says:

nārāyaṇa-parāḥ sarve na kutaścana bibhyati
svargāpavarga-narakeṣv api tulyārtha-darśinaḥ

Devotees solely engaged in the service of Nārāyaṇa never fear any condition of life. For them the heavenly planets, liberation and the hellish planets are all the same. SB 6.17.28

TEXT 59

bhagavān iva satyaṁ me
ta eva parama-priyāḥ
parama-prārthanīyaś ca
mama taiḥ saha saṅgamaḥ

Truly speaking, to me such devotees are as supremely dear as the Lord himself. My highest ambition is to have their association.

"These devotees of the Lord are dearest to me, and not my associates like Nandīśvara." Śiva says to the ten Pracetās:

atha bhāgavatā yūyaṁ priyāḥ stha bhagavān yathā
na mad bhāgavatānāṁ ca preyān anyo 'sti karhicit

You devotees are dear to me just as the Supreme Lord is dear to me. The devotees hold me dear, just as they hold the Lord dear. SB 4.24.30

TEXT 60

nāradāham idaṁ manye
tādṛśānāṁ yataḥ sthitiḥ
bhavet sa eva vaikuṇṭho
loko nātra vicāraṇā

In my opinion, dear Nārada, wherever such devotees are found is actually Vaikuṇṭha. There is no room for argument in this matter.

The devotees living on earth are not less than the residents of Vaikuṇṭha. Wherever (yataḥ) they are situated is Vaikuṇṭha. On this fact (atra), there is no deliberation (vicāraṇā) – such as considering that they are different because they live on earth. Where the devotees reside, there is the wealth of bhakti and the residence of the Lord, just as in Vaikuṇṭha. The Lord says:

nāhaṁ vasāmi vaikuṇṭhe
na yogi-hṛdaye ravau
mad-bhaktā yatra gāyanti
tatra tiṣṭhāmi nārada

I do not reside in Vaikuṇṭha, in the heart of the yogī or in the sun. I reside where my devotees sing. Padma Purāṇa.

TEXT 61

kṛṣṇa-bhakti-sudhā-pānād
deha-daihika-vismṛteḥ
teṣāṁ bhautika-dehe 'pi
sac-cid-ānanda-rūpatā

Having drunk the nectar of kṛṣṇa-bhakti, those devotees forget their material bodies and relationships. Thus even while living in material bodies, they assume the forms of eternity, knowledge, and bliss.

"The residents of earth have temporary bodies made of material elements and the residents of Vaikuṇṭha have bodies of eternity, knowledge and bliss." This verse answers. The devotees on earth do not think about gross and subtle bodies (deha) which give rise to material identity or to things related to the body (daihika) such as possessions, sons, family and material enjoyment. Because of this, though they have material bodies, the devotees on earth should have forms of eternity, knowledge and bliss.

The meaning is this. By continually drinking the nectar of happiness in bhakti, which causes destruction of all obstacles, because they are similar to the residents of Vaikuṇṭha, they actually have forms of eternity, knowledge and bliss though they have material bodies. Or their material bodies transform into forms of eternity, knowledge and bliss.

Maitreya says regarding Dhruva attaining the highest place:

parītyābhyarcya dhiṣṇyāgryaṁ pārṣadāv abhivandya ca
iyeṣa tad adhiṣṭhātuṁ bibhrad rūpaṁ hiraṇmayam

Circumambulating and worshipping the plane, offering respects to the two associates, assuming a golden form, he desired to board the plane. SB 4.12.29

Śrīdhara Svāmī explains this: Dhruva assumes a radiant (hiraṇmayam) form. It was radiant because it was spiritual. In the material world, by drinking a special potion, one can transform the body in a more beautiful form.

TEXT 62

paraṁ bhagavatā sākaṁ
sākṣāt krīḍā-paramparāḥ
sadānubhavituṁ tair hi
vaikuṇṭho 'pekṣyate kvacit

But only to continually relish a series of variegated pastimes with the Lord do devotees sometimes prefer to live in Vaikuṇṭha.

"Then why did you previously praise the residents of Vaikuṇṭha?" Two verses (62-63) explain. Everything else is perfect for the devotees on earth, but Vaikuṇṭha is sometimes preferred in order to experience continually and directly a series of variegated pastimes with the Lord. In Vaikuṇṭha, everything is naturally perfect, whereas in the material world this is not so at all times. Because Vaikuṇṭha is devoid of restriction on the continual flow of rasa, the planet's nature as Vaikuṇṭha is accomplished (Vaikuṇṭha means "the place without restrictions"). In the material world the Lord manifests in the heart and then disappears. Thus that devotee hankers for direct vision of the Lord with a manifestation of special prema.

TEXT 63

ato hi sarve tatratyā
mayoktāḥ sarvato 'dhikāḥ
dayā-viśeṣa-viṣayāḥ
kṛṣṇasya parama-priyāḥ

Hence, I say that the residents of Vaikuṇṭha are greater than everyone else. As the objects of Kṛṣṇa's special mercy, they are dearest.

The residents of Vaikuṇṭha (tatratyāḥ) are superior to everyone—to the liberated souls, to us and to devotees who have not attained Vaikuṇṭha. The main reason for saying this is given. They are the objects of the Lord's special mercy because they are dearest to him. Or since they are the special objects of Kṛṣṇa's mercy, they are dearest.

TEXT 64

śrī-pārvaty uvāca
tatrāpi śrīr viśeṣeṇa
prasiddhā śrī-hari-priyā
tādṛg-vaikuṇṭha-vaikuṇṭha-
vāsinām īśvarī hi yā

Pārvatī said: Furthermore, among them all, Lakṣmī is famous as especially dear to the Lord. She is indeed the queen of Vaikuṇṭha and its residents.

Not tolerating the situation, as if angry on hearing her husband speak without special glorification of Mahālakṣmī when describing Vaikuṇṭha, Pārvatī begins to describe Lakṣmī, her dear friend. In Vaikuṇṭha (tatra), Mahālakṣmī is dear to the Lord. This statement is connected to the previous statement that the devotees of Vaikuṇṭha are dearest to the Lord. She is particularly superior to all others. She who is śrī is known as Hari-priyā. That is her name. Or in Vaikuṇṭha, particularly, Śrī is well known to be dear to the Lord (hari-priyā). The reason is that she is the queen of all the residents of Vaikuṇṭha and of Vaikuṇṭha itself. She is most worshipable. This is certain (hi), because of established evidence.

TEXT 65

yasyāḥ kaṭākṣa-pātena
loka-pāla-vibhūtayaḥ
jñānaṁ viraktir bhaktiś ca
sidhyanti yad-anugrahāt

By her mercy the devatās obtain their powers and by her mercy one can attain knowledge, detachment, and devotion.

By the mercy of Lakṣmī, powers of the devatās, knowledge of jīva and Īśvara, detachment from material enjoyment and liberation and bhakti to the Lord are achieved.

yataḥ sattvaṁ tato lakṣmīḥ sattvaṁ-anusāri ca
niḥśrīkānāṁ kutaḥ sattvaṁ vinā tena guṇāḥ kutaḥ

Where there is strength of character there is Lakṣmī. It follows Lakṣmī. If Lakṣmī is not present, how can there be strength of character. Without strength of character, how can good qualities be present? Viṣṇu Purāṇa

Good qualities here means knowledge and detachment. Indra praises Lakṣmī:

yajña-vidyā mahā-vidyā guhya-vidyā ca śobhane
ātma-vidyā ca devi tvaṁ vimukti-phala-dāyinī

O glorious Lakṣmī! You are knowledge of sacrifice, you are great knowledge, you are secret knowledge, you are knowledge of ātmā. You give results of liberation. Viṣṇu Purāṇa

Or it is stated that Lakṣmī gives vibhūti (yajña-vidyā), detachment (mahā-vidyā), bhakti with material desires (guhya-vidyā), and brahma-jñāna (ātmā-vidyā). Four types of knowledge give four results (artha, dharma, kāma, mokṣa). And Lakṣmī also gives bhakti, the result of liberation.

TEXT 66

yā vihāyādareṇāpi
bhajamānān bhavādṛśān
vavre tapobhir ārādhya
nirapekṣaṁ ca taṁ priyam

Disregarding persons like you who worship her with great respect, she chose to worship her beloved Lord by austerities, even though he was indifferent to her.

Now, the greatness of Lakṣmī's worship of the Lord with the highest prema, with disregard for all else, is described. The Lord is described as indifferent (nirapekṣam) since he is ātmārāma and full in his desires. The cause of accepting her is her affection for him (priyam). This means that she was dedicated only to him. How did she gain the Lord who is ātmārāma? She worshipped the Lord with austerities or various services, while completely concentrating on him (tapobhiḥ). Plural is used in tapobhiḥ to indicate respect. It is said in the Tenth Canto:

kasyānubhāvo 'sya na deva vidmahe
tavāṅghri-reṇu-sparaśādhikārah
yad-vāñchayā śrīr lalanācarat tapo
vihāya kāmān su-ciraṁ dhṛta-vratā

O Lord, we do not know how the serpent Kāliya has attained this great opportunity of being touched by the dust of your lotus feet. For this end, the goddess of fortune performed austerities for centuries, giving up all other desires and taking austere vows. SB 10.16.36

Though Lakṣmī is the eternal consort of the Lord of Vaikuṇṭha, and does not need to attain him by worship like others, her expansions like the daughter of Bhṛgu (Bhārgavī) are described in scriptures as performing penances to attain the Lord. These forms are considered non-different from Lakṣmī in verses like the one quoted above.

TEXT 67

karoti vasatiṁ nityaṁ
yā ramye tasya vakṣasi
pati-vratottamāśeṣā-
vatāreṣv anuyāty amum

This most perfect of chaste wives resides permanently on his beautiful chest and follows him in all his incarnations.

"Since her expanded forms as avatāras presiding over material wealth show the fault of fickleness, does not that same fault appear in Mahālakṣmī in Vaikuṇṭha?" Refuting this doubt, her supreme greatness is established in this verse. She resides permanently on his chest which is attractive (ramye), being broad and most beautiful. This indicates Vāsudeva. She comes (anuyāti) with the Lord when he comes as avatāra, and takes a suitable form since she the best among chaste women. It is said in Viṣṇu Purāṇa:

evaṁ yathā jagat-svāmī deva-devo janārdanaḥ
avatāraṁ karoty eṣa tathā śrīs tat-sahāyinī

When Janārdana, master of the universe, lord of lords, appears as avatāra, Lakṣmī accompanies him.

devatve deva-deheyaṁ manuṣyatve ca mānuṣī
viṣṇor dehānurūpāṁ vai karoty eṣātmanas tanūm

She takes a body suitable to that of Viṣṇu. When he appears as a devatā she appears as a devatā and when he appears as a human, she appears as a human.

TEXT 68

śrī-parīkṣid uvāca
tataḥ parama-harṣeṇa
kṣobhitātmālapan muniḥ
jaya śrī-kamalā-kānta
he vaikuṇṭha-pate hare

Parīkṣit said: Then the sage, excited with extreme joy, exclaimed loudly, "Glories to you, O husband of the goddess Kamalā, O Hari, Lord of Vaikuṇṭha!"

Nārada exclaimed loudly (alapat). What he said in described in a verse and a half.

TEXT 69

jaya vaikuṇṭha-loketi
tatratyā jayateti ca
jaya kṛṣṇa-priye padme
vaikuṇṭhādhīśvarīty api

"Glories to you, O Vaikuṇṭha planet! Glories to the residents! And glories to you, O Padmā, Lord Kṛṣṇa's beloved, O queen of Vaikuṇṭha!"

"O Vaikuṇṭha planet! May you remain excellent! O residents of Vaikuṇṭha! May you remain excellent! O queen of Vaikuṇṭha! May you remain excellent!" Hearing the great glories of Lakṣmī and the residents of Vaikuṇṭha, losing control because of his great bliss, Nārada forgot about the Lord residing in the material world in Dvārakā. He wanted to go to Vaikuṇṭha because his heart was overcome. Thus he praised Viṣṇu, his planet, the residents and Mahālakṣmī of Vaikuṇṭha. First he praised Viṣṇu, the husband of Mahālakṣmī (kamalā-kānta). Then he praised the objects of mercy—the planet and the residents. Then he praises Lakṣmī, the supreme object of mercy.

TEXT 70

athābhinandanāyāsyā
vaikuṇṭhe gantum utthitaḥ
abhipretya hareṇoktaḥ
kare dhṛtvā nivārya saḥ

Then, eager to visit Vaikuṇṭha and personally offer respects to the Lakṣmī, Nārada stood up. Seeing this, Śiva grabbed by the hand to stop him and spoke to him.

Nārada was eager to go to Vaikuṇṭha in order to praise Lakṣmī with gentle worlds, saying that she is the greatest object of Kṛṣṇa's mercy and dearest to him. This could be understood from the signs he exhibited and by his glancing upwards and his praises of Vaikuṇṭha and its residents. Nārada was stopped from going by Śiva, who grabbed his hand and spoke to him.

TEXT 71

śrī-maheśa uvāca
kṛṣṇa-priya-janālokot-
sukatā-vihata-smṛte
na kiṁ smarasi yad bhūmau
dvārakāyāṁ vasaty asau

Maheśa said: My dear Nārada, you have lost your memory because of your eagerness to see the dearest devotees of Kṛṣṇa. Don't you remember that the Lord of Vaikuṇṭha is residing in Dvārakā on earth right now?

O Nārada, whose memory has been lost by eagerness to see the dear devotees of Kṛṣṇa! This is not a fault in you, since Kṛṣṇa creates the greatest bewilderment. The Lord of Lakṣmī resides in Dvārakā on earth. Do you not ascertain this?

TEXT 72

rukmiṇī sā mahā-lakṣmīḥ
kṛṣṇas tu bhagavān svayam
tasyā aṁśāvatārā hi
vāmanādi-samīpataḥ

Queen Rukmiṇī is Mahālakṣmī herself, and Kṛṣṇa is Bhagavān Svayam. Rukmiṇī's partial incarnations accompany Lord Vāmana and the other avatāras of the Lord.

"Where is Mahālakṣmī there? Is she the daughter of Bhīṣmaka, Rukmiṇī?" Yes, that is true. Rukmiṇī is Mahālakṣmī. "Does Mahālakṣmī ever give up company of the Lord?" She is with Kṛṣṇa, Svayam Bhagavān. "How is Lakṣmī seen with Vāmana, the thousand-headed form or Kapila, since Mahālakṣmī comes as Rukmiṇī?" Her portions accompany Vāmana and other forms. Thus the greatness of Mahālakṣmī, the queen of Vaikuṇṭha is proved.

TEXT 73

sampūrṇā paripūrṇasya
lakṣmīr bhagavataḥ sadā
niṣevate padāmbhoje
śrī-kṛṣṇasyaiva rukmiṇī

Rukmiṇī, the perfectly complete Lakṣmī, always serves lotus feet of Kṛṣṇa, the complete Bhagavān.

"Does an expansion of Lakṣmī stay at Kṛṣṇa's side?" No, Rukmiṇī is complete. The word eva (only) should be added to other phrases where appropriate. The complete Lakṣmī is Rukmiṇī alone. She always serves (sevate) to the highest degree (ni) the lotus feet of only (eva) Kṛṣṇa, who is also the complete form of Bhagavān.

TEXT 74

tasmād upaviśa brahman
rahasyaṁ paramaṁ śanaiḥ
karṇe te kathayāmy ekaṁ
parama-śraddhayā śṛṇu

So sit down, my dear brāhmaṇa, and I shall whisper in your ear a great secret. Please hear this with absolute faith.

"Since Lakṣmī has appeared with the Lord on earth, coming from Vaikuṇṭha (tasmāt), sit down. Giving up the desire to go to Vaikuṇṭha, sit here a moment." "I will immediately go to Dvārakā? Why should I sit here?" "I will whisper the greatest secret in your ear. Since it is the greatest secret, it should not be revealed to many people. Or I will whisper it since Pārvatī, the dear friend of Mahālakṣmī, will become envious. Your desire will not be accomplished by going to Dvārakā." Śiva will tell Nārada that Prahlāda is greater than Mahālakṣmī.

TEXT 75

tvat-tātato mad garuḍāditaś ca
śriyo 'pi kāruṇya-viśeṣa-pātram
prahlāda eva prathito jagatyāṁ
kṛṣṇasya bhakto nitarāṁ priyaś ca

A greater recipient of Kṛṣṇa's mercy than your father, me, Garuḍa, etc., and even Mahālakṣmī is Prahlāda. He is famous throughout the world as the dearmost devotee of Kṛṣṇa.

Now Śiva speaks so that Nārada will go to Prahlāda. Prahlāda is a greater recipient of mercy than your father Brahmā, than me, than the residents of Vaikuṇṭha like Garuḍa, Viṣvaksena and others, than even Mahālakṣmī. The reason is given: he is the greatest devotee (nitarām bhaktaḥ) and is the dearest (nitarām priyaḥ).

TEXT 76

bhagavad-vacanāni tvaṁ
kiṁ nu vismṛtavān asi
adhītāni purāṇeṣu
ślokam etaṁ na kiṁ smareḥ

Do you not remember the Lord's words about this. You must have read them in the Purāṇas and may remember the following verse:

In order to speak out the glories of devotees in general, showing that Prahlāda is famous in the world, Śiva makes Nārada remember. Do you not remember the famous verses? Yes, you remember.

TEXT 77

nāham ātmānam āśāse
mad-bhaktaiḥ sādhubhir vinā
śriyam ātyantikīṁ vāpi
yeṣāṁ gatir ahaṁ parā

"O brāhmaṇa! Without the devotees, who take shelter of only me, I do not desire to enjoy my own bliss or my six great qualities."

Without my devotees, I do not desire or do not rejoice in (āśāse) Lakṣmī. The Lord speaks this to Durvāsā in the Ninth Canto. Also the Lord says:

ahaṁ bhakta-parādhīno hy asvatantra iva dvija
sādhubhir grasta-hṛdayo bhaktair bhakta-jana-priyaḥ

O brāhmaṇa! I am completely under the control of my devotees. I am not at all independent. My heart is controlled by the pure devotees. What to speak of my devotee, even those who are devotees of my devotee are very dear to me. SB 9.4.63

mayi nirbaddha-hṛdayāḥ sādhavaḥ sama-darśanāḥ
vaśe kurvanti māṁ bhaktyā sat-striyaḥ sat-patiṁ yathā

As chaste women bring their gentle husbands under control by service, the pure devotees, who see others' suffering as their own and are completely attached to me in the core of the heart, bring me under their full control. SB 9.4.66

He says to Uddhava in the Eleventh Canto:

na tathā me priyatama ātma-yonir na śaṅkaraḥ
na ca saṅkarṣaṇo na śrīr naivātmā ca yathā bhavān

Neither Brahmā, Śiva, Saṅkarṣaṇa, the goddess of fortune nor even my deity form (ātmā) are as dear to me as you are. SB 11.14.15

The meaning is this. In this verse (SB 11.14.15) ātmā means the deity. The word bhavān should mean "devotee" in this verse, not just Uddhava. The word bhavān (you) is used because of the Lord's great bliss, which arose from describing the special greatness of his devotees.

TEXT 78

mad-ādi-devatā-yonir
nija-bhakta-vinoda-kṛt
śrī-mūrtir api sā yebhyo
nāpekṣyā ko hi nautu tān

The Lord's divine personal form is the source of all the devatās, including me, and gives great bliss to his devotees. But the Lord considers his own form worthless compared to the value of his devotees. Who can praise the Lord's devotees?

Two verses (78-79) express the conclusion. "The Lord is the source of me (Śiva), and others such as Brahmā and Indra (ādi). Even the mahāpuruṣa who is the source of Brahmā and others arises from the Lord. Or the Lord is the shelter of the devatās and others, since everyone serves him. Thus the beautiful form of the Lord is greater than all devatās. That form of Lord gives special, intense bliss (vinoda) to his devotees such as Śeṣa and Garuḍa (nija-bhakta). That form is indescribable (sā), with the greatest beauty and sweetness. Compared to the devotees, that form is not considered an object of respect by the Lord. Who can praise the devotees? No one can praise them sufficiently."

TEXT 79

tatrāpy aśeṣa-bhaktānām
upamānatayoditaḥ
sākṣād bhagavataivāsau
prahlādo 'tarkya-bhāgyavān

Moreover, among those countless devotees, Prahlāda is described as exemplary by the Lord himself. Prahlāda's good fortune is inconceivable.

Prahlāda's greatness among devotees in general has been described as superior to Brahmā and Śiva himself. Now he is described as greater that even Śeṣa and Garuḍa. Among the devotees, he has good fortune which is inconceivable. He is the special object of the Lord's affection. He is the best because of having the greatest good fortune. The Lord himself has directly said (uditaḥ) that among unlimited devotees he is the example.

In the Seventh Canto the Lord says:

bhavanti puruṣā loke mad-bhaktās tvām anuvratāḥ
bhavān me khalu bhaktānāṁ sarveṣāṁ pratirūpa-dhṛk

Those who follow your example will naturally become my devotees. You are the best example among all my devotees. SB 7.10.21

The meaning of the above verse is this. "Anyone who follows you becomes my devotee. Thus you are the best among all my devotees. Or my devotees will follow you. The reason is that you are most fortunate (having the greatest mercy.) "

TEXT 80

tasya saubhāgyam asmābhiḥ
sarvair lakṣmyāpy anuttamam
sākṣād dhiraṇyakaśipor
anubhūtaṁ vidāraṇe

We devatās and Lakṣmī directly perceived the incomparable good fortune of Prahlāda when the Lord tore apart Hiraṇyakaśipu.

"How did he become superior to Garuḍa and Mahālakṣmī since he was born in a demon family, and is a recent devotee?" "When Hiraṇyakaśipu was torn apart by the Lord, all of us—Brahmā, the devatās and Garuḍa, experienced his greatest good fortune. Since we experienced it, there is no need for logic or other words of proof." The details are given in the Seventh Canto in the prayers of the devatās in the story of Prahlāda.

TEXT 81

punaḥ punar varān ditsur
viṣṇur muktiṁ na yācitaḥ
bhaktir eva vṛtā yena
prahlādaṁ taṁ namāmy aham

"Lord Viṣṇu several times tried to offer him boons, but Prahlāda did not ask for liberation. Instead he chose only bhakti. I bow down before him."

In order to show his supreme excellence, first he is glorified for having the highest bhakti with disregard for liberation. The above verse is found in the Nārāyaṇa-vyūha-stava. To show the special glory of Prahlāda, Viṣṇu's insistence on giving him liberation is stressed. Thus words "again and again Viṣṇu offered boons" are used. But he did not ask for liberation. Or Viṣṇu wanted to give him boons but Prahlāda accepted only bhakti again and again. This indicates Prahlāda's firm desire or his special mood. Or it means "Prahlāda accepted bhakti birth after birth."

nātha yoni-sahasreṣu
yeṣu yeṣu vrajāmy aham
teṣu teṣv acyutā bhaktir
acyutāstu sadā tvayi

O Lord! O Acyuta! May I always have unfailing bhakti to you in all the thousands of births I accept.

By mentioning "thousands of births," Prahlāda indicates that he has no desire for liberation.

TEXTS 82–83

maryādā-laṅghakasyāpi
gurv-ādeśākṛto mune
asampanna-sva-vāg-jāla-
satyatāntasya yad baleḥ

dvāre tādṛg avasthānaṁ
tuccha-dāna-phalaṁ kim u

rakṣaṇaṁ duṣṭa-bāṇasya
kiṁ nu mat-stava-kāritam

My dear sage, Bali transgressed the rules by disobeying his spiritual master and failing to be true to his own words. Still, the Lord agreed to become the guard at Bali's door. Was that simply the fruit of Bali's insignificant charity? The Lord also granted protection to the wicked Bāṇa. Was that the result of my offering the Lord prayers?

One should not think that the Lord becoming Bali's doorkeeper indicates that he obtained more mercy than Prahlāda. To explain this Śiva speaks in two and half verses. Bali transgressed the rules (maryādā-laṅghakasya). Brahmā prescribed Svarga for the devatās and Pātalā for the demons. Bali transgressed, even (api) took the position of Indra, took the sacrificial offerings and took control of the sun and moon. The word api should be applied to the statements following this also. Bali did not even follow the order of his guru Śukrācārya, who said, "Do not fulfil the whole promise you made to Vāmana. Give only a little." Bali did not follow this instruction. He was even cursed by his guru for this. Śukadeva says:

evam aśraddhitaṁ śiṣyam anādeśakaraṁ guruḥ
śaśāpa daiva-prahitaḥ satya-sandhaṁ manasvinam

Thereafter, Śukrācārya, influenced by previous offense to the Lord, cursed his exalted, generous disciple Bali Mahārāja, who was fixed in fulfilling his promise, since he had become unfaithful to guru and willing to disobey his guru. SB 8.20.14

He could not accomplish (asampanna) being fixed (anta) in truthfulness to all his words (sva-vāg-jāla). He could not give the three steps of land taken by the Lord as he had promised. Bali had said:

yad yad vaṭo vāñchasi tat pratīccha me
tvām arthinaṁ vipra-sutānutarkaye
gāṁ kāñcanaṁ guṇavad dhāma mṛṣṭaṁ
tathānna-peyam uta vā vipra-kanyām
grāmān samṛddhāṁs turagān gajān vā
rathāṁs tathārhattama sampratīccha

O son of a brāhmaṇa! O brahmacārī! It appears that you have come here to ask me for something. Take from me whatever you want. O best of those who are worshipable! Take from me a cow, gold, a furnished house, palatable food and drink, the daughter of a brāhmaṇa for your wife, prosperous villages, horses, elephants, or chariots. SB 8.18.32

After the Lord requested three steps of land Bali said:

aho brāhmaṇa-dāyāda vācas te vṛddha-sammatāḥ
tvaṁ bālo bāliśa-matiḥ svārthaṁ praty abudho yathā

O son of a brāhmaṇa! Your words are agreeable to the learned and elderly persons. Nonetheless, you are a boy with inexperienced intelligence. You are not aware of your self-interest. SB 8.19.18

After the Lord replied he said:

ity uktaḥ sa hasann āha vāñchātaḥ pratigṛhyatām
vāmanāya mahīṁ dātuṁ jagrāha jala-bhājanam

When the Lord had thus spoken to Bali Mahārāja, Bali smiled and said, "All right. Take whatever you like." To confirm his promise to give Vāmanadeva the desired land, he then took up his water pot. SB 8.19.28

Was the Lord being situated as the guard at the door (tadṛg avasthānam) the result of Bali's insignificant offering of his body and the three worlds to the Lord? Bali told the Lord:

padaṁ tṛtīyaṁ kuru śīrṣṇi me nijam

Please, therefore, place your third lotus footstep on my head. SB 8.22.2

Was the Lord being his doorkeeper the result of this? Not at all. Affection for Prahlāda, the dearest devotee was the cause. Since Bali was described as transgressing the rules, disobeying his guru and not fulfilling his promise, it was impossible that the Lord would be his door keeper. It was also not because he gave away his kingdom of the three worlds. That was insignificant (tuccha) for the Lord.

Bāṇa's wicked actions are described in the Tenth Canto. He spoke to Śiva with arrogance:

doḥ-sahasraṁ tvayā dattaṁ paraṁ bhārāya me 'bhavat
tri-lokyāṁ pratiyoddhāraṁ na labhe tvad ṛte samam

These one thousand arms you bestowed upon me have become merely a heavy burden. Besides you, I find no one in the three worlds worthy to fight. SB 10.62.6

"He rejected bhakti to Viṣṇu, his family tradition, and hated the devatās, brāhmaṇa, and bhakti as a demon. He captured Aniruddha and fought with the Lord. This is understood from other Purāṇas also. I offered prayers to protect Bāṇa. Was the protection the Lord granted to Bāṇa because of my prayers? Not at all. The protection depended on affection for Prahlāda alone."

The most serious offenses to the Vaiṣṇavas is removed by the mercy of Vaiṣṇavas alone. By Bali and Bāṇa being the son and grandson of Prahlāda, by affection arising for Prahlāda, the Lord forgave all offenses and showed the highest mercy.

TEXT 84

kevalaṁ tan-mahā-preṣṭha-
prahlāda-prīty-apekṣayā
kiṁ brūyāṁ param atrāste
gaurī lakṣmyāḥ priyā sakhī

No, it was only on account of the Lord's affection for his most beloved devotee Prahlāda. But what more can I say in the presence of Gaurī, the close friend of Lakṣmī?

"If Prahlāda is the greatest object of mercy, please speak more about him." How much more can I say? I will lose my self-control because of manifesting the highest bliss on speaking of Prahlāda's great glories. And by speaking loudly, Pārvatī, who is present will hear everything. She is the dear friend of Mahālakṣmī. If she hears that Prahlāda is greater than Mahālakṣmī she will not tolerate that and will become angry. She will disrespect you and me. That would not be proper.

It does not seem proper that Prahlāda, a recent devotee is greater than Mahālakṣmī, who is the Lord's dear consort eternally, the queen of Vaikuṇṭha and who resides on the Lord's chest constantly. However, when Hiraṇyakaśipu, the leader of the demons, had by the boon of Brahmā overtaken the three worlds and created obstacles for bhakti and created the greatest disturbance to everyone, the Lord himself glorified Prahlāda more than the ancient or recent devotees, more than the residents of Vaikuṇṭha, more than his eternal associates and even more than Mahālakṣmī. He did this to show the glory of his devotee. This is made clear in the story in the Seventh Canto. Śiva has spoken in the same way:

"There is a greater recipient of Kṛṣṇa's mercy than your father, me, and other servants like Garuḍa, and even than the goddess of fortune. His name is Prahlāda. He is famous throughout the world as the greatest devotee of Kṛṣṇa and the dearest as well." (Bṛhad Bhāgavatāmṛta verse 75)

"When the Lord tore apart Hiraṇyakaśipu, I, all the devatās, and the goddess Lakṣmī witnessed with our own eyes the incomparable good fortune of Prahlāda." (Bṛhad Bhāgavatāmṛta verse 80)

Sometimes, such perfection is achieved by the will of the Lord and nothing else.

na tathā me priyatama ātma-yonir na śaṅkaraḥ
na ca saṅkarṣaṇo na śrīr naivātmā ca yathā bhavān

Neither Brahmā, Śiva, Saṅkarṣaṇa, the goddess of fortune nor even my own self are as dear to me as you (Uddhava) are. SB 11.14.15

nāham ātmānam āśāse mad-bhaktaiḥ sādhubhir vinā
śriyaṁ cātyantikīṁ brahman yeṣāṁ gatir ahaṁ parā

O brāhmaṇa! Without the devotees, who take shelter of only me, I do not desire to enjoy my own bliss by my six great qualities. SB 9.4.64

One hears of other recent devotees whom the Lord glorifies more than his eternal associates like Saṅkarṣaṇa and even Mahālakṣmī. Because Saṅkarṣaṇa and others by their natures have the highest pure prema, depending completely on the Lord, they have nothing to renounce. The recent devotees however, depending completely on the Lord, renounce everything in this world.

Or the Lord praises these devotees profusely in order to encourage everyone in bhakti, without interest in anything else. In all cases, they attain perfection.

However, Brahmā, Indra and others, have the good fortune of seeing the Lord directly. This is the highest result of all types of sādhana. Prahlāda, who mainly remembers the Lord, does not have this excellence. Prahlāda will say in the next chapter:

hanūmad-ādi-vat tasya
kāpi sevā kṛtāsti na
paraṁ vighnākule citte
smaraṇaṁ kriyate mayā

I have never performed any real service for the Lord like Hanumān and others. I have only remembered the Lord some-times, when my mind was troubled. (Bṛhad Bhāgavatāmṛta 1.3 20)

However, in the Fifth Canto Prahlāda's verses of praise and constantly seeing the deity form of Nṛsiṁha in Harivarṣa are famous (SB 5.18.7) Bali (Prahlāda's grandson) can also see the Lord directly, since Vāmana remains as his door keeper. Thus Bali's greatness is proved, what to speak of Prahlāda's greatness (who resides with Bali in Sutala).

Prahlāda speaks in this way since he is most humble as a great devotee, and is not satisfied with his position, which is born out of bhakti's nature. Thus Prahlāda is greater than the other devotees, since he is the recipient of the Lord's special mercy, according to the previous reasoning. Nothing more needs to be explained. Let us return to the subject.

TEXT 85

tad gatvā sutale śīghraṁ
vardhayitvāśiṣāṁ gaṇaiḥ
prahlādaṁ svayam āśliṣya
mad-āśleṣāvaliṁ vadeḥ

Go quickly to Sutala. Offer Prahlāda your countless blessings, embrace him, and offer him my countless embraces.

Therefore (tat) quickly go to Sutala, third of the lower planets to encourage him with blessings. This had been the Lord's order so that Prahlāda could see the Lord constantly:

vatsa prahrāda bhadraṁ te prayāhi sutalālayam
modamānaḥ sva-pautreṇa jñātīnāṁ sukham āvaha

My dear son Prahlāda, all good fortune unto you! Please go to the place known as Sutala while rejoicing and there enjoy happiness with your grandson and your other relatives. SB 8.23.9

nityaṁ draṣṭāsi māṁ tatra
gadā-pāṇim avasthitam
mad-darśana-mahāhlāda-
dhvasta-karma-nibandhanaḥ

All bondage of karma has already been destroyed by the great bliss of seeing me. Now you will constantly see me there with a club in my hand. SB 8.23.10

"Prahlāda is there now. First embrace him and experiencing great bliss, offer (vadeḥ) my embraces also." The potential case of the verb is used to indicate an order.

TEXT 86

aho na sahate 'smākaṁ
praṇāmaṁ saj-janāgraṇīḥ
stutiṁ ca mā pramādī syās
tatra cet sukham icchasi

Unfortunately, that foremost of saintly persons will not tolerate our bowing down to him. Also, if you wish to remain happy, do not make the mistake of praising him.

"It is proper to offer respects to the greatest of devotees?" Aho indicates lamentation. He does not tolerate even praise. Do not be inattentive (mā pramādī). Being careful, do not offer respects. "But I will be satisfied if I can offer respects and praises to such a great devotee." By acting in this way the great devotee will be unhappy. Thus you will not attain happiness or satisfaction from seeing this devotee.

Thus ends the third chapter of Canto One of Śrīla Sanātana Gosvāmī's Bṛhad-bhāgavatāmṛta, entitled "Prapañcātīta: Beyond the Material World."

Chapter Four

Bhakta: The Devotee

TEXT 1

śrī-parīkṣid uvāca
śrutvā mahāścaryam iveśa-bhāṣitaṁ
prahlāda-sandarśana-jāta-kautukaḥ
hṛd-yānataḥ śrī-sutale gato 'cirād
dhāvan praviṣṭaḥ puram āsuraṁ muniḥ

Parīkṣit said: After hearing the most amazing words of Śiva, Nārada was eager to see Prahlāda in person. He at once, therefore, traveled to Sutala by the vehicle of mind and entered running into the city of the demons.

In the Fourth Chapter Prahlāda criticizes glorification of himself and says Hanumān is superior. Hanumān says the Pāṇḍavas are superior to him.

He went quickly using the mind as a vehicle (hṛd-yānataḥ). When he thought in his mind "I will go to Sutala," he immediately arrived there.

TEXT 2

tāvad vivikte bhagavat-padāmbuja-
premollasad-dhyāna-viṣakta-cetasā
śrī-vaiṣṇavāgryeṇa samīkṣya dūrataḥ
protthāya vipraḥ praṇato 'ntikaṁ gataḥ

Prahlāda, the best of devotees, was in a solitary place, absorbed in glorious meditation on the Lord's lotus feet in prema. Seeing Nārada approaching from a distance, Prahlāda stood up and then offered respects as Nārada came close.

Nārada was seen from far off by Prahlāda, best of the devotees, in his meditation, as if he directly saw him. As Prahlāda gave up his meditation, Nārada quickly approached him. Prahlāda rose from his seat and offered respects. "What had he been doing?" His mind was absorbed in glorious meditation on the Lord's lotus feet in prema in a solitary place. For this reason he did not immediately rise up on seeing Nārada from afar.

TEXT 3

pīṭhe prayatnād upaveśito 'yaṁ
pūjāṁ purā-vad vidhinārpyamāṇām

sambhrānta-cetāḥ parihṛtya varṣan
harṣāsram āśleṣa-paro 'vadat tam

With some effort, Prahlāda made Nārada accept a seat and then began to worship him in accordance with standard rules, as was done previously. But Nārada, feeling great reverence for Prahlāda, refused the worship. He shed tears of joy and tried to embrace Prahlāda. Then he spoke as follows.

Though Nārada was offered a seat, he did not accept it. Prahlāda however was insistent, and then he sat down. He did not accept the worship being offered to him (arpyamānām) according to the rules, as was done previously. Or he did not accept the articles of worship such as foot water and arghya. With his mind confused by prema, he wanted to embrace Prahlāda. He shed tears of joy. Then he spoke to Prahlāda, best of Vaiṣṇavas.

TEXT 4

śrī-nārada uvāca
dṛṣṭaś cirāt kṛṣṇa-kṛpā-bharasya
pātraṁ bhavān me sa-phalaḥ śramo 'bhūt
ā-bālyato yasya hi kṛṣṇa-bhaktir
jātā viśuddhā na kuto 'pi yāsīt

Nārada said: Now, after so long, I have finally seen you — the true recipient of Kṛṣṇa's full mercy! Now my efforts have yielded results! From your very childhood you have been endowed with pure kṛṣṇa-bhakti, which did not exist anywhere previously.

"My efforts (śramaḥ) of studying, etc. or of starting in Prayāga and the southern states and wandering about, have yielded results." Nārada describes the characteristics of Prahlāda being the recipient of great mercy of the Lord. This continues for seven verses (4-10). "Starting from childhood you had developed pure kṛṣṇa-bhakti, which did not exist anywhere previously."

TEXT 5

yayā sva-pitrā vihitāḥ sahasram
upadravā dāruṇa-vighna-rūpāḥ
jitās tvayā yasya tavānubhāvāt
sarve 'bhavan bhāgavatā hi daityāḥ

By that bhakti, you overcame terrible obstacles, the thousands of violences your father committed against you. And by your influence all the demons became devotees.

By that bhakti you overcame thousands of disturbances created by your own father Hiraṇyakaśipu. These are described in the Seventh Canto:

prayāse 'pahate tasmin daityendraḥ pariśaṅkitaḥ
cakāra tad-vadhopāyān nirbandhena yudhiṣṭhira

O King Yudhiṣṭhira! When all the attempts failed, the King of the demons, Hiraṇyakaśipu, being most fearful, stubbornly tried other means to kill him. SB 7.5.42

dig-gajair dandaśūkendrair abhicārāvapātanaiḥ
māyābhiḥ sannirodhaiś ca gara-dānair abhojanaiḥ
hima-vāyv-agni-salilaiḥ parvatākramaṇair api
na śaśāka yadā hantum apāpam asuraḥ sutam
cintāṁ dīrghatamāṁ prāptas tat-kartuṁ nābhyapadyata

When Hiraṇyakaśipu could not kill his innocent son by throwing him beneath the feet of big elephants, throwing him among huge snakes, employing destructive spells, hurling him from the tops of hills, conjuring up illusory tricks, imprisoning him, administering poison, starving him, exposing him to severe cold, winds, fire and water, or throwing heavy stones on him to crush him, he began to contemplate the situation deeply. He did not succeed in killing him. SB 7.5.43-44

A description of the disturbances is given. They were obstacles to bhakti since they were frightening and difficult to escape (dāruṇa). The obstacles however were all conquered (jitāḥ). They could not affect Prahlāda. "And by your influence (anubhāvāt) the demons became devotees (bhāgavatāḥ). This is certain (hi)." Actually the demons' children became devotees, by instructions and later by seeing and touching him. The earth says in Nāradīya Purāṇa and Hari-bhakti-sudhodaya:

aho kṛtārthaḥ sutarāṁ nṛ-loko
yasmin sthito bhāgavatottamo 'si
spṛśanti paśyanti ca ye bhavantaṁ
bhāvāṁś ca yāṁs te hari-loka-bhājaḥ

Ah, this human world is now especially fortunate since you, the best of Vaiṣṇavas, are present in it. Everyone who touches you or sees you and the symptoms of your ecstatic emotions will become entitled to take up residence in Vaikuṇṭha.

TEXT 6

kṛṣṇāviṣṭo yo 'smṛtātmeva matto
nṛtyan gāyan kampamāno rudaṁś ca
lokān sarvān uddharan saṁsṛtibhyo
viṣṇor bhaktiṁ harṣayām āsa tanvan

While immersed in meditation on Kṛṣṇa, you seemed to forget your own existence. Dancing, singing, trembling, you called out loudly as if intoxicated. In this way you spread bhakti unto Lord Viṣṇu, delivering all the worlds from the cycle of material life and filling them with joy.

You act like a madman, or as if intoxicated by liquor (mattaḥ). You deliver people from the twenty-one kinds of material suffering, which are defined in nyāya scriptures (saṁsṛtibhyaḥ).

śrutvāty-adbhuta-vairāgyāj
janās tasyojjvalā giraḥ
aśrūṇi mumucuḥ kecid
vīkṣya ke 'py anamaṁś ca tam
līlayānye pare hāsyād
bhaktyā kecana vismayāt
janās taṁ saṅghaśo 'paśyan
sarvathāpi hatainasaḥ

Upon hearing his brilliant words, some people began to shed tears because of an extraordinary sense of detachment from material life. Others who saw him responded by bowing down to him. Others were amazed to see him playfully laugh and simply stood in groups watching him. All these persons were relieved of worldly contamination. Hari-bhakti-sudhodaya

These people had all their suffering of saṁsāra destroyed (hatainasaḥ). Not only was their suffering destroyed by his delivering them from saṁsṛti, but they attained the highest happiness by his spreading bhakti.

TEXT 7

kṛṣṇenāvirbhūya tīre mahābdheḥ
svāṅke kṛtvā lālito mātṛ-vad yaḥ
brahmeśādīn kurvato 'pi stavaughaṁ
padmāṁ cānādṛtya sammānito yaḥ

Lord Kṛṣṇa appearing on the shore of the ocean, placed you on his lap and caressed you like a mother. Thus he honored you, disregarding

Brahmā and the others devatās offering prayers, and even disregarding Lakṣmī.

You were kissed and embraced by the Lord who acted like a mother (lālitaḥ).

tataḥ kṣitāv eva niviśya nāthaḥ
kṛtvā tam aṅke sva-janaika-bandhuḥ
śanair vidhunvan kara-pallavena
spṛśan muhur mātṛ-vad āliliṅga

Sitting on the earth, the Lord, the only friend of the people, took Prahlāda on his lap, and gently rocking back and forth, stroked him with his lotus hand. He embraced him like a mother. Hari-bhakti-sudhodaya

The Lord disregarded Brahmā and others, not giving them a glance of mercy. Prahlāda was respected more (saṁ mānitaḥ) than Brahmā, Garuḍa and even Lakṣmī. The Lord gave him his glance of mercy, raised him up on his lap and touched him.

TEXT 8

vitrastena brahmaṇā prārthito yaḥ
śrīmat-pādāmbhoja-mūle nipatya
tiṣṭhann utthāpyottamāṅge karābjaṁ
dhṛtvāṅgeṣu śrī-nṛsiṁhena līḍhaḥ

Brahmā, terrified, begged you to approach Nṛsiṁha. And when you fell at the Lord's beautiful lotus feet, the Lord stood up and raised you from the ground. He placed his lotus hand upon your head and began to lick all your limbs.

There is a description of a related incident. Brahmā was terrified that the whole universe would be destroyed by the Lord's anger generated by violence to his devotee. He prayed to Prahlāda so that the Lord would mercifully withdraw his anger. Brahmā's request to Prahlāda is described in the Seventh Canto:

prahrādaṁ preṣayām āsa brahmāvasthitam antike
tāta praśamayopehi sva-pitre kupitaṁ prabhum

Brahmā requested Prahlāda, who was standing nearby. "My dear son, please go forward and appease the Lord who is angry at your father." SB 7.9.3

While the Lord stood, Prahlāda fell down like a stick at the shelter (mūle) of his beautiful (śrīmat) lotus feet. Placing his lotus hand on Prahlāda's head, he licked all of his limbs.

sva-pāda-mūle patitaṁ tam arbhakaṁ
vilokya devaḥ kṛpayā pariplutaḥ
utthāpya tac-chīrṣṇy adadhāt karāmbujaṁ
kālāhi-vitrasta-dhiyāṁ kṛtābhayam

When Lord Nṛsiṁhadeva saw the small boy prostrated at the soles of his feet, overcome with affection, he raised Prahlāda and placed upon the boy's head his lotus hand, which destroys fear in the minds of persons afraid of the snake of time. SB 7.9.5

Bṛhan-narasiṁha Purāṇa says lilihe tasya gātrāṇi sva-potasyeva keśarī: Lord Nṛsiṁha licked Prahlāda's limbs as a lioness licks her cub.

TEXT 9

yaś citra-citrāgraha-cāturī-cayair
utsṛjyamānaṁ hariṇā paraṁ padam
brahmādi-samprārthyam upekṣya kevalaṁ
vavre 'sya bhaktiṁ nija-janma-janmasu

When Lord Hari, with most attractive and clever enticements, tried to offer you the supreme abode, which is prayed for by Brahmā and by everyone else, you showed no interest in it. Rather, you asked only bhakti to the Lord, birth after birth.

You ignored liberation or Vaikuṇṭha (param padam) offered by the Lord with profuse cleverness, with insistence which was of many types or most astonishing (citra-citra).

prahrāda bhadra bhadraṁ te prīto 'haṁ te 'surottama
varaṁ vṛṇīṣvābhimataṁ kāma-pūro 'smy ahaṁ nṛṇām

O Prahlāda, most gentle devotee! Best in the family of the demons! Good fortune unto you. I am pleased with you. Please ask for a cherished benediction. I fulfill the desires of men (jīvas). SB 7.9.52

kurvatas te prasanno 'haṁ bhaktim avyabhicāriṇīm
yathābhilaṣito mattaḥ prahlāda vriyatāṁ varaḥ

O Prahlāda! Because you have been offering me devotional service without deviation, I am pleased with you. Please choose any benediction you would like from me. Viṣṇu Purāṇa

After giving Prahlāda the benediction of bhakti, Viṣṇu said:

mayi bhaktis tavāsty eva bhūyo py evaṁ bhaviṣyati
varaś ca mattaḥ prahlāda vriyatāṁ yas tavepsitaḥ

May you have bhakti for me now and in the future. O Prahlāda! Choose whatever benediction you desire.

The Lord also tells Prahlāda in the Hari-bhakti-sudhodaya:

sa-bhayaṁ sambhramaṁ vatsa mad-gaurava-kṛtaṁ tyaja
naiṣa priyo me bhakteṣu svādhīna-praṇayī bhava

Give up respect with fear, produced by my great position. I do not like this in my devotees. Be independently affectionate.

api me pūrṇa-kāmasya navaṁ navam idaṁ priyaṁ
niḥśaṅkaḥ praṇayād bhakto yan māṁ paśyati bhāṣate
sadā mukto 'pi baddho 'smi bhaktena sneha-rajjubhiḥ
ajito 'pi jito 'haṁ tair avaśyo 'pi vaśī-kṛtaḥ
tyakta-bandhu-dhana-sneho mayi yaḥ kurute ratim
ekas tasyāsmi sa ca me na hy anyo 'sty āvayoḥ suhṛt
nityaṁ ca pūrṇa-kāmasya janmāni vividhāni me
bhakta-sarveṣṭa-dānāya tasmāt kiṁ te priyaṁ vada

If a fearless devotee speaks or sees me out of affection, that is dear to me in newer and newer ways, though I am complete in my desires. Though I am eternally liberated I am bound by the devotee by his ropes of affection. Though I am unconquered, I am conquered by the devotees. Though not controlled by anyone, I am controlled by the devotees.

He who, giving up attachment to friends and wealth, develops attraction for me is mine, and I am his. Neither of us have any other friend. Though complete in my desires, I take various births to give everything to the devotee. Therefore say what you desire. Hari-bhakti sudhodaya

After Prahlāda replied the Lord said:

satyaṁ mad-darśanād anyad vatsa naivāsti te priyam
ata eva hi samprītis tvayi me 'tīva vardhate

O child! It is true. Nothing is dearer for you than seeing me. Thus my affection for you increases more.

api te kṛta-kṛtyasya mat-priyaṁ kṛtyam asti hi
kiñcic ca dātum iṣṭaṁ me mat-priyārthaṁ vṛṇuṣva tat

Though you are contented, I want to do something for you. I want to give something to you. Choose something to please me.

"You chose bhakti (bhaktim) to the Lord (asya), birth after birth." By choosing to take many births, Prahlāda showed his extreme disinterest in liberation.

TEXT 10

yaḥ sva-prabhu-prītim apekṣya paitṛkaṁ
rājyaṁ svayaṁ śrī-narasiṁha-saṁstutau
samprārthitāśeṣa-janoddhṛtīcchayā
svī-kṛtya tad-dhyāna-paro 'tra vartate

Considering your Lord's affection, you agreed to accept your father's throne. And as you told Lord Nṛsiṁha in your prayers, by doing this you wished to help deliver all people. You are still on that royal seat, fixed in meditation on Lord Nṛsiṁha.

"Then how did you take up the powers of the king?" Considering the affection of Nṛsiṁha, your master, you accepted your father's kingdom and remain in that post.

"How could the Lord be pleased by accepting a kingdom?" With a desire to deliver unlimited people, which you requested in praising the Lord, you (Prahlāda) would be able to deliver all jīvas and give them happiness, by spreading bhakti everywhere through your great power on ruling the kingdom. He said this in his prayer to the Lord. By desiring to do that, the Lord became pleased.

Or "Previously he did not accept liberation to please the Lord, even at the insistence of the Lord. Now, why did he accept the kingdom?" By his own desire to deliver unlimited people as expressed in his prayer, because of feeling pain at the people's suffering, he accepted the kingdom. By accepting the kingdom he did not destroy his own interest: he remained fixed in meditation on the Lord.

His prayer is given in the Seventh Canto:

evaṁ sva-karma-patitaṁ bhava-vaitaraṇyām
anyonya-janma-maraṇāśana-bhīta-bhītam
paśyañ janaṁ sva-para-vigraha-vaira-maitraṁ
hanteti pāracara pīpṛhi mūḍham adya

I see these people who have fallen in the material world by their karma, similar to the Vaitaraṇī River. They are filled with extreme fear concerning eating, birth and death, making friends, enemies, and quarrelling with family members and others. Oh Lord, you can help them cross the river! Deliver these fools today. SB 7.9.41

The meaning is this. I see foolish people who have fallen by their actions into saṁsāra, which is like the Vaitaraṇī River leading to hell, full of great pain, who fear both birth and death, who make enemies and friends, quarrelling with family members and others. O Lord situated beyond this! Ever-liberated Lord! It is difficult (aho)! Today save them from the Vaitaraṇī.

ko nv atra te 'khila-guro bhagavan prayāsa
uttāraṇe 'sya bhava-sambhava-lopa-hetoḥ
mūḍheṣu vai mahad-anugraha ārta-bandho
kiṁ tena te priya-janān anusevatāṁ naḥ

Guru of all beings! O Lord! What effort is required for you to deliver everyone, since you are the cause of creation, maintenance and destruction of the universe? O friend of the suffering! You are most compassionate to the fools. But why do you have to deliver us? We simply serve your dear devotees and get delivered. SB 7.9.42

The meaning is this. "O guru of everyone!" This indicates that it is suitable that the Lord give mercy to everyone. "What difficulty is there for you to deliver everyone?" There is no difficulty. Why? "It is not difficult for the person who is the cause of creating, maintaining and destroying the universe (asya). You should do it, since you are compassionate to fools." "I will deliver you and other devotees. Do not insist on delivering the whole world." "Why do you have to deliver us, who serve your devotees (priya-janān)? We naturally get delivered."

TEXT 11

yaḥ pīta-vāso-'ṅghri-saroja-dṛṣṭyai
gacchan vanaṁ naimiṣakaṁ kadācit
nārāyaṇenāhava-toṣitena
proktas tvayā hanta sadā jito 'smi

You once went to the Naimiṣaraṇya Forest to have darśana of Nārāyaṇa, who is known as "the Lord in yellow dress." While on the way you satisfied the Lord in combat, and he told you, "I am always conquered by you!"

This is a story found in Vāmana Purāṇa. Once Prahlāda went to see the most attractive Lord who wears yellow cloth and who was staying in Naimiṣaraṇya forest. On the way he saw a person dressed as an ascetic and holding a bow in his hand. Thinking the person to be imitator because of the contrary dress and conduct, he engaged in a great battle with him. He promised, "I will defeat you." But he could not do that.

One day, early in the morning, he worshipped his personal deity with devotion. In battle, seeing on the ascetic's chest the garland he had offered in worship, he understood that the person was Nārāyaṇa, his Lord, and satisfied the Lord with various verses of praise. The Lord relieved him of fatigue from fighting by the touch of his hand and comforted him. Prahlāda explained that he was at fault because he could not fulfil his promise to defeat the Lord. The Lord, satisfied with the previous fight, smiled and said, "I am always conquered by you."

TEXT 12

śrī-parīkṣid uvāca
evaṁ vadan nārado 'sau
hari-bhakti-rasārṇavaḥ
tan-narma-sevako nṛtyan
jitam asmābhir ity araut

Parīkṣit continued: Having said this, Nārada, the ocean of bhakti-rasa, began to dance. That intimate servant of the Lord shouted, "The Lord has been conquered by us!"

Nārada shouted in a loud voice (araut), "The Lord has been conquered by us!" This implies the Lord is conquered by all the devotees.

TEXT 13

śrī-nārada uvāca
bho vaiṣṇava-śreṣṭha jitas tvayeti kiṁ
vācyaṁ mukundo balināpi nirjitaḥ
pautreṇa daiteya-gaṇeśvareṇa te
saṁrakṣito dvāri tava prasādataḥ

Nārada then said: O best of Vaiṣṇavas, why should I say that Lord Mukunda has been conquered only by you? Your grandson Bali, chief of the Daityas, has also conquered him and keeps the Lord at the door by your grace.

"The Lord has also been completly brought under control (nirjitaḥ) by Bali, the leader of the demons. But this was only by your mercy. Bali did not do any sādhana." The signs of being brought under control are explained. The Lord is kept at the door as the guard. Prahlāda says in the Eighth Canto:

nemaṁ viriñco labhate prasādaṁ
na śrīr na śarvaḥ kim utāpare 'nye
yan no 'surāṇām asi durga-pālo
viśvābhivandyair abhivanditāṅghriḥ

We have attained mercy that Brahmā, Lakṣmī or Śiva, what to speak of others, have not attained. You, whose lotus feet are worshiped by the most respected person in the universe, are the protector of us demons in all respects. SB 8.23.6

In the Dvārakā-māhātmya of Prahlāda-saṁhitā, the Lord spoke to Durvāsa who had come from Dvārakā to bring the Lord from Sutala because the people of Dvārakā were suffering from defeat from the demon Kuśa.

parādhīno 'smi viprendra
bhakti-krīto 'smi nānyathā
baler ādeśa-kārī ca
daityendra-vaśa-go hy aham

O best of brāhmaṇas! I am dependent. I am purchased by bhakti alone. I follow the order of Bali. I am under the control of the king of the demons.

tasmāt prārthaya viprendra
daityaṁ vairocanaṁ balim
asyādeśāt kariṣyāmi
yad abhīṣṭaṁ tavādhunā

Therefore O best of the brāhmaṇas, request the demon Bali, son of Virocana. I will immediately do as you desire by his order.

When Bali refused Durvāsā's request, Bali then said to Durvāsā who was about to give up his life by fasting.

yad bhāvyaṁ tad bhavatu te yaj jānāsi tathā kuru
brahma-rudrādi-namitaṁ nāhaṁ tyakṣye pada-dvayam

What you want for the future, let it happen. What you understand is proper, do that. I cannot give up the lotus feet of the Lord which are worshipped by Brahmā, Śiva and others.

TEXT 14

itaḥ prabhṛti kartavyo
nivāso niyato 'tra hi
mayābhibhūya dakṣādi-
śāpaṁ yuṣmat-prabhāvataḥ

From now on I must stay here certain. By your influence I shall certainly be able to overcome the curses I received from Dakṣa and others.

I must stay here certainly (hi). Dakṣa and others had cursed Nārada so that could not remain in one place for long.

tantu-kṛntana yan nas tvam abhadram acaraḥ punaḥ
tasmāl lokeṣu te mūḍha na bhaved bhramataḥ padam

O cause of separation from sons! O fool! Because you have created misfortune for me, you will wander about without a permanent place in all the planets. SB 6.5.43

Other people cursing him includes Jarā.

mayi saṁrabhya vipulam
adāc chāpaṁ suduḥsaham
sthātum arhasi naikatra
mad-yācñā-vimukho mune

Angry with me, she uttered a great, intolerable curse. "O sage! You cannot stay in one place since you have refused my request." SB 4.27.22

TEXT 15

śrī-parīkṣid uvāca
sva-ślāghā-sahanāśakto
lajjāvanamitānanaḥ
prahlādo nāradaṁ natvā
gauravād avadac chanaiḥ

Parīkṣit said: Unable to tolerate hearing his own praise, Prahlāda lowered his face in embarrassment, bowed down before Nārada, and respectfully addressed him in a soft voice.

Prahlāda was embarrassed at hearing himself being praised. He thought Nārada must be joking, since what Nārada had said was impossible. He lowered his head. Since Nārada was respectable (gauravāt). Prahlāda spoke in a soft voice (śanaiḥ). Otherwise he would have spoken loudly in anger, since he was unable to tolerate himself being praised.

TEXT 16

śrī-prahlāda uvāca
bhagavan śrī-guro sarvaṁ
svayam eva vicāryatām
bālye na sambhavet kṛṣṇa-
bhakter jñānam api sphuṭam

Prahlāda said: My lord and guru, please reconsider everything you have said. At a young age how can there be a clear understanding of bhakti?.

"Please consider what you said." He then explains in four and a half verses (16-20). It is clear (sphuṭam) that a child cannot understand bhakti. Or, at a young age there is no c lear understanding (sphutām jñānam) of bhakti . At a young age how can bhakti be perfected?

TEXTS 17–18

mahatām upadeśasya
balād bodhottame sati
harer bhaktau pravṛttānāṁ
mahimāpādakāni na

vighnānabhibhavo bāleṣ-
ūpadeśaḥ sad-īhitam
ārta-prāṇi-dayā mokṣa-
syānaṅgī-karaṇādi ca

When one receives special knowledge by the power of instructions of great souls, then one can engage in bhakti to the Lord. Therefore, it is not a sign of greatness that ordinary persons like me can persevere despite terrible disturbances, give spiritual instructions to children, behave like saintly persons, show compassion to suffering souls, or refuse the boon of liberation.

By the power of great souls like Nārada (mahatām), when there is special knowledge of the greatness of bhakti and the devotees (bodhottame) arising from having no regard for artha, dharma, kāma or mokṣa, due to understanding their uselessness, then people become engaged in bhakti to the Lord.

Not being overcome by obstacles, teaching to the children of the demons, behaving (ihitam) like a devotee (satām) by dancing, etc., being merciful to suffering living entities and not accepting liberation, and pleasing people (ca) do not make qualified one understand the greatness (or they are not causes of greatness) of persons beginning devotion, what to speak of the greatness of persons fixed in devotion.

These two verses are an answer to Nārada's two and half verses of praise. He rejects some statements completely and accepts others a little, but with a different meaning.

For instance as a young boy, he did not accept at all pure bhakti since he lacked special jñāna and kriyā śakti as a child. Though he accepts conquering over the disturbance caused by obstacles to bhakti created by his father, he rejects that praise by saying it was caused by the greatness of bhakti. Though he accepted that he made the demons into devotees, he did something improper, since it is not proper to reveal what is taught by great souls to children. Paropadeśe pāṇḍityaṁ sarveṣāṁ sukaraṁ nṛṇām: it is easy for all men to show learning by giving teachings to others.

He did not accept being absorbed in Kṛṣṇa, since that is highly secret and produces embarrassment to the devotee. He accepted that he danced and sang, but he did this as a necessity, as a sādhana. What is a characteristic for siddhas is a practice for sādhakas.

"Everything took place by the natural power of beginning bhakti (bodhottame). This beginning takes place by the power of the teachings of great devotees (mahatāṁ upadeśasya-balāt). This is the causeless mercy of those devotees. Thus I have no quality by which I could be considered great."

TEXT 19

kṛṣṇasyānugraho 'py ebhyo
nānumīyeta sattamaiḥ
sa cāvirbhavati śrīmann
adhikṛtyaiva sevakam

The best of saints do not infer the Lord's mercy on person merely by such symptoms. Kṛṣṇa's mercy, O Nārada, appears only in a truly worthy servant.

The characteristics of the Lord's special mercy are as follows. Persons who know the power of bhakti at Kṛṣṇa's feet do not infer the characteristics of Lord's special mercy by symptoms like enduring obstacles. "I am not qualified for what is called the Lord's mercy. O Nārada, endowed with a wealth of service to the Lord (śrīman)! That mercy manifests in those who do service, not in persons who do not do service. Since the mercy of the Lord is eternal, cognizant and blissful like the Lord and since it exists everywhere at all times, it just appears and disappears at some time and some place (by his will)."

TEXT 20

hanūmad-ādi-vat tasya
kāpi sevā kṛtāsti na
paraṁ vighnākule citte
smaraṇaṁ kriyate mayā

I have never performed any real service for the Lord like Hanumān and others. I only remember the Lord sometimes, when my mind is troubled.

"Since you are a devotee, that mercy has come to you." I have not served Kṛṣṇa. I have only (param) meditated (smaraṇam) on him. The present tense is used to indicate that even now he does this. And even in meditation it is not steady.

"Among the nine types of bhakti defined as service, one engages the mind, the chief of all the senses, thinking of the Lord. Smaraṇam is the chief engagement or service. Since you have done that, you are the chief devotee and have received the Lord's great mercy." I remember the Lord in my mind to overcome with obstacles such as sleep and distraction. Because my mind is overcome with obstacles, I cannot remember the Lord completely. Or since memory is the nature of the mind and its nature is to be overcome with obstacles, smaraṇam is not the chief process.

This will be explained later with logic in the glorification of Goloka.

TEXT 21

yan mad-viṣayakaṁ tasya
lālanādi praśasyate
manyate māyikaṁ tat tu
kaścil līlāyitaṁ paraḥ

You praise me because he caressed me and showed affection. But some consider such affectionate behavior merely a false show of māyā, and others just a display of his pastimes.

"Caressing you indicates his mercy to you." What is done by Kṛṣṇa (yat) such as caressing is considered māyā by the Māyāvādīs fixed in Advaita, since such acts are not possible in the Supreme Brahman. Those on the path of bhakti consider such actions as pastimes, not māyā, since various acts full of eternity, knowledge and bliss are possible by the śakti of eternity, knowledge and bliss. However, such actions are not a sign of his great mercy since they are not in themselves the highest result.

TEXT 22

svābhāvikaṁ bhavādṛk ca
manye svapnādi-vat tv aham
satyaṁ bhavatu vāthāpi
na tat kāruṇya-lakṣaṇam

Persons like you regard such affectionate behaviour as natural expression of love, but I consider them no more real than a dream. And even if we accept them as real, they are still not signs of his mercy.

Persons like you (bhavādṛk) consider that these actions were done out of the Lord's natural affection and soft nature (svābhāvikam). But like fire, it amounts to spreading general mercy everywhere, just as fire destroys cold. "But that is mercy." I consider it like a dream (svapna), fantasy or illusion (ādi). It manifests for only a moment. I consider it false.

According to Māyāvādīs, things do not exist at all. According to me, it is false in the sense that it manifests to me temporarily, as a dream does.

"But this is famous everywhere. It is seen by the sages and devatās. You have experienced it in plenty. Why do you consider it like a dream? Why deny the signs of the wealth of the Lord's mercy, which is evident by your understanding the truth in childhood and by your devotional actions?" They may be real. However, caressing, etc. (tat) are not signs of mercy.

TEXT 23

vicitra-sevā-dānaṁ hi
hanūmat-prabhṛtiṣv iva
prabhoḥ prasādo bhakteṣu
mataḥ sadbhir na cetarat

Saintly authorities consider that the Lord's real mercy is when he gives various kinds of direct services, a blessing he gives to such devotees as Hanumān. Nothing else counts as his mercy.

The reason is explained. This is because (hi) the best devotees consider that giving various services is the Lord's mercy. Nothing else, like the Lord's caresses, are considered his mercy.

"What are the varieties of such service?" Or "In which persons does such mercy exist?" An example is given. This mercy is found in Hanumān and others such as the Pāṇḍavas and Sugrīva (prabhṛtiṣu). The mercy found in Hanumān and others is not found in Prahlāda. How can Prahlāda be glorified as the object of great mercy? This refutes the statement "When Lord Kṛṣṇa appeared on the shore of the ocean, he placed you (Prahlāda) on his lap and caressed you like a mother." (verse 7)

TEXT 24

śrīman-nṛsiṁha-līlā ca
mad-anugrahato na sā
sva-bhakta-devatā-rakṣāṁ
pārṣada-dvaya-mocanam

Also, Nṛsiṁha performed his pastimes not to show mercy to me but to protect his devotees – the devatās, and deliver his two eternal servants.

"Was not the Lord's appearance in an astonishing form to kill Hiraṇyakaśipu when he created obstacles to your bhakti the greatest mercy to you?" This verse answers. The pastime of appearing in that most astonishing from and killing Hiraṇyakaśipu was for protecting the devatās headed by Indra, and to free his two Vaikuṇṭha door keepers from the curse of the Kumāras.

TEXT 25

brahma-tat-tanayādīnāṁ
kartuṁ vāk-satyatām api
nija-bhakti-mahattvaṁ ca
samyag darśayituṁ param

He also wished to make the words of Brahmā, Brahmā's sons and others come true, and fully display the greatness of bhakti. These were the only reasons for his pastimes.

He performed the pastimes to make the words of Brahmā and the Kumāras, as well as the words of his door keeper Jaya in the form of Hiraṇyakaśipu and the words of Nārada (ādīnām) come true. By appearing as Narasiṁha, Brahmā's words came true and by killing

Hiraṇyakaśipu, the Kumāras' words came true. It is said satyaṁ vidhātuṁ nija-bhṛtya-bhāṣitam: to make true what was spoken by his servants. (SB 7.8.17) Śrīdhara Svāmī explains these words in detail. The explanation is not given here.

Prahlāda had said "These acts are not mercy to me." Now, the Lord's showing respect for Prahlāda while ignoring Brahmā, Śiva and others is rejected as the Lord's mercy. He did this only (param) to show the greatness of bhakti. Or he did this to show the supreme (param) greatness of bhakti. It would otherwise be unsuitable to disrespect eternal associates like Garuḍa and Mahālakṣmī. This was explained previously. The statement refutes the statement made in verse 7.

TEXT 26

paramākiñcana-śreṣṭha
yadaiva bhagavān dadau
rājyaṁ mahyaṁ tadā jñātaṁ
tat-kṛpāṇuś ca no mayi

O greatest of devotees who have nothing material to possess, when the Lord gave me a kingdom, I understood that I had not received even a speck of his mercy.

"The Lord did not show any mercy to me, but rather punished me." This is explained in three verses (26-28). "O Nārada best of the devotees, who have given up even the desire for liberation and its happiness! You know the faults of attachment to kingdom. There is not a speck of mercy of the Lord in me. I understood this at that time."

TEXT 27

taṁ bhraṁśayāmi sampadbhyo
yasya vāñchāmy anugraham
ity-ādyāḥ sākṣiṇas tasya
vyāhārā mahatām api

As the Lord says, "When I wish to favor someone I deprive him of opulence." Such statements as this are evidence, and so also are the statements of his exalted devotees.

Proof is given. The Lord speaks these words to Indra in the Tenth Canto (SB 10.27.16). These words of the Lord (tasya) are proof (sākṣinaḥ). Ādayaḥ indicates other statements. The Lord speaks to Yudhiṣṭhira:

yasyāham anugṛhṇāmi hariṣye tad-dhanaṁ śanaiḥ
tato 'dhanaṁ tyajanty asya svajanā duḥkha-duḥkhitam

If I especially favor someone, I gradually deprive him of his wealth. Then the relatives and friends of such a poverty-stricken man abandon him. In this way he suffers one distress after another. SB 10.88.8

The words of the devotees (mahatām) are also proof. Śrīdāmā says:

bhaktāya citrā bhagavān hi sampado
rājyaṁ vibhūtīr na samarthayaty ajaḥ
adīrgha-bodhāya vicakṣaṇaḥ svayaṁ
paśyan nipātaṁ dhaninām madodbhavam

To a devotee who lacks spiritual insight, the Supreme Lord will not grant the wonderful powers of this world—kingly power and material assets. In his infinite wisdom the unborn Lord knows how the intoxication of pride can cause the downfall of the wealthy. SB 10.81.37

Vṛtra says:

puṁsāṁ kilaikānta-dhiyāṁ svakānāṁ
yāḥ sampado divi bhūmau rasāyām
na rāti yad dveṣa udvega ādhir
madaḥ kalir vyasanaṁ samprayāsaḥ

My Lord does not give the wealth of heaven, earth or lower planets to his devotees who are dedicated only to him, because that wealth becomes the cause of hatred, agitation, anxiety, pride, quarrel, calamity and endeavor. SB 6.11.22

TEXT 28

paśya me rājya-sambandhād
bandhu-bhṛtyādi-saṅgataḥ
sarvaṁ tad-bhajanaṁ līnaṁ
dhig dhiṅ māṁ yan na rodimi

Just see how my worship of the Lord has disappeared by my attachment to ruling my kingdom and by my ties to family members, servants, and others! Fie on me, for not crying in remorse!

"This applies to persons who have no spiritual vision (adīrgha-bodhāya SB 10.81.37 cited above). But it is not a fault to have a kingdom for a spiritual person like you." The Lord says to Mucukunda:

pralobhito varair yat tvam apramādāya viddhi tat
na dhīr ekānta-bhaktānām āśīrbhir bhidyate kvacit

Understand that I enticed you with benedictions just to prove that you would not be deceived. The intelligence of my unalloyed devotees is never diverted by material blessings. SB 10.51.59

The Lord says to Uddhava:

bādhyamāno 'pi mad-bhakto viṣayair ajitendriyaḥ
prāyaḥ pragalbhayā bhaktyā viṣayair nābhibhūyate

If my devotee has not fully conquered his senses, he may be harassed by material desires, but because of his generally strong bhakti, he will not be defeated by sense gratification. SB 11.14.18

"That is true. But because I do not have the Lord's mercy, there is certainly a fault." Prahlāda speaks in misery. "Look! Worship of the Lord (tasya) or the previous worship has disappeared (līnam)." Since bhakti is full of eternity, knowledge and bliss, and cannot be destroyed, it can only disappear from the individual. This was previously explained in relation to mercy appearing (verse 19).

TEXT 29

anyathā kiṁ viśālāyāṁ
prabhuṇā viśrutena me
punar jāti-svabhāvaṁ taṁ
prāptasyeva raṇo bhavet

Why else would I have fought with the famous Lord at Viśālā, as if I had reverted to the low conditioning of my birth?

He confirms this statement by showing his negative actions. The Lord is well known to have lived at Viśālā or Badarī:

turye dharma-kalā-sarge nara-nārāyaṇāv ṛṣī
bhūtvātmopaśamopetam akarod duścaraṁ tapaḥ

Fourth, appearing in the wife of Dharma, he became Nara-Nārāyaṇa, and performed severe austerities which give peace to the soul. SB 1.3.9

evaṁ sura-gaṇais tāta bhagavantāv abhiṣṭutau
labdhāvalokair yayatur arcitau gandhamādanam

O Vidura! The Supreme Lords Nara-Nārāyaṇa, thus worshipped and praised by the devatās who had received their glance, departed for Gandhamādana Hill. SB 4.1.58

"How could I fight with the famous Lord (prabhunā) there, unless my bhakti had disappeared (anyathā)?" Potential verb is used to show possibility. "Battle would not be possible if I had mercy. I had attained the nature of hating the Lord (svabhāvam) because of being born in the demon's family (jāti). I could not give up that unsuitable nature because of low qualities. Or I had attained a nature like that of my father (jāti-svabhāvam)." The word iva indicates disregard for the Lord.

TEXT 30

ātma-tattvopadeśeṣu
duṣpāṇḍitya-mayāsuraiḥ
saṅgān nādyāpi me śuṣka-
jñānāṁśo 'pagato 'dhamaḥ

Inferior dry jñāna has not left me even now because of my association with demons who have bad learning concerning teachings about ātmā.

Even previous to this material acquisition, my bad nature as a demon had not been removed. Because of association with demons who understood spirituality only from the viewpoint of jñāna without bhakti, false teachings about the nature of jīva being Brahman (ātma-tattva), a trace of that dry jñāna devoid of bhakti, has not gone from me. That dry jñāṇa is most wicked (adhamaḥ) since it is a disturbance to the rasa of bhakti.

TEXT 31

kuto 'taḥ śuddha-bhaktir me
yayā syāt karuṇā prabhoḥ
dhyāyan bāṇasya daurātmyaṁ
tac-cihnaṁ niścinomi ca

So how could any pure bhakti arise in me that would indicate the Lord's mercy? I discerned this sign from the wickedness of Bāṇāsura.

"For that reason (ataḥ), how could I have bhakti devoid of karma and jñāna. It could not arise." Vopadeva in Mukta-phala has quoted the words of Kapila to describe pure bhakti:

lakṣaṇaṁ bhakti-yogasya nirguṇasya hy udāhṛtam
ahaituky avyavahitā yā bhaktiḥ puruṣottame

It is said that the quality of bhakti beyond the guṇas is absence of results other than bhakti and lack of obstructions from other processes. SB 3.29.12

By that pure bhakti, mercy of the Lord arises. I have understood clearly the characteristics of that absence of bhakti. I have discerned the sign from the wicked nature (dauryātmyam) of Bāṇa—who took shelter of others while rejecting Viṣṇu, the deity of his family, and who tied up Aniruddha.

No pure bhakti or being the recipient of mercy of the Lord is possible for one who had such wicked person in his family. This statement refutes Śiva's statement that Prahlāda got the Lord's mercy since Bāṇa was protected by the Lord. "It would have been better to kill Bāṇa."

TEXT 32

baddhvā saṁrakṣitasyātra
rodhanāyāsty asau baleḥ
dvārīti śrūyate kvāpi
na jāne kutra so 'dhunā

I have heard somewhere that now, after arresting and imprisoning Bali, the Lord stays as a doorman just to keep him captive. In any case, I cannot say where the Lord is now.

"How does the Lord act as Bali's door keeper without your having pure bhakti or the Lord's mercy?" The Lord remains in Sutala at the door to confine Bali there (rodhanāya). I have heard this somewhere, among some sages. In Hari-vaṁśa Kuṣmāṇḍa speaks to Bāṇa:

balir viṣṇu-balākrānto baddhas tava pitā nṛpa
salilaughād viniḥsṛtya kvacid rājyam avāpsyati

O king! Overcome by Viṣṇu's strength, Bali, your father, is tied up. Sometimes in the future, escaping from the water, he will attain a kingdom.

A similar statement is found in Rāmāyaṇa, Uttara-kāṇda, when Rāvaṇa conquers Pātāla. The Lord is not situated at Bali's door out of mercy but to confine him. In this way his confinement previously mentioned is confirmed. This verse refutes Nārada's words stating that Bali also conquered the Lord. (verse 13)

"The Lord of Vaikuṇṭha, who is rarely seen by Śiva and Brahmā, is seen at the door of Bali constantly. This indicates great mercy." I do not know where the Lord is at present (adhunā). Where can he be seen? By saying "now" he indicates that sometimes the Lord can be seen, but not always.

TEXT 33

kadācit kārya-gatyaiva
dṛśyate rāvaṇādi-vat
durvāsasekṣito 'traiva
viśvāsāt tasya darśane

On rare occasions some persons like Rāvaṇa can see the Lord here. Durvāsa saw the Lord here because Durvāsā had strong faith in being able to see the Lord.

"It can be understood that the Lord remains at all times at the door because there is the story of how the Lord, holder of the club, kicked Rāvaṇa with his big toe when he entered Sutala, Bali's city." He is sometimes seen when he accepts the post as a doorkeeper (kārya-gatyā). If the Lord did not come, Bali would have been conquered by Rāvaṇa. The word ādi indicates persons like Durvāsā.

"It must be accepted that Rāvaṇa saw the Lord in Sutala, since the Lord manifested directly there to confine Bali. Durvāsā came to Sutala to inform the Lord of his suffering caused by demons headed by Kuśa at Kuśasthalī. There he saw the Lord. One can understand that the Lord resides there constantly according to Prahlāda-saṁhitā."

The Lord was seen by Durvāsā in Sutala because of his faith in seeing the Lord there at Bali's door, not because he resided there as the door keeper. Durvāsā had faith in Nārada, who instructed, "The Lord who respects brāhmaṇas is presently at Bali's door. You will see him there very soon." Durvāsā went there at once and saw the Lord. This story is told in the Dvārakā-māhātmya of Prahlāda-saṁhitā.

TEXT 34

yasya śrī-bhagavat-prāptāv
utkaṭecchā yato bhavet
sa tatraiva labhetāmuṁ
na tu vāso 'sya lābha-kṛt

Wherever one develops an intense desire to achieve the Supreme Lord, then one can obtain him. But the Lord is not obtained even at his residence.

"How can faith arise unless the Lord is at a fixed location?" At whatever place (yataḥ) one develops intense desire or greed to see the Lord—longing in prema, not just a little desire, one will obtain the Lord (amum) there. A person does not attain (lābha-kṛt) the Lord at his residence or place (vāsaḥ). If that were the case, Vāsudeva, who resides everywhere, would be obtained by everyone everywhere.

Trust in the Lord arises by the strong desire to attain the Lord. Though one can sometimes see the Lord in Vṛndāvana without faith in his dear pastimes, that is because of the great power of the special place which is dearest to the Lord. This is not true of all places where the Lord resides.

TEXT 35

prākaṭyena sadātrāsau
dvāre varteta cet prabhuḥ
kiṁ yāyāṁ naimiṣaṁ dūraṁ
draṣṭuṁ taṁ pīta-vāsasam

If my Lord were always visibly present here, why would I go to Naimiṣāraṇya to see him, who is dressed in yellow garments?

The Lord does not reside here at all times in person. That is made clear in this verse. "If the Lord were visibly present here why would I go to Naimiṣāraṇya to see him in his real form (tam)?"

TEXT 36

bhavatād bhavataḥ prasādato
bhagavat-sneha-vijṛmbhitaḥ kila
mama tan-mahimā tathāpy aṇur
nava-bhakteṣu kṛpā-bharekṣayā

By your mercy the Supreme Lord developed some affection for me. But my greatness is just like a tiny speck before the heaps of mercy the Lord bestows on his recent devotees.

It would be improper for Prahlāda to criticize the words of his guru Nārada, even if he did so politely. Thinking in this way, Prahlāda accepted Nārada's words but refutes them in another way. May your words be true (bhavatāt). "Because of your mercy, affection of the Lord for me developed. My greatness that you described is a small particle compared to the great mercy shown to Hanumān and other recent devotees. Similarly, a pond seems small when one sees the great ocean."

TEXT 37

nirupādhi-kṛpārdra-citta he
bahu-daurbhāgya-nirūpaṇena kim
tava śug-jananena paśya tat-
karuṇāṁ kimpuruṣe hanūmati

O Nārada, your heart overflows with unconditional mercy. What is the use of describing all my misfortunes which simply make you unhappy? Instead please consider the Lord's mercy on Hanumān of the Kimpuruṣas.

"You should clearly describe how your mercy is meagre." O Nārada, whose heart is soft with mercy (ardra) because it is unconditional (nirupādhi). Your teaching to me was out of the greatest mercy, not because of my qualities. What is the use of describing in detail my misfortunes? There is no use at all. Rather it becomes a fault. Why should I cause you to lament (kiṁ śuk-jananena), out of affection for a disciple or from being unable to tolerate my great suffering.

"Is there another object of the Lord's great mercy, so that my goal will be fulfilled?" See the mercy of the Lord given to Hanumān who lives in Kimpuruṣa-varṣa. Directly experience it.

TEXT 38

bhagavann avadhehi mat-pitur
hananārthaṁ narasiṁha-rūpa-bhṛt
sahasāvirabhūn mahā-prabhur
vihitārtho 'ntaradhāt tadaiva saḥ

My Lord, please know that the Supreme Lord appeared suddenly in the form of Narasiṁha just to kill my father and disappeared as soon as the purpose was fulfilled.

To describe that mercy in detail, first Prahlāda explains his meagre good fortune in two verses (38-39). "Having fulfilled his purpose (vihitārthaḥ) of killing the demon, he disappeared immediately (tadā)."

TEXT 39

yathā-kāmam ahaṁ nāthaṁ
samyag draṣṭuṁ ca nāśakam
mahodadhi-taṭe 'paśyaṁ
tathaiva svapna-vat prabhum

I haven't been able to directly see my Lord at will. So when I saw him once on the shore of the ocean, it was just like seeing a dream.

I have been unable to even (ca) see the Lord, what to speak of perform bhakti to him. I was not able to see him completely because of fear and reverence, and because he appeared for a very short time when he manifested as Nṛsiṁha from the pillar. With fear similar to that on seeing him the first time, I saw him on the shore of the ocean. The details are given in Hari-bhakti-sudhodaya.

TEXT 40

hanūmāṁs tu mahā-bhāgyas
tat-sevā-sukham anvabhūt
su-bahūni sahasrāṇi
vatsarāṇām avighnakam

But Hanumān is much more fortunate. He has experienced the bliss of serving the Lord constantly, for many thousands of years without obstruction.

What can be said? Hanumān saw the Lord to full satisfaction. And he has experienced continually the bliss of service for thousands of years. According to Rāmāyaṇa he served Rāma for a little over eleven thousand years. According to Bhāgavatam he served over thirteen thousand years.

tata ūrdhvaṁ brahmacaryaṁ dhāryann ajuhot prabhuḥ
trayodaśābda-sāhasram agnihotram akhaṇḍitam

After mother Sītā entered the earth, Rāmacandra observed complete celibacy and performed an uninterrupted sacrifice for thirteen thousand years. SB 9.11.18

bubhuje ca yathā-kālaṁ kāmān dharmam apīḍayan
varṣa-pūgān bahūn nṝṇām abhidhyātāṅghri-pallavaḥ

Without transgressing the religious principles, Rāmacandra, whose lotus feet are worshiped by devotees in meditation, enjoyed desired objects as long as he wanted. SB 9.11.36

Hanumān served without a touch of obstacles (avighnakam) at all.

TEXT 41

yo baliṣṭha-tamo bālye
deva-vṛnda-prasādataḥ

samprāpta-sad-vara-vrāto
jarā-maraṇa-varjitaḥ

He is most powerful person, having obtained many wonderful beneditions from the devatās in his childhood. Thus he became immune to old age and death.

Hanumān's great fortune will be described. First his strength is mentioned since it assists him in the happiness of continual service to the Lord without obstacles. The statement continues till three-quarters of the next verse. Even at a young age he attained great benedictions. Five items are described. The short narrative is well known in the Rāmāyaṇa.

As soon as he was born, on seeing the sun rise, he jumped at it to swallow it, thinking it was a ripe tāla fruit. Going upwards to catch the sun, he was struck on his jaw by a thunderbolt of Indra, who wanted to protect the sun. He fell to the earth and fainted. Vāyu, out of grief for his son, began to withdrawn himself from everything. Seeing that the life airs of all beings were in danger, Brahmā and other devatās gathered and brought Hanumān to good health. They gave him various great benedictions.

TEXT 42

aśeṣa-trāsa-rahito
mahā-vrata-dharaḥ kṛtī
mahā-vīro raghu-pater
asādhāraṇa-sevakaḥ

He is devoid of all fear, maintains great vows, and is very learned. He is a great warrior and is an exceptional servant of the Lord of the Raghus.

He maintains a vow of brahmacārya (mahā-vrata-dharaḥ). He knows all scriptures and is a great poet (kṛtī). He is a great warrior (mahā-vīraḥ). Or, he has many types of enthusiasm (vīra) such as charity, dharma, etc.

dāna-vīraṁ dharma-vīraṁ yuddha-vīraṁ tathaiva ca
rasaṁ vīram api prāha brahmā tri-vidham eva hi

Brahmā has explained that the rasa (secondary) of vīra has three types: enthusiasm to give in charity, enthusiasm to act according to dharma, and enthusiasm to fight. Bharata, Nātya-śāstra

He is a servant without compare (asādhāraṇa).

TEXT 43

helā-vilaṅghitāgādha-
śata-yojana-sāgaraḥ
rakṣo-rāja-pura-sthārta-
sītāśvāsana-kovidaḥ

He sportively jumped across thousands of miles of abyssal ocean. And he expertly comforted the distressed Sītā, in the capital of the Rākṣasa king.

His service is described. The description continues till verse 49.

TEXT 44

vairi-santarjako laṅkā-
dāhako durga-bhañjakaḥ
sītā-vārtā-haraḥ svāmi-
gāḍhāliṅgana-gocaraḥ

He threatened his enemies, burned Laṅkā, and destroyed its fortifications. When he returned with news of Sītā, he received his master's tight embrace.

He gave fear (saṁtarajakaḥ) to the enemies such as Rāvaṇa and the Rākṣasas, by killing Rāvaṇa's son Akṣaya-kumāra and the sons of Rāvaṇa's ministers. Out of joy on attaining news of Sītā, Rāma embraced him tightly. He indicates successively greater and greater causes of great service.

TEXT 45

sva-prabhor vāhaka-śreṣṭhaḥ
śveta-cchatrika-pucchakaḥ
sukhāsana-mahā-pṛṣṭhaḥ
setu-bandha-kriyāgraṇīḥ

He was the Lord's best carrier, with his tail as a royal white umbrella, and his broad back as a comfortable seat for the Lord. And it was Hanumān who was the leader in building the bridge over the ocean.

From Kiṣkindha to the ocean, Hanumān carried Rāma on his back. He was the best carrier since his back was wide, beautiful and soft. He was the best among carriers like Garuḍa. Even though he was the carrier during the battle with Rāvaṇa, the events listed are according to the order given in Rāmāyaṇa, starting with jumping over the ocean, and ending with giving happiness to Sītā. As the best carrier he is further described. His tail became an umbrella and his huge back became comfortable seat or an auspicious throne. A white umbrella is a symbol of a king. The word pucchakaḥ is formed according to Pāṇini 5.4.151, in bāhu-vrīhi compound. He was the chief person in building the bridge over the ocean. One time he brought many huge mountains for the bridge.

TEXT 46

vibhīṣaṇārtha-sampādī
rakṣo-bala-vināśa-kṛt
viśalya-karaṇī-nāmau-
ṣaudhy-ānayana-śaktimān

He fulfilled the purposes of Vibhīṣaṇa and destroyed the military force of the Rākṣasas. And he had the special power to deliver viśalya-karaṇī - a healing herb .

He fulfilled the purpose of Vibhīṣaṇa, taking shelter of Rāmacandra's lotus feet. Hanumān told him of Rāma previously, and then arranged a meeting with the Lord when he came to the shore of the ocean.

The services of Hanumān described in the Bālya, Kiṣkindha and Sundara kāṇḍas have been summarized. Now the services in the Yuddha-kāṇda are described till verse 49. The full stories can be understood from studying the Rāmāyaṇa. Since they are well known they are not described here in detail.

When all the monkeys became unconscious when Indrajit fought using illusory powers, which created night, and when Lakṣmaṇa, struck by Rāvaṇa's unfailing spear, played the pastime of fainting, fulfilling Brahmā's words, Hanumān, following the instructions of Suṣeṇa, a physician, had the power to bring twice in the middle of the night the herb called viśalya-karaṇī. He had to defeat the Gandharvas, and uproot the Gandhamādana Mountain, carry it and quickly return. The suffix mān on śakti means he had an abundance of power.

TEXT 47

sva-sainya-prāṇa-daḥ śrīmat-
sānuja-prabhu-harṣakaḥ
gato vāhanatāṁ bhartur
bhaktyā śrī-lakṣmaṇasya ca

He was the very life of his soldiers. Always giving great joy to his glorious Lord and the Lord's younger brother Lakṣmaṇa, he devotedly served as carrier for them both.

He gave joy to Rāma, who had great glory (śrīmat), by removing injury caused to the soldiers during battle, out of affection for the devotees and for his younger brother Lakṣmaṇa. This is not the actual sequence in the narrative. Actions repeated twice are mentioned as one. In the fight with Indrajit, he acts as the carrier for Lakṣmaṇa, who is devoted to Rāma, out of affection for his master Rāma.

TEXT 48

jaya-sampādakas tasya
mahā-buddhi-parākramaḥ
sat-kīrti-vardhano rakṣo-
rāja-hantur nija-prabhoḥ

Supremely intelligent and valorous, he brought victory for the Lord. He increased the spotless fame of his Lord, who killed the king of the Rākṣasas.

He produced victory for Rāma or for Lakṣmaṇa (tasya). He had great valor, showing this during battle, and showed intelligence by giving advice on how to kill Indrajit and Rāvaṇa. He increased the fame of Rāma and Lakṣmaṇa by performing necessary actions for killing Rāvaṇa and jumping over the ocean. This is a summary of his services during the battle.

TEXT 49

sītā-pramodanaḥ svāmi-
sat-prasādaika-bhājanam
ājñayātmeśvarasyātra
sthito 'pi virahāsahaḥ

He engladdened Sītā and by the Lord's order, this true recipient of his master's favor, still lives in this world, though unable to bear separation from the Lord.

He gave great joy to Sītā (pramodanaḥ), bringing her news that Rāvaṇa was killed and bringing her to Rāma. Having described Hanumān's service to his master, he now describes his attainment of special mercy as a result of his service. After Rāma's coronation as King of Ayodhyā, he was the recipient of the Lord's great mercy. Rāma gave him Sītā's gold necklace and bestowed on him permanent, pure prema.

"Then why did he leave the side of his master and remain here?" By the order of his own master (ātmeśvarasya) he remains here on earth. Or by the order of the unconditional benefactor of all jīvas (ātmeśvarasya) he remains here, giving the greatest benefit and happiness by promoting bhakti to all people. He remains here even though he cannot tolerate separation from his Lord. He accomplished the greatest service by fulfilling the order coming directly from his master's mouth.

TEXT 50

ātmānaṁ nitya-tat-kīrti-
śravaṇenopadhārayan
tan-mūrti-pārśvatas tiṣṭhan
rājate 'dyāpi pūrva-vat

He sustains himself by constantly hearing the glories of Lord Rāma. Remaining at side of the Lord's deity, he is present even today with the same brilliance as always.

"How can he remain alive without the Lord?" He keeps himself alive by constantly hearing the glorification of his Lord (tat) or by hearing the indescribable (tat) glories. Or he keeps himself alive by hearing recitations sung in sweet melodies by Ārṣṭiṣeṇa and others in Kimpuruṣa-varsa. Or he keeps himself near them by hearing Ārṣṭiṣeṇa singing about the Lord.

Or he keeps his soul within his body by reasoning, though it tends to leave (upadhārayan). He remains always at the side of a deity of Rāma in Kimpuruṣa-varṣa, performing various services. Even today he manifests brilliance as he serves the Lord as when he previously performed services.

kimpuruṣe varṣe bhagavantam ādi-puruṣaṁ lakṣmaṇāgrajaṁ sītābhirāmaṁ rāmaṁ tac-caraṇa-sannikarṣābhirataḥ parama-bhāgavato hanumān saha kimpuruṣair avirata-bhaktir upāste.

My dear King, in Kimpuruṣa-varṣa the great devotee Hanumān is always engaged along with the inhabitants of that land in devotional service to Lord Rāmacandra, the elder brother of Lakṣmaṇa and dear husband of Sītādevī.

ārṣṭiṣeṇena saha gandharvair anugīyamānāṁ parama-kalyāṇīṁ bhartṛ-bhagavat-kathāṁ samupaśṛṇoti svayaṁ cedaṁ gāyati.

Hanumān, along with Ārṣṭiṣeṇa, constantly hears with rapt attention the most auspicious glories of his master, sung by Gandharvas. Hanumān chants the following mantras. SB 5.19.1-2

TEXT 51

svāmin kapi-patir dāsye
ity-ādi-vacanaiḥ khalu
prasiddho mahimā tasya
dāsyam eva prabhoḥ kṛpā

O master, Hanumān's greatness is well known from scriptural statements like "The chief of the monkeys attained perfection by serving the Lord." His servitude is proof of the Lord's mercy.

This is a summary. O Nārada! This verse is famous.

śāraṅgi-śravaṇe parīkṣid abhavad vaiyāsakiḥ kīrtane

prahlādaḥ smaraṇe tad-aṅghri-bhajane lakṣmīḥ pṛthuḥ pūjane akrūras tv abhivandane kapi-patir dāsye 'tha sakhye 'rjunaḥ

sarva-svātma-nivedane balir abhūd bhaktaḥ kathaṁ varṇyate

Parīkṣit is an example of hearing about the Lord and Śukadeva is an example of chanting the glories of the Lord. Prahlāda is an example of remembering the Lord and Lakṣmī is an example of serving the lotus feet of the Lord. Pṛthu is an example of performing deity worship of the Lord. Akrūra is an example of attaining perfection by offering prayers to the Lord. Hanumān is an example of service with the attitude of a servant of the Lord. Arjuna is an example of friendship with the Lord. Bali is an example of offering the self to the Lord. How can one describe the devotee? BRS 1.2.265

Śārṅgi becomes śāraṅgi for metrical reasons. Substituting the words śṛi-viṣṇoḥ is a modern version. Dāsyam here refers to acts predominated by menial services and not the offering of prescribed karmas to the Lord, which is Śrīdhara Svāmī's explanation. Dāsyam here means sevā or service. Bodily service means using all the senses since both external and internal senses take shelter of the body. Similarly by bodily purification through bathing, all the senses are purified. Dāsyam is superior to smaraṇam and this service was directly to Rāmacandra. Smaraṇam is generally indirect action. Thus it is proper that Prahlāda praises Hanumān as being superior to himself.

TEXT 52

yadṛcchayā labdham api
viṣṇor dāśārathes tu yaḥ
naicchan mokṣaṁ vinā dāsyaṁ
tasmai hanūmate namaḥ

"Although obtaining from the son of Daśaratha the boon of liberation without striving for it, Hanumān never wanted to accept it without the opportunity to serve. To that Hanumān I offer my obeisances."

The previous verse mentioned other verses (ādi-vacanaiḥ) were famous as well in praising Hanumān. He thus quotes another verse that glorifies Hanumān. Hanumān did not want liberation, though he attained it as an accompanying benefit without his endeavor. He did not even desire it, what to speak of accepting it, since it was contrary to the rasa of bhakti. He desired only dāsyam (vinā dāsyam). He did not desire anything else. May my bhakti continue to flow, even though saṁsāra with birth and death is destroyed.

Or I offer respects to Hanumān who, rejecting liberation (mokṣam vinā), even though it came to him as a secondary result, and who, not an ordinary jīva (na), only prayed for pure dāsyam. This verse is found in Nārāyaṇa-vyūha-stava.

TEXT 53

mad-anuktaṁ ca māhātmyaṁ
tasya vetti paraṁ bhavān
gatvā kimpuruṣe varṣe
dṛṣṭvā taṁ modam āpnuhi

You certainly know glories of his other than what I spoke. Why not go to Kimpuruṣa-varṣa, see him yourself, and be enlivened?

"You know glories of Hanumān such as being completely dedicated to Rāma's lotus feet, other than what I spoke. What can I describe? Therefore seeing Hanumān, attain bliss." The imperative (āpnuhi-become joyful) indicates sympathy for Nārada

TEXT 54

śrī-parīkṣid uvāca
aye mātar aho bhadram
aho bhadram iti bruvan

utpatyāsanataḥ khena
muniḥ kimpuruṣaṁ gataḥ

Parīkṣit said: O mother, the sage Nārada then jumped up from his seat and flew through the sky to Kimpuruṣa-varṣa, all the while repeating, "How auspicious! How auspicious!"

Nārada rose from his seat, from a lower position to a higher place, and then travelled through the sky.

TEXT 55

tatrāpaśyad dhanūmantaṁ
rāmacandra-padābjayoḥ
sākṣād ivārcana-rataṁ
vicitrair vanya-vastubhiḥ

There in Kimpuruṣa-varṣa, Nārada saw Hanumān absorbed in worshiping lotus feet of Lord Rāmacandra's deity with varied items from the forest, as if serving the Lord personally as before.

Just as previously he had directly worshipped Rāma's lotus feet (sākṣāt iva), now also he was absorbed in worshipping them with articles from the forest. Or, giving up awareness of the deity form, he worshipped the form as if the Lord were personally present.

TEXT 56

gandharvādibhir ānandād
gīyamānaṁ rasāyanam
rāmāyaṇaṁ ca śṛṇvantaṁ
kampāśru-pulakācitam

Listening to the nectarean Rāmāyaṇa recited by Gandharvas and other celestial singers, Hanumān was in ecstasy. His limbs trembled, while he was covered with goose bumps and tears.

Hanumān is described in more detail in two verses (56-57). He saw Hanumān who was listening to stories about Ṛāma (rāmāyaṇam), and was covered (ācitam) with goose bumps and tears, while he trembled. The stories were being sung by Gandharvas and others residing in Kimpuruṣa-varṣa and were the shelter of attraction for all the worlds (rasāyanam) or were the shelter of rasas like śṛṅgāra, or were a great, sweet medicine nourishing bhakti, which destroyed the disease of saṁsāra. They sung with bliss, and Hanumān listened in bliss.

TEXT 57

vicitrair divya-divyaiś ca
gadya-padyaiḥ sva-nirmitaiḥ
stutim anyaiś ca kurvāṇaṁ
daṇḍavat-praṇatīr api

Glorifying the Lord with various excellent prose and poetry verses of his own, and also reciting prayers from the scriptures, he repeatedly offered respects, falling like a stick.

He recited prayers he himself had composed, in verse and prose, which were more attractive than the attractive (divya-divyaiḥ) prayers from the Purāṇas and Vedas (anyaiḥ). He offered respects, touching eight limbs to the ground.

TEXT 58

cukrośa nārado modāj
jaya śrī-raghunātha he
jaya śrī-jānakī-kānta
jaya śrī-lakṣmaṇāgraja

Nārada cried out in joy, "Glories to You, Raghunātha! Glories to the beloved of Jānakī! Glorles to the elder brother of Lakṣmaṇa!"

Nārada, arriving through the air, seeing him, shouted loudly in joy. His words are described.

TEXT 59

nijeṣṭa-svāmino nāma-
kīrtana-śruti-harṣitaḥ
utplutya hanūmān dūrāt
kaṇṭhe jagrāha nāradam

Delighted to hear the singing of the names of the Lord he worshiped, Hanumān jumped into the sky and embraced Nārada by the neck.

Out of joy on hearing the singing of the names of Rāma, he jumped up high into the sky.

TEXT 60

tiṣṭhan viyaty eva muniḥ praharṣān
nṛtyan padābhyāṁ kalayan karābhyām

premāśru-dhārāṁ ca kapīśvarasya
prāpto daśāṁ kiñcid avocad uccaiḥ

Situated in the sky, Nārada danced with his feet out of great joy, and with his hands he wiped away the flood of loving tears from the eyes of the lord of the monkeys. Attaing the state of highest prema, Nārada spoke in a loud voice.

Nārada danced with his feet only, since he could not move his other limbs. Hanumān was holding him by his neck. He wiped away the tears or accepted (kalayan) the tears of Hanumān with his hands. Having attained the state of the highest prema, he spoke.

TEXT 61

śrī-nārada uvāca
śrīman bhagavataḥ satyaṁ
tvam eva parama-priyaḥ
ahaṁ ca tat-priyo 'bhūvam
adya yat tvāṁ vyalokayam

Nārada said: O blessed one, truly you are the dearest devotee of the Supreme Lord! Just by seeing you today, I too have become dear to the Lord.

O Hanumān endowed with the wealth of the highest bhakti (śrīman)! Even (ca) I have become dear to the Lord today because (yat) I have seen you.

TEXT 62

śrī-parīkṣid uvāca
kṣaṇāt svasthena devarṣiḥ
praṇamya śrī-hanūmatā
raghu-vīra-praṇāmāya
samānītas tad-ālayam

Parīkṣit said: In a moment Hanumān became sober and bowed down to the sage among the devatās. Hanumān then brought him to the temple of Lord Rāmacandra, the hero of the Raghus, so that Nārada could offer obeisances.

Nārada was offered respects by Hanumān who had returned to his previous state, having controlled his disturbance of prema. Nārada was brought to the temple of Rāma (tad ālayam).

TEXT 63

kṛtābhivandanas tatra
prayatnād upaveśitaḥ
sampattiṁ prema-jāṁ citrāṁ
prāpto vīṇāśrito 'bravīt

Having paid respects and being seated, Nārada felt he had now obtained an amazing treasure born from prema for the Lord. He picked up his vīṇā and spoke.

Having offered respects to the deity of Rāma in the temple (tatra), Nārada, having attained a wealth of trembling, perspiration, goose bumps, choked voice and tears, took up his vīṇā, but could not play it. Or he took support of his vīṇā because he was worried that he would stumble because of ecstasy.

TEXT 64

śrī-nārada uvāca
satyam eva bhagavat-kṛpā-bhara-
syāspadaṁ nirupamaṁ bhavān param
yo hi nityam ahaho mahā-prabhoś
citra-citra-bhajanāmṛtārṇavaḥ

Nārada said: Yes, you are the greatest recipient of the mercy of the Supreme Lord. No one can compare to you. Ah! You are eternally an ocean of excellect ecstatic worship of the Lord.

It is true that you alone (param) are the shelter of incomparable mercy of the Lord. Aho indicates amazement. You are an ocean of worship, very sweet and destroying saṁsāra (amṛta), which is more astonishing than the astonishing or more variegated than the variegated (citra-citra).This is certain (hi).

TEXT 65

dāsaḥ sakhā vāhanam āsanaṁ dhvaja-
cchatraṁ vitānaṁ vyajanaṁ ca vandī
mantrī bhiṣag yodha-patiḥ sahāya-
śreṣṭho mahā-kīrti-vivardhanaś ca

You are the Lord's servant, friend, carrier, seat, flag, umbrella, canopy, fan, bard, adviser, doctor, general, best assistant, and the expander of his infinite glories.

His service is described in two verses (65-66). Since Prahlāda described the services previously (verse 43 etc.), Nārada here only briefly describes them. You are dāsa because you serve the Lord. You are a friend or one who is trusted. Rāma gave him his ring and sent him to inform Sītā. He is a flag, since he is always at Rāma's side and announces from far off Rāma's presence like a flag, since his body is huge. Or while acting as Rāma's vehicle, his raised tail is seen from far off like a flag. His tail acts as an umbrella, by blocking the hot sun. His tail acts as a canopy and fan. He is a fan in the sense that his tail acts as a fan. The two are considered non-different. He is a vandī since he recites various verses of praise. His is a physician since he cured wounds of a lance by the medicine called viśalya-karaṇī. He was the best of the monkey assistants since he had most outstanding intelligence and prowess.

TEXT 66

samarpitātmā parama-prasāda-bhṛt
tadīya-sat-kīrti-kathaika-jīvanaḥ
tad-āśritānanda-vivardhanaḥ sadā
mahat-tamaḥ śrī-garuḍādito 'dhikaḥ

Having offered yourself completely to the Lord, having received his supreme mercy, having dedicated your life to narrations of his transcendental glories, you always increase the bliss of his sheltered devotees. You are the best of saints, greater even than others like Garuḍa.

He had offered himself completely to the Lord (sampārītātmā) since he employed all his senses in serving or since he was unattached to activities related to the body, because of his exclusive devotion to Rāma. His very life was topics related only to Rāma. Without those topics he would die in separation from the Lord. It is well known that where there are topics about Rāma, Hanumān comes. He increased the bliss of Rāma's devotees at that time and increases the bliss at the present. The word sadā (constantly) can be applied to many of the statements. He is greater than Garuḍa and others. Or he is the greatest (mahattamaḥ) among all the devotees since his service is superior to that of Garuḍa and others.

The exalted Vaiṣṇava Yāmunācārya describes Garuḍa's service:

dāsaḥ sakhā vāhanam āsanaṁ dhvajo
yas te vitānanaṁ vyajanaṁ trayī-mayaḥ

upasthitaṁ te purato garutmatā
tvad-aṅghri-sammardakiṇāṅka-śobhinā

When will your lotus feet, present in front of Garuḍā endowed with glorious limbs, who massages those feet, and who, composed the three Vedas, who acts as servant, friend, carrier, seat, flag, canopy, and fan, decorate my head? Stotra-ratna

Hanumān's service is greater than that.

TEXT 67

aho bhavān eva viśuddha-bhaktimān
paraṁ na sevā-sukhato 'dhimanya yaḥ
imaṁ prabhuṁ vācam udāra-śekharaṁ
jagāda tad-bhakta-gaṇa-pramodinīm

Indeed, your devotion for the Lord is absolutely pure, for you consider nothing more valuable than the pleasure of service. You gave joy to all the Lord's devotees by speaking to that best of generous Lords these words:

Now Nārada glorifies Hanumān for his constant devotion with disregard for all else. Aho indicates surprise. You do not consider anything better than the happiness of service (sevā-sukhataḥ). Service alone is the best type of devotion. Everything else is inferior. Nārada spoke to the crest jewel of generosity, he who was eager to give everything (udhāra-śekharam). Hanumān spoke words which give joy to the devotees of the Lord. Considering only service to the Lord, Hanumān would completely reject liberation as it was contrary to the service of the Lord (dāsyam).

TEXT 68

bhava-bandha-cchide tasyai
spṛhayāmi na muktaye
bhavān prabhur ahaṁ dāsa
iti yatra vilupyate

"Even though liberation destroys the bondage of material existence, I have no desire for liberation, in which I would forget that you are the master and I am your servant."

I do not desire liberation which cuts the bondage of saṁsāra, birth and death, what to speak of accepting it. This is because in liberation there is no distinction of self and Lord, which is contrary to the happiness of bhakti. The verse is very famous.

TEXT 69

śrī-parīkṣid uvāca
tato hanūmān prabhu-pāda-padma-
kṛpā-viśeṣa-śravaṇendhanena
pradīpitādo-virahāgni-tapto
rudan śucārto munināha sāntvitaḥ

Parīkṣit said: Then Hanumān,buring in a fire of separation that was set ablaze by hearing of the special mercy at the feet of the Lord, cried sorrowfully, and then, calmed by the sage, he spoke.

He became completely enflamed by the dry wood of hearing of special mercy at the feet of the Lord, in the form of his service, and burned up with the fire of separation from those lotus feet. Later, calmed by Nārada's sweet words, he spoke.

TEXT 70

śrī-hanūmān uvāca
muni-varya kathaṁ śrīmad-
rāmacandra-padāmbujaiḥ
hīnaṁ rodayase dīnaṁ
naiṣṭhurya-smāraṇena mām

Hanumān said: O best of sages, hy do you make me, who am such a wretch devoid of the lotus feet of Rāmacandra, cry by reminding me of how the Lord has neglected me?

I have been rejected by the lotus feet of Rāma (padābujaiḥ hīnam), because he left. Plural of feet is used instead of dual to indicate respect. Why do you make me, who am devoid of his feet and miserable, cry by reminding me of his hard heart (naiṣṭhuryam).

TEXT 71

yadi syāṁ sevako 'muṣya
tadā tyajyeya kiṁ haṭhāt
nītāḥ sva-dayitāḥ pārśvaṁ
sugrīvādyāḥ sa-kośalāḥ

If I were the Lord's servant, then why would he forcibly abandon me when he took with him to his spiritual kingdom his dear devotees, including Sugrīva and all the residents of Kośala?

If I were Rāma's servant, why was I given up by him, by force? Though I really wanted to go with him, he did not take me (haṭhāt). He kept me here using various logical arguments.

He did not bring me to his side but he brought to his side those dear to him like Sugrīva and Aṅgada and the residents of Ayodhyā (sa-koṣalāḥ).

TEXT 72

sevā-saubhāgya-hetoś ca
mahā-prabhu-kṛto mahān
anugraho mayi snigdhair
bhavadbhir anumīyate

You are very kind to me. Because I have had the great fortune of his service, you conclude that the Lord has given me his mercy.

Though he rejects completely his good fortune of receiving great mercy, since he experienced the bad fortune of being left alone at the end, out of respect, he accepts that he has received great mercy of service to the Lord as described by Nārada, or what is inferred by him, when he served the Lord directly in his presence. But still he rejects this in another way in three verses (72-74).

The great mercy of the Lord upon me caused by the good fortune of service is inferred by you, who are very affectionate to me. You say this out of affection, not because it is the truth.

TEXTS 73–74

so 'dhunā mathurā-puryām
avatīrṇena tena hi
prāduṣkṛta-nijaiśvarya-
parā-kāṣṭhā-vibhūtinā

kṛtasyānugrahasyāṁśaṁ
pāṇḍaveṣu mahātmasu
tulayārhati no gantuṁ
sumeruṁ mṛd-aṇur yathā

But now the Lord has appeared in Mathurā-purī, where he displays the pinnacle of his opulences and powers. All the mercy he has shown me

cannot equal even a speck of the mercy he has shown the saintly Pāṇḍavas, any more than a speck of dirt can equal Mount Sumeru.

That mercy cannot compare to a small portion of the mercy shown now by the Lord to the Pāṇdavas. The cause of the special mercy is explained. The Lord has appeared in Mathurā, manifesting a wealth of his highest powers.

One cannot compare a speck of dirt to the great golden Sumeru Mountain. The great mercy shown to the Pāṇḍavas is the opposite of what the Lord showed to me.

TEXT 75

sa yeṣāṁ bālyatas tat-tad-
viṣādy-āpad-gaṇeraṇāt
dhairyaṁ dharmaṁ yaśo jñānaṁ
bhaktiṁ premāpy adarśayat

By sending poison and many other calamities, one after another, to trouble the Pāṇḍavas from their childhood, the Lord deliberately showed their fortitude, dharma, fame, wisdom, bhakti, and prema.

The mercy to the Pāṇdavas is described in two verses (75-76). By sending dangers such as poison which were many or indescribable (tat tat), from childhood, the Lord announced to the world the fortitude, dharma, fame, knowledge, bhakti, and prema of the Pāṇḍavas, since amidst all the dangers they maintained their good qualities. He alone sent the dangers in order to manifest their greatness. How else was it possible for such things to happen to the Pāṇḍavas?

TEXT 76

sārathyaṁ pārṣadatvaṁ ca
sevanaṁ mantri-dūtate
vīrāsanānugamane
cakre stuti-natīr api

He acted as their charioteer, court attendant, servant, adviser, and messenger. He kept watch for them at night, followed behind them and even offered them praise and obeisances.

Having described what the Lord did invisibly, he now describes mercy which he showed in person. As a follower (prāṣadatvam) he acted as the leader of their assembly or acted as their friend at all times, being constantly at their side. He took the mentality of a menial servant (sevanam), or at the rājasūya-yajña washed the guests' feet. He acts as a minister and as a messenger. He stayed awake at night with a sword in his hand (vīrāsanam).

He followed behind them (anugamane) or wherever they went he followed them. He praised them and offered them respects.

sārathya-pāraṣada-sevana-sakhya-dautya-
vīrāsanānugamana-stavana-praṇāmān
snigdheṣu pāṇḍuṣu jagat-praṇatiṁ ca viṣṇor
bhaktiṁ karoti nṛ-patiś caraṇāravinde

Hearing through their praises that Kṛṣṇa acted as charioteer, follower, servant, friend and messenger of the dear Pāṇḍavas and that Viṣṇu was respected by the whole world, he expressed devotion to the lotus feet of the Lord. SB 1.16.16

All the things like being the charioteer arise from sakhya. They are functions of sakhya and thus sakhya is not explicitly mentioned, though it is mentioned in the next verse. Or sakhya is included within pārṣadatvam.

TEXT 77

kiṁ vā sa-sneha-kātaryāt
teṣāṁ nācarati prabhuḥ
sevā sakhyaṁ priyatvaṁ tad
anyonyaṁ bhāti miśritam

Out of his affectionate concern for them, what would the Lord not do? The Lord and Pāṇḍavas mutually exchange a mixture of service, friendship and affection.

What else would he not do? He even gave up his promise not to fight. For instance he accepted the attack of Bhīṣma. "Since he holds all beings dear as the highest being, he is friendly. But why should he serve and have faith in lowly humans?" Service, friendship and affection mixed together are glorious. Friendship without service, or affection without friendship or friendship without affection are not glorious. Rather each would be false.

Service, friendship and affection performed mutually between the Pāṇḍavas and Kṛṣṇa are glorious. If Kṛṣṇa does no service when the

Pāṇḍavas do service, it is not glorious. The items are proper when mixed together and mutually exchanged.

TEXT 78

yasya santata-vāsena
sā yeṣāṁ rājadhānikā
tapo-vanaṁ maharṣīṇām
abhūd vā sat-tapaḥ-phalam

Because the Lord resides constantly with the Pāṇḍavas, their capital city has become a forest of austerity for sages, and residing in that city awards one the same pious benefits as performing austerities.

Because the Lord resides in their capital city constantly the city of the Pāṇḍavas became a forest of austerity—a place where sages reside and attain perfection of austerities. That was because the sages always came there to see Kṛṣṇa and by seeing Kṛṣṇa they automatically attained the highest austerities. Nārada says to Yudhiṣṭhira in the Seventh Canto:

yūyaṁ nṛ-loke bata bhūri-bhāgā
lokaṁ punānā munayo 'bhiyanti
yeṣāṁ gṛhān āvasatīti sākṣād
gūḍhaṁ paraṁ brahma manuṣya-liṅgam

You Pāṇḍavas are most fortunate in this world. Sages who purify the planets come to your houses because the Supreme Brahman personally resides in your houses in a human form. SB 7.15.75

What to speak of attaining perfection in austerity, they attained the highest result of austerity. Vā indicates an alternative. Rather, the city became result of the topmost (sat) austerity. Or austerity in this context means concentration of the mind. Sat can modify phalam instead of tapaḥ. The city was the best result of concentration of the mind for the sages: they saw Kṛṣṇa directly at all times. The word phalam (result) is used instead of phala-da (the city was the giver of the result) since the cause and the effect are considered the same since at all times the city gave that result.

TEXT 79

śrī-parīkṣid uvāca
śṛṇvann idaṁ kṛṣṇa-padābja-lālaso
dvāravatī-santata-vāsa-lampaṭaḥ

utthāya cotthāya mudāntarāntarā
śrī-nārado 'nṛtyad alaṁ sa-hūṅkṛtam

Parīkṣit said: Upon hearing these words, Nārada became most eager to see the lotus feet of Kṛṣṇa. He simply wanted to live in Dvārakā forever. Standing up again and again, he danced enthusiastically, filled with inner joy, and made loud cries.

Nārada became completely joyful by hearing of the great glories of Kṛṣṇa's devotees. Hearing what Hanumān had said (idam śṛnvan), he became most eager to serve his lotus feet constantly. He became greedy to live constantly in Dvārakā.

govinda-bhuja-guptāyāṁ dvāravatyāṁ kurūdvaha
avātsīn nārado 'bhīkṣṇaṁ kṛṣṇopāsana-lālasaḥ

O best of the Kurus! Eager to engage in the worship of Kṛṣṇa, Nārada Muni stayed constantly in Dvārakā, which was always protected by the arms of Govinda. SB 11.2.1

In joy he stood up again and again during the conversation (antarā antarā) and danced wildly (alam) while shouting. Repetition of utthāya indicated he again and again stood up.

TEXT 80

pāṇḍavānāṁ hanūmāṁs tu
kathā-rasa-nimagna-hṛt
tan-nṛtya-vardhitānandaḥ
prastutaṁ varṇayaty alam

Hanumān's heart was absorbed in special sweetness from speaking about the Pāṇḍavas. With his joy raised higher by Nārada's dancing, he continued to speak about the topics.

"Why did Hanumān not dance with Nārada in such a celebration?"

His heart was absorbed in attraction or special sweetness (rasa) in speaking stories of the Pāṇḍavas. Or his mind became absorbed in the sweet, intoxicating liquor of the topics, which made him forget the material world and bestowed the highest happiness.

Moreover, his joy because of the topics increased by Nārada's dancing. Thus he described elaborately the glories under discussion.

TEXT 81

śrī-hanūmān uvāca
teṣām āpad-gaṇā eva
sattamāḥ syuḥ su-sevitāḥ
ye vidhāya prabhuṁ vyagraṁ
sadyaḥ saṅgamayanti taiḥ

Hanumān said: All the calamities that befell the Pāṇḍavas were most worshipable and pure because those calamities made the Lord anxious to meet with the Pāṇḍavas quickly.

The various calamities which were most worshipable (susevitāḥ) and most pure (sattamāḥ), making the Lord anxious to go to them (vyagram), giving up many other duties, caused him to meet with the Pāṇḍavas (taiḥ). As great devotees make the Lord appear, so even the calamities of the Pāṇḍavas made the Lord appear. What to speak of the greatness of their good fortune! His killing Jarāsandha and washing the feet of the guests at the rājasūya-yajña are famous. Previously Hanumān explained that their misfortunes were not actual, but arranged by the Lord to show their good qualities. Now however the calamities are explained from the commoner's point of view. Those calamities bestowed the best results.

TEXT 82

are prema-parādhīnā
vicārācāra-varjitāḥ
niyojayatha taṁ dautye
sārathye 'pi mama prabhum

O Pāṇḍavas, prema has subdued you! Devoid of discrimination and etiquette, you engage my Lord as your messenger and charioteer.

Overcome with the highest bliss, Hanumān addresses the Pāṇḍavas as if they were present. "O Pāṇḍavas, you are controlled by prema. You are devoid of discrimination. The Lord of the universe, the controller of Brahmā, should not be engaged as a messenger. You are devoid of proper conduct. The servant should not engage the master. But you engage my master. Out of special prema Hanumān regards Kṛṣṇa as his master (instead of Rāma)."

TEXT 83

nūnaṁ re pāṇḍavā mantram
auṣadhaṁ vātha kiñcana

lokottaraṁ vijānīdhve
mahā-mohana-mohanam

Ah, you Pāṇḍavas know some herb or mantra that can enchant the most powerful enchanter.

"They may be devoid of discrimination because of prema, but why does the Lord accept that treatment?" Nūnam indicates conjecture. You know some herb or mantra that can control (moham) the Lord who is the greatest bewilderer, being the controller of māyā. It is beyond human capacity (lokottaram). Actually he acts in this way because he is bewildered by the great prema of his devotees. The truth will be revealed in verse 85.

TEXT 84

ity uktvā hanūmān mātaḥ
pāṇḍaveya-yaśasvini
utplutyotplutya muninā
muhur nṛtyati vakti ca

[Parīkṣit Mahārāja said:] O mother, O celebrated wife Abhimanyu, after Hanumān said this he repeatedly jumped up high into the air, joining the sage Nārada in dancing. He then continued to speak.

O mother, famous wife of Abhimanyu! The glory of the Pāṇḍavas spreads to you as well. Having explained how the Lord is controlled by the devotee (ity uktvā), Hanumān, jumping high in the air with Nārada, danced constantly and spoke constantly.

TEXT 85

aho mahā-prabho bhakta-
vātsalya-bhara-nirjita
karoṣy evam api svīya-
cittākarṣaka-ceṣṭita

O master of all masters, you are completely controlled by your great affection for your devotees! This is how you attract their hearts.

What did he say? Aho indicates astonishment or an exclamation in prema. O master of all lords of the universe (mahāprabho)! You act in this way (as a charioteer, etc.). All this is possible. O Lord, completely controlled by great affection for your devotees! Since you are not independent, you act according to the devotees. The Lord says in the Ninth Canto:

ahaṁ bhakta-parādhīno hy asvatantra iva dvija
sādhubhir grasta-hṛdayo bhaktair bhakta-jana-priyaḥ

O brāhmaṇa! I am completely under the control of my devotees. I am not at all independent. My heart is controlled by the pure devotees. What to speak of my devotee, even those who are devotees of my devotee are very dear to me. SB 9.4.63

"Why do the devotees not suffer mentally (feeling guilty) when the Lord acts under the control of the devotees?" O Lord whose actions attract the hearts of his devotees! Because the actions produce the highest bliss and because the actions are performed for satisfaction of his devotees out of great affection, devotees never feel unhappiness at any time, since the Lord is always affectionate to the devotees (bhakta-jana-priyaḥ). The Lord himself says this in the above verse. In conclusion the Lord does everything out of affection for the devotees.

The Lord says:

muhūrtenāpi saṁhartuṁ
śakto yady api dānavān
mad-bhaktānāṁ vinodārthaṁ
karomi vividhāḥ kriyāḥ
darśana-dhyāna-saṁsparśair
matsya-kūrma-vihaṅgamāḥ
svāny apatyāni puṣṇanti
tathāham api padmaja

Even though I can kill the demons in a moment, I perform various actions to give pleasure to my devotees. Just as the fish by seeing, the turtle by thought and the bird by touch, nourish their young, I nourish my devotees. Padma Purāṇa

TEXT 86

mamāpi paramaṁ bhāgyaṁ
pārthānāṁ teṣu madhyamaḥ
bhīmaseno mama bhrātā
kanīyān vayasā priyaḥ

It is my greatest fortune that Pṛthā's middle son, Bhīma, is also my dear younger brother.

"I am unfortunate, but by being related to to the Pāṇḍavas, I have become most fortunate." He praises his good fortune in order to relate their good fortune. Bhīma is the middle son of Pṛthā, though Arjuna would be the middle son among all the Pāṇḍavas. Pṛthā was also a great devotee. Bhīma was great because of being born from such a great devotee. Hanumān considers himself fortunate for having Bhīma as a brother. By age (vayasā) Bhīma was younger. But it is hinted by qualities Bhīma was elder. Thus he is the object of my affection (priyaḥ). That is my great fortune.

TEXT 87

svasṛ-dānādi-sakhyena
yaḥ samyag anukampitaḥ
tena tasyārjunasyāpi
priyo mad-rūpavān dhvajaḥ

Lord Kṛṣṇa showed Arjuna special mercy by acts of friendship like giving his sister in marriage to him. That Arjuna carries my image on the treasured flag of his chariot.

Among the Pāṇḍavas, Arjuna was shown special (samyak) mercy by Kṛṣṇa, who acted as a friend by consenting to Arjuna's marriage with his sister Subhadrā and by acting as Arjuna's charioteer (ādi). The flag dear to Arjuna is endowed with my form.

TEXT 88

prabhoḥ priya-tamānāṁ tu
prasādaṁ paramaṁ vinā
na sidhyati priyā sevā
dāsānāṁ na phalaty api

Without the unconditional mercy of the Lord's dearest associates, a devotee's loving service can never succeed or bear fruit.

Having given this description, Hanumān indicates that Nārada must go to Dvārakā, having himself become eager to go there because of arousal of prema. Four verses describe this (88-91). The service performed by the servants or dāsyam - which is dear to the servants (priyā sevā), since the Lord is their only object of affection - cannot be performed, and though done, cannot bear results, without the mercy of the Lord's dearest associates. It will not produce the highest prema, since the Lord is dependent on the dear associates.

TEXT 89

tasmād bhāgavata-śreṣṭha
prabhu-priyatamocitam
tatra no gamanaṁ teṣāṁ
darśanāśrayaṇe tathā

Therefore, O best of Vaiṣṇavas, dearest to the Lord, let us go together to see the Pāṇḍavas and take shelter of them.

O Nārada, dearest to the Lord! O best of the devotees! By addressing Nārada with these two phrases, Hanumān indicates that Nārada also has good fortune like the Pāṇḍavas. By association with Nārada, Hanumān also developed the desire to see the Pāṇḍavas.

It is proper for us servants to go to the Pāṇḍavas' house. Not only will we go, but we will serve them (āśrayaṇe), by guarding them at night. Tathā indicates all that was said, or in the manner that the Lord served the Pāṇḍavas. Or āśrayaṇe can mean accepting shelter of the Pāṇḍavas, with an act of śaraṇāgati or surrender.

TEXTS 90–91

ayodhyāyāṁ tadānīṁ tu
prabhuṇāviṣkṛtaṁ na yat
mathuraika-pradeśe tad
dvārakāyāṁ pradarśitam

paramaiśvarya-mādhurya-
vaicitryaṁ vṛndaśo 'dhunā
brahma-rudrādi-dustarkyaṁ
bhakta-bhakti-vivardhanam

Never in Ayodhyā did the Lord disclose what he now reveals in a district of Mathurā known as Dvārakā: countless varieties of supreme opulence and sweetness, one after another, which Brahmā, Rudra, and other devatās can hardly fathom. These glories devotion of his devotees.

Moreover there will the greatest attainment there. With enthusiasm to go he speaks. What was not shown in Ayodhyā is now revealed in one area of Mathurā known as Dvārakā.

Hari-vaṁśa confirms this in the words of Madhu himself, spoken about his son-in-law to Vikadru:

svāgataṁ vatsa haryaśva prīto 'smi tava darśanāt
yad etan mama rājyaṁ vai sarvaṁ madhu-vanaṁ vinā
dadāmi tava rājendra vāsaś ca pratigṛhyatām
pālayainaṁ śubhaṁ rāṣṭraṁ samudrān upabhūṣitam
go-samṛddhaṁ śriyā juṣṭam ābhīra-prāya-mānuṣam
atra te vasatas tāta durgaṁ giri-puraṁ mahat
bhavitā pārthivāvāsaḥ surāṣṭra-viṣayo mahān
anupaviṣayaś caiva samudrānte nirāmayaḥ
ānartaṁ nāma te rāṣṭraṁ bhaviṣyaty āyataṁ mahat

Welcome, dear boy Haryaśva! I am happy to see you. Let me give you this, my entire kingdom, except for the Madhuvana forest. Please agree to live here and rule this splendid kingdom. Graced by the shores of the ocean, it is rich with cows and peopled mostly by Ābhīra cowherds. During your stay here, in the district of Saurāṣṭra there will come to be a great mountain fortress, fit for the residence of kings and unequaled by any other royal estate. Your vast kingdom will be called Ānarta.

It is understood that the kingdom of Mathurā extended till the ocean. Of course Vāmana Purāṇa says viṁśati-yojanānāṁ tu māthuraṁ mama maṇḍalam: my area of Mathurā extends for twenty yojanas. This is stated because this limited place has the most purifying qualities, since it was the area in which Kṛṣṇa's lotus feet played. The glorification of Dvārakā ends in a glorification of Mathurā. There is a display of the greatest powers in Dvārakā but Dvārakā depends on Mathurā. Now let us return to the topic.

The greatest variety of power and sweetness are now shown plentifully to the highest degree (pradarśanam) in Dvārakā. That variety cannot be understood by Brahmā and Śiva. Going there, we can experience it all directly. My cherished service will increase significantly now. These manifestations in Dvārakā increase the devotion of the devotees, since by realizing those manifestations one's prema manifests in a greater way.

TEXT 92

śrī-nārada uvāca
āḥ kim uktam ayodhyāyām
iti vaikuṇṭhato 'pi na
uttiṣṭhottiṣṭha tat tatra
gacchāvaḥ satvaraṁ sakhe

Nārada said: Ah, what are you saying? Something unseen in Ayodhyā? It is not seen even in Vaikuṇṭha! Rise up, rise up, my friend! We should go there immediately.

Āh indicates great lamentation. The variety of power and sweetness is not manifested in Ayodhyā. Did you say that? It is not manifested even in Vaikuṇṭha. Therefore rise up, rise up. This is repeated to indicate great insistence. We will go to Dvārakā or to the Pāṇḍavas' city (tatra).

TEXT 93

śrī-parīkṣid uvāca
atha kṣaṇaṁ niśaśvāsa
hanūmān dhairya-sāgaraḥ
jagāda nāradaṁ natvā
kṣaṇaṁ hṛdi vimṛśya saḥ

Parīkṣit said: Hanumān, an ocean of soberness, then sighed for a moment, and after thinking for a few moments, he bowed down to Nārada and spoke.

Hanumān sighed, and became sober, sadden by thinking of his oath of loyalty to Rāma alone. Though he had a desire to see Dvārakā, and rose to go there on Nārada's inspiration, he began to consider that this would break his oath to Rāma. He bowed to Nārada in order to remove the offense of disrespect caused by his words.

TEXT 94

śrī-hanūmān uvāca
śrīman-mahā-prabhos tasya
preṣṭhānām api sarvathā
tatra darśana-sevārthaṁ
prayāṇaṁ yuktam eva naḥ

Hanumān said: Certainly it would be fitting for us to visit Dvārakā to see and serve the Pāṇḍavas, for they are in all respects most dear to the Lord and his consort.

Travelling there for the purpose of seeing and serving the Pāṇḍavas was most proper. Or travelling just for seeing them, which is the highest worship (sevā) , is most proper.

TEXT 95

kintu tenādhunājasraṁ
mahā-kāruṇya-mādhurī
yathā prakāśyamānās te
gambhīrā pūrvato 'dhikā

But the Lord is now displaying uncommonly intense mercy and sweetness, more profound than anything he has ever shown before.

TEXT 96

vicitra-līlā-bhaṅgī ca
tathā parama-mohinī
munīnām apy abhijñānāṁ
yayā syāt paramo bhramaḥ

Those wonderful sportive pastimes are so supremely enchanting that they bewilder even self-realized sages.

However, just as the Lord now reveals unlimitedly great mercy and sweetness, he reveals most enchanting actions in various pastimes.

The statements and the following verses are connected with verse 98. Because of the actions in his pastimes (tat) I am afraid of committing offenses (viśaṅkhe aparādhataḥ). If I were to become bewildered like others because of sometimes seeing those pastimes, I would commit offense. Because of this, I have great fear.

These pastimes are more difficult to understand or are more unrestricted than the previous pastimes (gambhirā)—the pastimes of Rāma and other avatāras. Even the sages are bewildered by the actions in these pastimes.

By the activities of the pastimes (yayā) there will be great bewilderment concerning Kṛṣṇa as an avatāra or avatārī.

TEXT 97

aho bhavādṛśāṁ tāto
yato loka-pitāmahaḥ
veda-pravartakācāryo
mohaṁ brahmāpy avindata

Oh! Even your father, Brahmā, grandfather of the world, the teacher of the propagators of the Vedas, was confused by the pastimes of Kṛṣṇa.

How astonishing (aho)! From the activities in the pastimes (yataḥ) even (api) Brahmā, the teacher of propagators of the Vedas such as Vyāsa and

Manu (veda-pravartakācāryaḥ), became bewildered. By seeing the most amazing things when he stole the calves and cowherd boys, Brahmā lost his power of knowing and doing.

TEXT 98

vānarāṇām abuddhīnāṁ
mādṛśāṁ tatra kā kathā
vetsi tvam api tad-vṛttaṁ
tad viśaṅke 'parādhataḥ

So what can be said about unintelligent monkeys like me?You know the bewildering nature of his pastimes. I am afraid of committing offenses.

I would definitely be bewildered by the pastimes in Dvārakā. I would become bewildered just by seeing a little.

"Learned sages may become bewildered. Brahmā may become bewildered because of his high position. How can the devotees become bewildered by the pastimes?"

Even you, the greatest devotee, are bewildered. You know what happened (vṛttam) because of his actions. Nārada became bewildered on seeing Kṛṣṇa in each of the queen's palaces.

TEXT 99

āstāṁ vānanya-bhāvānāṁ
dāsānāṁ paramā gatiḥ
prabhor vicitrā līlaiva
prema-bhakti-vivardhinī

Let the wonderfully variegated pastimes of the Lord be the supreme shelter of his servants who think of nothing but him. For such devotees, those pastimes always increase their prema-bhakti.

"Can the Lord, most worthy of service, not been seen by the fully devoted servants?" That is accepted but Hanumān rejects his own going to Dvārakā for other reasons in six verses (100-105). Let the pastimes be the shelter in all calamities for those who have bhāva for nothing except seeing Kṛṣṇa or for nothing except experiencing his variegated pastimes. The variegated pastimes of Kṛṣṇa are not only their shelter, but increase in a remarkable way (vivardhinī) their service (bhakti) by prema.

TEXTS 100–104

athāpi sahajāvyāja-
karuṇā-komalātmani
avakra-bhāva-prakṛtāv
ārya-dharma-pradarśake

eka-patnī-vrata-dhare
sadā vinaya-vṛddhayā
lajjayāvanata-śrīmad-
vadane 'dho-vilokane

jagad-rañjana-śīlāḍhye
'yodhyā-pura-purandare
mahā-rājādhirāje śrī-
sītā-lakṣmaṇa-sevite

bharata-jyāyasi preṣṭha-
sugrīve vānareśvare
vibhīṣaṇāśrite cāpa-
pāṇau daśarathātmaje

kauśalyā-nandane śrīmad-
raghunātha-svarūpiṇi
svasminn ātyantikī prītir
mama tenaiva vardhitā

Even so, I simply feel more attracted to the Supreme Lord in his eternal identity as Raghunātha, the son of Daśaratha and joy of Mother Kauśalyā. His heart always soft with natural, undeceptive compassion. His nature is devoid of crookedness. He demonstrates how to follow dharma properly, and he upholds the strict vow of having only one wife. He has a beautiful face always lowered with modesty because of increased politeness. His exalted character is pleasing to all. He stands with bow in hand, the king of kings, the hero of the city Ayodhyā, served by Sītā and Lakṣmaṇa, and as Bharata's elder brother. He rules the race of monkeys as the dear friend of Sugrīva and gives shelter to Vibhīṣaṇa. By my hearing of the pastimes of Kṛṣṇa, the intense love I feel for my own master has increased.

By Kṛṣṇa, son of Devakī (tena), my fixed, intense love for my Lord Rāmacandra, endowed with greatest glory, has increased, even though it is proper to go to Dvārakā to see Kṛṣṇa. He describes Rāma with seventeen remarkable terms according to his natural affection.

His heart or nature is soft with natural, undeceptive compassion. His nature is devoid of crookedness. He institutes by his own conduct the most respectable dharma (ārya – conduct).

He has a beautiful face (śrīmad-vadane) always lowered with modesty because of increased politeness. Thus his glance is lowered, not wandering here and there. He is endowed (āḍhye) with a nature or activities (śīla) which attract the whole world (jagad-rañjana). He is the great friend of Sugrīva. He is the lord of the monkeys like me. He became the shelter for Vibḥīṣaṇa.

TEXT 105

tasmād asya vasāmy atra
tādṛg rūpam idaṁ sadā
paśyan sākṣāt sa eveti
pibaṁs tac-caritāmṛtam

Therefore I think I shall stay here, constantly seeing him in this deity form and drinking the nectar of his pastimes.

Because my affection for Rāma has increased (tasmāt), I will stay here in Kimpuruṣa-varṣa, seeing this deity form of Kṛṣṇa (asya) I have described above (tadṛk) which is present (idam), understanding it as Rāma himself (sa iti), while drinking the nectar of his pastimes through Ārṣṭiṣena and others. I have no independence. Nothing is accomplished by my desire.

TEXT 106

yadā ca māṁ kam apy artham
uddiśya prabhur āhvayet
mahānukampayā kiñcid
dātuṁ sevā-sukhaṁ param

And when the Lord may sometimes call me for some purpose, by his great mercy he might give me the happiness of serving him.

“If the Lord desires, then I will go there.” This is expressed in two verses (106-107).

Kṛṣṇa may call me, ordering some particular goal such as causing fear in the Kaurava troops during the battle, or otherwise (param) to give me the happiness of serving by his great mercy. Wherever he calls from, Dvārakā or Hastinapura, I will quickly be there (āśu bhaveyam, verse 108). I will go there immediately.

Or "Service to the Lord is most pleasing to him. What is the use of anything else?" This verse answers. I will go when Kṛṣṇa calls for some purpose. Executing that order gives me the highest happiness (param) of service.

TEXT 107

kiṁ vā mad-viṣaya-sneha-
preritaḥ prāṇato mama
rūpaṁ priya-tamaṁ yat tat
sandarśayitum īśvaraḥ

Or, inspired by affection for me, the Lord may call me just to show me the beautiful form which is dearer than my own life.

"You can execute the orders here." Hanumān gives another reason for going. Inspired by his affection for me, he may call me in order to show me the form of Rāma, which is dearer to me than my life. This form is most indescribable (yat tat) or completely manifests the sweetness of all the pastimes. Here, there will not always be a direct realization of the special sweetness in the pastimes through the skill of sweet words.

How will this be accomplished? Kṛṣṇa is capable of doing everything (īśvaraḥ). Or Kṛṣṇa is directly Bhagavān, since he is the avatārī, source of all avatāras (īśvaraḥ).

One should examine this famous story. Once, wanting to break the pride of Garuḍa and others, to show outstanding devotion to his lotus feet, the Lord in Dvārakā ordered Garuḍa, "Letting him hear my order, bring Hanumān to me from Kiṁpuruṣa-varṣa." Garuḍa went to Kiṁpuruṣa-varṣa and said, "O Hanumān! The king of the Yadus is calling you. Quickly come!"

Hanumān, fixed in devotion to the lotus feet of Rāma, ignored his words. Garuḍa became angry and grabbed him with force to take him to Kṛṣṇa. Hanuman threw him away casually with the tip of his tail. He immediately fell in Dvārakā. Seeing him confused, the Lord said, "O Garuḍa! Go and tell him 'Rama is calling you.' " Kṛṣṇa transformed himself into Rāma and Balarāma became Lakṣmaṇa. But Satyabhāmā could not be made into Sītā. Kṛṣṇa laughed and made Rukmiṇī into Sītā and placed her at his side in Dvārakā.

Garuḍa went to Hanumān again and spoke. Hearing his words, Hanumān immediately became filled with the highest bliss and, running, arrived at

Dvārakā. He saw his Lord and praised him with devotion. He obtained desired benedictions because the Lord was most pleased.

TEXT 108

tadā bhaveyaṁ tatrāśu
tvaṁ tu gacchādya pāṇḍavān
teṣāṁ gṛheṣu tat paśya
paraṁ brahma narākṛti

Then I must be ready to immediately present myself in front of him. But now you please visit the Pāṇḍavas at their home and see the Supreme Brahman in his human-like form.

Let us return to the subject. "Now I will go with you." No, you go now. He explains the reason. He shows the great mercy of the Lord to Pāṇḍavas. See directly with your eyes the Supreme Brahman, Nārāyaṇa in person, in the Pāṇḍava's house since he has manifested two arms in a most beautiful human form. That form is glorious with a variety of indescribable sweetness.

TEXT 109

svayam eva prasannaṁ yan
muni-hṛd-vāg-agocaram
manohara-taraṁ citra-
līlā-madhurimākaram

Lord Kṛṣṇa is fully satisfied in himself. He is beyond the minds and words of the sages. He is the supreme enchanter because his wonderful pastimes are the source of endless attraction.

"How did the Pāṇḍavas obtain that rarest form of the Lord?" He was pleased with them, without their performing any sādhana (svayam prasannam). He was most merciful to them. They were especially great because this good fortune was constant. To show their special greatness in attaining the unobtainable, the rarity of others' seeing him is described.

He is beyond the minds and words of the sages. His great beauty is indicated. He is most attractive (manoharatam) because of the sweetness of his various pastimes. Or he is a mine (ākāram) of amazing pastimes and amazing sweetness, since he is attractive even to Cupid by contacting a small portion of him.

TEXT 110

bṛhad-vrata-dharān asmāṁs
tāṁś ca gārhasthya-dharmiṇaḥ
sāmrājya-vyāpṛtān matvā
māparādhāvṛto bhava

Do not become covered with offense by thinking we are brahmacārīs and they are householders, distracted by political affairs.

"It is improper for persons like me, fixed in detachment, to associate with the Pāṇḍavas who are endowed with power and enjoyment of material objects." We (asmān) refers to Nārada, the Kumāras and others, who are fixed in brahmacārya. Tān refers to the Pāṇḍavas, householders, situated in the house, endowed with household dharma, as well as ruling a kingdom and being involved in its duties (vyāpṛtān). Do not become covered with offense by thinking we are brahmacārīs and they are householders. It is an offense to think of the great devotees in this way. Such an offense never disappears. Thus do not be like this.

TEXT 111

nispṛhāḥ sarva-kāmeṣu
kṛṣṇa-pādānusevayā
te vai parama-haṁsānām
ācāryārcya-padāmbujāḥ

Those Pāṇḍavas never desire anything material, because they constantly serve Lord Kṛṣṇa's lotus feet. And indeed their own lotus feet are worshiped by the leaders of the paramahaṁsas.

What is the problem with a kingdom since they have the highest bhakti, with complete detachment from all material objects, in spite of having the kingdom? They have no desire at all for pleasurable objects of this world. Their lotus feet are fit to be worshipped by the gurus of the top renounced people, since these renouncers are attracted to the insignificant happiness of liberation, whereas the Pāṇḍavas taste bhakti filled with the highest bliss.

TEXT 112

teṣāṁ jyeṣṭhasya sāmrājye
pravṛttir bhagavat-priyāt

ato bahu-vidhā deva-
durlabhā rājya-sampadaḥ

The eldest of these brothers rules the state out of affection for the Lord. Thus his kingdom is rich in all sorts of assets rarely enjoyed by the devatās.

"If they are so detached, what happens to the kingdom?" The eldest of them, Yudhiṣṭhira rules the kingdom, considering everything in relation to affection for the Lord (bhagavat-priyāt). Though he rules the kingdom, by instituting bhakti, all the citizens attain the highest benefit. The Lord is pleased with his noble actions.

apīpalad dharma-rājaḥ pitṛvad rañjayan prajāḥ
niḥspṛhaḥ sarva-kāmebhyaḥ kṛṣṇa-pādānusevayā

Yudhiṣṭhira, like his father, freed from personal desires by engaging in service to the Lord, satisfied and protected the citizens. SB 1.12.4

Sūta explains that the king satisfied the citizens by promoting bhakti and like a father protected them. Nārada says to Śaunaka:

aho 'ti-dhanyo 'si yataḥ samasto
janas tvayeśa prabalī-kṛto 'yam
utpādayed yo 'tra bhavārditānāṁ
bhaktiṁ harau loka-pitā sa dhanyaḥ

You are most fortunate because all people have become strong because of you. He who promotes bhakti for the people suffering from material life is the father of the people and most fortunate. Hari-bhakti-sudhodaya

Because of what was said, he attained a wealth rare for even the devatās. This statement is connected with verse 115 which says that the kingdom could not contaminate Yudhiṣṭhira at all with material desire.

Rājyam means the king's actions of protecting the people, etc. There was a wealth of dharma, since he attained one sixth of the pious acts of the citizens. Or rājyam refers to the kingdom. The wealth of the kingdom however was actually the wealth of dharma since that was most prominent. Later their material wealth is mentioned. The eldest ruled, but the other brothers also engaged in ruling. By mentioning only Yudhiṣṭhira, it is indicated that by being together as one unit with great friendship, there was greatness of proper dharma, protection of the people, etc.

TEXT 113

rājasūyāśvamedhādi-
mahā-puṇyārjitās tathā
viṣṇu-lokādayo 'trāpi
jambu-dvīpādhirājatā

By sacrifices like the Rājasūya and Aśvamedha, he has earned great puṇya enough for attaining Vaikuṇṭha planets. And while still in this world, he rules the entire tract of Jambudvīpa.

Vaikuṇṭha and other planets were attained by the great puṇya of sacrifices like Rājasūya and Aśvamedha, directly performed by the king. The puṇya was actually bhakti, since everything was offered to Bhagavān in the sacrifices. Tathā means "all this" or "in this way" or "such." The Vaikuṇṭha planets are mentioned since Vaikuṇṭha planets are the main places, being the best of all and being situated above all places. By attaining Vaikuṇṭha, all other planets were attained. By attaining the ocean of happiness in Vaikuṇṭha, the happiness of all other places was attained. Or by his desire he could go to Vaikuṇṭha after visiting all the upper planets in order (ādi). After mentioning the spiritual attainment, the material world is mentioned. Even here in this world (atra) rulership of Jambudvīpa was attained. Three verses (113-115) explain the material wealth.

TEXT 114

trai-lokya-vyāpakaṁ svacchaṁ
yaśaś ca viṣayāḥ pare
surāṇāṁ spṛhaṇīyā ye
sarva-doṣa-vivarjitāḥ

His pure fame is known throughout the three worlds. His faultless possessions evoke the envy of the devatās.

Other objects (pare) are desired by the devatās, but not obtained by them. Previously the spiritual wealth was unobtainable by the devatās. Now even the worldly possessions are desired by the devatās. It is not repetition. The cause of desiring is mentioned. Those objects are devoid of faults like being temporary, since they arose by the mercy of Kṛṣṇa. They were not earned by karma.

TEXT 115

kṛṣṇa-prasāda-janitāḥ
kṛṣṇa eva samarpitāḥ

nāśakan kām api prītiṁ
rājño janayituṁ kvacit

The king achieved all this opulence by Kṛṣṇa's mercy, and has offered it all to Kṛṣṇa. The opulence was never able to please him.

"But these objects would be full of faults like heat in fire and would thus cause disturbance." That is true, but by offering to the Lord, even the material objects attain spiritual natures. Those objects cannot at all produce faults. On the contrary they produce the best results. The objects are offered without material desire to Kṛṣṇa.

TEXT 116

kṛṣṇa-premāgni-dandahya-
mānāntaḥ-karaṇasya hi
kṣud-agni-vikalasyeva
vāsaḥ-srak-candanādayaḥ

Because his heart always burns with the fire of prema for Kṛṣṇa, those clothes, garlands, and sandalwood pulp attract him no more than they would attract a man afflicted by the fire of hunger.

He describes the king, speaking of the results of offering to Kṛṣṇa, in order to show another, chief reason for the king's being unable to manifest affection for material objects. The king's heart burns with the fire of prema for Kṛṣṇa. That prema is called a fire because it burns up unlimited faults just by its touch. It is caused by pain in separation. But even at the time of meeting, the heart burns with the worry of future separation. Or the highest bliss has the natural quality great energy, like fire. The kings' mind burns intensely (dandahyamāna) with that fire of prema. Hi indicates a reason or means certainly.

āśliṣya sama-śītoṣṇaṁ prasūna-vana-mārutam
janās tāpaṁ jahur gopyo na kṛṣṇa-hṛta-cetasaḥ

Except for the gopīs, whose hearts had been stolen by Kṛṣṇa, the people could forget their suffering by embracing the wind coming from the flower-filled forest, which was neither hot nor cold. SB 10.20.45

This verse describes the autumn season. Experiencing the autumn wind filled with the fragrance of flowers, all people became relieved of suffering, but the gopīs were not relieved of suffering, because their hearts were stolen by Kṛṣṇa. They were severely burned by the fire of kṛṣṇa-prema. They suffered more. Autumn season was an uddīpana for their prema.

An example is given. A person suffering from the fire of hunger, though accepting objects like fine cloth or sandalwood, cannot become happy. He simply suffers. The word ādayaḥ refers to family and sons, etc. Just as by eating, the person becomes peaceful and happy, so Yudhiṣṭhira destroys the fire of separation and obtains happiness by attaining Kṛṣṇa. Or the example is used to show the absence of power to produce attraction in material objects.

TEXT 117

aho kim apare śrīmad-
draupadī mahiṣī-varā
tādṛśā bhrātaraḥ śrīmad-
bhīmasenārjunādayaḥ

What more shall I say? His exhalted queen is none other than Draupadī, and his brothers are such men as the blessed Bhīmasena, Arjuna, etc.

"But he has great attraction for his wife Draupadī and his younger brothers." Two verses (117-118) explain this. What to speak of objects like enjoyment of wealth and friends (apare) being attractive to him. These objects could not attract his wife or his brothers as well.

TEXT 118

na priyā deha-sambandhān
na catur-varga-sādhanāt
paraṁ śrī-kṛṣṇa-pādābja-
prema-sambandhataḥ priyāḥ

They are dear to him not because of bodily relationships or because they help him achieve the four goals of material life but because of their relationship of prema with Kṛṣṇa's lotus feet.

Yudhiṣṭhira's affection for them which is seen, is not because of bodily relationships, but because of a relationship with kṛṣṇa-bhakti.

Or for Yudhiṣṭhira who had affection for Kṛṣṇa alone, there was affection for nothing else (apare). What to speak of himself, Draupadī and his brothers had affection for nothing else. This is expressed in the two verses, which are connected.

Draupadī was the best among the queens since she was decorated with all good qualities and form. Her form and qualities were indescribable (śrīmat).

The kings' affection for them was not caused by relationship of bodies through birth or marriage, or because they helped produce dharma, artha, kāma and mokṣa. It is said:

mātā tīrthām pitā tīrthaṁ bhāryā tīrthaṁ tathaiva ca putra-tīrtham

The mother is a holy tīrtha, the father, the wife and the son are holy tīrthas (capable of producing puṇyas). Padma Purāṇa

According to this statement, Draupadī and his younger brothers, who were like sons were also tīrthas. They could help Yudhiṣṭhira attain the four goals. But they were dear to him only (param) because they had a relationship of prema with the lotus feet of Kṛṣṇa or or because Krsna's lotus feet had prema for them. The word priyaḥ is repeated to express the great affection for them because of relationship with kṛṣṇa-prema.

It is well known that because the nature of bhakti is friendliness among the devotees, that affection produces great happiness from tasting that rasa of bhakti. And thus the qualities of one devotee become the qualities in all other devotees. One should see the glorification of Yudhiṣṭhira as a glorification of all of the Pāṇḍavas, since the younger members follow the elder.

The topic is explained in the following verse:

sampadaḥ kratavo lokā mahiṣī bhrātaro mahī
jambūdvīpādhipatyaṁ ca yaśaś ca tri-divaṁ gatam
kiṁ te kāmāḥ sura-spārhā mukunda-manaso dvijāḥ
adhijahrur mudaṁ rājñaḥ kṣudhitasya yathetare

O brāhmaṇa! He had all wealth, sacrifices, planets, queens, brothers, the earth, lordship over Jambudvīpa, and fame in Svarga, desirable even for the devatās. Did these things give joy to the King, whose mind was only fixed on Mukunda without deviation and nothing else? SB 1.12.5-6

TEXT 119

vānareṇa mayā teṣāṁ
nirvaktuṁ śakyate kiyat
māhātmyaṁ bhagavan vetti
bhavān evādhikādhikam

But what can a monkey like me describe the glories of the Pāṇḍavas? You already know much more than I.

How much can a monkey like me describe the glories of the Pāṇdavas? I cannot describe anything. Why? I have the form of a monkey. What can I describe? "Then how can I (Nārada) know about the Pāṇḍavas?" O omniscient one (bhagavan)! You know more than what I spoke. Prema in Nārada was aroused. He was thus anxious to go to Dvārakā.

Thus ends the fourth chapter of Canto One of Śrīla Sanātana Gosvāmī's Bṛhad-bhāgavatāmṛta, entitled "Bhakta: The Devotee."

Chapter Five

Priya: The Beloved

TEXT 1

śrī-parīkṣid uvāca
tatra śrī-nārado harṣa-
bharākrāntaḥ sa-nartanam
kuru-deśaṁ gato dhāvan
rājadhānyāṁ praviṣṭavān

Parīkṣit said: Nārada, beside himself with joy, arrived dancing at the kingdom of the Kurus and raced into their capital city.

In the Fifth Chapter, the Pāṇḍavas refute Nārada's glorification of them, and speak of the glories of the Yadus and Uddhava. Nārada danced as he ran there. He entered the capital city of Yudhiṣṭhira (rājādhānyām).

TEXTS 2–3

tāvat kasyāpi yāgasya
vipat-pātasya vā miṣāt
kṛṣṇam ānāyya paśyāma
iti mantrayatā svakaiḥ

dharma-rājena taṁ dvāri
tathā prāptaṁ mahā-munim
niśamya bhrātṛbhir mātrā
patnībhiś ca sahotthitam

Yudhiṣṭhira was just then consulting his inner circle about how to bring Kṛṣṇa on the pretext of some sacrifice or calamity so as to see him. When the king heard that the great sage was at the door, he at once stood up with his brothers, mother, and wives.

While Nārada was entering the city, Yudhiṣṭhira was discussing how to bring Kṛṣṇa. When he heard from the door keepers that Nārada had arrived at the gate, he rose up from his seat from consulting with others along with his brothers. He had been consulting with his brothers and ministers (mantrayatā) on how to bring Kṛṣṇa, on the pretext (miṣāt) of some sacrifice like Aśvamedha, from Dvārakā to Hastināpura by sending Bhīma there so that they could see him. But he might not come quickly because of that. Thus another pretext was calamity so that Kṛṣṇa would prevent (pātasya) the threat (vipad) from wicked elements or he would come quickly (pātasya) because of the threat. Though such attack was not possible it could happen so that they could see Kṛṣṇa. And they spoke of sacrifices and attacks out of greed to see Kṛṣṇa.

There are two types of calamities, according to what was said. Some are arranged by the Lord himself in order to broadcast the glories of the Pāṇḍavas. Some are arranged by the Pāṇḍavas in order to see the Lord. This applies to other devotees as well.

TEXT 4

sa sambhramaṁ dhāvatā tu
so 'bhigamya praṇamya ca
sabhām ānīya sat-pīṭhe
prayatnād upaveśitaḥ

Yudhiṣṭhira eagerly rushed forward to meet Nārada, approached him and offered respects. He then brought Nārada into the assembly hall and with some effort made him accept a seat of honor.

Nārada was brought forward by Yudhiṣṭhira and offered respects with eight parts of the body.

TEXT 5

rājñā pūjārtham ānītaiḥ
pūrva-vad dravya-sañcayaiḥ
mātas tvac-chvaśurān eva
sa-bhṛtyān ārcayat sa tān

O mother, the king brought the articles for worshiping Nārada, as had been done previously. But Nārada took those items and instead worshiped your fathers-in-law and their servants.

Verse 3 mentioned dharma-rājena (by Yudhiṣṭhira) and this verse mentions rajñā (by the king). The repetition indicates that the king had the power to immediately gather unlimited articles for worshipping Nārada. He had brought the articles for worshipping Nārada, as had been done previously. But he did not offer them. As soon as he started to worship Nārada with the articles, Nārada instead began worshipping Yudhiṣṭhira and his servants. By calling them fathers-in-law to his mother, Parīkṣit indicates her similar greatness also. He calls out to his mother in great astonishment (mātaḥ).

TEXT 6

hanūmad-gaditaṁ teṣu
kṛṣṇānugraha-vaibhavam
muhuḥ saṅkīrtayām āsa
vīṇā-gīta-vibhūṣitam

Nārada, playing his vīṇā, extensively glorified the greatness of Kṛṣṇa's favor on the Pāṇḍavas which Hanumān had spoken of.

Nārada extensively glorified the greatness or amount (vaibhavam) of Kṛṣṇa's mercy to the Pāṇḍavas. As he glorified them, he played the vīṇā while singing. This means it was very sweet.

TEXT 7

śrī-nārada uvāca
yūyaṁ nṛ-loke bata bhūri-bhāgā
yeṣāṁ priyo 'sau jagad-īśvareśaḥ
devo gurur bandhuṣu mātuleyo
dūtaḥ suhṛt sārathir ukti-tantraḥ

Nārada said: You all are indeed the most fortunate on earth! The Lord of all lords of the universe is your dearest friend. He is your God, guru, blood relative, maternal cousin, messenger, well-wisher, order carrier, and charioteer.

The glorification is described. This continues till verse 44. The Pāṇḍavas are the most fortunate on earth (nṛ-loke). One is not qualified for the special mercy of the Lord without being naturally detached from the great enjoyment and wealth of Svarga. They had attained the highest level (bhūri) of good fortune or worship (bhāgāḥ) characterized by special bhakti caused by great mercy of the Lord. Or they had attained a portion (bhāgāḥ) of the Lord's great mercy. Why? The Lord was the object of their affection (priyaḥ).

Who is he? He is the controller of Brahmā, Śiva and others (jagadīvareśvaraḥ). He can produce their good fortune. Moreover, he is worthy of worship, protecting them from all dangers (devaḥ). He gives all instructions personally (guru). He is the best relative among all relationships caused by birth. He is a cousin, an object of special affection, since cousins show special friendship like brothers. Or he is a cousin among relatives: he most friendly, related to them through their mother.

He was their messenger, being sent from Upaplava in the Virāṭa to Hastināpura, to Duryodhana's assembly. He is their well-wisher, performing beneficial actions without cause, always willing to help without expectation of reward. He was their charioteer, driving Arjuna's horses during the Kurukṣetra war.

He obeyed orders (ukti-tantraḥ). Arjuna said, "O Acyuta! Drive the chariot between the two armies."(BG 1.21) Kṛṣṇa immediately followed his order and took the chariot where he ordered. Or following orders is a summary of the previous terms such as being charioteer, messenger, etc. Or what more can be said? He followed your orders: when you give the order, at that moment he undertakes it.

Or ukti-tantraḥ means he is a servant. However the words sevaka is not used as it is harsh to the ears. This indicates staying up at night guarding, services that Hanumān had mentioned. This also shows how the Lord is their dear friend (priyaḥ) and thus he acted as their protector (devaḥ).

Or priyaḥ can also be applied to all the words describing Kṛṣṇa. For instance Kṛṣṇa is the priyaḥ devaḥ: he is their worshippable deity, worshipped constantly out of prema. (Similarly he is priyaḥ dūtaḥ, etc.)

The word priyaḥ distinguished the relationship with Kṛṣṇa from relationship with others. For instance, Arjuna worshipped Śiva (deva) and Droṇa (guru), but his worship of Kṛṣṇa as deva and guru was most distinct in terms of the affection (priyaḥ). Being dear to them is included in all the items of the list. Each item proves that he was the object of their love. Kṛṣṇa is the controller of Brahmā and Śiva. But Kṛṣṇa was the dear object of the Pāṇḍavas.

Or others are worshipable as controllers but the Pāṇḍavas worship Kṛṣṇa because he is dear. He is the teacher because he is dear. Thus the Pāṇḍavas are superior to Brahmā, Śiva and others.

TEXT 8

yo brahma-rudrādi-samādhi-durlabho
vedokti-tātparya-viśeṣa-gocaraḥ
śrīmān nṛsiṁhaḥ kila vāmanaś ca
śrī-rāghavendro 'pi yad-aṁśa-rūpaḥ

For Brahmā, Rudra, and other devatās he is difficult to realize even in samādhi. The words of the Vedas describe him only indirectly. Nṛsiṁha, Vāmana, and Rāghavendra are his plenary expansions.

"Our greatness occurs by having Kṛṣṇa as our object of affection. If he is most rare to attain, how can he be easily available at our house? Are you are not giving exaggerated praise to us?"

To answer this, Nārada glorifies the rarity of attaining Kṛṣṇa until verse 28. First, the great rarity of attaining him is described in a half a verse. Brahmā and Śiva cannot attain Kṛṣṇa even when they are in samādhi. Why? The words of the Vedas only describe him indirectly (tātparya), but do not do so directly (sākṣāt vṛtti). One can understand him only as the essence (viśeṣa) of the general purport (tātparya). He cannot be described in the same way that Brahman is indicated – by negating the unreal, since Kṛṣṇa is a sweet form of eternity, knowledge and bliss.

"Would Nṛsiṁha and other forms of the Lord be similarly unreachable?" Kṛṣṇa is different from them. Though Nṛsiṁha is frightening and Vāmana is a dwarf, they are beautiful (śrīmat).

Nṛsiṁha appeared from the pillar with such a ferocious form out of affection for his devotee. Vāmana showed a form of the universe to Bali stepping over the three worlds. Rāmacandra, like them, is a portion of Kṛṣṇa, an avatāra. Though he is directly Bhagavān, he is perceived as an avatāra, not revealing all his powers. This is well known (kila). Ete cāṁśa-kalāḥ puṁsaḥ kṛṣṇas tu bhagavān svayam (SB 1.3.28) Thus it is proved that the Pāṇḍavas are greater then Prahlāda, Vāli and Hanumān, servants of Nṛsiṁha, Vāmana and Rāmacandra.

TEXT 9

anye 'vatārāś ca yad-aṁśa-leśato
brahmādayo yasya vibhūtayo matāḥ
māyā ca yasyekṣaṇa-vartma-vartinī
dāsī jagat-sṛṣṭy-avanānta-kāriṇī

All other incarnations of the Lord are mere portions of his plenary portions. Brahmā and others are considered his vibhūtis. And Māyā is his maidservant. Standing always in view ready to serve him, she enacts the creation, protection, and destruction of the universe.

Other avatāras such as Matsya and Kūrma appear from portions (aṁśa) and Pṛthu and others appear as smaller portions (leśataḥ). Brahmā and others are considered his vibhūtis or servants, not līlāvatāras, by the knowers of scriptures. Brahmā says to Nārada:

ahaṁ bhavo yajña ime prajeśā
dakṣādayo ye bhavad-ādayaś ca
svarloka-pālāḥ khaga-loka-pālā
nṛloka-pālās talaloka-pālāḥ
gandharva-vidyādhara-cāraṇeśā
ye yakṣa-rakṣoraga-nāga-nāthāḥ
ye vā ṛṣīṇām ṛṣabhāḥ pitṝṇāṁ
daityendra-siddheśvara-dānavendrāḥ
anye ca ye preta-piśāca-bhūta-
kūṣmāṇḍa-yādo-mṛga-pakṣy-adhīśāḥ
yat kiṁ ca loke bhagavan mahasvad
ojaḥ-sahasvad balavat kṣamāvat
śrī-hrī-vibhūty-ātmavad adbhutārṇaṁ
tattvaṁ paraṁ rūpavad asva-rūpam

I; Śiva; Viṣṇu; the Prajāpatis such as Dakṣa; you, Nārada; and others like the Kumāras; the protectors of Svarga, Bhuvar-loka, Bhū-loka and the lower planets; leaders of the Gandharvas, Vidyādharas, and Cāraṇas;[14] the leaders of the Yakṣas, Rakṣas, Uragas and Nāgas;[15] the best of the sages and Pitṛṣ, the leaders of the Daityas, Dānavas[16] and Siddhas, the leaders of the Pretas, Piśācas, Bhūtas, Kūṣmāṇdas, aquatics, beasts and birds[17] — whatever in this universe possesses glory, influence, strength of mind, senses and body; whatever is endowed with patience, beauty, shame at doing the sinful, excellence, intelligence, or astonishing syllables: whatever has form or no form—none of these are the svarūpa of the Lord.

prādhānyato yān ṛṣa āmananti
līlāvatārān puruṣasya bhūmnaḥ

---

[14] Leader of the Gandharvas is Viśvāvasu. Leader of the Cāraṇas is Puṣpadanta.

[15] Kuvera is head of the Yakṣas. Nirṛti is head of the Rākṣasas. Vāsuki is head of the Uragas and Ananta is head of the Nāgas. Head of the sages is Vasiṣṭha. Head of the Pitṛs is Yama. Head of the Daityas is Prāhlada. Head of the Siddhas is Sanaka. Head of the Dānavas is Vṛṣaparva.

[16] Dānavas are the sons of Danu and Kaśyapa. Daityas are sons of Diti and Kāśyapa.

[17] Pretas and Piśācas are type of Bhūtas or ghosts. The leader of the Piśācas is Ghaṇṭākarṇa. The leader of the Bhūtas is Bhairava. The leader of the Kūṣmāṇḍas is Bhṛṅgi. The leader of the aquatics is the timiṅgila. Head of the beasts is the lion. This list is taken from Vijayadhvaja-tīrtha's commentary.

āpīyatāṁ karṇa-kaṣāya-śoṣān
anukramiṣye ta imān supeśān

I will now speak in order about the beautiful līlāvatāras of the Supreme Lord, whose topics dry up the desire to hear anything else and which the sages glorify for their valuable content. SB 2.6.43-46

Śrīdhara Svāmī explains those verses. I (Brahmā); Śiva (bhavaḥ); Viṣṇu (yajñaḥ); the leaders of the prajās such as Dakṣa; brahmacārīs like you (Nārada); the loka-pālas; the leaders of Pātāla-loka; the leaders of the Gandharvas, Vidhyādharas and Cāraṇas; the lords of the Yakṣas, Rākṣasas, and snakes; the best of the sages and Pitṛs; the leaders of the Pretas and others—all of them are Kṛṣṇa's vibhūtis (tattvaṁ param). They are endowed with the Lord's powers of tejas (mahasvat), power of the senses (ojaḥ) and mind (sahasvad), and firmess (balavat). As well, they may be endowed with beauty (śrī), lack of entanglement of karma (hrī), wealth (vibhūti), intelligence (ātmā), astonishing color (adbhutārṇam). These are all vibhūtis. They are not the Lord's svarūpa (asvarūpa).

According to the list in Bhagavad Gītā, Chapter 10, the guṇāvatāras are also vibhūtis. In verse 46 he speaks to introduce the līlāvatāras who are filled with eternity, knowledge and bliss. I will speak about the chief avatāras (imān) in order. There are many other lesser avatāras not so famous.

avatārā hy asaṅkhyeyā hareḥ sattva-nidher dvijāḥ |
yathāvidāsinaḥ kulyāḥ sarasaḥ syuḥ sahasraśaḥ ||

Unlimited avatāras arise from the Lord, the treasure house of the highest mercy, just as thousands of small rivers flow from an inexhaustible lake. SB 1.3.26

The avatāras, arising from the Lord, a treasure house of the highest mercy (sattva) are innumerable, like thousands of rivers flowing from an inexhaustible lake.

Though Brahmā, Śiva and Viṣṇu are guṇāvatāras, and not vibhūtis, Brahmā and Śiva are counted among the vibhūtis sometimes since they spread bhakti like the devotees. To help the two, Viṣṇu appears as Yajña and other forms in every manvantara period, as the protector of the period. Yajña is also counted as a līlāvatāra.

jāto rucer ajanayat suyamān suyajña
ākūti-sūnur amarān atha dakṣiṇāyām

loka-trayasya mahatīm aharad yad ārtiṁ
svāyambhuvena manunā harir ity anūktaḥ

The Lord called Suyajña, the son of Ākūti and Ruci, gave birth to the devatās called Suyamās in his wife Dakṣiṇā. When he relieved the three worlds of great suffering, Svāyambhuva named him Hari. SB 2.7.2

But he is counted as a vibhūti as a protector of Svayambhuva manvantara or for taking the post of Indra. The main līlāvatāras can be understood from the list in the Bhāgavatam.

Having shown the Lord as the cause of the vibhūtis, the Lord is shown to be rarely attained since māyā cannot attain him directly. As a maidservant, extremely dependent, she stands far away on the path, accepting his glance. She causes creation, maintenance and destruction of the material world. All the personalities such as Brahmā, being dependent, are servants by their nature.

TEXT 10

yasya prasādaṁ dharaṇī-vilāpataḥ
kṣīroda-tīre vrata-niṣṭhayā sthitāḥ
brahmādayaḥ kañcana nālabhanta
stutvāpy upasthāna-parāḥ samāhitāḥ

When Brahmā and other devatās responded to the lamentation of Mother Earth, together they all stood on the shore of the Milk Ocean, observing strict vows. They recited prayers and worshiped the Supreme Lord, meditating with full concentration. Nonetheless, they were unable to obtain his mercy.

How Brahmā cannot meet the Lord in samādhi is described through a history. The word api (even) can be applied to many of the phrases of the verse. Because of the earth's lamentation, even though they stood on the shore of the Milk Ocean - which was the father of Lakṣmī (since she appeared from the churning of the Milk Ocean), controlling their breath and eating, even though they engaged in worship and prayers (upasthānam), even with steadiness externally and internally (samāhitāḥ), praising the Lord with puruṣa-sūkta and other verses, they did not obtain mercy in the form of receiving consolation by seeing the Lord. How could they attain him (since he is rarely attained)? This is described at the beginning of the Tenth Canto.

TEXT 11

brahmaṇaiva samādhau khe
jātām adhigatāṁ hṛdi
yasya prakāśya tām ājñāṁ
sukhitā nikhilāḥ surāḥ

Brahmā, in samādhi, then perceived in his heart the Lord's command, which manifested in the sky. He repeated that command to the devatās, and they all became satisfied.

"But the worship of the Lord never goes in vain." That is true. But because it was not possible to immediately solve the problem, since their request was profound, the Lord remains difficult to attain.

Brahmā revealed the well-known (tat) order of Lord (yasya).

puraiva puṁsāvadhṛto dharā-jvaro
bhavadbhir aṁśair yaduṣūpajanyatām
sa yāvad urvyā bharam īśvareśvaraḥ
sva-kāla-śaktyā kṣapayaṁś cared bhuvi

Kṛṣṇa is already aware of the distress on earth. For as long as the source of all forms of the Lord remains visible on earth to diminish its burden, all of you devatās should appear as sons and grandsons along with his eternal associates in the family of the Yadus at the proper time.

vasudeva-gṛhe sākṣād bhagavān puruṣaḥ paraḥ
janiṣyate tat-priyārthaṁ sambhavantu sura-striyaḥ

The Supreme Lord Kṛṣṇa, who has full potency, will personally appear as the son of Vasudeva. Therefore all the wives of the devatās should also appear in order to satisfy him.

vāsudeva-kalānantaḥ sahasra-vadanaḥ svarāṭ
agrato bhavitā devo hareḥ priya-cikīrṣayā

The expansion of Kṛṣṇa is Saṅkarṣaṇa, who is unlimited and has a thousand heads and exists along with Kṛṣṇa. He is worshipped by all. Previous to the appearance of Kṛṣṇa, this Saṅkarṣaṇa will appear as Baladeva, just to please the Supreme Lord Kṛṣṇa in his pastimes.

viṣṇor māyā bhagavatī yayā sammohitaṁ jagat
ādiṣṭā prabhuṇāṁśena kāryārthe sambhaviṣyati

The potency of the Lord, full of power, who bewilders the whole world, will also appear by the request of her master to perform her actions, as a servant of the Lord. SB 10.1.22-25

Brahmā received the Lord's message through knowledge (adhigatam), by concentration of his mind, withdrawing the functions of his external senses. That also came from the sky, in the form of a voice speaking. He did not directly see the Lord. Brahmā revealed this message to the devatās, though it was most confidential. By this he satisfied the devatās.

TEXT 12

kasminn api prājña-varair vivikte
gargādibhir yo nibhṛtaṁ prakāśyate
nārāyaṇo 'sau bhagavān anena
sāmyaṁ kathañcil labhate na cāparaḥ

Only in some solitary place did wise sages like Garga divulge who Kṛṣṇa really is: He whom Lord Nārāyaṇa equals only in some aspects, no one else even coming close.

"He is directly Nārāyaṇa, Bhagavān." In two verses (12-13), he glorifies Kṛṣṇa as superior to Nārāyaṇa in order to how that the Pāṇḍavas are greater than Garuḍa and others in Vaikuṇṭha. The revelation of Garga to Nanda is not clearly mentioned. It was not proper to mention Nanda at this time since later Nanda and other will be describes as the highest objects of mercy. Garga revealed Kṛṣṇa to Nanda in a solitary place, and very quietly (nibhṛtam). "What did he reveal?" Nārāyaṇa was equal to Kṛṣṇa in some ways, such as beauty and being the source of avatāras. But he was not completely equal. Narāyaṇa is Bhagavān.

aiśvaryasya samagrasya vīryasya yaśasaḥ śriyaḥ
jñāna-vairāgyayoś caiva ṣaṇṇāṁ bhaga itīṅganā

The six bhagas are complete control, influence, good qualities, wealth, knowledge and renunciation. Viṣṇu Purāṇa

Nārāyaṇa means he who sees (ayate) all the jīvas (nāra) with great mercy, who protects them by giving them jñānā and kriya śaktis, and who inspires them to do proper activity. And others (na ca aparaḥ), such as the mahā-puruṣa (Garbhodakaśāyī), are not different: they cannot be compared to Kṛṣṇa

etan nānāvatārāṇāṁ nidhānaṁ bījam avyayam
yasyāṁśāṁśena sṛjyante deva-tiryaṅ-narādayaḥ

He is the indestructible source of various avatāras. His expansion is Brahmā and Brahmā's expansions are Marīci and others. Through them the Lord creates the devatās, animals and human beings. SB 1.3.5

Though the mahā-puruṣa is the source of avatāras, he does not have the sweet qualities and pastimes of Kṛṣṇa.

Or ca means "even." There is no one superior to Kṛṣṇa, since he is the best. Even Nārāyaṇa is not at all equal to Kṛṣṇa since he does not reveal the abundance of sweetness of form, qualities and pastimes which spread the highest, special prema. Garga says to Nanda:

tasmān nandātmajo 'yaṁ te nārāyaṇa-samo guṇaiḥ
śriyā kīrtyānubhāvena gopāyasva samāhitaḥ

In conclusion, therefore, O Nanda Mahārāja, this child of yours is as good as Nārāyaṇa by his qualities, opulence, fame and influence. You should protect this child very carefully. SB 10.8.19

Nārāyaṇa is equal in some qualities but not in distributing special pastimes and special sweetness. Or Kṛṣṇa to whom Nārāyaṇa is equal, is endowed with special qualities.

Another meaning is Kṛṣṇa is endowed with a wealth of love (āya) for the cowherds (gopa). Or he is supremely engaged (sumāhitaḥ—one version has gopāya-susamāhitaḥ) in the good fortune (aya) of the cowherds. Or he is engaged for the wealth and safety (sva-gopāya-sva-sumāhitaḥ) of the cowherds.

Thus the meaning is "Kṛṣṇa is directly Bhagavān, greater than Nārāyaṇa, since he manifests special form, qualities and pastimes which are not manifest in Vaikuṇṭha."

TEXT 13

ataḥ śrī-madhu-puryāṁ yo
dīrgha-viṣṇur iti śrutaḥ
mahā-harir mahā-viṣṇur
mahā-nārāyaṇo 'pi ca

Thus, in Mathurā City, Kṛṣṇa is well known as Dīrgha-viṣṇu, Mahā-hari, Mahā-viṣṇu, and Mahā-nārāyaṇa.

According to what we heard, the son of Devakī is well known (śrutaḥ) as Dīrgha-viṣṇu in Mathurā.[18] He is also known as Mahā-nārāyaṇa, though this is not so famous (api ca).

[18] Before the wrestling match in Mathurā, Kṛṣṇa expanded his form similar to Vāmana to convince his friends that he could kill Kaṁsa. The temple is the oldest in Mathurā.

TEXT 14

yasya prasādaḥ san-mauna-
śānti-bhakty-ādi-sādhanaiḥ
prārthyo naḥ sa svayaṁ vo 'bhūt
prasanno vaśa-varty api

We can only pray to satisfy him through our sādhana of silence, peace, bhakti, etc. But being naturally satisfied with you, he has even submitted himself to your control.

You are greater than the great sages worshipped by the world. We pray for Kṛṣṇa's mercy by excellent (sat) conduct as ātmārāmas (mauna), by liberation (śānti), by nine types of bhakti, and by seeing the deity and associating with devotees (ādi). But even today we have not attained that mercy. We will not attain it. He is pleased with you, even without doing sādhana. Not only is he pleased but he is controlled by you, taking orders from you. Nārada speaks to Yudhiṣṭhira:

yūyaṁ nṛ-loke bata bhūri-bhāgā
lokaṁ punānā munayo 'bhiyanti
yeṣāṁ gṛhān āvasatīti sākṣād
gūḍhaṁ paraṁ brahma manuṣya-liṅgam

You Pāṇḍavas are most fortunate in this world. Sages who purify the planets come and visit your houses because the Supreme Brahman personally resides in your houses in a human form.

sa vā ayaṁ brahma mahad-vimṛgya-
kaivalya-nirvāṇa-sukhānubhūtiḥ
priyaḥ suhṛd vaḥ khalu mātuleya
ātmārhaṇīyo vidhi-kṛd guruś ca

Kṛṣṇa definitely expands as the Brahman, the realization of bliss without qualities, which is sought by great sages. He also resides in your house as the object of affection, a friend, a cousin, as your soul, as a person worthy of worship, as a servant and as a guru.

na yasya sākṣād bhava-padmajādibhī
rūpaṁ dhiyā vastutayopavarṇitam
maunena bhaktyopaśamena pūjitaḥ
prasīdatām eṣa sa sātvatāṁ patiḥ

The truth about Kṛṣṇa is not perceived as it actually is by Brahmā or others by their intelligence. May the Lord of the devotees, who is worshipped by vows of silence, bhakti and control of the mind, be pleased with us! SB 7.10.48-50

Nārada, seeing the Pāṇḍavas, spoke the three verses quoted above after finishing the story of Prahlāda. Yudhiṣṭhira lamented, thinking that Prahlāda had received such mercy from the Lord and thought himself unfortunate.

Sages gather from all over at your houses. Why? The secret Supreme Brahman with human form resides directly there. They come to see him. Having mentioned his secretive nature, rarity of attaining him is mentioned. He is Brahman sought by Brahmā, the Kumāras and other great sages. Or he is sought out in the Vedas by Brahmā and others, but is not directly attained.

He gives an experience of unconditional bliss (kaivalya-nirvāṇa-sukhsānubhūtiḥ).

"He who is indescribable is your dear friend. He shows affection for you (priyaḥ). He is an unconditional benefactor (suhṛt). He is the object of the highest affection (ātmā). He is worthy of worship. He carries out your orders." He points out Kṛṣṇa sitting in the assembly (ayam). "Though he is most rare, he has become visible to all at this time by his special mercy to you. You are most fortunate."

"If he is the supreme Brahman, why does he have attraction to sixteen thousand women? How does he set an example of dharma?" The truth (rūpam) about him is not perceived by the intelligence of Brahmā and Śiva. Or one limb of that beautiful form directly seen cannot be described directly as this or that by your intelligence or by Brahmā and Śiva. What to speak of describing his wealth of pastimes. And what to speak of people being able to describe him.

"He is pleased with you, but we must simply pray for his mercy while performing sādhanas of the ātmārāmas, etc." Eśāḥ also indicates pointing out the Lord with the finger.

The meaning is this. "The Lord does not reside in Prahlāda's house. And sages do not come there to see the Lord. Nor does the Lord exist as a cousin for Prahlāda. Nor is the Lord personally pleased. Thus you alone are more fortunate than the great sages, than Brahmā and Śiva, and then us devotees."

TEXT 15

aho śṛṇuta pūrvaṁ tu
keṣāñcid adhikāriṇām
anena dīyamāno 'bhūn
mokṣaḥ sthitir iyaṁ sadā

Oh! Please listen: Previously, Kṛṣṇa gave the gift of liberation only to a qualified few. And this has always been the rule.

A manifestation of great, uncommon fortune in the form of Kṛṣṇa's sweetness is the cause of your attaining all excellences just described. This is indicated in ten verses (15-24). "It is astonishing (aho)! Among those qualified for liberation, liberation was given to a few (keśañcit) by Kṛṣṇa (anena). This has always been the rule. There has never been any deviation from this."

TEXTS 16–17

kālanemir hiraṇyākṣo
hiraṇyakaśipus tathā
rāvaṇaḥ kumbhakarṇaś ca
tathānye ghātitāḥ svayam

muktiṁ na nītā bhaktir na
dattā kasmaicid uttamā
prahlādāya paraṁ dattā
śrī-nṛsiṁhāvatārataḥ

Kālanemi, Hiraṇyākṣa, Hiraṇyakaśipu, Rāvaṇa, Kumbhakarṇa, and others were killed by the Supreme Lord, but none of them attained liberation. And pure bhakti was given only to Prahlāda, who received it from the incarnation Nṛsiṁha.

Anena from verse 15 is understood in this verse. Kālanemī was killed in a battle between the devatās and demons by the Lord directly, as the Lord of Vaikuntha. Hiraṇyākṣa was killed by Varāha. Hiraṇyakaśipu was killed by Nṛsiṁha. Rāvaṇa and Kumbhakarṇa were killed by Rāma. Other demons, Rākṣasas, and their relatives were also killed. Though they were personally killed by the Lord they did not attain liberation. Since Kṛṣṇa did give liberation to those he killed, he is considered much greater. Did they attain bhakti to the Lord? Prema or pure bhakti (uttamā) was given only (param) to Prahlāda. But from later statements it is understood that it was mixed with jñāna. This was also explained by Prahlāda previously.

TEXTS 18–19

hanūmān jāmbuvān śrīmān
sugrīvo 'tha vibhīṣaṇaḥ
guho daśaratho 'py ete
nūnaṁ katipaye janāḥ

raghunāthāvatāre 'smāc
chuddhāṁ bhaktiṁ tu lebhire
viśuddhasya ca kasyāpi
premṇo vārtāpi na sthitā

Indeed a few — Hanumān, Jāmbavān, the fortunate Sugrīva, Vibhīṣaṇa, Guha, and Daśaratha obtained pure bhakti from Lord Raghunātha. But in relation to those devotees we never hear of spontaneous prema.

A few jīvas or servants (janāḥ) like Hanumān achieved pure bhakti, unmixed with karma or jñāna, during the appearance of Rāma, from the son of Devakī (asmāt). This is connected with the previous verses discussing Kṛṣṇa. The word śrīmān means "endowed with a wealth of good fortune." This word modifies all the individuals like Hanumān. Nūnam means certainly or supposition, since the pure bhakti is inferred by their qualities. Or even Daśaratha attained pure bhakti. Because of Brahmā's curse, he died of grief from separation from his son. There is doubt whether he attained pure bhakti. But pure bhakti was possible because of his affection for his son. The word api (even) is used to emphasize this.

Viśuddhasya means prema which is not dependent on certain qualities or form (spontaneous). At that time, there is no mention of even one type (kasya) among the various spontaneous prema (viśuddhasya) manifested with bhāvas of the Lord as husband or son, etc., what to speak of anyone attaining it. Or there is no mention of indescribable prema (kasya), special prema for Kṛṣṇa like that of the gopīs.

TEXT 20

idānīṁ bhavadīyena
mātuleyena no kṛtāḥ
muktā bhaktās tathā śuddha-
prema-sampūritāḥ kati

But now so many persons have not only been liberated, and made devotees, but also filled with pure prema, all by your maternal cousin!

How many were not liberated, made devotees or filled with pure prema? Many attained liberation, many were made into devotees and many were filled with pure prema, by your cousin. This indicates that the Pāṇḍavas have a relationship with Kṛṣṇa, who has such glory. Thus they have similar glory.

TEXT 21

ātmanā māritā ye ca
ghātitā vārjunādibhiḥ
narakārhāś ca daiteyās
tan-mahimnāmṛtaṁ gatāḥ

And by his power, demons fit for hell have attained immortality after being slain by him or by him through Arjuna and others.

Even (ca) all (vā) the demons such as Pūtanā (daiteyāḥ) killed by Kṛṣṇa, or killed by him through Arjuna and others, such as Karṇa, Duryodhana, etc., who were considered demons because demons had entered them, and who even though deserving hell since they attacked Viṣṇu and the devotees, attained liberation (amṛtam) by the greatness of Kṛṣṇa, your cousin.

ye ca pralamba-khara-dardura-keśy-ariṣṭa-
mallebha-kaṁsa-yavanāḥ kapi-pauṇḍrakādyāḥ
anye ca śālva-kuja-balvala-dantavakra-
saptokṣa-śambara-vidūratha-rukmi-mukhyāḥ
ye vā mṛdhe samiti-śālina ātta-cāpāḥ
kāmboja-matsya-kuru-sṛñjaya-kaikayādyāḥ
yāsyanty adarśanam alaṁ bala-pārtha-bhīma-
vyājāhvayena hariṇā nilayaṁ tadīyam

The demons headed by Pralambha, Dhenuka, Baka, Keśī, Ariṣṭa, the wrestlers, Kuvalayāpīḍa, Kaṁṣa, Kālayavana, Dvivida, Pauṇḍraka, Śālva, Narakāsura, Balvala, Dantavakra, the seven bulls, Śambara, Vidūratha and Rukmi, as well as those with bow in hand glorious in fighting on the battlefield, such as the Kāmbojas, Matsyas, Kurus, Sṛñjayas, and Kaikayas will attain sāyujya or Vaikuṇṭha by the Lord or through his instruments Balarāma, Arjuna, Bhīma and others. SB 2.7.34-35

The meaning is this. "All these will attain (yāsyanti) extreme (alam) liberation (nilayam), which is invisible or devoid of again seeing (adarśanam), since liberation is a state of absolute absence. Or that liberation is most detestable, most unsightly since it prevents bhakti." Dardura means Baka. Kapi means Dvivida.

"Balarāma killed Dhenuka, Dvivida and Balvala. Bhīma and Arjuna killed the Kambhojas and others. Śambara was killed by Pradumnya. Yavana was killed by Mucukunda. Kṛṣṇa did not kill them." They were killed by the Lord or by the substitute (vyājāhvayena) names of Bhīma, Arjuna, Balarāma, etc.

If nilayam tadīyam means Vaikuṇṭha then the reference to liberation in verse 20 means that by taking them to Vaikuṇṭha, they became liberated from the bondage of saṁsāra.

TEXTS 22–23

tapo-japa-jñāna-parā
munayo ye 'rtha-sādhakāḥ
viśvāmitro gautamaś ca
vaśiṣṭho 'pi tathā pare

te kurukṣetra-yātrāyāṁ
gatvā kṛṣṇa-prasādataḥ
bhaktiṁ taṁ prārthya tāṁ prāpyā-
bhavaṁs tad-bhakti-tatparāḥ

Viśvāmitra, Gautama, Vasiṣṭha and other sages with various goals in life were intent on tapasya, japa, and jñāna. But while they were on pilgrimage at Kurukṣetra, Kṛṣṇa mercifully inspired them to pray to him for bhakti. Thus obtaining it, they became fully dedicated to bhakti to him.

Now those who attained bhakti are explained in two verses. Viśvamitra was engaged in tapasya, Gautama was engaged in japa and Vaśiṣṭha was engaged in jñāna. They were engaged in dharma, artha, kāma and mokṣa. Even they obtained bhakti. They prayed to Kṛṣṇa for bhakti. That is explained in the Tenth Canto:

tasyādya te dadṛśimāṅghrim aghaugha-marṣa-
tīrthāspadaṁ hṛdi kṛtaṁ su-vipakva-yogaiḥ
utsikta-bhakty-upahatāśaya jīva-kośā
āpur bhavad-gatim athānugṛhāna bhaktān

Today we have directly seen your feet, the source of the holy Ganges, which washes away volumes of sins. Perfected yogīs can at best meditate upon your feet within their hearts. But only those who render you wholehearted devotional service and in this way vanquish the soul's covering—the material mind—attain you as their final destination. Therefore kindly show mercy to us, your devotees. SB 10.84.26

Śrīdhara Svāmī explains the verse. Today by good fortune we have seen your feet which are the shelter of the Gaṅgā (tīrtha) which destroys (marṣa) heaps of sin (aghaugha) which yogīs keep in their hearts but cannot see. Be merciful to us. Making us into devotees show mercy to us. "What is the use of bhakti? Perform austerities as previously." Only those who have destroyed the material mind by intense bhakti attain the supreme destination. Others do not.

TEXT 24

sthāvarāś ca tamo-yoni-
gatās taru-latādayaḥ
śuddha-sāttvika-bhāvāptyā
tat-prema-rasa-varṣiṇaḥ

Even immobile creatures such as trees, creepers, and so on which are born in tamas have been raised to pure sattva. Now those trees and creepers are raining down a nectar-sap of kṛṣṇa-prema.

Now being filled with prema is described. Even plants (ca) shower prema. The trees and creepers of Vṛndāvana, are born in tamas since they are incapable of using external senses, but even they showered prema. Though there is no tamas in Vṛndāvana, this is said from the point of view of ordinary plants. Or this may be speaking of Hastināpura plants, for Kuntī speaks to the Lord in the First Canto in the same way:

ime jana-padāḥ svṛddhāḥ supakvauṣadhi-vīrudhaḥ
vanādri-nady-udanvanto hy edhante tava vīkṣitaiḥ

This thriving land, filled with ripe herbs and fruit-laden trees, forests, mountains and rivers, has grown prosperous by your glance. SB 1.8.40

By your (the Lord's) glance the trees increase with attainment of a wealth of the highest prema (edhante).

By attaining the state of the highest Vaiṣṇavas with ecstatic symptoms or attaining a state untouched by rajas or tamas, they shower the rasa of prema of the Lord. This means that by flowing with streams of honey constantly, they produced a shower like tears of prema.

TEXT 25

he kṛṣṇa-bhrātaras tasya
kiṁ varṇyo 'pūrva-darśitaḥ
rūpa-saundarya-lāvaṇya-
mādhuryāścaryatā-bharaḥ

O Kṛṣṇa's brothers, how can one describe the infinite wonders of his form, beauty, effulgence and charm, which have never been seen in anyone else.

Having described Kṛṣṇa's greatness in giving liberation, bhakti and prema, now Nārada describes in two verses (25-26) the greatness of Kṛṣṇa form and qualities, which act as a cause for his giving liberation, etc.

How can one describe the abundance of astonishment in his form, his beauty, his effulgence, and sweetness (in his smile, brow, dancing and side glance), not manifested in Vaikuṇṭha or in the avatāras (pūrva-darśitaḥ)? One cannot describe it at all.

TEXT 26

apūrvatvena tasyaiva
yo vismaya-vidhāyakaḥ
tathā līlā guṇāḥ premā
mahimā keli-bhūr api

Those unprecedented attractive features of Kṛṣṇa leave one struck with wonder as do his pastimes, qualities, prema, greatness, and pastime places.

The astonishing abundance of his form, beauty, luster, etc. cause wonder (viṣmayam vidhāyakaḥ) because of their amazing nature (apūrvatvena) or because they were never seen before, but somehow are now manifested. Similar to his form and beauty are his pastimes or variegated actions, his qualities like mercy, prema for the devotees or their prema for him, etc., his greatness (mahimā)—showing affection for the suffering souls or being dependent on the devotees, and his place of pastimes such as Vṛndāvana (keli-bhūḥ). O brothers of Kṛṣṇa! You know and experience these things completely. You alone are most fortunate.

TEXT 27

manye 'trāvatariṣyan na
svayam evam asau yadi

tadāsya bhagavattaivā-
bhaviṣyat prakaṭā na hi

I think that if Kṛṣṇa did not appear on earth in his original form, the world would never have known his true identity as the Supreme Lord.

"If these things (attractive features of Kṛṣṇa) were not previously existing, their eternal nature would be falsified. If they were previously existing (prior to his descent), then Kṛṣṇa could not be the best (of the *avatāras*)." Two verses (27-28) answer. I (Nārada) think that if Kṛṣṇa did not appear on earth or in Mathurā (atra), his nature as the Supreme Lord would not be clear. What to speak of his astonishing form, no one would be able to realize his pastimes etc. That is certain (hi). Or if he did not appear in Mathurā his form, qualities, etc. would not be manifest. They would be unmanifested.

TEXT 28

idānīṁ paramāṁ kāṣṭhāṁ
prāptābhūt sarvataḥ sphuṭā
viśiṣṭa-mahima-śreṇī-
mādhurī-citratācitā

Now his identity as the Lord, reaching the highest perfection, has become visible everywhere, adorned with his exceptional glories and marked by varieties of his charming sweetness.

Now, in this avatāra, his nature as the Lord has become completely clear and reached its highest point. This nature is spread with a great variety of sweetness of the greatest (viśiṣtha) glories. This indicates Kṛṣṇa as the avatārī (source of all avatāras), and as avatāra (having manifested in this world). Simultaneously the greatest powers and greatest sweetness combine in him.

TEXT 29

kṛṣṇasya kāruṇya-kathās tu dūre
tasya praśasyo bata nigraho 'pi
kaṁsādayaḥ kāliya-pūtanādyā
baly-ādayaḥ prāg api sākṣiṇo 'tra

We speak of Kṛṣṇa's kindness, but even his administered punishments are worthy of praise. Kaṁsa, Kāliya, and Pūtanā and, in the more distant past, Bali and others bear witness to this.

Having described the greatness of the Lord's mercy briefly, the special greatness of the Lord's punishments is described. Bata indicates joy. Even Kṛṣṇa's punishments are most worthy of praise. Kaṁsa and others are proof of the praiseworthy punishment. When Kaṁsa was the ruler of Mathurā, Kaṁsa thought as follows:

āsīnaḥ saṁviśaṁs tiṣṭhan bhuñjānaḥ paryaṭan mahīm
cintayāno hṛṣīkeśam apaśyat tanmayaṁ jagat

While sitting on his throne or in his sitting room, while lying on his bed, or while situated anywhere, and while eating or walking, Kaṁsa saw only the Supreme Lord. His world became filled with the Lord. SB 10.2.24

While living, he attained a state rare for great yogīs. While dying he directly saw the face of Kṛṣṇa, and Kṛṣṇa's lotus feet were on his chest after he had been pulled from the stage and jumped upon by Kṛṣṇa. After Kaṁsa had died, Kṛṣṇa, surrounded by the Yadus and cowherds, performed his funeral rites which were befitting a great king. He consoled Kaṁsa's wives like the greatest friend. He offered the throne to Kaṁsa's father. Kaṁsādāyaḥ means Kaṁsa and wrestlers like Cānura, kings like Jarāsandha, excluding Śiśupāla and Dantavakra. Those two deserved mercy since they were previously devotees, but had offended the Kumāras.

Because of the order of Kaṁsa, in order to fight with the Lord, the wrestlers and kings developed a mentality similar to Kaṁsa's (absorption in hatred). The Lord, fighting with the wrestlers, gave them great mercy by embracing them as if they were cowherd boys. He performed the funeral rites even for them:

rāja-yoṣita āśvāsya bhagavāû loka-bhāvanaḥ
yām āhur laukikīṁ saṁsthāṁ hatānāṁ samakārayat

After consoling the royal ladies, Kṛṣṇa, sustainer of all the worlds, arranged for the prescribed funeral rites to be performed. SB 10.44.49

Jarāsandha, caught by Balarāma, was released by Kṛṣṇa repeatedly in order to show Jarāsandha's great valor. Finally, Kṛṣṇa went to Jarāsandha's house with his friends and clearly established in the world Jarāsandha's great fame for having incomparable generosity to brāhmaṇas.

Pauṇḍraka and others are also included in this list. Text 21 mentioned that those who were killed by Kṛṣṇa attained liberation.

vaireṇa yaṁ nṛpatayaḥ śiśupāla-pauṇḍra-
śālvādayo gati-vilāsa-vilokanādyaiḥ
dhyāyanta ākṛta-dhiyaḥ śayanāsanādau
tat-sāmyam āpur anurakta-dhiyāṁ punaḥ kim

Inimical kings like Śiśupāla, Pauṇḍraka and Śālva, while they were lying down, sitting or engaging in other activities, enviously meditated upon the bodily movements of the Lord, his sporting pastimes, and his loving glances. Being thus always absorbed in Kṛṣṇa, they achieved positions in the spiritual world. What then can be said of the benedictions offered to those who constantly fix their minds on Lord Kṛṣṇa in a favorable, loving mood? SB 11.5.48

The demons who went to Gokula are distinguished from the others mentioned in the verse. In fighting with the Lord, Kāliya received the direct embrace of Kṛṣṇa with more great fortune than the wrestlers like Cānura. He also received the good fortune of the touch of the dust from his lotus feet. Kāliya's wives say:

kasyānubhāvo 'sya na deva vidmahe
tavāṅghri-reṇu-sparaśādhikāraḥ
yad-vāñchayā śrīr lalanācarat tapo
vihāya kāmān su-ciraṁ dhṛta-vratā

O Lord, we do not know how the serpent Kāliya has attained this great opportunity of being touched by the dust of your lotus feet. For this end, the goddess of fortune performed austerities for centuries, giving up all other desires and taking austere vows. SB 10.16.36

He got the specially joyful touch of the dust when Kṛṣṇa danced on his heads. Each head became the Lord's dancing arena. Kāliya also worshiped and praised Kṛṣṇa, received orders as mercy, and obtained a comfortable place to live in Ramaṇaka Island which he had given up previously because of fear of Garuḍa. He became great friends with Garuḍa who is the natural enemy of snakes, and was respected by Garuḍa since he held imprinted on his head the rare mark of the cakra from Kṛṣṇa's lotus foot.

Pūtanā went to Gokula dressed in the most excellent clothing among all the cowherd people. Śukadeva says:

na yatra śravaṇādīni rakṣo-ghnāni sva-karmasu
kurvanti sātvatāṁ bhartur yātudhānyaś ca tatra hi

Wherever people in any position perform chanting and hearing about the devotees and the Lord while doing their duties, there cannot be any danger from bad elements. Therefore there was no need for anxiety about Gokula while the Supreme Lord was personally present. SB 10.6.3

Thus, it was only by special fortune that she could enter Gokula. She placed Kṛṣṇa's lotus feet, meditated upon by Brahmā and others, in her lap with great affection. Then she caressed him. Yaśodā was most astonished:

tāṁ tīkṣṇa-cittām ativāma-ceṣṭitāṁ
vīkṣyāntarā koṣa-paricchadāsivat
vara-striyaṁ tat-prabhayā ca dharṣite
nirīkṣyamāṇe jananī hy atiṣṭhatām

Although seeing her within the room, Yaśodā and Rohiṇī, overwhelmed by her affection, thinking her to be the best of women, simply stood and gazed at her, though her heart was most cruel—because she displayed the gentlest behavior, like a knife hidden in a sheath. SB 10.6.9

By caring for Kṛṣṇa like a mother, Pūtanā attained the position of a mother.

pūtanā loka-bāla-ghnī rākṣasī rudhirāśanā
jighāṁsayāpi haraye stanaṁ dattvāpa sad-gatim

Pūtanā was always hankering for the blood of human children, and with that desire she came to kill Kṛṣṇa; but because she offered her breast to him, she attained him. SB 10.6.35

Brahmā says:

sad-veṣād iva pūtanāpi sa-kulā tvām eva devāpitā

You awarded yourself even to Pūtanā and her family members because she wore the disguise of a nurse. SB 10.14.35

Uddhava says:

aho bakī yaṁ stana-kāla-kūṭaṁ
jighāṁsayāpāyayad apy asādhvī
lebhe gatiṁ dhātry-ucitāṁ tato 'nyaṁ
kaṁ vā dayāluṁ śaraṇaṁ vrajema

Oh! Evil Pūtanā, who offered her poisonous breast to Kṛṣṇa to drink with the intention of killing him, attained the position of a nurse in the spiritual world. How else is so merciful? I surrender to him! SB 3.2.23

And even when she was dead, the Lord played joyfully on her chest.

bālaṁ ca tasyā urasi krīḍantam akutobhayam
gopyas tūrṇaṁ samabhyetya jagṛhur jāta-sambhramāḥ

Without fear, the child Kṛṣṇa was playing on the upper portion of Pūtanā Rākṣasī's breast, and when the gopīs saw the child's wonderful activities, they immediately came forward with great jubilation and picked him up. SB 10.6.18

In burning the material body of Pūtanā a fragrance better than aguru spread in all directions.

dahyamānasya dehasya dhūmaś cāguru-saurabhaḥ
utthitaḥ kṛṣṇa-nirbhukta- sapady āhata-pāpmanaḥ

Because Kṛṣṇa had sucked the breast of Pūtanā, when he killed her she was immediately freed of all material contamination. When her gigantic body was being burnt, the smoke emanating from her body was fragrant like aguru incense. Anyone who smelled this smoke had their sinful reactions destroyed. SB 10.6.34

Like Kāliya the yamalārjuna trees obtained mercy. They were allowed to enter into the astonishing pastime when Dāmodara was tied up. They were released from the curse of Nārada, offered prayers and received the benediction of prema-bhakti from Kṛṣṇa.

Kṛṣṇa with his friends entered into the huge body of Aghāsura as if he were a friend. He attained liberation, which was astonishing to the whole universe. His dead body became a place for Kṛṣṇa's playing.

rājann ājagaraṁ carma śuṣkaṁ vṛndāvane 'dbhutam
vrajaukasāṁ bahu-tithaṁ babhūvākrīḍa-gahvaram

O King Parīkṣit, when the python-shaped body of Aghāsura dried up, becoming merely a big skin, it astonished the inhabitants of Vṛndāvana and became a cave for the boys' sporting for many days. SB 10.12.36

Many others like Baka, Ariṣṭa, and Keśī clearly received his mercy. Kṛṣṇa's fault of giving up the gopīs in the rāsa dance was to increase their prema. Since he gave them up in order to become absorbed in hearing their expressions of prema in separation. Since he is attracted to intense prema, his fault became a great quality. This is clear in the Lord's own words:

nāhaṁ tu sakhyo bhajato 'pi jantūn
bhajāmy amīṣām anuvṛtti-vṛttaye

yathādhano labdha-dhane vinaṣṭe
tac-cintayānyan nibhṛto na veda

But the reason I do not immediately reciprocate the affection of living beings even when they worship Me, O gopīs, is that I want to intensify their loving devotion. They then become like a poor man who has gained some wealth and then lost it, and who thus becomes so anxious about it that he can think of nothing else. SB 10.32.20

This will become clear later. The great mercy applies to the avatarī Kṛṣṇa, but it applies to the previous avatāras of Kṛṣṇa Vāmana as well (prāg api). He announced the great tolerance of Bali by tying him up. Though Bali lost Svarga, the Lord gave him the great post of ruling Sutala, which was wealthier than Svarga, and the Lord remained as his door keeper. He protected Bali by preventing Rāvaṇa from entering as he acted as the door keeper. Even when Durvāsa prayed painfully for the Lord's help when afflicted by the demon Kuśa, he did not give up this post as the doorkeeper without Bali's permission.

These stories are well known in Bhāgavatam and other scriptures. But whatever Kṛṣṇa did as Vāmana avatāra in a similar manner ultimately meant greater glorification of the avatārī Kṛṣṇa at this time. Balyādāyaḥ means demons like Madhu, Kaiṭabha and Kālanemi. The great mercy shown to them when the Lord fought with them is well known in the Purāṇas.

TEXT 30

śrī-parīkṣid uvāca
iti pragāyan rasanāṁ munir nijām
aśikṣayan mādhava-kīrti-lampaṭām
aho pravṛttāsi mahattva-varṇane
prabhor apīti sva-radair vidaśya tām

Parīkṣit said: While singing excellently in this way, the sage instructed his own tongue, which was greedy to glorify Lord Mādhava, "Oh, you are engaged in describing the greatness of our master!" To stop that tongue, he then bit it with his teeth.

Singing excellently in this way (pragayan) he instructed his tongue which was speaking, which was greedily tasting the fame or kīrtana of the Lord who arose as the moon in the ocean of the Madhu dynasty. What did he do before giving instructions? He bit his tongue. Why? You are engaged in describing the greatness of Kṛṣṇa in an unsuitable way. If Brahmā with four mouths and Śeṣa with thousands of mouths cannot describe Kṛṣṇa, how can you describe him? Since you are incapable, your action shows your rashness.

TEXT 31

rasane te mahad bhāgyam
etad eva yad īhitam
kiñcid uccārayaivaiṣāṁ
tat-priyāṇāṁ sva-śaktitaḥ

"O tongue, you are very fortunate to have attempted to speak these words. Please speak about the dear devotees of Kṛṣṇa, according to your ability."

What did Nārada instruct? Api here means eva (even) and can be applied to many phrases in the verse. "Describe the activities of at least the devotees, if not those of the Lord. And describe even the activities, if you cannot describe their glories. You can do that even a little if you cannot describe everything. You should at least pronounce the words (uccāraya) if you cannot glorify completely. That is your good fortune.

Even though the glories of the devotees are indescribable, like the glories of the Lord, it is difficult to describe the glories of the Lord because that is beyond your knowledge, since those glories are without beginning and end and difficult to understand. Since the devotees are similar to you and can be directly understood, it is possible to describe them according to what you have seen of their activities. The devotees, being affectionate to the fallen, can forgive the offenses committed by you for describing what is not true. You should describe the devotees' glories." The deep meaning is that describing the glories of the devotees is superior to describing the glories of the Lord.

TEXT 32

śrī-nārada uvāca
mahānubhāvā bhavatāṁ tu tasmin
prati-svakaṁ yaḥ priyatā-viśeṣaḥ
bhavatsu tasyāpi kṛpā-viśeṣo
dhṛṣṭena nīyeta sa kena jihvām

Nārada continued: O great souls, can anyone be bold enough to let the tongue describe the unique love that each of you has for Kṛṣṇa or his special mercy on each of you?

Having described the glories of all of the Pāṇḍavas in general, now, in order to give special glorification to each of them as objects of the Lord's mercy, first Nārada worries about his own qualification to describe the Pāṇḍavas.

TEXT 33

mātā pṛtheyaṁ yadu-nandanasya
snehārdram āśvāsana-vākyam ekam
akrūra-vaktrāt prathamaṁ niśamya
prema-pravāhe nimamajja sadyaḥ

When your mother, Pṛthā, once heard from the mouth of Akrūra a single statement of affectionate consolation by Kṛṣṇa, she immediately plunged into a swiftly flowing current of prema.

Since he relishes glorification of the devotees, Nārada further describes their glories in seven verses (33-39), unable to give them up. "Your mother, or the mother of persons even like me, heard Kṛṣṇa's words of consolation:

sa bhavān suhṛdāṁ vai naḥ śreyān śreyaś-cikīrṣayā
jijñāsārthaṁ pāṇḍavānāṁ gacchasva tvaṁ gajāhvayam

You (Akrura) are the best of us Yadus and our relatives, so please go to Hastināpura and, as the well-wisher of the Pāṇḍavas, find out how they are doing. SB 10.48.32 "

She had not heard such words before (prathamam).

TEXT 34

vicitra-vākyair bahudhā ruroda
sphuṭen nṛṇāṁ yac-chravaṇena vakṣaḥ
bhavatsv api sneha-bharaṁ paraṁ sā
rarakṣa kṛṣṇa-priyatām apekṣya

She often lamented with poignant words hearing which the hearts of men would shatter even today. And she maintained affection for you only because you are very dear to Lord Kṛṣṇa.

Her absorption in the rasa of prema is described. Her various words (vicitra-vākyaih) are described in the Tenth Canto:

kṛṣṇa kṛṣṇa mahā-yogin viśvātman viśva-bhāvana
prapannāṁ pāhi govinda śiśubhiś cāvasīdatīm

Kṛṣṇa, Kṛṣṇa! O great yogī! O Supreme Soul and protector of the universe! O Govinda! Please protect me, who have surrendered to you. I and my sons are being overwhelmed by trouble.

nānyat tava padāmbhojāt paśyāmi śaraṇaṁ nṛṇām
bibhyatāṁ mṛtyu-saṁsārād īsvarasyāpavargikāt

For persons fearful of death and rebirth, I see no shelter other than your lotus feet, which award liberation, for you are the Supreme Lord. SB 10.49.11-12

Hearing the words or hearing the lamentation (yat śravaṇena) the hearts of men would break (sphuṭet) even today. The potential verb indicates possibility.

"Then why could she have affection for us sons?" She maintained affection for you since Kṛṣṇa had prema for you. Of course (api) you were qualified, being great sons and she was Pṛthā. Or you had prema for Kṛṣṇa. She considered only (param) their prema for Kṛṣṇa. Because of her natural devotion to Kṛṣṇa, she tended to reject affection for sons and everything else. However, she maintained that affection because they were devotees of Kṛṣṇa. The past tense is used (rarakṣa) in order to strengthen the meaning, even though the maintaining affection continues in the present.

TEXT 35

cireṇa dvārakāṁ gantum
udyato yadu-jīvanaḥ
kāku-stutibhir āvṛtya
sva-gṛhe rakṣyate 'nayā

After a long time, Kṛṣṇa, the life of the Yadus, tried to leave for Dvārakā, but by capturing him with plaintive prayers she kept him in her home.

Kṛṣṇa stayed a long time with the Pāṇdavas because of the Kurukṣetra war. He should have gone to the Yadus to give them life since they were almost dying in separation (yadu-jīvanaḥ). He was captured (āvṛtya) by her plaintive prayers.

namasye puruṣaṁ tvādyam īśvaraṁ prakṛteḥ param
alakṣyaṁ sarva-bhūtānām antar bahir avasthitam

I offer my respects to you, the Supreme Person, the original one, the controller, beyond the control of prakṛti, unseen by material senses, and existing inside and outside of all living beings. SB 1.8.18

He was kept by her (anayā) in her house. The present tense (rakṣyate) is used to indicate that this happened many times.

TEXT 36

yudhiṣṭhirāyāpi mahā-pratiṣṭhā
loka-dvayotkṛṣṭatarā pradattā
tathā jarāsandha-vadhādinā ca
bhīmāya tenātmana eva kīrtiḥ

To Yudhiṣṭhira the Lord gave great fame, greater than that of anyone else in the upper and lower worlds. And by allowing Bhīma to kill Jarāsandha, Kṛṣṇa granted Bhīma unequaled fame.

Yudhiṣṭhira was prominently given (pradattāḥ) great fame (mahā-pratiṣṭhā) by Kṛṣṇa, since Kṛṣṇa assisted in his performing the rājasūya-yajña. Thus one of the thousand names of the Lord is yudhiṣṭhira-pratiṣṭhatā: the Lord gave Yudhiṣṭhira fame. His own (ātmanaḥ) fame was given to Bhīma since Kṛṣṇa had many opportunities to kill Jarāsandha but did not do so.

TEXT 37

bhagavān ayam arjunaś ca tat-
priya-sakhyena gataḥ prasiddhatām
na purāṇa-śataiḥ parair aho
mahimā stotum amuṣya śakyate

Arjuna attained fame throughout the world by being the dear friend of Kṛṣṇa. It is not possible for the Purāṇas or hundreds of others to praise his glories.

Arjuna is addressed as bhagavān to show him great respect. Or bhagavān is used with the following meaning:

utpattiṁ pralayaṁ caiva bhūtānām āgatiṁ gatim
vetti vidyām avidyāṁ ca sa vācyo bhagavān iti

The person who knows creation and destruction, the coming and going of living beings, knowledge and ignorance, may be called bhagavān. Viṣṇu Purāṇa

Or he is called bhagavān because he is equal to the Lord by his qualities. He attained fame by being the dear friend of Kṛṣṇa. It is not possible for hundreds of other or the best (paraiḥ) Purāṇas to praise Arjuna's (amuṣya) glories. Aho indicates astonishment.

TEXT 38

nakulaḥ sahadevaś ca
yādṛk-prīti-parau yamau
agra-pūjā-vicārādau
sarvais tad vṛttam īkṣitam

And as for the twins Nakula and Sahadeva, their love for Kṛṣṇa was witnessed by everyone during the deliberations on whom to worship first in the Rājasūya and their behavior in other matters.

Yamau means the twins. The conduct of one was the conduct of the other. They deliberated on who could be the person to be worshipped first at the rājasūya-yajña and performed various actions (ādau) as well. Their conduct (vṛttim) denoting their prema for Kṛṣṇa was observed by all at the the rājasūya-yajña.

TEXT 39

śrī-draupadī ca hariṇā svayam eva rāja-
sūyādiṣūtsava-vareṣv abhiṣikta-keśā
sambodhyate priya-sakhīty avitātri-putra-
duḥśāsanādi-bhayato hṛta-sarva-śokā

During the rājasūya-yajña and other festivals, Kṛṣṇa personally anointed Draupadī's hair. He would address Draupadī as "O dear friend." He relieved her of fear of Atri's son Durvāsā and fear of others, including Duḥśāsana. He removed all her sorrow.

Her hairs was sprinkled with pots of water sanctified by mantras, which were held by Kṛṣṇa's hands personally. She was addressed by Kṛṣṇa as "O dear friend!" She was protected (avitā) from fear of Durvāsa (atri-putra) and Duhśāsana. She was saved when Durvāsa came with many disciples on being invited by Dharmarāja. It was impossible to feed him since food could not be generated from the pot. Sūrya gave the benediction that the pot would give enough food only till they had finished eating. The Pāṇḍavas had already finished eating. Kṛṣṇa saved them from Durvāsā's wrath by eating a remaining morsel. Durvāsā and all his disciples no longer had any hunger. They left without eating, fearing offense by not eating. Duḥśāsana attemped to disrobe Draupadī in the assembly and Kṛṣṇa saved her by supplying cloth. All her sorrow of being brought to the assembly was removed by the killing of Duḥśāsana.

TEXT 40

āsvādanaṁ śrī-viduraudanasya
śrī-bhīṣma-niryāṇa-mahotsavaś ca
tat-tat-kṛta-tvādṛśa-pakṣa-pāta-
syāpekṣayaiveti vicārayadhvam

Kṛṣṇa tasted and praised the food Vidura offered and organized the funeral-festival of Bhīṣma. Please consider that this depended on the fact that Vidura and Bhīṣma took your side.

"But it seems that Vidura was given more mercy, since the Lord ate his food and Bhīṣma was given more mercy than us Pāṇḍavas, since the Lord arranged a festival at his passing."

Kṛṣṇa tasted and praised the food offered by Vidura. At the time of Bhīṣma's death (niryāṇa "final going") Kṛṣṇa arranged a festival. Or niryāṇa can mean not taking birth again or liberation: he merged with the Lord attaining similarity to the Lord in order to attain Vaikuṇṭha. This attainment was the festival. When it is said that the devotees merge with the Lord, it means that they attain similarity to the Lord by accepting a form of eternity, knowledge and bliss, and thus become qualified to enter Vaikuṇṭha. This will be explained later.

But this happened because they helped you or had great affection for you (tādṛśa-pakṣa-pātasya). Kṛṣṇa favored them because of this relationship with you, and not because of their proper conduct. It was impossible for them to attain such great mercy by their small acts of service alone. You should know this by considering the matter (vicāryadhvam). This shows that the Pāṇdavas had greater good fortune as objects of the Lord's great mercy than both of these famous persons.

TEXT 41

aho bata mahāścaryaṁ
kavīnāṁ geyatāṁ gatāḥ
bhavadīya-pura-strīṇāṁ
jñāna-bhakty-uktayo harau

O, it is amazing that the words of the women of your city spoken with knowledge and bhakti about Kṛṣṇa are praised in songs by accomplished poets.

Enough of speaking about you. The citizens related to you have astonishing greatness. The words of the city women spoken with knowledge and bhakti about Kṛṣṇa have attained qualification to be sung by poets like Vyāsa. In five verses (SB 1.10.21-25) they speak with knowledge:

sa vai kilāyaṁ puruṣaḥ purātano
ya eka āsīd aviśeṣa ātmani
agre guṇebhyo jagad-ātmanīśvare
nimīlitātman niśi supta-śaktiṣu

Kṛṣṇa is certainly that ancient puruṣa who alone existed without expansions before the agitation of the guṇas and during devastation, when all the jīvas along with their identities were merged within him, the soul of prakṛti. SB 1.10.21

They speak four verses (SB 1.10.26-29) with bhakti:

aho alaṁ ślāghyatamaṁ yadoḥ kulam
aho alaṁ puṇyatamaṁ madhor vanam
yad eṣa puṁsām ṛṣabhaḥ śriyaḥ patiḥ
sva-janmanā caṅkramaṇena cāñcati

Oh! Most praiseworthy is the family of Yadu! Most purifying is Mathurā-maṇḍala, which Kṛṣṇa, the best of men, the Lord of auspiciousness, respects by taking birth there, moving about and performing pastimes. SB 1.10.26

TEXT 42

sahaika-pautreṇa kayādhu-nandano
'nukampito 'nena kapīndra ekalaḥ
sa-sarva-bandhuḥ sva-janā bhavādṛśā
mahā-hareḥ prema-kṛpā-bharāspadam

Prahlāda along with his grandson, Bali, attained the favor of the Lord while Hanumān, the best of monkeys was favored alone. But you rare souls have received the complete prema and mercy of the great Lord Hari with all your family members and servants.

Summarizing Nārada indicates that the Pāṇḍavas have greater fortune than Prahlāda and Hanumān. Prahlāda along with one grandson Bali was shown mercy by Kṛṣṇa (anena).

bahavo mat-padaṁ prāptās tvāṣṭra-kāyādhavādayaḥ
vṛṣaparvā balir bāṇo mayaś cātha vibhīṣaṇaḥ

Vṛtrāsura, Prahlāda Mahārāja and others like them also achieved my abode by association with my devotees, as did personalities such as Vṛṣaparvā, Bali Mahārāja, Bāṇāsura, Maya, Vibhīṣaṇa. SB 11.12.5

Hanumān alone (ekalaḥ) was shown mercy. He did not have any sons since he was a lifelong brahmacārī. You sons and wives (bāndhavāḥ) and the citizens and ministers (sva-janāḥ) received mercy. Or bāndhavāḥ can refer to relatives like Drupada and Virāṭa. Relatives like Duryodhana (sva) and servants and citizens (janāḥ) were the objects of great mercy endowed with prema from Kṛṣna, the most attractive person, the supreme avatārī (mahā-hareḥ).

TEXT 43

uddiśya yān kaurava-saṁsadaṁ gataḥ
kṛṣṇaḥ samakṣaṁ nijagāda mādṛśām
ye pāṇḍavānāṁ suhṛdo 'tha vairiṇas
te tādṛśā me 'pi mamāsavo hi te

Once, in the court of the Kauravas, in the presence sages like me, Kṛṣṇa said of you, "A well-wisher of the Pāṇḍavas is my well-wisher, and their enemy is my enemy. The Pāṇḍavas are my very life."

It is now shown that those related to the Pāṇḍavas were objects of Kṛṣṇa's mercy. In the presence of great sages (mādṛśām) he spoke. The statement was thus known by the great sages and accepted as truth. What did he say? "Those who do beneficial acts for the Pāṇḍavas (suṛdaḥ) are my benefactors as well. Those who are their enemies are my enemies as well. This is because (hi) the Pāṇḍavas are my very life. They are very dear to me." Kṛṣṇa says in Mahābhārata:

yas tān dveṣṭi sa māṁ dveṣṭi
yas tān anu sa mām anu
aikātmyam āgataṁ viddhi
pāṇḍavair dharma-cāribhiḥ

He who hates the Pāṇḍavas hates me. He who follows the Pāṇḍavas follows me. Know that I have become one with the Pāṇḍavas, who follow dharma. Mahābhārata

Kṛṣṇa also says:

dviṣad-annaṁ na bhoktavyaṁ
dviṣantaṁ naiva bhojayet

pāṇḍavān dviṣase rājan
mama prāṇā hi pāṇḍavāḥ

One should not eat the food of a person who hates the Pāṇḍavas, and one should not feed those who hate them. O King! You hate the Pāṇḍavas. The Pāṇḍavas are my very life. Mahābhārata

TEXT 44

dhārṣṭyaṁ mamāho bhavatāṁ guṇān kila
jñātuṁ ca vaktuṁ prabhavet sa ekalaḥ
nirṇītam etat tu mayā mahā-prabhuḥ
so 'trāvatīrṇo bhavatāṁ kṛte param

Oh my arrogance! Kṛṣṇa alone is capable of knowing and describing your qualities. But at least I am convinced that the Lord has descended to this world for your sake only.

He summarizes. "Kṛṣṇa alone can know and speak about your qualities." Others cannot, since he alone can manifest behavior suitable to the Pāṇḍavas. Kila indicates certainty or conjecture (Is it not so?). "Others cannot understand, since his nature is indescribable. My inclination to describe them is impudence. What misfortune for me (aho). What is the use of speaking further? What has been defined by me? Kṛṣṇa (mahāprabhuḥ) has appeared in this world for you Pāṇḍavas in order to distribute your special glory—your treasure of happiness."

TEXT 45

śrī-parīkṣid uvāca
atha kṣaṇaṁ lajjayeva
maunaṁ kṛtvātha niḥśvasan
dharma-rājo 'bravīn mātṛ-
bhrātṛ-patnībhir anvitaḥ

Parīkṣit said: For a moment, Yudhiṣṭhira was silent as if embarrassed. Then he sighed and he spoke along his mother, brothers, and wife.

For a moment Yudhiṣṭhira was silent as if embarrassed. Actually he thought Nārada's words were a great mockery. He lamented, with mental anguish, being unsatisfied. He released a heavy sigh. Though it is stated that he spoke along with his brothers, wife and mother, they actually spoke in turns. That is stated later.

TEXT 46

vāvadūka-śiro-dhārya
naivāsmāsu kṛpā hareḥ
vicāryābhīkṣṇam asmābhir
jātu kāpy avadhāryate

Yudhiṣṭhira said: O crest jewel of eloquent speakers, the Lord does not show us mercy at all. We are not aware of any mercy he has shown us, even after we consider this for a long time.

O crest jewel of eloquent speakers! O best of speakers! You have spoken with skill, but not considering the highest truth. The Lord does not show us mercy at all. Considering this constantly, we are certainly never aware of it.

TEXT 47

prākṛtānāṁ janānāṁ hi
mādṛg-āpad-gaṇekṣayā
kṛṣṇa-bhaktau pravṛttiś ca
viśvāsaś ca hrased iva

If materialists see the many disasters that have afflicted us, their faith and inclination for kṛṣṇa-bhakti are likely to decrease.

He shows this with reasons in ten verses (47-56). By seeing the many disasters that afflicted us, the faith that nothing unfortunate happens to Kṛṣṇa's devotees will decrease for those who see with external vision. The inclination for bhakti will also decrease. The word iva indicates that actually that loss of faith has not happened till now.

TEXT 48

etad evāti-kaṣṭaṁ nas
tad-eka-prāṇa-jīvinām
vinānnaṁ prāṇināṁ yadvan
mīnānāṁ ca vinā jalam

This would surely cause us great distress, for Kṛṣṇa is our only life and breath. We would be just like living beings without food or like fish deprived of water.

The decrease in their faith and bhakti would cause us distress, not the series of disasters. Kṛṣṇa or kṛṣṇa-bhakti is our chief or only life air, or the sūtrātmā which maintains our bodies. Two examples are given. Without water the fish cannot live. We cannot tolerate the terrible situation of decrease of faith or bhakti for a moment.

TEXT 49

ato 'rthitaṁ mayā yajña-
sampādana-miṣād idam
niṣṭhāṁ darśaya bhaktānām
abhaktānām api prabho

Therefore, on the pretext of arranging a sacrifice, I requested him, "O Lord, please show the condition of the devotees and the nondevotees."

"For that reason (ataḥ) on the pretext of the rājasūya-yajña I asked him this." He did not perform the sacrifice for material benefits. Or this verse is connected with the following verses that explain what he really intended by the sacrifice. "Please show the condition of the devotees and nondevotees. Your devotees enjoy unlimited wealth in this world. Others are the opposite."

tad deva-deva bhavataś caraṇāravinda-
sevānubhāvam iha paśyatu loka eṣaḥ
ye tvāṁ bhajanti na bhajanty uta vobhayeṣāṁ
niṣṭhāṁ pradarśaya vibho kuru-sṛñjayānām

Therefore, O Lord of lords, let the people of this world see the power of devotional service rendered to your lotus feet. Please show them, O almighty one, the position of those Kurus and Sṛñjayas who worship you, and the position of those who do not. SB 10.72.5

TEXTS 50–51

lokayanto yato lokāḥ
sarve tvad-bhakta-sampadaḥ
aihikāmuṣmikīś citrāḥ
śuddhāḥ sarva-vilakṣaṇāḥ

bhūtvā parama-viśvastā
bhajantas tvat-padāmbujam
nirduḥkhā nirbhayā nityaṁ
sukhitvaṁ yānti sarvataḥ

"By this, all people will see the variegated, pure and exceptional wealth of your devotees in this life and the next. Then, becoming convinced,

people will worship your lotus feet and become ever free of sorrow and fear, and will attain happiness in all respects."

By showing the condition of your devotees (yataḥ) all the people, seeing the wealth of your devotees, will develop great faith and will worship your lotus feet. Being free of all sorrow, constantly being free of fear, they will attain happiness everywhere. Two verses are connected. What is this wealth? It is the wealth of this life, such as the ingredients for the rājasūya-yajña and the wealth of next life, which is worshippable by the devatās. That wealth has many varieties (citrāḥ) and is devoid of all faults (śuddhāḥ). That wealth is exceptional (vilakṣanā), different from all the wealth of the material planets attained by following dharma.

TEXT 52

sampraty abhaktān asmākaṁ
vipakṣāṁs tān vināśya ca
rājyaṁ pradattaṁ yat tena
śoko 'bhūt pūrvato 'dhikaḥ

Now that our nondevotee enemies have been destroyed, and the kingdom given to us — our lamentation is greater than ever before.

"But now with the disappearance of calamities, your desires have been accomplished. Why do you lament?"

Now that our enemies like Jarāsandha, Śiśupāla and Duryodhana have been destroyed at the root, since they will not be born again (vināśya), with the bestowal of kingdom, the lamentation is greater than previously, when there were calamities.

TEXT 53

droṇa-bhīṣmādi-guravo
'bhimanyu-pramukhāḥ sutāḥ
pare 'pi bahavaḥ santo
'smad-dhetor nidhanaṁ gatāḥ

Teachers like Droṇa and Bhīṣma, sons headed by Abhimanyu and many other devotees of Kṛṣṇa have met their demise on our account.

He gives the reason for lamentation in three verses (53-55). "Many devotees of Kṛṣṇa (santaḥ) have died (nidhanam gatāḥ), but this was because of us—so that we could gain the kingdom."

TEXT 54

sva-jīvanādhika-prārthya-
śrī-viṣṇu-jana-saṅgateḥ
vicchedena kṣaṇaṁ cātra
na sukhāṁśaṁ labhāmahe

The association of those devotees of Viṣṇu is more desirable to us than our own lives. Separated from that association, we can not find even a momentary particle of happiness.

Because of separation from the association of devotees, more desirable than our own lives, or desired as the greatest people in our lives (adhika-prārthya) we do not have, even (ca) for a moment, a particle of happiness.

TEXT 55

śrī-kṛṣṇa-vadanāmbhoja-
sandarśana-sukhaṁ ca tat
kadācit kārya-yogena
kenacij jāyate cirāt

The happiness of seeing Kṛṣṇa's lotus face occurs only once in a while, when after long times of absence he visits us on some business.

That happiness, previously experienced (tat), or indescribable, of seeing Kṛṣṇa's lotus face, happens only once in a while, after a long time, during opportunities like a horse sacrifice. In other words, now we have developed the greatest lamentation.

TEXT 56

yādavān eva sad-bandhūn
dvārakāyām asau vasan
sadā parama-sad-bhāgya-
vato ramayati priyān

He always lives in Dvārakā with the Yādavas, who alone are his true relatives. He is always gives pleasure to those dear and supremely fortunate relatives.

"Kṛṣṇa has no dearer friends than you. He has gone somewhere for your purpose and after completing the task he will return." That is not so. The Yādavas are dearer to him than we are. To say this, the Yādavas' special good fortune is described. "He lives with the Yādavas, who are excellent relatives (bandhūn) and thus dear." Why? "Because they have the greatest good fortune (sad-bhāgyavataḥ), in the form of special bhakti for Kṛṣṇa. Thus Kṛṣṇa gives them pleasure at all times. Lacking that good future of bhakti, we are ignored by him and are vile. The Yādavas are most fortune."

TEXT 57

asmāsu yat tasya kadāpi dautyaṁ
sārathyam anyac ca bhavadbhir īkṣyate
tad bhūri-bhāra-kṣapaṇāya pāpa-
nāśena dharmasya ca rakṣaṇāya

Your lordship has seen how he occassionaly carries our messages, drives our chariots, and does other services for us. But he does these things only for relieving the earth of its burden by destroying sins, and for protecting dharma.

"If that is so, why does he act as your messenger, etc.?" His acting as our messenger, driving a chariot or giving instructions (anyat), which are seen by you, are for protecting dharma and relieving the earth of its burden, by destroying adharma or causes of adharma (pāpa). He does all this for those purposes, not out of affection for us.

TEXT 58

śrī-parīkṣid uvāca
atha śrī-yādavendrasya
bhīmo narma-suhṛttamaḥ
vihasyoccair uvācedaṁ
śṛṇu śrī-kṛṣṇa-śiṣya he

Parīkṣit continued: Then Bhīma, jovial friend of Kṛṣṇa, laughed loudly and said, "Please listen, O disciple of Kṛṣṇa."

Bhīma was Kṛṣṇa's greatest friend in uttering jokes. Thus he laughed loudly and said as follows. "O disciple of Kṛṣṇa! You have been taught by him to speak deceptive words. It is not your fault. "

TEXT 59

amuṣya durbodha-caritra-vāridher
māyādi-hetoś caturāvalī-guroḥ
pravartate vāg-vyavahāra-kauśalaṁ
na kutra kiṁ tan na vayaṁ pratīmaḥ

Kṛṣṇa is an ocean of incomprehensible pastimes. He is the original cause of māyā. He is the preceptor of a host of cheaters. Where does he not show cleverness in speech and action? Thus, we have no faith his skills.

Kṛṣṇa is an ocean of incomprehensible pastimes (durbodha-caritra). He is the original cause of māyā. He is the instructor of a host of cheaters. This means he is a leader among the best cheaters. He is thus at speaking and performing actions. Or where does he not show cleverness in speech and action? He does this sometimes out of great playfulness, sometimes through great illusory powers, and sometimes by great craftiness. He does not act out of friendship or out of respect for the highest truth. Thus, understanding all of this, we have no faith in his skills.

TEXT 60

śrī-parīkṣid uvāca
sa-śokam avadan mātas
tato mama pitāmahaḥ
kṛṣṇa-prāṇa-sakhaḥ śrīmān
arjuno niḥśvasan muhuḥ

Parīkṣit said: Then, dear mother, my grandfather Arjuna, the intimate friend of Kṛṣṇa, spoken in lamentation, while sighing constantly.

Arjuna who was a friend equal to Kṛṣṇa's own life, or who was the dearest friend, and thus endowed with all glories (śrīmān) spoke in lamentation, remembering Kṛṣṇa's cruelty, while sighing constantly.

TEXT 61

śrī-bhagavān arjuna uvāca
bhavat-priyatameśena
bhagavann amunā kṛtaḥ
kṛpā-bharo 'pi duḥkhāya
kilāsmākaṁ babhūva saḥ

The great Arjuna said: O godly Nārada, the great mercy your beloved Lord supposedly bestowed upon us has simply made us miserable.

That great mercy bestowed by Kṛṣṇa, the charioteer (amunā), your beloved master (priyatameśena), has made us miserable. Previously Bhīma, Kṛṣṇa's narma-sakha sighed because the mercy shown by Kṛṣṇa was done out of pastimes, māyā or craftiness, not with the highest intentions. Since Arjuna was a prāṇa-sakha, he accepted all the mercy, but rejected it on other grounds.

TEXTS 62–63

sva-dharmaika-paraiḥ śuṣka-
jñānavadbhiḥ kṛtā raṇe
bhīṣmādibhiḥ prahārā ye
varma-marma-bhido dṛḍhāḥ

te tasyāṁ mat-kṛte svasya
śrī-mūrtau cakra-pāṇinā
varyamāṇena ca mayā
soḍhāḥ svī-kṛtya vāraśaḥ

Dedicated to their sva-dharma and influenced by dry jñāna, Bhīṣma and others on the battlefield fiercely attacked Kṛṣṇa, piercing his armor and flesh. Kṛṣṇa, for my sake, tolerated those repeated attacks on his body, although I tried to stop him.

He supports his statement with reasoning in nine verses (62-70). The attacks done by Bhīṣma and others during the Kurukṣetra war were tolerated and accepted by Kṛṣṇa (cakra-paṇinā) on his body (mūrtau), which was most delicate, and which was my very life, many times, so that I could attain victory (mat-kṛte).

Bhīṣma and others were dedicated to their sva-dharma, thinking "The kṣatriya must kill even one's father in battle." This had to be done. But it was highly improper to attack Kṛṣṇa who was the very form of the result of all proper dharma. They were endowed with śuṣka-jñāna, thinking "Since Kṛṣṇa is the Supreme Brahman he cannot suffer pain from our weapons." They acted while being devoid of prema, since, not being inclined to bhakti, they lacked the special knowledge and taste of the nectar of Kṛṣṇa's lotus feet.

They could pierce the armor and vital points of others (varma-marma-bhidaḥ). Thus they were very resolute (dṛḍhāḥ). Or Kṛṣṇa showed flowing perspiration that became flowing blood out of affection for his devotee. He let Bhīṣma attack so that people could understand the great affection he had for his devotee.

I tried to stop Kṛṣṇa from accepting these attacks. "O Lord! Though you swore not to fight, why are you so eager to kill Bhīṣma and others? Why do you accept on yourself the attacks of Bhagadatta and others, in my presence?" By words and by taking his hand, I tried to stop him. Kṛṣṇa was the holder of the cakra. Even though the cakra could immediately kill everyone and prevent all the attacks easily, he tolerated the attacks and did not fight, in order to give me fame. He tolerated and accepted the attacks. Very easily he could have avoided the blows but he did not, in order to attain happiness.

TEXT 64

tan me cintayato 'dyāpi
hṛdayān nāpasarpati
duḥkha-śalyam ato brahman
sukhaṁ me jāyatāṁ katham

Remembering that even today, the arrow of suffering doesn't leave my heart. O Brāhmaṇa, how then can I feel any happiness?

Remembering those attacks, the arrow of suffering does not leave my heart. If one has an arrow in one's heart, one cannot be happy with all sorts of objects of enjoyment.

TEXT 65

karmaṇā yena duḥkhaṁ syān
nija-priya-janasya hi
na tasyācaraṇaṁ prīteḥ
kāruṇyasyāpi lakṣaṇam

Acts that bring pain to a dear one are not a sign of compassion arising from affection.

"Those actions were signs of the compassion of a great friend." Accomplishment (ācaraṇam) of his actions by which a friend suffers is not a sign of any sort of compassion out of prema (prīteḥ).

TEXTS 66–67

bhīṣma-droṇādi-hananān
nivṛttaṁ māṁ pravartayan
mahā-jñāni-varaḥ kṛṣṇo
yat kiñcid upadiṣṭavān

yathā-śrutārtha-śravaṇāc
chuṣka-jñāni-sukha-pradam

mahā-duḥkha-kṛd asmākaṁ
bhakti-māhātmya-jīvinām

When I refused to kill Bhīṣma, Droṇa, and others, Kṛṣṇa, the best of the great jñānis, instructed me to induce me to fight. Hearing only the literal meaning of his instructions may please dry jñānīs, but to us whose life and soul lies in glorifying pure bhakti, those instructions by the Lord give great pain.

"If Kṛṣṇa were not merciful, why did he teach you the essence of the Upaniṣads – Bhagavad-gītā?" This is explained in five verses(66-70). Kṛṣṇa instructed me (who was unwilling to kill Bhīṣma and others) in order to persuade me to do the killing (pravartayan).

Hearing those words literally, persons desiring liberation, who distinguish ātmā from non-ātmā, get happiness, but we become greatly pained. Why? Our very life comes from glorification of bhakti or our lives are full of glorification of bhakti (bhakti-māhātmya-jīvinām).

TEXT 68

tātparyasya vicāreṇa
kṛtenāpi na tat sukham
kiñcit karoty utāmuṣya
vañcanāṁ kila bodhanāt

Even carefully considering the purport of his words I do not get happiness. Rather, they only make me remember how he deceived us.

"You should look at the general purport of his instructions. That indicates glorification of bhakti. This will bring happiness to devotees like you." Considering the purport of his words, I do not get happiness, but rather, from remembrance, understand his cheating us.

TEXTS 69–70

yat sadā sarvathā śuddha-
nirupādhi-kṛpākare
tasmin satya-pratijñe san-
mitra-varye mahā-prabhau

viśvastasya dṛḍhaṁ sākṣāt
prāptāt tasmān mama priyam
mahā-manoharākārān
na para-brahmaṇaḥ param

He is a mine of pure unconditional mercy at all times and places, he is true to his promise, the best of all well-wishing friends, who does everything for me. He has given himself to me, who have complete faith in him. No one is dearer to me than Kṛṣṇa, the Supreme Brahman with his most attractive form.

In two verses, he explained the reason for feeling cheated. There is no dear result for me other than (param) Kṛṣṇa (tasmāt). I have firm faith in him. Four characteristics act as causes of this faith: At all times and places, he was the mine of pure, unconditional mercy; true to his promise - my devotee never perishes (BG 9.31); the best of all excellent benefactors (sanmitra-varye); doing anything for me (mahā-prabhau).

He has a most attractive form, which is parabrahma, the son of Devakī. Directly he gave himself as a friend without obstruction (sākṣāt prāptāt). Because of my great faith in him, there can be no other goal for me. Thus his instructions become useless and are cheating. He gave the instructions only so that I would kill Bhīṣma and Droṇa. Similarly, Yudhiṣṭhira also said that Kṛṣṇa acted as he did only to relieve the earth of its burden.

TEXTS 71–72

śrī-nakula-sahadevāv ūcatuḥ
yad vipad-gaṇato dhairyaṁ
vairi-varga-vināśanam
aśvamedhādi cāsmākaṁ
śrī-kṛṣṇaḥ samapādayat

yac ca tena yaśo rājyaṁ
puṇyādy apy anya-durlabham
vyatanod bhagavaṁs tena
nāsya manyāmahe kṛpām

Nakula and Sahadeva said: Yes, Kṛṣṇa gave us courage in the face of many calamities. He arranged for the destruction of all our enemies and for our success in the Aśvamedha and other pious acts. He expanded our fame, kingdom, and pious credits, which were rare for others. But, O godly Nārada, we do not consider this the evidence of his mercy.

He arranged for horse sacrifices and other pious acts (ādi). By all arrangements, he expanded our fame, kingdom and pious credits, which were rare for others. O Nārada (bhagavan)! We do not consider Kṛṣṇa merciful by spreading our fame, since we do not see him for a long time. Seeing him is the best result.

TEXT 73

kintv aneka-mahā-yajño-
tsavaṁ sampādayann asau
svī-kāreṇāgra-pūjāyā
harṣayen naḥ kṛpā hi sā

Rather, he gave us real mercy when, arranging the festival of many great sacrifices, he delighted us by accepting the first worship.

When he arranged for the sacrifices, we could see him constantly. Expanding our fame, etc. is not mercy, because (hi) real mercy was giving us pleasure by accepting the first worship.

TEXT 74

adhunā vañcitās tena
vayaṁ jīvāma tat katham
tad-darśanam api brahman
yan no 'bhūd ati-durghaṭam

Now he has cheated us. How can we continue to live? Before, O brāhmaṇa, at least we had the sight of him, so difficult to obtain!

How can we live, being ignored by him, since we saw him, though it is most difficult to accomplish, when he arranged for a festival, accepting the first worship.

TEXT 75

śrī-parīkṣid uvāca
tac chrutvā vacanaṁ teṣāṁ
draupadī śoka-vihvalā
saṁstabhya yatnād ātmānaṁ
krandanty āha sa-gadgadam

Parīkṣit said: Hearing the words of the Pāṇḍavas, Draupadī was overcome with sorrow. Calming herself with great effort, she spoke, crying, in a choked voice.

Draupadī had covered her sorrow, but hearing the words of Yudhiṣṭhira and others who spoke previously, she became overcome with sorrow. Later, controlling herself, she spoke.

TEXT 76

śrī-kṛṣṇovāca
śrī-kṛṣṇena mama prāṇa-
sakhena bahudhā trapā
nivāraṇīyā duṣṭāś ca
māraṇīyāḥ kiledṛśaḥ

Kṛṣṇā [Draupadī] said: Many times my intimate friend Kṛṣṇa saved me from embarrassment, and many times he killed evil persons!

Kṛṣṇa killed many who committed unspeakable acts or who were followers of Duryodhana and Duḥśāsana (īdṛśāḥ).

TEXT 77

kartavyo 'nugrahas tena
sadety āsīn matir mama
adhunā patitās tāta-
bhrātṛ-putrādayo 'khilāḥ

I thought he would always show us mercy, but now my father, brother, and sons have all dropped dead.

I thought he would show mercy at all times. Īdṛśāḥ from the previous verse can also modify anugrahaḥ in this verse—mercy such as preventing my shame by supplying cloth. But my father Drupada, my brother Dhṛṣṭādyumna, and my sons headed by Prativindhya and others were killed.

TEXT 78

tatrāpi vidadhe śokaṁ
na tad-icchānusāriṇī
kintv aicchaṁ prāptum ātmeṣṭaṁ
kiñcit tat-tac-chalāt phalam

Nonetheless I don't lament, conforming with the Lord's desire. But I had hoped that on one pretext or another I would have my desires fulfilled.

But I do not lament. Rather, I consider it proper, with the hope of fulfilling my desires. In spite of my father, brother and sons being killed, I do not lament, because I follow the desire of Kṛṣṇa, according to the maxim "Pleasing the dear one produces the highest happiness for oneself." I desired to achieve a result dear to me on the pretext of the killing of my relatives or the sorrow caused by that.

TEXT 79

tena sāntvayitavyāhaṁ
hata-bandhu-janā svayam
śrī-kṛṣṇenopaviśyātra
mat-pārśve yukti-pāṭavaiḥ

After my family members were killed, Kṛṣṇa personally sat here by my side and pacified me with persuasive arguments.

Two verses (79-80) explain this. I was satisfied by him personally, by his sweet words.

TEXT 80

tāni tāni tatas tasya
pātavyāni mayā sadā
madhurāṇi manojñāni
smita-vākyāmṛtāni hi

I always drink the immortal nectar of those sweet words, endowed with his smiles and so pleasing to the mind.

Because of those words (tataḥ) I always drink his sweet words endowed with smiles, which are nectar.

TEXT 81

tad astu dūre daurbhāgyān
mama pūrva-vad apy asau
nāyāty ato dayā kāsya
mantavyā mayakā mune

All that is distant now due to my misfortune. He no longer comes here. Therefore, O sage, what mercy should I think he has shown me?

Let the smiles and sweet words be distant (tad astu dūre) because of my misfortune! Kṛṣṇa (asau) does not come. For that reason (ataḥ) what mercy of Kṛṣṇa should be considered to have been given to me? None at all.

TEXT 82

śrī-parīkṣid uvāca
śokārteva tataḥ kuntī
kṛṣṇa-darśana-jīvanā
sāsraṁ sa-karuṇaṁ prāha
smarantī tat-kṛpākṛpe

Parīkṣit said: Mother Kuntī, for whom the sight of Kṛṣṇa was life, seemed tormented with grief. Pitifully and tearfully she spoke remembering Kṛṣṇa's mercy and lack of it.

She should not have lamented since she was the object of Kṛṣṇa's great mercy. Thus the word iva (as if) is added to the statement. She seemed tormented with sorrow like an ordinary woman. This sorrow was intense.

TEXT 83

śrī-pṛthovāca
anāthāyāḥ sa-putrāyā
mamāpad-gaṇato 'sakṛt
tvarayā mocanāt samyag
devakī-mātṛto 'pi yaḥ
kṛpā-viśeṣaḥ kṛṣṇasya
svasyām anumito mayā

Pṛthā [Kuntī] said: Having no protection, I and my sons were immediately freed from calamities many times by Kṛṣṇa. From this I understood that his mercy on me was special, and greater than his mercy on his mother, Devakī.

Because immediately and many times he freed me completely from calamities, I understood that I had more mercy that Devakī, his mother.

yathā hṛṣīkeśa khalena devakī
kaṁsena ruddhāticiraṁ śucārpitā
vimocitāhaṁ ca sahātmajā vibho
tvayaiva nāthena muhur vipad-gaṇāt

O master of the senses! O Lord! Just as you protected Devakī imprisoned by evil Kaṁsa one time, you, my master, released me along with my sons repeatedly from even greater dangers, since I was afflicted with great suffering.

viṣān mahāgneḥ puruṣāda-darśanād
asat-sabhāyā vana-vāsa-kṛcchrataḥ
mṛdhe mṛdhe 'neka-mahārathāstrato
drauṇy-astrataś cāsma hare 'bhirakṣitāḥ

You saved us from Bhīma getting poisoned, from the burning house of lac, from the sight of Rākṣasas like Hiḍimba, from the gambling den, from the hardships of living in the forest, from unlimited weapons thrown by great warriors in countless battlefields, and from the brahmāstra of Aśvatthāmā. SB 1.8.23-24

The meaning of the two verses is this. "You have more affection for me than for Devakī. O Hṛṣīkeśa! Just as Devakī, imprisoned by Kaṁsa, was freed by you, I was freed from dangers." But was it similar? "She was imprisoned a long time and released once. She lamented greatly and her sons were not saved. She had a master (not Kṛṣṇa). But I was saved from many dangers constantly and quickly along with my sons by you, my master."

The dangers are shown. "You saved Bhīma from the poison cake, you saved us from the house of lac, from the sight of Hiḍimba and Rākṣasas, and from the gambling match in the immoral assembly." This is a list of the dangers (āpada) mentioned in the verse.

TEXT 84

sa cādhunātmano 'nyeṣām
api geheṣu sarvataḥ
strīṇāṁ nihata-bandhūnāṁ
mahā-rodana-saṁśruteḥ
manasy api padaṁ jātu
na prāpnoti kiyan mama

But now in our home and the homes of our others, I hear the loud wailing of the women whose relatives have been killed, and the thought of his mercy doesn't enter my mind.

Now she speaks of his indifference. I can perhaps think of that special mercy now, but it does not have any place at all in speaking to others, since in our and others' homes I hear loud lamentation.

TEXT 85

atas tad-darśana-tyaktāḥ
sampadaḥ parihṛtya vai
āpadaḥ prārthitās tasmin
mayā tad-darśanāpikāḥ

Therefore, deprived of his sight, I prayed for our wealth to be taken away and to be given more calamities so as to bring him again within our sight.

We should think, "This wealth and kingdom will not give us any happiness, since we cannot see him anymore." This is the intention of the verse.

Since wealth brings sorrow (ataḥ) I prayed to Kṛṣṇa (tasmin) to take away our wealth and give calamities, since they cause Kṛṣṇa to be seen.

vipadaḥ santu tāḥ śaśvat tatra tatra jagad-guro
bhavato darśanaṁ yat syād apunar bhava-darśanam

O guru of the universe! May we have dangers in such situations continually, because in those dangers we will see you, and by that we will gain release from this material world. SB 1.8.25

The meaning is this. "May we have dangers, because in those dangers we will see you and not see the sorrows of saṁsāra (apunar bhava-darśanam). Or we will see you and we understand that liberation is useless. The bliss of seeing you reveals the insignificance of the happiness of liberation, just as seeing the great ocean makes a large pond insignificant."

TEXT 86

dattvā niṣkaṇṭakaṁ rājyaṁ
pāṇḍavāḥ sukhitā iti
matvādhunā vihāyāsmān
dvārakāyām avasthitam

Thinking that "having been given the kingdom freed from thorns, the Pāṇḍavas are now satisfied," he has abandoned us and resides in Dvārakā.

"Why do you lament? He will again come here." This is explained in one and half verses. Kṛṣṇa is situated without moving (avasthitam) in Dvārakā since now we are out of danger.

TEXT 87

ato 'tra tasyāgamane
'py āśā me 'pagatā bata
manye 'dhunātmanaḥ śīghra-
maraṇaṁ tad-anugraham

Alas, I have even given up hope that he will ever come. Now I think his real mercy would be my quick death.

How unfortunate (bata)! I have given up hope of that he will come, so we can see him. Living is inappropriate. I think that my dying, not seeing him, would be Kṛṣṇa's mercy. He is completely indifferent now.

TEXT 88

bandhu-vatsala ity āśā-
tantur yaś cāvalambate
sa truṭyed yadubhis tasya
gāḍha-sambandha-marśanāt

The thread of hope — that Kṛṣṇa is most affectionate to his relatives — can easily break if I consider how strongly he is attached to the Yadus.

As a reason for giving up hope, she indicates in two verses (88-89) that the Yadus are greater objects of mercy than the Pāṇḍavas, as was mentioned by Yudhiṣṭhira. The thread of hope that Kṛṣṇa is most affection to his relatives may be cut, if I consider his strong relationship (as son and brother) with the Yadus unbreakable, since he was born in that dynasty. Or considering the strong relationship of server and served, unbreakable because of special exchange of affection, the thread will be cut. He will ignore weaker relations in preference to stronger relationships.

TEXT 89

tad yāhi tasya parama-priya-varga-mukhyān
śrī-yādavān nirupama-pramadābdhi-magnān
teṣāṁ mahattvam atulaṁ bhagavaṁs tvam eva
jānāsi tad vayam aho kim u varṇayema

Therefore, go to the Yādavas, the topmost of the beloved associates of the Lord, who are immersed in an unlimited ocean of bliss. O lord, you know very well their unequalled greatness. What can I tell you about their glories?

Therefore, go to the Yadus. Pursue them or attain them because they are the chief among those dearest to him—such as Brahmā, Garuḍa, Prahlāda, Hanumān and us. They are outstanding (nirupamān) and immersed in an unlimited ocean of bliss (pramada). By seeing them, you will develop special bliss. By associating with us, you feel misery. Quickly go to them and see.

"Please describe their glories." You know their greatness—that they are object of Kṛṣṇa's special affection—exceptional (atulam), which others do not have. O Nārada, who knows everything (bhagavan), or who is most fortunate, always living in Dvārakā! You know their glories. Aho expresses lamentation or astonishment. Therefore (tat) why should we explain those glories? Or you know and no one else does. Thus how can we inferior beings describe those glories?

TEXT 90

śrī-parīkṣid uvāca
bho yādavendra-bhaginī-suta-patni mātaḥ
śrī-dvārakāṁ muni-varas tvarayāgato 'sau
daṇḍa-praṇāma-nikaraiḥ praviśan purāntar
dūrād dadarśa su-bhagān yadu-puṅgavāṁs tān

Parīkṣit said: O mother, O wife of the son of Kṛṣṇa's sister, the exalted sage Nārada, swiftly arriving at Dvārakā, entered the inner city, repeatedly offering obeisances, and saw from a distance the fortunate Yadu heroes.

O wife of Abhimanyu, who was the son of Subhadrā, Kṛṣṇa's sister! You are most fortunate like the Yadus. He saw the Yadu heroes as described by the Pāṇḍavas as dearest to Kṛṣṇa, or who were indescribable (tān).

TEXT 91

sabhāyāṁ śrī-sudharmāyāṁ
sukhāsīnān yathā-kramam
nija-saundarya-bhūṣāḍhyān
pārijāta-srag-ācitān

They were comfortably sitting in the assembly hall called Sudharmā, in order of from oldest to youngest. They were ornamented with their own bodily beauty, and were further adorned with garlands of pārijāta.

They are described in six verses (91-96). They were sitting in the assembly hall called Sudharmā, the hall of the devatās, beautiful because the Yadus were comfortably sitting there (śrī-sudharmāyām), in order from oldest to youngest. They were ornamented with their natural beauty and covered with garlands of pārijāta flowers from the tree from Svarga.

TEXT 92

divyāti-divya-saṅgīta-
nṛtyādi-paramotsavaiḥ
sevyamānān vicitroktyā
stūyamānāṁś ca vandibhiḥ

They were being worshipped by a festival of most attractive singing and dancing, and praised by bards in wonderful words.

They were constantly worshipped (sevyamānān) by a festival of most complete singing (saṅgīta) and dancing, as well as instrumental music and dramatic performances (ādi) performed by residents of Svarga (divya) and Vaikuṇṭha (ati-divya) or more attractive than the most attractive (divyāti-dviya). This was because they were served by all great siddhis which acted like servant girls.

TEXT 93

anyonyaṁ citra-narmokti-
kelibhir hasato mudā
sūryam ākrāmataḥ svābhiḥ
prabhābhir mādhurī-mayān

The Yadus exchanged clever jokes among one another and laughed, the effulgence of their bodies surpassing that of the sun, their personalities full of charm.

They were filled with sweetness by their playful gestures and astonishing or various (citra) joking words, joyful laughing and their personal effulgence which subdued (ākrāmataḥ) the sun. That bright effulgence did not pain the eyes of anyone but caused pleasure: it caused joy in all people (mādhurīmayān).

TEXT 94

nānā-vidha-mahā-divya-
vibhūṣaṇa-vicitritān

kāṁścit pravayaso 'py eṣu
nava-yauvanam āpitān
śrī-kṛṣṇa-vadanāmbhoja-
sudhā-tṛptān abhīkṣṇaśaḥ

Many kinds of precious ornaments decorated the Yadus. And even some of the most elderly members of the assembly had attained youth by constantly enjoying the nectar of Kṛṣṇa's lotus face.

To indicate that all of them were young, the youthful appearance of the elders is described. Among the Yadus even the elders had attained youth by the Lord or by the special power of bhakti.

tatra pravayaso 'py āsan yuvāno 'ti-balaujasaḥ
pibanto 'kṣair mukundasya mukhāmbuja-sudhāṁ muhuḥ

Even the most elderly inhabitants of the city appeared youthful, full of strength and vitality, for with their eyes they constantly drank the elixir of Mukunda's lotus face. SB 10.45.19

TEXT 95

ugrasenaṁ mahā-rājaṁ
parivṛtya cakāśataḥ
pratīkṣamāṇān śrī-kṛṣṇa-
devāgamanam ādarāt

Surrounding Mahārāja Ugrasena, the Yadus glowed brilliantly, as they respectfully awaited the arrival of Kṛṣṇa.

They surrounded Ugrasena, who was sitting among everyone on an excellent throne, furnished with a white umbrella and cāmaras, insignia of a king, and who appeared glorious (cakāśataḥ). In spite of such happiness caused by great powers and wealth, they depended only on Kṛṣṇa. They all desired that Kṛṣṇa, the most worshipable (deva) since he was dearest to them, would come to the assembly.

TEXT 96

tad-antaḥ-pura-vartmekṣā-
vyagra-mānasa-locanān
tat-kathā-kathanāsaktān
asaṅkhyān koṭi-koṭiśaḥ

Countless millions of Yadus waited, absorbed in talk about Kṛṣṇa, their minds and eyes anxiously looking at the path from Kṛṣṇa's private chambers.

Their eyes and minds were anxiously looking at the path from his private chambers. They were absorbed in speaking about his previous pastimes or topics to be raised when he came to the assembly. They were indifferent to everything else. Their numbers were uncountable.

yadu-vaṁśa-prasūtānāṁ puṁsāṁ vikhyāta-karmaṇām
saṅkhyā na śakyate kartum api varṣāyutair nṛpa

The Yadu dynasty produced innumerable great men of famous deeds. Even in tens of thousands of years, O King, one could never count them all.

tisraḥ koṭyaḥ sahasrāṇām aṣṭāśīti-śatāni ca
āsan yadu-kulācāryāḥ kumārāṇām iti śrutam

I have heard from authoritative sources that the Yadu family employed 38,800,000 teachers just to educate their thousands of children. SB 10.90.40-41

Śrīdhara Svāmī explains: the children were unlimited (sahasrāṇām). Each children had many teachers. The numbers were heard, but not directly known. The number of children could not be counted. What to speak of the number of the Yadus.

TEXT 97

jñātvā taṁ yadavo 'bhyetya
dhāvantaḥ sambhramākulāḥ
utthāpya prasabhaṁ pāṇau
dhṛtvā ninyuḥ sabhāntaram

Understanding that Nārada had arrived, they eagerly came out running. Quickly raising him from the ground, they took him by his hands, and led him into the assembly hall.

Understanding that Nārada had come, by messages from the door keepers or by directly seeing him, they were overcome with eagerness. They rushed to meet him face to face and forcibly raised him up since he had offered respects on the ground. They forcibly took his hand and led him within the hall.

TEXT 98

mahā-divyāsane datte
'nupaviṣṭaṁ tad-icchayā
bhūmāv evopaveśyāmuṁ
paritaḥ svayam āsata

They offered him a large heavenly seat, but he refused to sit on it. Yielding to his desire, they gave him a seat on the ground, and they all sat around him.

By the desire of Nārada, because that satisfied his mind, they sat him on the ground and they sat around him.

TEXT 99

devarṣi-pravaro 'mībhiḥ
pūjā-dravyaṁ samāhṛtam
natvā sāñjalir utthāya
vinīto muhur āha tān

When they brought articles for worship, Nārada bowed his head to it with folded hands. He then stood up and humbly spoke to them at length.

Nārada offered respects to the articles of worship since he was overcome with great devotion. He then spoke to the Yadus (tān).

TEXT 100

śrī-nārada uvāca
bhoḥ kṛṣṇa-pādābja-mahānukampitā
lokottarā mām adhunā dayadhvam
yuṣmākam evāviratam yathāhaṁ
kīrtiṁ pragāyan jagati bhrameyam

Nārada said: O greatest recipients of the mercy of Kṛṣṇa's lotus feet, O transcendental persons, please be merciful to me today, so that I may wander throughout the universe singing your glories incessantly.

O Yadus, the best of all people, or persons beyond this world (lokottarāḥ)! Be merciful to me. How? Be merciful so that I can wander throughout the universe singing only (eva) your glories.

TEXT 101

aho alaṁ ślāghya-tamaṁ yadoḥ kulaṁ
cakāsti vaikuṇṭha-nivāsito 'pi yat
manuṣya-loko yad-anugrahād ayaṁ
vilaṅghya vaikuṇṭham atīva rājate

O, the family of the Yadus is most praiseworthy! You are more radiant than the residents of Vaikuṇṭha! By your mercy this world of men has surpassed Vaikuṇṭha and attained supreme glory.

Describing their glory with reasons, out of great respect he speaks indirectly. Aho indicates surprise. The family of the Yadus has become praiseworthy to the highest degree (alam). That family shines more brilliantly than the inhabitants of Vaikuṇṭha such as Garuḍa. By the mercy of the Yadu family, which spreads bhakti everywhere, even humans subject to death shine brightly, surpassing Vaikuṇṭha-loka since Kṛṣṇa does not show such mercy in Vaikuṇṭha.

TEXT 102

vṛttā dharitri bhavatī saphala-prayāsā
yasyāṁ janur vasatiḥ keli-cayaḥ kilaiṣām
yeṣāṁ mahā-harir ayaṁ nivasan gṛheṣu
kutrāpi pūrvam akṛtai ramate vihāraiḥ

O fortunate earth! By your fruitful endeavors these Yadus have manifest upon your surface their birth, residence, and pastimes. The Supreme Lord Hari resides in their homes and enjoys with them unprecedented transcendental pastimes.

Giving up glorifying the Yadus' family members because of extreme bliss, he addresses earth in five verses (102-106). On earth all the Yadus (eṣām) are born, live and play. That is certain (kila). In the Yādavas' houses the son of Devakī (mahā-hariḥ) enjoys pastimes which he never performed previously in Vaikuṇṭha or Ayodhyā (akṛtaiḥ).

TEXTS 103–105

yeṣāṁ darśana-sambhāṣā-
sparśānugamanāsanaiḥ
bhojanodvāha-śayanais
tathānyair daihikair dṛḍhaiḥ

duśchedaiḥ prema-sambandhair
ātma-sambandhato 'dhikaiḥ

baddhaḥ svargāpavargecchāṁ
chittvā bhaktiṁ vivardhayan

kṛṣṇo vismṛta-vaikuṇṭho
vilāsaiḥ svair anu-kṣaṇam
navaṁ navam anirvācyaṁ
vitanoti sukhaṁ mahat

Kṛṣṇa has now forgotten Vaikuṇṭha, for he is bound by intense, unbreakable relationships of prema with these Yadus. He sees the Yadus, talks with them ,touches them, follows them when they walk, sits with them, eats and sleeps with them, takes part in their marriage ceremonies, and shares in their other activities of embodied life. These relations are more tangible than the yogīs' union with him in meditation. Thus, by his pastimes Kṛṣṇa spreads among the Yadus infinite pleasure, ever fresh and indescribable, destroying any desire they might have for Svarga or liberation, and increasing more and more their bhakti to him.

Not only does he enjoy but he gives enjoyment constantly to the Yadus. That is explained in three verses. Bound by relationships of prema, by actions related to the body, by seeing, touching, talking to the Yadus, Kṛṣṇa spreads happiness by his extraordinary pastimes. He increases prema in a special way (vivardhayan), after destroying their desire for Svarga and liberation (apavarga), by bringing the Sudharmā hall and the pārijāta tree to Dvārakā. The Yadus may have thought, "We will go to Svarga and enjoy with the Lord." It would be impossible for them to appear with the Lord again and again if they stopped the process of birth (another meaning of apavarga).

Tathā means "all things mentioned" or "such things." Anyaiḥ (other things) refers to welcoming them as guests. The words daihika-sambandaiḥ do not mean that the actions were temporary, since the relationships were superior to relationships with the ātmā by dhāraṇa or samādhi (ātma-sambandhataḥ). The relationships were firm (dhṛdhaiḥ) and could not be cut by anything at any time at all (duśchedaiḥ).

He spread happiness which was newer and newer at every moment (anukṣaṇam) and which was impossible to describe (anirvācyam). The meaning is this. The Yādavas had bodies of eternity, knowledge and bliss. There was no worry of anything being temporary. By samādhi one could enjoy only a little happiness. But by relationships involving body and limbs and senses, one can attain variegated, intense happiness. Yudhiṣṭhira speaks at Kurukṣetra:

yad-viśrutiḥ śruti-nutedam alaṁ punāti
pādāvanejana-payaś ca vacaś ca śāstram
bhūḥ kāla-bharjita-bhagāpi yad-aṅghri-padma-
sparśottha-śaktir abhivarṣati no 'khilārthān
tad-darśana-sparśanānupatha-prajalpa-
śayyāsanāśana-sayauna-sapiṇḍa-bandhaḥ
yeṣāṁ gṛhe niraya-vartmani vartatāṁ vaḥ
svargāpavarga-viramaḥ svayam āsa viṣṇuḥ

His fame, as broadcast by the Vedas, the water that has washed his feet, and the words he speaks in the form of the revealed scriptures—these thoroughly purify this universe. Although the earth's good fortune was ravaged by time, the touch of his lotus feet has revitalized her, and thus she is raining down on us the fulfillment of all our desires. The same Lord who pervades everything, who makes one forget the goals of Svarga and liberation has now entered into marital and blood relationships with you, who otherwise travel on the hellish path of family life. Indeed, in these relationships you see and touch him directly, walk beside him, converse with him, and together with him lie down to rest, sit at ease and take your meals. SB 10.82.29-30

The meaning is this. His fame (yad viśrutiḥ) praised (nutā) by the Vedas completely (alam) purifies the universe (idam). The water that washed his feet, the Gaṅgā, purifies the universe. His words in the form of the Vedic scriptures purifies the universe. Though the earth's good fortune was destroyed by time, by the touch of his feet, manifesting power (uttha-śaktiḥ), she showers everywhere all things upon us.

Though you live in houses which are a cause of saṁsāra (niraya-vartmani), Kṛṣṇa, bound up (bandhaḥ) by seeing, following (anupatha), discussing (prajalpa) and by marriage (sayauna) and blood relationships (sapiṇḍa), making you detached from Svarga and liberation, remains here. He remains, giving the highest bliss.

TEXT 106

śayyāsanāṭanālāpa-
krīḍā-snānāśanādiṣu
vartamānā api svān ye
kṛṣṇa-premṇā smaranti na

While sleeping, sitting, walking, speaking, playing, bathing, eating, etc., the Yadus are so absorbed in kṛṣṇa-prema that they even forget their own families and possessions.

While sleeping, etc. because of their prema for Kṛṣṇa, they did not remember their possessions or their sons and wives (svān). Or they did not remember themselves. Where are we standing? What are we doing? They were not able to understand their situation, since they were absorbed completely in Kṛṣṇa. This shows that though they had a wealth of enjoyable objects, they were absorbed in Kṛṣṇa-prema.

śayyāsanāṭanālāpa-krīḍā-snānādi-karmasu
na viduḥ santam ātmānaṁ vṛṣṇayaḥ kṛṣṇa-cetasaḥ

The Vṛṣṇis were so absorbed in Kṛṣṇa that they forgot their own bodies while sleeping, sitting, walking, conversing, playing, bathing and so on. SB 10.90.46

Padma Purāṇa says:

ete hi yādavāḥ sarve mad-gaṇā eva bhāmini
sarvadā mat-priyā devi mat-tulya-guṇa-śālinaḥ

All the Yādavas are my people. At all times they are dear to me. They possess qualities equal to mine.

TEXT 107

mahā-rājādhirājāyam
ugrasena mahādbhutaḥ
mahā-saubhāgya-mahimā
bhavataḥ kena varṇyatām

O Ugrasena, king of exalted kings! Who can describe the greatness of your good fortune?

Having described things in general, now Nārada speaks of the glories of Ugrasena in three and half verses (107-110). He calls Ugrasena the best because he is the special object of the Lord's mercy and because he is the king among them all. O Ugrasena, the king of all great kings like Yudhiṣṭhira! Who can describe the greatness of your good fortune, which is famous (ayam) or directly perceived? No one can describe it.

TEXT 108

aho mahāścaryataraṁ
camatkāra-bharākaram
paśya priya-jana-prīti-
pāra-vaśyaṁ mahā-hareḥ

Oh, just see the wonderful astonishing ways in which the Lord Hari submits to the love of his dear devotees!

In order to describe Ugrasena's good fortune, Nārada speaks of the special affection that Kṛṣṇa has for his devotees. See his dependence on the prema of his devotees, which is the cause (ākāram) of great astonishment.

TEXT 109

yadu-rāja bhavantaṁ sa
niṣaṇṇaṁ paramāsane
agre sevaka-vat tiṣṭhan
sambodhayati sādaram

O king of the Yadus, as you sit on your great throne, that same Hari stands facing you like a servant and reverentially addresses you.

This submission is described. He stands facing (agre) you, as you sit on an excellent throne, worthy of a king.

TEXT 110

bho nidhāraya deveti
bhṛtyaṁ mām ādiśeti ca
tad bhavadbhyo namo 'bhīkṣṇaṁ
bhavat-sambandhine namaḥ

He says, "O lord, Please be attentive. Please order me, your servant." I therefore offer constant respects to you and to all your relatives.

Kṛṣṇa is described. "O lord (bho!) Please be attentive (nidhāraya). Order me, your servant (bhṛtyam) or dependent." The Lord says:

mayi bhṛtya upāsīne bhavato vibudhādayaḥ
baliṁ haranty avanatāḥ kim utānye narādhipāḥ

Since I am present in your entourage as your personal attendant, all the devatās and other exalted personalities will come with heads bowed to offer you tribute. What, then, to speak of others, the rulers of men? SB 10.45.14

Uddhava says:

tat tasya kaiṅkaryam alaṁ bhṛtān
no viglāpayaty aṅga yad ugrasenam
tiṣṭhan niṣaṇṇaṁ parameṣṭhi-dhiṣṇye
nyabodhayad deva nidhārayeti

O Vidura! Kṛṣṇa's acting as a servant of Ugrasena gives us servants great pain. Standing in from of Ugrasena sitting on the king's throne he informed him, "O king of kings! Please establish me in your service." SB 3.2.22

Therefore, I offer respects to you (bhavadbhyaḥ). Using the plural (bhavadbhyaḥ) in the last quotation indicates great respect for Ugrasena or indicates all the Yādavas. I offer respects to anyone related to you (sambandhine). What to speak of offering respects to them, I must offer respects to you. Or everything results in a glorification of the Lord. Summarizing he offers respects to the Lord, who is related to Ugrasena.

TEXT 111

śrī-parīkṣid uvāca
tato brahmaṇya-devānu-
vartino yadavo 'khilāḥ
sa-pāda-grahaṇaṁ natvā
mātar ūcur mahā-munim

Parīkṣit said: The Yādavas were all followers of the Lord, who respects brāhmaṇas. Dear mother, those Yādavas then, bowing down and touching the feet of the great sage, spoke as follows.

O mother Uttara (mātaḥ)! After Nārada had spoken (tataḥ) to the Yādavas, followers of the Lord, who respects brāhmaṇas, the Yādavas held Nārada's feet with devotion. This means they offered respects.

TEXT 112

śrī-yādavā ūcuḥ
śrī-kṛṣṇasyāpi pūjyas tvam
asmadīya-mahā-prabhoḥ
katham asmān mahā-nīcān
nīca-van namasi prabho

The Yādavas said: You are worshipable even by Śrī Kṛṣṇa, who is the supreme master of us all. Why then, O venerable sage, are you acting like a lowly person by offering respects to us, the most lowly?

O Nārada, whose feet are most worshipable (prabho)!

TEXT 113

jita-vāk-pati-naipuṇya
yad idaṁ nas tvayoditam
tad asambhāvitaṁ na syād
yādavendra-prabhāvataḥ

You can defeat the wit of even Brahmā, the master of speech. And so, by the power of Kṛṣṇa, what you have spoken about us cannot be untrue.

O Nārada, whose skill in words can defeat even Brahmā! You have spoken using words, not without consideration of truth. All the glorification (yad idam) which was spoken by you, cannot be untrue because of the power of Kṛṣṇa. It must be true.

TEXT 114

tasya kenāpi gandhena
kiṁ vā kasya na sidhyati
mahā-dayākaro yo 'yaṁ
nirupādhi-suhṛttamaḥ

If one has even a slight relationship with Kṛṣṇa, is there anything one cannot achieve? Kṛṣṇa is a reservoir of great mercy and one's unconditional best friend.

Speaking of the cause for the truth of the words, they glorify Kṛṣṇa in two verses (114-115). By even a distant relationship (gandhena) with Kṛṣṇa, what cannot be achieved by anyone? The reason is given. He who is the king of the Yadus is the originating place (ākaraḥ) of great mercy. "But great mercy cannot be repaid." He is the best of unconditional helpers (suhṛttamaḥ).

TEXT 115

mahā-mahima-pāthodhiḥ
smṛta-mātro 'khilārtha-daḥ

dīna-nāthaika-śaraṇaṁ
hīnārthādhika-sādhakaḥ

He is the ocean of all greatness. Simply remembering him brings all results. He is the master and only shelter of the most fallen, the provider of everything desirable to those who have nothing to possess.

He does not just fulfil desires but gives more than what is desired. He is a fixed ocean – beyond limit or depth – of greatness in the form of giving beyond what one desires. He does this not after a long time or according to qualification. Just remembering him brings all results (smṛti-mātraḥ). Another version has smṛti-mātreṇa: just by thinking of him in the mind, he gives all puruṣārthas. He is the sole protector or shelter (śaraṇam) for persons with no shelter (anātha), for persons with nothing or in pain (dīna). He provides more than everything to persons devoid of dharma, jñāna and bhakti or to the lowest persons (hīna).

Because he has special greatness of being most merciful, and we are the most miserable (dīna) and lacking (hīna), it is fitting that he is merciful to us. By his power everything comes to us. Therefore, by considering carefully, everything should credited to him, not to us. To glorify us is mere clever use of words.

TEXT 116

kintv asmāsūddhavaḥ śrīmān
paramānugrahāspadam
yādavendrasya yo mantrī
śiṣyo bhṛtyaḥ priyo mahān

But among us, blessed Uddhava has received Kṛṣṇa's greatest mercy. He is Kṛṣṇa's adviser, his student, his servant, and his extremely dear friend.

Though accepting all of what was said, the Yadus glorified Uddhava as the object of Kṛṣṇa's special mercy, in order to denigrate their own glorification, which is natural to bhakti. This is expressed in ten verses (116-125). "Among us, he who is the object of the greatest mercy of Kṛṣṇa, who is thus endowed with all treasures (śrīman), who is Uddhava, is Kṛṣṇa's great advisor, his great student, his great servant and is dearest to him. Though we are also advisors, students, servants and dear to him, we are inferior because we lack greatness in those roles."

TEXT 117

asmān vihāya kutrāpi
yātrāṁ sa kurute prabhuḥ
na hi tad-duḥkham asmākaṁ
dṛṣṭe tv asminn apavrajet

Sometimes the Lord abandons us to go somewhere on a trip. This gives us such distress that even when we see him again the pain does not go away.

Two verses (117-118) illustrate this. The distress arising from his going away (tad-duḥkham) does not go away, even when we see him (asmin).

TEXT 118

na jānīmaḥ kadā kutra
punar eṣa vrajed iti
uddhavo nityam abhyarṇe
nivasan sevate prabhum

We do not know when he might go somewhere else. But Uddhava is always by Kṛṣna's side, serving his master, and residing with him.

The reason their suffering does not go away is explained. "We cannot be happy in seeing him, because we worry about future separation. Uddhava however is always happy."

TEXT 119

sva-gamya eva viṣaye
preṣayed bhagavān amum
kauravāvṛta-sāmbīya-
mocanādi-kṛte kvacit

Sometimes the Lord sends Uddhava on missions on which the Lord himself should have gone. For example, the Lord sent him to arrange the release of Sāmba, whom the Kauravas had taken captive.

"Sometimes Uddhava has separation, when he is sent to Gokula or Hastināpura." Sometimes the Lord sends him somewhere for a particular purpose, when the Lord himself should go. Sāmba, son of Jāmbavatī, was surrounded and capture by Bhīṣma, Dhuryodhana and the other Kauravas because he took Duryodhana's daughter. Uddhava was sent to arrange his release. He was also sent to console the people of Vraja (ādi). Because this was confidential information, it was not revealed directly. But he gets greater happiness through releasing or consoling his dear devotees than by association with the Lord.

TEXT 120

yas tiṣṭhan bhojana-krīḍā-
kautukāvasare hareḥ
mahā-prasādam ucchiṣṭaṁ
labhate nityam ekalaḥ

Uddhava stays alone with Kṛṣṇa during the Lord's joyful pastime of eating. So he is the only person who always obtains the Lord's mahā-prasāda remnants.

It was said that Uddhava was constantly with the Lord. That is described till verse 123. At the time of his joyful pastime of eating Uddhava alone obtains the food remnants.

TEXT 121

pādāravinda-dvandvaṁ yaḥ
prabhoḥ saṁvāhayan mudā
tato nidrā-sukhāviṣṭaḥ
śete svāṅke nidhāya tat

With great pleasure Uddhava massages his master's lotus feet and then happily falls asleep with the Lord's feet on his lap.

After massaging the Lord's feet Uddhava becomes absorbed in happiness of sleep also, placing the Lord's feet on his lap and dozing. Even during sleeping he is not separated from the Lord.

TEXT 122

rahaḥ-krīḍāyāṁ ca kvacid api sa saṅge bhagavataḥ
prayāty atrāmātyaḥ pariṣadi mahā-mantra-maṇibhiḥ
vicitrair narmaughair api hari-kṛta-ślāghana-bharair
manojñaiḥ sarvān naḥ sukhayati varān prāpayati ca

When the Lord goes out for confidential pastimes, Uddhava sometimes goes with him. And when Uddhava serves as the Lord's minister in this assembly hall, his precious gems of advice and his flood of witty and charming comments earn abundant praise from the Lord. They also delight all of us and fulfill all our desires.

When the Lord sometimes goes for confidential pastimes such as visiting Kubjā, Uddhava also goes. He is not only a confidential servant, but in the assembly also, being the best, he gives happiness even to us. He is an excellent (mahān) minister (amātyaḥ). By his excellent advice, with a host of various joking words, which are praised by Kṛṣṇa, he delights us and grants what we desire—the Lord's food remnants, etc.

TEXT 123

kiṁ tasya saubhāgya-kulaṁ hi vācyaṁ
vātulatāṁ prāpa kilāyam evam
ā-śaiśavād yaḥ prabhu-pāda-padma-
sevā-rasāviṣṭatayocyate 'jñaiḥ

What can be said of his continuous good fortune? Since childhood he has been so absorbed in the taste of serving his master's lotus feet that foolish people call him insane.

His extraordinary absorption in serving from childhood is described. Those who are ignorant of the truth say that Uddhava has become afflicted with a wind (vāta) disease (making him insane). Why? Because, starting from childhood, he was completely attached to or absorbed (āviṣṭatayā) in the rasa of service to the Lord's lotus feet. He appeared to be insane because he would speak incoherently as if haunted by ghosts, being completely unaware of the external world.

TEXT 124

aho sadā mādhava-pāda-padmayoḥ
prapatti-lāmpaṭya-mahattvam adbhutam
ihaiva mānuṣya-vapuṣy avāpa
svarūpam utsṛjya hareḥ svarūpatām

Just see how amazing is his great eagerness to surrender always at the lotus feet of Lord Mādhava! He has even given up the normal bodily features of a human birth and instead assumed a form closely resembling that of Hari.

Enough of explaining his qualities! Even the excellence of his form is most astonishing. This is explained in two verses (124-125). It is the secondary result of being absorbed in service. His great taste (lampaṭya) for serving (prapatti) the lotus feet of Kṛṣṇa is astonishing. In this world or in this birth (iha), in a human form, or even while having a human body, he attained a form similar to Kṛṣṇa's; it was beautiful and dark, giving up the natural golden complexion of a kṣatriya in the middle states of India.

TEXT 125

pradyumnād ramya-rūpaḥ prabhu-dayitataro 'py eṣa kṛṣṇopabhuktair
vanya-srak-pīta-paṭṭāṁśuka-maṇi-makarottaṁsa-hārādibhis taiḥ
nepathyair bhūṣito 'smān sukhayati satataṁ devakī-nandanasya
bhrāntyā sandarśanena priya-jana-hṛdayākarṣaṇotkarṣa-bhājā

Uddhava has a more beautiful form than even Pradyumna, and Uddhava is even dearer to Kṛṣṇa than Pradyumna is. When bedecked with jewels, pearl necklaces, yellow silk dress, forest-flower garlands, makara-shaped earrings, and other ornaments, Uddhava delights us, and we mistake him for the son of Devakī Himself. No one attracts the hearts of Kṛṣṇa's devotees more than Uddhava.

That form is described. Uddhava (eṣaḥ) has a form more beautiful that Pradyumna's, even though Pradyumna's form is most beautiful. He is dearer to Kṛṣṇa than Pradyumna. Thus he is decorated with extraordinary ornaments and garlands used by Kṛṣṇa. Thus, when Kṛṣṇa cannot be seen, he is able to give us happiness.

The forest garland (vanya-srak) is defined as a garland made of leaves and flowers. The jewel (maṇi) is the Kaustubha. His earrings are shaped like makaras. The necklace is a string of pearls. Ādi indicates unguents and head ornaments. On seeing him, we mistake him for Kṛṣṇa. He manifests excellence in attracting the hearts of the devotees.

The meaning is this. When they see Uddhava from far off, when Kṛṣṇa is not seen, they think he is Kṛṣṇa. By seeing him, in this mistaken way, they become happy since he is most attractive.

Or he makes us happy on seeing him going here and there constantly to serve the Lord (bhrāntyā), because he has the excellence of attracting the hearts of Kṛṣṇa's devotees—since he has the same form as Kṛṣṇa.

Or he makes us constantly happy by appearing everywhere, here and there (bhrāntyā) with a beautiful form similar to Kṛṣṇa's (sandarśanena), even though we know he is Uddhava, because he has the excellence of attracting the devotees' hearts.

TEXT 126

śrī-parīkṣid uvāca
mātar ity-ādikaṁ śrutvā
mahā-saubhāgyam uttamam
uddhavasya munir gehaṁ
gantuṁ harṣa-prakarṣataḥ

Parīkṣit said: O mother, after hearing these and other exalted glories of Uddhava, Nārada, overjoyed, became eager to go to Uddhava's house.

Hearing of the great fortune of Uddhava that had been just spoken, as well unspoken things which will be mentioned, Nārada, filled with bliss, rose from the assembly to go to the house of Uddhava.

TEXT 127

utthāya tasya dig-bhāga-
vartmādātuṁ samudyataḥ
jñātvokto yadu-rājena
citra-prema-vikāra-bhāk

Showing various symptoms of prema, Nārada stood up, ready to set off on in that direction. Noticing this, King Ugrasena spoke.

He was eager to get the correct path and direction to Uddhava's house. Noticing him in this condition, Ugrasena spoke to him. Nārada had various or astonishing (citra) transformations arising from prema, such as perspiration, hairs standing end and tears.

TEXT 128

śrīmad-ugrasena uvāca
bhagavann uktam evāsau
kṣaṇam ekam api kvacit
nānyatra tiṣṭhatīśasya
kṛṣṇasyādeśato vinā

Ugrasena told Nārada: My lord, we already said that without Kṛṣṇa's order Uddhava never leaves the Lord's presence even for a moment.

We already said (uktam) that he is at the Lord's side constantly. This is again explained. If the Lord gives the order, then Uddhava will stay elsewhere. This is because he cannot disobey the order of the Lord (īśasya). This was also previously stated.

TEXT 129

yathāhaṁ prārthya tat-saṅga-
sthitiṁ nāpnomi karhicit
tan-mahā-lābhato hīno
'satyayā rājya-rakṣayā

In contrast, despite my begging to stay in Kṛṣṇa's company, I never obtain that blessing, being deprived of it because of my degraded occupation of protecting the kingdom.

By saying that Uddhava was always at the Lord's side, Ugrasena discourages Nārada from going to Uddhava's house. He now rejects Nārada's glorification of himself and glorifies Uddhava till the end of the chapter.

Begging to stay in Kṛṣṇa's presence (saṅga-sthitim), I never attained that situation. I have been cheated by Kṛṣṇa. No one has been cheated in this manner as I have (yathā tathā see verse 31). I have been deprived of that great attainment – being in his association, because I have to protect the kingdom. But this protection is non-existent (asatyayā), since it is impossible for enemies to defeat a kingdom given by the mercy of the Lord. Or it is deceptive order of protection, since the kingdom given by the Lord cannot ever be afflicted by troubles. The order given by the Lord "I am going elsewhere. You protect the kingdom while I am gone" amounts to deception.

tiṣṭha tvaṁ nṛpa-śārdūla
bhrātrā me sahito nṛpa
kṣatriyā nikṛta-prajñāḥ
śāstra-niścita-darśanāḥ
purīṁ śūnyām imāṁ vīra
jaghanyā māsma pīḍayan

O tiger among kings, please stay here with my brother. There are many warriors who externally follow the rules of scripture but whose intelligence is perverted. When these kings find the city vacant, with no ruler in place, they will attack it and impose terror.

Ugrasena replied:

tvayā vihīnāḥ sarve sma
na śaktāḥ sukham āsitum
pure 'smin viṣayānte ca
pati-hīnā yathā striyaḥ
tvat-sanāthā vayaṁ tāta
tvad-bāhu-balam āśritāḥ

bibhīmo na narendrāṇāṁ
sendrāṇām api māna-da
vijayāya yadu-śreṣṭha
yatra yatra gamiṣyasi
tatra tvaṁ sahito 'smābhir
gacchethā yādavarṣabha

Without Your presence none of us citizens can live peacefully in this city or its outlying districts, just as women cannot live happily without their husbands. Dear son, we all consider you our master. We depend on the shelter of your mighty arms. Therefore, O creator of our honor, we fear no earthly kings nor even Indra, king of heaven. Wherever you go to find victory in battle, O first and best of the Yadus, You should please take us with you. Hari-vaṁśa

TEXT 130

ājñā-pālana-mātraika-
sevādara-kṛtotsavaḥ
yathā ca vañcito nītvā
mithyā-gaurava-yantraṇām

I delight in only one service: following Kṛṣṇa's orders. But the false honor he shows me simply torments me and leaves me feeling cheated.

"Then why do you rule the kingdom? But since it is a great offense to disobey the Lord's order, why do you lament?"

I have the highest bliss (ustavaḥ) produced by faith (ādara) in one service—following his order. As much as that is so, I feel cheated, having the torment of useless respect. "You, the king of the Yadus, respected grandfather, sit on the throne and order us." He would rise from his seat when I came. Giving me such respect caused me pain.

In Hari-vaṁśa, Kṛṣṇa is described entering Dvārakā after being anointed as the king. Coming down from his chariot at the city's gate, Kṛṣṇa saw Ugrasena standing on the ground to receive him with arghya in his hands. Kṛṣṇa then told Ugrasena:

yan mayā sv-abhiṣiktas
tvaṁ mathureśo bhavān iti
na yuktam anyathā
kartuṁ mathurādhipate
na dātum arhase rājann

eṣa me manasaḥ priyaḥ svayam
arghyam ācamanaṁ caiva
pādyaṁ cātha niveditam

Because I officially anointed you king of Mathurā, it is improper for you to act in a contrary way. You should not present me these offerings of arghya, ācamana, and pādya waters, dear king. That is pleasing to my mind. Hari-vaṁśa

Cheating me by such words, I suffer greatly. What is my good fortune?

TEXT 131

kṛṣṇena na tathā kaścid
uddhavaś ca mahā-sukhī
tat-pārśva-sevā-saubhāgyād
vañcitaḥ syāt kadāpi na

No one else has ever been cheated like this by the Lord. But as for Uddhava, he enjoys the greatest happiness. Privileged to stay always by Kṛṣṇa's side, he is never deprived of Kṛṣṇa's association.

No one else has been cheated in this way. I do not have the good fortune of Sātyaki and others, what to speak of having the good fortune of Uddhava. He alone has the greatest fortune since he will never be cheated of the good fortune of service at the Lord's side. He always serves the Lord in close association.

TEXT 132

tat tatra gatvā bhavatāśu mādṛśāṁ
sandeśam etaṁ sa nivedanīyaḥ
adyātyagād āgamanasya velā
sva-nātham ādāya sabhāṁ sa-nāthaya

Therefore please go to Uddhava quickly and convey from us this message: The time for the Lord's arrival is already past . Kindly bring Kṛṣṇa and grace the assembly with our master's presence.

Today we will be happy by his mercy alone. Since Uddhava has these good qualities (tat), go quickly to the Lord's inner chambers (tatra). Uddhava (saḥ) should be given this message. The time for your or the Lord's coming to the assembly has passed. Bring the Lord quickly (sva-nātham ādāya) and fill (sanāthaya) the Sudharmā hall. Without seeing the Lord all of us are without a master. Even you, Nārada, are more fortunate than us since you can go close to the Lord at will.

Thus ends the fifth chapter of Canto One of Śrīla Sanātana Gosvāmī's Bṛhad-bhāgavatāmṛta, entitled "Priya: The Beloved."

CHAPTER SIX

PRIYATAMA: THE MOST BELOVED

TEXTS 1–3

śrī-parīkṣid uvāca
tac chrutvārye mahā-prema-
rasāveśena yantritaḥ
mahā-viṣṇu-priyo vīṇā-
hasto 'sau vismṛtākhilaḥ

sadā-dvāravatī-vāsā-
bhyastāntaḥ-pura-vartmanā
prabhu-prāsāda-deśāntaḥ-
praveśāścarya-vāhinā

pūrvābhyāsād ivābhyāsaṁ
prāsādasya gato muniḥ
bhūtāviṣṭo mahonmāda-
gṛhītaś ca yathetaraḥ

Parīkṣit said: O noble lady, after hearing Ugrasena's advice, Nārada, the dear devotee of Lord Mahā-viṣṇu, became absorbed in the taste of exalted love of God, which seized him in its grip. Forgetting everything else, he started off, vīṇā in hand. Having spent much time before in Dvārakā, Nārada automatically took the familiar roads to the center of the city, amazing roads that led to the neighborhood of the Lord's palaces, and came to a palace of Kṛṣṇa's that he knew how to reach from earlier visits. Under the spell of intense transcendental agitation, Nārada seemed like an ordinary person haunted by a ghost.

O mother (ārye)! Hearing the glories of Uddhava, the sage Nārada (asau) went near (abhyāsam) the Lord's palace (prasadasya). Three verses are joined together. Nārada had his vīṇā in his hand but did not play it because he had forgotten (vismṛtākhilaḥ) everything concerning his body.

How did he go to the palace? He went from previous practice. He went by the road to the palace, a road familiar because he always lived in Dvārakā, a road producing (vāhinā) great varieties of astonishment, with various turns and paths, which led to the vicinity of Kṛṣṇa's palace. He went because he had previously gone many times. The word iva is used to suggest that though he was under the control of great prema, he could not forget the road to the Lord. Or the word iva is used without special meaning. Controlled by great bewilderment, he went like an ordinary person haunted by a ghost. Or he became like a person haunted by a ghost. Ca means vā (or). Or he went just like a person controlled by madness.

TEXT 4

bhūmau kvāpi skhalati patati kvāpi tiṣṭhaty aceṣṭaḥ
kvāpy utkampaṁ bhajati luṭhati kvāpi rodity athārtaḥ
kvāpy ākrośan plutibhir ayate gāyati kvāpi nṛtyan
sarvaṁ kvāpi śrayati yugapat prema-sampad-vikāram

He sometimes tripped and fell to the ground and sometimes stood motionless. Sometimes his body trembled, or he rolled on the ground, or he wept in great distress. He sometimes shouted and jumped about, sometimes sang and danced. And sometimes all the transformations of priceless prema converged in him at once.

His insane activities are described. He moved by jumping (plutibhiḥ). Sometimes or at some places, simultaneously his whole body developed ecstatic symptoms like shivering perspiration, standing of hairs on end and crying.

TEXT 5

he man-mātar idānīṁ tvaṁ
sāvadhāna-tarā bhava
sthiratāṁ prāpayantī māṁ
sa-dhairyaṁ śṛṇv idaṁ svayam

O my mother, please now be fully attentive. Making me steady, listen soberly to what I am about to say.

"O my mother!" He calls out to her, since she should develop special prema by concentrating her mind on the astonishing activities of the Lord which will be spoken. "Listen carefully now." He was about to praise the special, most enchanting activities of the Lord. "Make me remain steady or make me return to normal state if I develop intense prema. Hear what I will speak with composure."

TEXTS 6–8

tasminn ahani kenāpi
vaimanasyena veśmanaḥ

antaḥ-prakoṣṭhe suptasya
prabhoḥ pārśvaṁ vihāya saḥ

adūrād dehalī-prānte
niviṣṭaḥ śrīmad-uddhavaḥ
baladevo devakī ca
rohiṇī rukmiṇī tathā

satyabhāmādayo 'nyāś ca
devyaḥ padmāvatī ca sā
pravṛtti-hāriṇī kaṁsa-
mātā dāsyas tathā parāḥ

That day, Lord Kṛṣṇa was for some reason disturbed in mind and asleep in the inner quarters, and Uddhava had left him and sat down nearby on a terrace at the edge of the palace. There Uddhava was joined by Baladeva, Devakī, and Rohiṇī and queens of Kṛṣṇa like Rukmiṇī and Satyabhāmā, as well as various maidservants and other ladies, including Kaṁsa's mother, Padmāvatī, a lady who had the habit of making public gossip out of Kṛṣṇa's personal affairs.

The disturbance to his mind is not specified (kenāpi), since it should be revealed later, or because Parīkṣit feared his mother would faint. The Lord had become absent minded or was suffering mentally (vaimanasyena). Because of the Lord's mental suffering, Uddhava gave up the Lord's side as he slept in an inner room of his palace. Uddhava, who was glorious as described or sought by Nārada (saḥ), was sitting at the edge of a raised terrace. Baladeva and others were also sitting there. The famous Padmāvatī, Kaṁsa's mother, was also there. She was famous because she was cheated by the demon Durmila who disguised himself as Ugrasena (and by him bore Kaṁsa as her son). She would broadcast to the public news about Kṛṣṇa. She lived there at all times.

TEXT 9

tūṣṇīm-bhūtāś ca te sarve
vartamānāḥ sa-vismayam
tatra śrī-nāradaṁ prāptam
aikṣantāpūrva-ceṣṭitam

All of them sat there silent, perplexed. They saw that Nārada had arrived and that he was acting in an astonishing manner.

Perplexed because the Lord was sleeping untimely, they remained there with him. They saw Nārada, endowed with wealth of special prema or with beauty caused by that prema (śrī), who had come near the Lord's palace. Nārada was acting in an astonishing manner, or in a way previously unseen (apūrva-ceṣṭitam).

TEXT 10

utthāya yatnād ānīya
svāsthyaṁ nītvā kṣaṇena tam
premāśru-klinna-vadanaṁ
prakṣālyāhuḥ śanair laghu

Standing up, they brought him carefully to where they had been sitting. They took a moment to restore him to a condition closer to normal and wiped dry his face, moist with tears of prema. Then they spoke to him, simply and gently.

He stood at a distance. Forcibly they brought him close (ānīya). They wiped his face which was moist with tears of prema. They spoke to him softly and with few words, since they worried that the Lord's sleep would be broken or feared the Lord would be disturbed in mind.

TEXT 11

adṛṣṭa-pūrvam asmābhiḥ
kīdṛśaṁ te 'dya ceṣṭitam
ākasmikam idaṁ brahmaṁs
tūṣṇīm upaviśa kṣaṇam

They said: We have never seen you behave like this. What is this sudden change in you, dear brāhmaṇa? Please sit here quietly for a moment.

This astonishing behavior consisted of actions like stumbling, etc. They urged him to be quite because of the fear of waking the Lord or disturbing his mind as previously explained.

TEXT 12

śrī-parīkṣid uvāca
sa-gadgadam uvācāśru-
dhārā-mīlita-locane
yatnād unmīlayan natvā
sa-kampa-pulakācitaḥ

Parīkṣit said: Nārada replied in a choking voice, tears flowing from his eyes. As he began to speak, he opened his eyes with difficulty and bowed down to offer respects. He was trembling, and the hairs on his body stood erect.

He opened his eyes which were closed because of streams of tears. He offered them respects (natvā).

TEXT 13

śrī-nārada uvāca
manojña-saubhāgya-bharaika-bhājanaṁ
mayā samaṁ saṅgamayadhvam uddhavam
tadīya-pādaika-rajo 'tha vā bhavet
tadaiva śāntir bata me 'ntar-ātmanaḥ

Nārada said: Please arrange for me to meet with Uddhava, the only true object of exquisite good fortune. Or else let me have from his feet one particle of dust. Then alone will I have peace of mind.

Uddhava was present there very close, but Nārada did not see him because of his prema. Nārada said, "Please arrange for Uddhava to meet with me." Thinking that meeting Uddhava would be improper for him, he then suggested obtaining dust from his feet. "Then I will have peace of mind (antarātmanaḥ). I am in this condition because I have not attained Uddhava." This is thus an answer about his strange behavior that day.

TEXT 14

purātanair ādhunikaiś ca sevakair
alabdham āpto 'lam anugrahaṁ prabhoḥ
mahat-tamo bhāgavateṣu yas tato
mahā-vibhūtiḥ svayam ucyate ca yaḥ

He has received an abundance of our Lord's mercy never gained by the Lord's other servants, in the past or even now. Because Uddhava is the greatest of all Vaiṣṇavas, the Lord himself calls Uddhava one of his own special expansions.

He glorifies Uddhava with reasons in five verses (14-18). Uddhava has received the greatest (alam) mercy of Kṛṣṇa. Because of that (tataḥ) he is the best (mahattamaḥ) among the Lord's devotees. Uddhava is called a great vibhūti (mahā-vibhūtiḥ) by the Lord himself. Among all the Lord's vibhūtis he is the best.

vāsudevo bhagavatāṁ tvaṁ tu bhāgavateṣv aham
kimpuruṣāṇāṁ hanuman vidyādhrāṇāṁ sudarśanaḥ

Among those entitled to the name Bhagavān, I am Vāsudeva, and indeed, you, Uddhava, represent me among the devotees. I am Hanumān among the Kimpuruṣas, and among the Vidyādharas, I am Sudarśana. SB 11.16.29

TEXT 15

pūrve pare ca tanayāḥ kamalāsanādyāḥ
saṅkarṣaṇādi-sahajāḥ suhṛdaḥ śivādyāḥ
bhāryā ramādaya utānupamā sva-mūrtir
na syuḥ prabhoḥ priya-tamā yad-apekṣayāho

No one has ever been as dear to the Lord — neither the Lord's direct sons like Brahmā, nor friends like Śiva, nor brothers like Balarāma, nor the goddess Ramā or the Lord's other wives. Not even his own form is as dear.

What can be said! He is greater than any other servant or even the Lord's sons. Brothers like Balarāma, friends like Śiva, and even the Lord's own extraordinary form are not as dear as Uddhava. Aho indicates surprise. He is dearer than all of them.

na tathā me priyatama ātma-yonir na śaṅkaraḥ
na ca saṅkarṣaṇo na śrīr naivātmā ca yathā bhavān

Neither Brahmā, Śiva, Saṅkarṣaṇa, the goddess of fortune nor even my own self are as dear to me as you are. SB 11.14.15

According to Śrīdhara Svāmī, Kṛṣṇa should have said yathā bhaktaḥ but used the word bhāvan (you). This verse was quoted in the glorification of Prahlāda. However, here the word bhāvan refers to Uddhava directly.

TEXTS 16–18

bhagavad-vacanāny eva
prathitāni purāṇataḥ
tasya saubhāgya-sandoha-
mahimnāṁ vyañjakāny alam

tasmin prasāda-jātāni
śrī-kṛṣṇasyādbhutāny api
jagad-vilakṣaṇāny adya
gītāni yadu-puṅgavaiḥ

pravisya karṇa-dvāreṇa
mamākramya hṛd-ālayam
madīyaṁ sakalaṁ dhairya-
dhanaṁ luṇṭhanti hā haṭhāt

The Lord's own words, disclosed in the Purāṇas, tell the abounding glories of Uddhava's good fortune. Those words, born of Kṛṣṇa's causeless mercy, are unlike any others heard in this world. The Yādava heroes now tell those words in songs. Alas, when those words enter the abode of my heart through the gateway of the ears, they steal all my wealth of sobriety.

Saying that the Lord's words and their results are proof, he shows Uddhava's glories. They had asked Nārada, "What is this extraordinary behavior of yours?" He answers here. You asked the question and here I speak the answer. It is because of Uddhava's great glories. In three verses he describes those glories.

The Lord's words of praise are as follows:

athaitat paramaṁ guhyaṁ
śṛṇvato yadu-nandana
su-gopyam api vakṣyāmi
tvaṁ me bhṛtyaḥ suhṛt sakhā

O beloved of the Yadu dynasty! Because you are my servant, well-wisher and friend, I shall now speak to you, who listen well, the supreme secret. SB 11.11.49

noddhavo 'ṇv api man-nyūno
yad guṇair nārditaḥ prabhuḥ
ato mad-vayunaṁ lokaṁ
grāhayann iha tiṣṭhatu

Uddhava is not less than me, because he is master of māyā and not at all lacking in any spiritual quality. He should remain on this earth, giving knowledge of me to the world. SB 3.4.31

The words arise from Kṛṣṇa's mercy to Uddhava (tasmin prasāda-jātāni). The words are sung in the assembly with great joy and pleasant voice by Ugrasena, best of the Yadus. The words enter the abode of my heart through the ears and forcibly spread, and plunder the treasure of my self-control by force.

The words are famous in the Purāṇas such as Bhāgavatam. They reveal profoundly the glories of Uddhava with his abundant good fortune. The words which arose from the mercy of the Lord are most astonishing, since they are unique in the universe (vilakṣaṇāni). They are like a thief who, bewildering people, enters a house and steals everything.

TEXTS 19–21

śrī-parīkṣid uvāca
uddhavo 'tyanta-sambhrānto
drutam utthāya tat-padau
nidhāyāṅke samāliṅgya
tasyābhipretya hṛd-gatam

hṛt-prāpta-bhagavat-tat-tat-
prasāda-bhara-bhāg-janaḥ
tadīya-prema-sampatti-
vibhava-smṛti-yantritaḥ

rodanair vivaśo dīno
yatnād dhairyaṁ śrito munim
avadhāpyāha mātsaryāt
sāttvikāt pramudaṁ gataḥ

Parīkṣit said: Impelled by great respect for Nārada, Uddhava suddenly stood up, held Nārada's feet, and embraced them. Aware of what Nārada was thinking, Uddhava remembered many devotees who had received the Lord's special mercy. As Uddhava meditated on those devotees, their prema for the Lord, and the wealth of their loving ecstasies, he felt distress, thinking himself fallen, and cried helplessly. Only with some effort was he able to regain his composure. Then he became joyful and spoke to the sage, moved by the sāttvika emotion of jealousy.

Three verses make one sentence. Uddhava spoke, directing himself to Nārada. All had been sitting down. Previously, they had told Nārada to sit for a while to recover. They all sat with him. Now Uddhava rose from his seat. Uddhava took Nārada's feet on his lap and embraced them. He could understand (abhipretya) that Nārada (tasya) was trying to find the Lord's object of mercy (hṛd-gatam). He remembered those who had obtained the great indescribable (tat tat) mercy of the Lord. Or he remembered the many famous devotees (tat tat) such as Rādhā who had received the Lord's great mercy.

He became pained on remembering how they, endowed with a wealth of prema, cried in pain (vibhava), or on remembering the weeping in

Lakṣmī's (sampatti) prema. Or he became pained on remembering the manifestation (vibhava) of a wealth (sampatti) of symptoms of prema like perspiration, shivering and hairs standing on end.

Great prema had manifested in Uddhava. Thus he was miserable (dīnaḥ). With efforts of Nārada, Balarāma and others, or by his own attempts he became peaceful (dhairyaṁ śritāḥ). He felt joy arising from envy—hatred of another person's good fortune (mātsaryāt), which arose from sattva-guṇa (actually śuddha-sattva), not rajas or tamas, since the lower guṇas were absent in him. Since hatred does not exist in śuddha-sattva, mental suffering or envy cannot occur. Rather by describing exalted devotees with absorption resembling rivalry, he attained the highest bliss.

TEXTS 22–23

śrīmad-uddhava uvāca
sarva-jña satya-vāk-śreṣṭha
mahā-muni-vara prabho
bhagavad-bhakti-mārgādi-
guruṇoktaṁ tvayeha yat

tat sarvam adhikaṁ cāsmāt
satyam eva mayi sphuṭam
varteteti mayā jñātam
āsīd anyair api dhruvam

Uddhava said: O omniscient Nārada, most truthful speaker, greatest of sages, you are the master who teaches the means and the end of bhakti to the Supreme Lord. All you just said about me, and more, is self-evident to me. I knew it was true before you said it, and so did others.

O omniscient Nārada! This means "You know Rādhā and others, the great objects of Kṛṣṇa's mercy." O best among speakers of truth like Yudhiṣṭhira! This means "What you have said to me is all true." O best among the sages like Vyāsa! You alone can describe their glories. No one else can. O Lord! Whatever you desire must be followed. You are the first guru on the path of bhakti (bhagavad-bhakti-margādi-gurunā). Thus you must be the recipient of the Lord's great mercy, because of your devotion to the Lord. Bhakti will spread everywhere by your teachings. You alone are the recipient of the Lord's great mercy.

Or Uddhava calls out to Nārada many times because his prema was awakened. And more than what you said is true. This is known to others like Ugrasena as well.

TEXT 24

idānīṁ yad vraje gatvā
kim apy anvabhavaṁ tataḥ
mahā-saubhāgya-māno me
sa sadyaś cūrṇatāṁ gataḥ

Recently having gone to Vraja, I experienced something which crushed my pride in my good fortune .

I experienced something indescribable (yat kim api) when I went to Vraja. Because of that experience (tataḥ) my pride in my good fortune was immediately (sadyaḥ) crushed. Or the indescribable pride in my good fortune, which was described by you and known by me, was immediately crushed. This suggests that his pride was huge like Sumeru but was easily crushed.

TEXT 25

tata eva hi kṛṣṇasya
tat-prasādasya cādbhutā
tat-premṇo 'pi mayā jñātā
mādhurī tadvatāṁ tathā

Since then I have understood the amazing sweetness of Kṛṣṇa's mercy, prema, and those who possess that prema.

From that realization (tataḥ) I have understood the amazing sweetness of Kṛṣṇa's mercy, prema and his devotees possessing prema (tadvatām).

TEXT 26

tad-darśanenaiva gato 'ti-dhanyatāṁ
tarhy eva samyak prabhuṇānukampitam
tasya prasādātiśayāspadaṁ tathā
matvā svam ānanda-bharāpluto 'bhavam

Just by what I saw in Vraja, I came to be most blessed. I was swept away in an ocean of ecstasy, thinking myself completely favored by the Lord, a recipient of his most extreme mercy.

Just by seeing the inhabitants of Vraja (tad-darśanena) or by that realization, I became extremely fortunate. At that time, I considered myself to be completely the object of his mercy. Tathā means "all this." Understanding myself to be the object of Kṛṣṇa's mercy, I became filled with great bliss. I was inundiated in an ocean of the highest bliss.

TEXT 27

gāyaṁ gāyaṁ yad-abhilaṣatā yat tato 'nutiṣṭhitaṁ yat
tat sarveṣāṁ su-viditam itaḥ śakyate 'nyan na vaktum
natvā natvā muni-vara mayā prārthyase kākubhis tvaṁ
tat-tad-vṛtta-śravaṇa-rasataḥ saṁśrayethā virāmam

Everyone here knows very well what I then sang in my ecstasy, what desires I had, and what I did. Better for now not to speak on those matters further. O best of sages, I bow down to you again and again, and I beseech you: Please curb your eagerness to relish those various affairs.

Everyone knows what I sang because of that realization (tataḥ) or because of that realization in Vraja. He sang as follows:

etāḥ paraṁ tanu-bhṛto bhuvi gopa-vadhvo
govinda eva nikhilātmani rūḍha-bhāvāḥ
vāñchanti yad bhava-bhiyo munayo vayaṁ ca
kiṁ brahma-janmabhir ananta-kathā-rasasya

Among all persons on earth, these cowherd women alone have attained prefect bodies, for they have achieved mahābhāva for Govinda, the source of all forms of the Lord. Their pure love is desired by those who fear material existence, by great sages, and by ourselves as well. For one who has tasted the narrations of the infinite Lord, what is the use of taking birth as a high-class brāhmaṇa, or even as Brahmā himself? SB 10.47.58

He desired to be a shrub to take the foot dust of the gopīs:

āsām aho caraṇa-reṇu-juṣām ahaṁ syāṁ
vṛndāvane kim api gulma-latauṣadhīnām
yā dustyajaṁ sva-janam ārya-pathaṁ ca hitvā
bhejur mukunda-padavīṁ śrutibhir vimṛgyām

The gopīs of Vṛndāvana have given up the association of their husbands, sons and other family members, who are very difficult to give up, and they have forsaken their relatives and the path of dharma to obtain the lotus feet of Mukunda, Kṛṣṇa, which even the Vedas pursue. Oh, let me be fortunate enough to be one of the bushes, creepers or herbs in Vṛndāvana, because the gopīs bless them with the dust of their lotus feet. SB 10.47.61

His action was offering respects:

vande nanda-vraja-strīṇāṁ pāda-reṇum abhīkṣṇaśaḥ
yāsāṁ hari-kathodgītaṁ punāti bhuvana-trayam

I repeatedly offer my respects to the dust from the feet of the women of Nanda Mahārāja's cowherd village. When these gopīs loudly chant the glories of Kṛṣṇa, the vibration purifies the three worlds.SB 10.47.63

Everyone knows very well what I sang, what I desired and what I did. Though it should not be kept secret that Rādhā is the greatest object of Kṛṣṇa's mercy since it is well known, it cannot be spoken elsewhere (itaḥ anyat) or else only in a general way. Satyabhāmā and others will become unhappy at the glorification of the gopīs, since the queens will fear the competition. Or we fear that the Lord will develop great pain from intense prema.

"By hearing these topics I can determine who is the greatest recipient of his mercy. I am persistent in finding this out. Therefore, please speak in detail."

Please give up greed (rasataḥ) for hearing about the various topics or the topics of the gopīs and Kṛṣṇa (tat tat vṛtta). Otherwise great calamity will occur.

TEXT 28

śrī-parīkṣid uvāca
tad-vākya-tattvaṁ vijñāya
rohiṇī sāsram abravīt
cira-gokula-vāsena
tatratya-jana-sammatā

Parīkṣit said: Because Rohiṇī had long lived in Gokula, its residents held her in high regard. She knew the inner meaning of Uddhava's words. So with tears in her eyes, she decided to speak.

However, when dedicated devotees of Kṛṣṇa gather, this topic cannot be suppressed. Rohiṇī, understanding the import (tattva) of Uddhava, spoke with tears. The import was: the people of Vraja and no one else were the objects of Kṛṣṇa's great mercy. Rohiṇī was very dear to the people of Gokula (sammatā). Or she held them dear.

TEXTS 29–30

śrī-rohiṇy uvāca
ās tān śrī-hari-dāsa tvaṁ

mahā-durdaiva-māritān
saubhāgya-gandha-rahitān
nimagnān dainya-sāgare

tat-tad-vāḍava-vahny-arcis-
tāpyamānān viṣākulān
kṣaṇācintā-sukhinyā me
mā smṛteḥ padavīṁ naya

Rohiṇī said: Alas, dear servant of Hari, the residents of Vraja have by evil fate been all but slain. They have lost the last trace of good fortune and are drowning in an ocean of misery. There they suffer, poisoned and scorched, in the flames of an underwater fire. So please do not destroy my moment of happiness by reminding me of them.

Ā indicates great sorrow. O servant of the Lord, Uddhava! Do not make me remember the people of Vraja. The reason is given. They have been completely overcome (māritān) by great misfortune which is inconceivable. Thus they are devoid of a trace of the good fortune of being favored by Kṛṣṇa. They are not touched by anything related to good fortune. Submerged in an ocean of misery, they are burned by the vāḍava fire of lamentation. They are bewildered as if by poison, because of increased prema. I was happy (sukhinyāḥ) not thinking of them for a moment. Do not give me such sorrow by remembering them.

Uddhava sung of the gopīs particularly. Rohiṇī uses the masculine plural, whereas he does not. However Rohiṇī's statement indicates that all the people of Vraja suffered, since she was affectionate to all of them. Of course Yaśodā and others were terribly afflicted and she mentioned them next.

TEXTS 31–32

ahaṁ śrī-vasudevena
samānītā tato yadā
yaśodāyā mahārtāyās
tadānīntana-rodanaiḥ

grāvo 'pi rodity aśaner
apy antar dalati dhruvam
jīvan-mṛtānām anyāsāṁ
vārtāṁ ko 'pi mukhaṁ nayet

When Vasudeva brought me back from Gokula, the cries of the greatly distraught Yaśodā made even stones shed tears and lightning bolts shatter. And who can let the mouth speak about the other women of Vraja, who after Kṛṣṇa left became like living corpses?

Not being able to tolerate the situation, she describes what happened in two verses. "When I was brought from Gokula (tataḥ), the stones, though very hard, wept. They became liquid. Thunderbolts, even harder, split open (antar dalati). Harder than that was someone's heart. It did not melt from the cries of Yaśodā. What person, man or woman, can speak about the condition of other women—Rādhā and the gopīs?"

TEXT 33

athāgataṁ guru-gṛhāt
tvat-prabhuṁ prati kiñcana
saṅkṣepeṇaiva tad-vṛttaṁ
duḥkhād akathayaṁ ku-dhīḥ

But I am not very intelligent. After your Lord returned from the house of his guru, my sadness drove me to tell him briefly how the Vraja-vāsīs were faring.

After I had been brought from Gokula (atha), I spoke very briefly about Vraja to Kṛṣṇa when he returned from Sāndīpani's house. I spoke a little because I feared his lamentation. Though I knew that I would not achieve the result I wanted, I spoke, because I was suffering, according to the maxim "On revealing one's suffering one becomes happy." If I did not speak, I would suffer. But it is unsuitable to speak at the wrong place. I spoke because I was unintelligent (kudhīḥ).

TEXT 34

na hi komalitaṁ cittaṁ
tenāpy asya yato bhavān
sandeśa-cāturī-vidyā-
pragalbhaḥ preṣitaḥ param

This, though, did not soften his heart, because all he did in response was send you, an expert in the clever art of delivering messages.

By my speaking the news, his heart did not soften. It was certain (hi). The symptom was that Uddhava was sent there. Only you were sent, and Kṛṣṇa did not go in person. "But that should also be auspicious." You are skillful in the art of clever speaking. Or you are skillful in knowing how to speak cleverly. By that speaking, the people of Vraja become more grief-stricken and not at all pacified.

TEXT 35

ayam eva hi kiṁ teṣu
tvat-prabhoḥ paramo mahān
anugraha-prasādo yas
tātparyeṇocyate tvayā

Is this your Lord's greatest favor and mercy on them, as your words imply?

Is his behavior endowed with mercy to them? Or was he pleased to give mercy to them, which was implied by your words, though not spoken directly (tātparyena)?

TEXTS 36–38

mama pratyakṣam evedaṁ
yadā kṛṣṇo vraje 'vrajat
tato hi pūtanādibhyaḥ
keśy-antebhyo muhur muhuḥ

daityebhyo varuṇendrādi-
devebhyo 'jagarāditaḥ
tathā cirantana-svīya-
śakaṭārjuna-bhaṅgataḥ

ko vā nopadravas tatra
jāto vraja-vināśakaḥ
tatratyās tu janāḥ kiñcit
te 'nusandadhate na tat

My own experience is this: When Kṛṣṇa lived in Vraja, so many calamities threatened to destroy it. Vraja was disturbed by demons, from Pūtanā to Keśī, by devatās like Varuṇa and Indra, by creatures like the python, and by the falling of familiar things at Kṛṣṇa's house like the cart and the arjuna trees. But to these dangers the residents paid no regard.

And when Kṛṣṇa was there, they did not at all have happiness. Rohiṇī speaks with great suffering. I experienced this misery (pratyākṣam) since I lived in Vraja for a long time, even before Kṛṣṇa came there. Starting from the time when Kṛṣṇa came there, Vraja was disturbed by demons like Pūtanā and by devatās like Varuṇa, who stole Nanda, and Indra who poured rain on Vraja, by animals like the python which tried to swallow Nanda at Sarasvatī tīrtha, as well as (āditaḥ) Kāliya who, on Kaṁsa's order, poisoned the Yamunā. Vraja was disturbed by the breaking of the ancient cart and the arjuna trees. The cart is called "his own" (svīya) because it served as his cart and umbrella.

But the people did not lose affection for Kṛṣṇa. Rather their affection increased. What danger did not arise there? The people did not pay attention to the appearance of dangers (tat) or did not consider it a danger at all. They did not at all consider, "Some unhappy situation has occurred for us. Let us counteract this."

TEXT 39

mohitā iva kṛṣṇasya
maṅgalaṁ tatra tatra hi
icchanti sarvadā svīyaṁ
nāpekṣante ca karhicit

As if entranced, in each event they only wanted Kṛṣṇa's welfare. They never thought about themselves.

The cause is explained. They were as if (iva) bewildered. Kṛṣṇa had taken away their sense of discernment, since actually they could not be bewildered materially. Or they were like (iva) other people who become tricked by magic, because (hi) at all times they desired only Kṛṣṇa's safety in all these dangers. They did not consider their own safety.

TEXT 40

svabhāva-sauhṛdenaiva
yat kiñcit sarvam ātmanaḥ
asyopakalpayante sma
nanda-sūnoḥ sukhāya tat

Out of natural fondness for the son of Nanda, they fully dedicated everything they owned to his pleasure.

They offered (upakalpayante) or provided everything to Kṛṣṇa for his happiness because of prema alone, which was their nature. There was no particular cause. Seeing him as the son of Nanda (nanda-sunoḥ) they did not consider him the Supreme Lord, using terms like "son of the Yadu dynasty." They related with him out of manifestation of the highest prema.

TEXT 41

tadānīm api nāmīṣāṁ
kiñcit tvat-prabhuṇā kṛtam
idānīṁ sādhita-svārtho
yac cakre 'yaṁ kva vacmi tat

Even then your Lord did nothing to help them. And who could bear to hear me say what he has been doing now to accomplish the goals of his other devotees?

She draws the conclusion. "He did not do anything for the people of Vraja (amīṣām). He also fulfilled his purpose with his relatives (sva), and lived happily with them in Mathurā."

Or he accomplished his own purpose of killing Kaṁsa by living incognito with the people of Vraja. To whom will I say that (yat) your master has given up his devotees? I cannot say this to anyone, since there is no one suitable at this place, or because I fear criticizing Kṛṣṇa.

TEXT 42

śrī-parīkṣid uvāca
tac chrutvā duṣṭa-kaṁsasya
jananī dhṛṣṭa-ceṣṭitā
jarā-hata-vicārā sā
sa-śiraḥ-kampam abravīt

Parīkṣit said: Upon hearing this, the mother of the wicked Kaṁsa spoke out, her head shaking, her manner bold, her intelligence spoiled by old age.

The mother of Kaṁsa was bold in her actions, being without shyness, because she had a son (Kaṁsa) born through the demon Drumila. The three adjectives describing her (mother of Kaṁsa, boldness, and lack of intelligence because of old age) are the cause of her bad words. She was well known for her lack of intelligence, since she greatly lamented the death of her son Kaṁsa. She shook her head because of old age or to show cleverness at criticizing Rohiṇī's words.

TEXT 43

padmāvaty uvāca
aho batācyutas teṣāṁ
gopānām akṛpāvatām
ā-bālyāt kaṇṭakāraṇye
pālayām āsa go-gaṇān

Padmāvatī said: Just see! Since childhood our Kṛṣṇa has stayed in the forest full of thorns to guard the cows of those merciless cowherds.

How unfortunate (aho)! Kṛṣṇa, steady in spite of the hardships (acyutaḥ), herded the cows of the merciless cowherds.

TEXT 44

pāduke na dadus te 'smai
kadācic ca kṣudhāturaḥ
go-rasaṁ bhakṣayet kiñcid
imaṁ badhnanti tat-striyaḥ

They never even gave him shoes! And if when tormented by hunger he sometimes drank a little milk, the cowherd women would tie him up.

Their merciless nature is shown till verse 45. The cowherds did not give shoes to Kṛṣṇa. Exhausted from hunger, if he drank some butter milk, the cowherd women would tie him up with cow ropes. This relates to the Dāmodara story.

vatsān muñcan kvacid asamaye krośa-sañjāta-hāsaḥ
steyaṁ svādv atty atha dadhi-payaḥ kalpitaiḥ steya-yogaiḥ

Your son sometimes comes to our houses before the milking of the cows and releases the calves, and when the master of the house becomes angry, your son merely smiles. Sometimes he devises some process by which he steals palatable curd, butter and milk, which he then eats and drinks. SB 10.8.29

TEXT 45

ākrośanti ca tad duḥkhaṁ
kāla-gatyaiva kṛtsnaśaḥ
kṛṣṇena soḍham adhunā
kiṁ kartavyaṁ batāparam

And they also scolded him. Because he was young, Kṛṣṇa had no choice but to tolerate all this pain. But what does he have to do for those people now?

The suffering in herding the cows was because of his youth (kāla-gatya), when he did not consider suffering. Or he had to endure the suffering at that time in order to live secretly, to fool Kaṁsa. Bata indicates lamentation. What else (anyat) should he do for these people now?

TEXT 46

śrī-parīkṣid uvāca
prajñā-gāmbhīrya-sampūrṇā
rohiṇī vraja-vallabhā
tasyā vākyam anādṛtya
prastutaṁ saṁśṛṇoti tat

Parīkṣit said: Rohiṇī, the darling of Vraja, was fully endowed with gravity and wisdom. Ignoring Padmāvatī's remarks, she went on finish what she was saying.

Rohiṇī ignored Padmāvatī's (tasyāḥ) foolish words, as if she did not hear them and finished her own statement. She was endowed with a depth of wisdom or with wisdom and gravity (prajñā-gambhīrya-saṁpūrṇāḥ).

TEXT 47

śrī-rohiṇy uvāca
rājadhānīṁ yadūnāṁ ca
prāptaḥ śrī-mathurām ayam
hatāri-vargo viśrānto
rāja-rājeśvaro 'bhavat

Rohiṇī said: Then Kṛṣṇa went to Mathurā, the capital of the Yadus. He killed many enemies, relaxed for a while, and became king of the rulers of kings.

"After completing his remaining tasks in other places today or tomorrow he will return to Vraja." That is answered in two verses (47-48). Kṛṣṇa (ayam) went Mathurā and recovered (viśrāntaḥ) from the fatigue of fighting by enjoying there. Or it can mean that he went to live comfortably in Dvārakā.

TEXT 48

nirjitopakṛtāśeṣa-
devatā-vṛnda-vanditaḥ

aho smarati citte 'pi
na teṣāṁ bhavad-īśvaraḥ

Now, honored by countless devatās, whom he has sometimes defeated and sometimes helped, this Lord of yours no longer even thinks about the residents of Vraja.

He is worshipped by the unlimited host of devatās whom he sometimes defeated (as in taking the pārijāta tree) and sometimes helped (by killing Naraka, etc.) Aho indicates lamentation. He does not even remember the people of Vraja, what to speak of going there.

TEXT 49

śrī-parīkṣid uvāca
tad-vaco 'sahamānāha
devī kṛṣṇasya vallabhā
sadā kṛta-nivāsāsya
hṛdaye bhīṣma-nandinī

Parīkṣit said: Kṛṣṇa's dear queen Rukmiṇī, Bhīṣmaka's daughter, who always lived in Kṛṣṇa's heart, found these words unbearable. And so she spoke up.

Rukmiṇī lives on the chest (hṛdi) of Kṛṣṇa. She knows in truth what is happening within his heart.

TEXT 50

śrī-rukmiṇy uvāca
bho mātar nava-nītāti-
mṛdu-svāntasya tasya hi
avijñāyāntaraṁ kiñcit
katham evaṁ tvayocyate
yūyaṁ śṛṇuta vṛttāni
tarhi tarhi śrutāni me

Rukmiṇī said: O mother, you don't understand the inner feelings of Kṛṣṇa at all. His heart is softer than freshly churned butter. Why are you saying these things? Just hear from me what I have heard.

You do not know the internal condition (antaram) of Kṛṣṇa, whose heart is softer than butter. If you know, you will never speak about it.

TEXT 51

kim api kim api brūte rātrau svapann api nāmabhir
madhura-madhuraṁ prītyā dhenūr ivāhvayati kvacit
uta sakhi-gaṇān kāṁścid gopān ivātha mano-harāṁ
samabhinayate vaṁśī-vaktrāṁ tri-bhaṅgi-parākṛtim

Sometimes at night he says this and that in his sleep. Sometimes, in a most sweet voice, he affectionately utters names as if calling his cows. Sometimes he calls his girlfriends or some of the cowherd boys. And sometimes while asleep he acts as if he were placing his flute to his mouth and assumes his enchanting threefold-bending form.

She describes his internal condition in four verses (51-54). He acts in this way even while sleeping, what to speak of his waking state. Sometimes he affectionately calls the cows by name, such as "Gaṅgā, Yamunā, Dhavalā, Kālindī." Uta indicates "all". He calls out to the cowherds with affection by name. Sometimes he acts as if the flute were in his mouth or imitates the deity form (ākṛtim) with his feet, hands and head slightly bent (tri-bhaṅgi). Kṛṣṇa is the subject of all these statements.

TEXT 52

kadācin mātar me vitara nava-nītaṁ tv iti vadet
kadācic chrī-rādhe lalita iti sambodhayati mām
kadāpīdaṁ candrāvali kim iti me karṣati paṭaṁ
kadāpy asrāsārair mṛdulayati tūlīṁ śayanataḥ

While asleep he sometimes says, "Mother, give me some fresh butter." Sometimes He calls out to me, "O Rādhā!" or "O Lalitā!" Sometimes he pulls my cloth and asks me, "Candrāvalī, what are you doing?" And sometimes he drenches the pillow on his bed with torrents of tears.

He calls out to me, thinking of stealing my clothes. "Why do you cheat me? What are you acting like this?" Saying this, he sometimes pulls my cloth. He sometimes moistens the pillow of the bed with torrents of tears.

TEXT 53

svapnād utthāya sadyo 'tha
rodity ārta-svarais tathā
vayaṁ yena nimajjāmo
duḥkha-śoka-mahārṇave

Then at times suddenly waking up, he rises from bed, and cries in a pitiful voice, drowning us in an ocean of pain and grief.

Having described his activities during sleep, now Rukmiṇī describes his actions during waking state in two verses (53-54). "After that (atha), waking up, rising from sleep, he cries. All of us queens (vayam) drown in an ocean of sorrow." She does not feel competition from the other queens, having special bhakti for the Lord.

TEXT 54

adyāpi dṛṣṭvā kim api svapan niśi
krandan śucāsau vimanaskatāturaḥ
dattvāmbaraṁ mūrdhani supta-vat sthito
nityāni kṛtyāny api nācarad bata

Just last night he must have seen something in a dream, because today he has been weeping sorrowfully and is beside himself with agitation. Now he is lying in bed as if asleep, his cloth pulled over his head. He has not even performed his daily duties.

What to speak of other days, today this has happened. Seeing something in a dream, he cries in lamentation even in the day while awake. He speaks with lamentation. He covers his head with his yellow silk cloth. This is a sign of great lamentation. He pretends to sleep. Because of great mental anguish, he cannot sleep. Remaining in bed (sthitaḥ), he does not perform his daily duties. Or he remained there, pretending to sleep.

TEXT 55

śrī-parīkṣid uvāca
sa-sapatnī-gaṇā serṣyaṁ
satyabhāmāha bhāminī
he śrī-rukmiṇi nidrāyām
iti kiṁ tvaṁ prajalpasi

Parīkṣit said: Then temperamental Satyabhāmā, surrounded by other wives, spoke out of jealousy. She said, "Dear Rukmiṇī, why are you prattling on like this? Why talk only about what he does while asleep?

Satyabhāmā spoke out of jealousy. Why do you talk of what he does while sleeping?

TEXT 56

kim api kim api kurvan jāgrad apy ātma-citte
śayita iva vidhatte tādṛśaṁ tādṛśaṁ ca

vayam iha kila bhāryā nāmato vastutaḥ syuḥ
paśupa-yuvati-dāsyo 'py asmad asya priyās tāḥ

"Even while active and awake, he seems to have his mind on something else, as if dreaming. Indeed, we are his wives in name only; his young cowherd maidservants are in fact dearer to him than we are."

What is he thinking even while awake? He acts as if he were asleep: calling the cows, etc. as you described. He does this repeatedly (tādṛṣām tādṛśām). Or the repetition indicates that waking and sleeping states are the same. Thus we are his wives in name only. Actually, even the menial servants of the young cowherd girls are dearer to Kṛṣṇa than we are.

TEXT 57

śrī-parīkṣid uvāca
aśaktas tad-vacaḥ soḍhuṁ
gokula-prāṇa-bāndhavaḥ
rohiṇī-nandanaḥ śrīmān
baladevo ruṣābravīt

Parīkṣit said: Baladeva, the darling son of Rohiṇī and intimate friend of all Gokula, couldn't tolerate hearing these words. He replied angrily.

Hearing the words of Rukmiṇī and others, Balarāma, most dear to the people of Gokula, who gave joy to Rohiṇī by the words he would speak (rohiṇī-nandanaḥ), spoke in anger, since he considered those words false or since he could analyze the deception of Kṛṣṇa.

TEXT 58

śrī-baladeva uvāca
vadhvaḥ sahaja-tatratya-
dainya-vārtā-kathā-parān
asmān vañcayato bhrātur
idaṁ kapaṭa-pāṭavam

Baladeva said: O ladies, all this is nothing but my brother's clever deception. We are intent on speaking about the natural miserable condition of the residents of Vraja — misery all too real — and he is simply cheating us.

O ladies! Kṛṣṇa's actions while sleeping are a skillful deception. He cheats us. All the actions are for deceiving us, who are intent on speaking about the natural miserable condition of the people of Vraja. Though the information is true, what efforts will he not make by deception to give us enjoyment? By inferring his deception, understand the truth about my brother. He manifests this deception in order to satisfy us. He cannot fool us by skillful words in speaking naturally. Being skillful in actions, he acts in this way to fool us.

TEXT 59

tatra māsa-dvayaṁ sthitvā
teṣāṁ svāsthyaṁ cikīrṣatā
tan na śaktaṁ mayā kartuṁ
vāgbhir ācaritair api

I stayed there in Vraja for two months and tried to restore the Vraja-vāsīs to normality, but nothing I said or did was of any avail.

He illustrates what he said in four verses (59-62). Wanting to restore the people of Vraja to normal condition, I stayed there for two months, but could not normalize their condition, by words or by actions. He spoke as follows. "Kṛṣṇa is suffering from separation from you. He sent me here quickly to pacify you. Destroying the enemies, he will come soon." He played in the Yamunā waters and built houses for Kṛṣṇa's pastimes in various places.

TEXT 60

ananya-sādhyaṁ tad vīkṣya
vividhaiḥ śapathaiḥ śataiḥ
tān yatnād īṣad āśvāsya
tvarayātrāgataṁ balāt

Seeing no other way to achieve my purpose, I made hundreds of promises to them and with great effort finally pacified them to some extent. Then I managed to pull myself away and hurried back here.

Seeing it was not possible to console them except by bringing Kṛṣṇa (ānanda). I said "Kṛṣṇa will definitely come. I will go there and bring him here." By such words I pacified the people of Vraja (tān) a little. Quickly I came to Dvārakā by force, since they did not permit me to leave.

TEXT 61

kātaryād gaditaṁ kṛṣṇa
sakṛd goṣṭhaṁ kayāpi tat

gatvā prasaṅga-saṅgatyā
rakṣa tatratya-jīvanam

I anxiously requested, "O Kṛṣṇa, please find some excuse to go to your cowherd village drowning in sorrow just once and save the lives of the people there."

Go once to that village (goṣṭham) which is the place of your infant pastimes (tat), or which is drowning in an ocean of sorrow, by some (kayā) means (saṅgatyā) such as an event or connected to some issue (prasaṅga). Protect the lives of Nanda and others (tatraya-jīvanam). I said this because of their great grief (which was previously described.)

TEXT 62

gantāsmīti mukhe brūte
hṛdayaṁ ca na tādṛśam
mānasasya ca bhāvasya
bhavet sākṣi prayojanam

With his mouth he said, "Certainly I shall go," but in his heart he thought otherwise. Indeed, the truth about a person's mind can be known from how he acts.

His heart is not similar to his words since (hi) actions (prayojanam) reveal (sākṣī) intentions in the mind (mānasya bhāvasya). Since he will not go, his words and his heart are different. This proves his deceptive nature.

TEXT 63

śrī-parīkṣid uvāca
idam ākarṇya bhagavān
utthāya śayanād drutam
priya-prema-parādhīno
rudann uccair bahir gataḥ

Parīkṣit said: Hearing this, the Lord, who is controlled by the prema of his devotees, suddenly got up from his bed and came outside, loudly weeping.

Hearing what Balarāma had said, he went out of the room and wept loudly. "How was this possible for the Lord?" He is controlled by the love of his devotees. This is the nature of Bhagavān.

TEXT 64

praphulla-padma-netrābhyāṁ
varṣann aśrūṇi dhārayā
sa-gadgadaṁ jagādedaṁ
parānugraha-kātaraḥ

From his fully blossoming lotus eyes rained a flood of tears. With a choking voice, tormented by compassion for others, he spoke as follows.

Helpless (kātaraḥ) with the highest compassion (parānugraha) he spoke. Or he who is filled with compassion even for the enemies (para) spoke. Thus he must act for his devotees.

TEXT 65

śrī-bhagavān uvāca
satyam eva mahā-vajra-
sāreṇa ghaṭitaṁ mama
idaṁ hṛdayam adyāpi
dvidhā yan na vidīryati

The Supreme Lord said: Yes, it is true. My heart is a thunderbolt. It must be so, because it has not yet split into two.

My heart does not split (vidīryati) in two parts.

TEXT 66

bālyād ārabhya tair yat tat
pālanaṁ vihitaṁ ciraṁ
apy asādhāraṇaṁ prema
sarvaṁ tad vismṛtaṁ mayā

Those devotees took care of me for so long, from the very beginning of my childhood, and still I have forgotten all about their exceptional prema.

The cause for his heart splitting is explained in two verses (66-67). Protection, indescribable or famous (tat), was given by the people of Vraja (taiḥ). I forgot all their prema.

TEXT 67

astu tāvad dhitaṁ teṣāṁ
kāryaṁ kiñcit kathañcana

utātyantaṁ kṛtaṁ duḥkhaṁ
krūreṇa mṛdulātmanām

Be that as it may, I must somehow do something to benefit them. I have indeed been cruel to have caused those gentle souls such extreme grief.

By some means (kathañcana), by some little help (kiñcit), I must act for their benefit. Let that be (tāvad astu). Rather (uta) I have made the people of Vraja, having tender natures, most unhappy, because I am cruel.

TEXT 68

bhrātar uddhava sarva-jña
preṣṭha-śreṣṭha vada drutam
karavāṇi kim ity asmāc
chokābdher māṁ samuddhara

O brother Uddhava, you are all-knowing, and you are the best of my dear friends. Please tell me at once what I should do. Please lift me from this ocean of distress.

Overcome with grief, as if not knowing what to do, he asks Uddhava. O best of dear friends! Tell me what I should do. Deliver me from the ocean of distress caused by Vraja (asmāt).

TEXT 69

śrī-parīkṣid uvāca
nanda-patnī-priya-sakhī
devakī putra-vatsalā
āhedaṁ dīyatāṁ yad yad
iṣyate taiḥ suhṛt-tamaiḥ

Parīkṣit said: Devakī was affectionate to her son and was a dear friend to Nanda's wife. She said, "You should give your best well-wishers whatever they desire!"

Worrying that Uddhava would say that Kṛṣṇa should return to Vraja, and that she would be separated from her son, Devakī spoke before Uddhava could speak. Being the dear friend of Yaśodā, Devakī said, "Give them what they desire" since she was affectionate to her son. Whatever is desired by the people of Vraja, the best well-wishers (suhṛttamaiḥ), should be given by you to them.

TEXTS 70–72

tataḥ padmāvatī rājya-
dāna-bhītā vimūḍha-dhīḥ
mahiṣī yadu-rājasya
vṛddhā mātāmahī prabhoḥ

apy uktāśravaṇāt pūrvaṁ
rāma-mātrāvahelitā
sva-bhartū rakṣituṁ rājyaṁ
cāturyāt parihāsa-vat

vyāhāra-paripāṭyānya-
cittatāpādanena tam
yadu-vaṁśyaika-śaraṇaṁ
vidhātuṁ svastham abravīt

Then, fearing that the kingdom was about to be given away, old Padmāvatī, the Lord's grandmother, the queen of the Yadu king Ugrasena, gathered her muddled wits and cleverly feigned a joking spirit. To protect her husband's kingdom, she spoke up again, even though Balarāma's mother had snubbed her by ignoring her previous remarks. Invoking eloquence, Padmāvatī tried to change the mood, to bring Kṛṣṇa, the exclusive shelter of the Yadu dynasty, back to normal.

After that (tataḥ), or because of Devakī's words, Padmāvatī feared the kingdom would be given away. She spoke as if joking. Three verses are connected. She was the queen of Ugrasena and therefore the Kṛṣṇa's grandmother. Not hearing what Padmāvatī had previously said, Rohiṇī had offended her. She spoke skillfully with joking, but without intelligence, because she wanted to protect her husband's kingdom. Or what she spoke, that appeared to be a joke, was spoken with cleverness.

"It is unsuitable to speak in this way when Kṛṣṇa is in great lamentation." She spoke to bring Kṛṣṇa to a normal state by changing the mood (anya-cittatā). Why? Kṛṣṇa was the shelter of persons such as Ugrasena in the Yadu dynasty (eka-śaranam). If Kṛṣṇa was not well, the Yadus would perish.

TEXTS 73–75

padmāvaty uvāca
tvayānutapyate kṛṣṇa
kathaṁ man-mantritaṁ śṛṇu

yad ekādaśabhir varṣair
nanda-gopasya mandire

dvābhyāṁ yuvābhyāṁ bhrātṛbhyām
upabhuktaṁ hi vartate
tatra dadyān na dadyād vā
go-rakṣā-jīvanaṁ sa te

sarvaṁ tad garga-hastena
gaṇayitvā kaṇāṇuśaḥ
dvi-guṇī-kṛtya mad-bhartrā
tasmai deyaṁ śape svayam

Padmāvatī said: Kṛṣṇa, why should you lament? Just listen to my advice. While living eleven years in the home of Nanda, you two brothers enjoyed various comforts. For that, I swear, my husband will repay Nanda twice over. My husband will see to it that Garga Muni calculates the amount to the smallest fraction and delivers it by his own hand. And if Nanda owes you payment for tending his cows, let him pay you or not, as he wishes.

Why should you lament? You two enjoyed in Nanda's house for eleven years. My husband Ugrasena will give Nanda twice that amount. Let Nanda pay or not pay you two for tending the cows. If Nanda just accepts this payment for boarding you two, you and I do not have to insist on charging him for your taking care of the cows. The amount can be calculated to the cent. This shows the generosity of her husband. Garga will calculate the amount. Being an astrologer, he could calculate without making mistakes. Nanda will receive the total amount due.

Her hidden meaning was that Nanda would not be overpaid. Referring to Nanda as a cowherd (gopa) she indicates that other than cow products, Nanda did not have other items of enjoyment. The amount should be paid for the upkeep of the two brothers. However, no amount should be paid for Rohiṇī who also stayed in Vraja with her maid servants, since Padmāvatī was angry with her for ignoring her words.

tato nanda-vrajam itaḥ
pitrā kaṁsād vibibhyatā
ekādaśa samās tatra
gūḍhārciḥ sa-balo 'vasat

His father, afraid of Kaṁsa, brought him to Vraja and for eleven years he lived there with Balarāma, like a covered flame. SB 3.2.26

He stayed for eleven years hidden. This does not mean that he stayed longer but not hidden. Akrūra came to take him to Mathurā when he was in his kaiśora period.

kiśorau śyāmala-śvetau śrī-niketau bṛhad-bhujau
su-mukhau sundara-varau bala-dvirada-vikramau

One of those two mighty-armed youths, the shelters of the goddess of fortune, had a dark-blue complexion, and the other's was white. With their fine-featured faces they were the most beautiful of all persons. They walked with the gait of young elephants, glancing about with compassionate smiles. SB 10.38.29

When the young women of Mathurā saw Kṛṣṇa he was of kaiśora age.

kva vajra-sāra-sarvāṅgau mallau śailendra-sannibhau
kva cāti-sukumārāṅgau kiśorau nāpta-yauvanau

What comparison can there be between these two professional wrestlers, with limbs as strong as lightning bolts and bodies resembling mighty mountains, and these two young, immature boys with exceedingly tender limbs? SB 10.44.8

Kiśora means eleven years old. After killing Kaṁsa Kṛṣṇa received his sacred thread. This is given at the age of eleven according to kṣatriya custom. The Lord says to Devakī and Vasudeva at the wrestling arena:

nāsmatto yuvayos tāta nityotkaṇṭhitayor api
bālya-paugaṇḍa-kaiśorāḥ putrābhyām abhavan kvacit

Dear Father, because of us, your two sons, you and mother Devakī always remained in anxiety and could never enjoy our childhood, boyhood or youth. SB 10.45.3

The meaning is this. They did not have the happiness of the two boys during their childhood, boyhood and youth. They did not have the happiness of their kaiśora pastimes. Since in Mathurā he revealed pastimes with great power, the sweetness of his Vraja kaiśora pastimes were not manifested there. Vasudeva and Devakī could not experience that type of happiness.

It is said that in Mathurā he manifested tāruṇya (after kaiśora) form and activities. But this actually means that he had special beauty, in an intense manner, even during kaiśora age, which was equivalent to his childhood period. It does not mean that he was older, since it is accepted that his age was actually kaiśora.

Or Kṛṣṇa went from Gokula to Mathurā at the very end of his kaiśora period when he was fifteen years old, since Bilvamaṅgala and others describe that he manifested yauvana in Vraja and manifested adult pastimes there. Though it is not impossible for Kṛṣṇa to manifest adult qualities even in his bālya period, since he manifests great strength, his being fifteen years old is widely accepted since it is most attractive, with manifestation of special rasa and a mature form. There should be no worry that this is incorrect, since because Kṛṣṇa was naturally very tender, it appeared that he has just entered kaiśora period (even at the end of the period). Thus it is concluded (by some) that he lived in Vraja for fifteen years. For the first four years of his life he drank his mother's breast milk. Subtracting that from fifteen years, one is left with eleven years (which is used to calculate how much of Nanda's milk he consumed and thus determines the amount of payment due to him by Ugrasena).

TEXT 76

śrī-parīkṣid uvāca
tac ca śrī-bhagavān kṛtvā
śrutam apy aśrutaṁ yathā
ajānann iva papraccha
śoka-vegād athoddhavam

Parīkṣit said: Although the Lord must have heard these words, he pretended he had not. Driven by sorrow, he then inquired from Uddhava as though ignorant.

Though he must have heard Padmāvatī's words (tat-śrutam) with full attention, he seemed not to hear the words at all, since he did not acknowledge them. Though he knew what he should do and knew what the people of Vraja desired, because of great lamentation he appeared not to know. Thus after his lamentation he inquired from Uddhava.

TEXT 77

śrī-bhagavān uvāca
bho vidvad-vara tatratyā-
khilābhiprāya-vid bhavān
teṣām abhīṣṭaṁ kiṁ tan me
kathayatv avilambitam

The Supreme Lord said: O best of learned scholars, you know all the thoughts of the residents of Vraja. Please tell me without delay what they desire.

O you who know the mentality of the people of Vraja! Please tell what they desire. Devakī has said that they should been given what they desired. Though he knows that their desires will not be fulfilled by giving anything, and that only his going to Vraja will satisfy them, he asks the question with the motive that if the best of advisors says that he must go, using logical words, no one present could prevent him. Thus he asks the question. Previously he was motived by his lamentation.

TEXT 78

śrī-parīkṣid uvāca
tac chrutvā bhagavad-vākyam
uddhavo hṛdi duḥkhitaḥ
kṣaṇaṁ niśvasya vismeraḥ
sānutāpaṁ jagāda tam

Parīkṣit said: Having heard these words from the Lord, the despondent Uddhava was taken aback. He sighed briefly and then answered, full of remorse.

Uddhava because of intense prema did not understand the purport of the Lord's words. Hearing the words literally, he became despondent. Hearing the words of such a (tat) Lord who is omniscient or a lion of mercy, he felt sad in his heart, because he thought Kṛṣṇa was cheating again. He was surprised because he thought that acting in this way, giving the dear devotees of Vraja some gift was not proper. Sighing loudly for a moment, he spoke to the Lord (tat) in a remorseful way or he spoke something (tat) which was filled with remorse.

TEXT 79

śrīmad-uddhava uvāca
na rāja-rājeśvaratā-vibhūtīr
na divya-vastūni ca te bhavattaḥ
na kāmayante 'nyad apīha kiñcid
amutra ca prāpyam ṛte bhavantam

Uddhava said: The people of Vraja don't want from you the power and wealth of emperors, nor the enjoyments found in heaven, nor anything

else obtainable in this world or the next. They do not desire anything except you.

The people like Nanda (te) do not desire wealth or power as rulers of kings or heavenly objects like the pārijāta, or anything attainable in this world (iha) or the next (amutra) from you. They do not desire anything except you. They desire the Lord only.

TEXT 80

avadhāna-prasādo 'tra
kriyatāṁ jñāpayāmi yat
paścād vicārya kartavyaṁ
svayam eva yathocitam

Kindly favor me with your attention. Think over what I am about to say and then act as you see fit.

Uddhava speaks so that Kṛṣṇa will understand what he will describe. What I will tell you, should be mercifully heard by you with attention (avadhāna-prasādaḥ). You should do what I will reveal to you (svayam).

TEXT 81

pūrvaṁ nandasya saṅgatyā
bhavatā preṣitāni te
bhūṣaṇādīni dṛṣṭvocur
mitho magnāḥ śug-ambudhau

Previously, when the cowherds met Nanda and saw the jewels and other gifts you had sent with him, they spoke among themselves, all of them immersed in an ocean of grief:

Previously, after Kaṁsa was killed (pūrvam), the people of Vraja, Yaśodā, Rādhā, and others (te), seeing the ornaments sent by you, spoke among themselves, drowning in an ocean of grief. The feminine gender is not used since the subject of the gopīs is secret.

TEXT 82

aho bata mahat kaṣṭaṁ
vayam etad-abhīpsavaḥ
etat-prasāda-yogyāś ca
jñātāḥ kṛṣṇena samprati

"Oh, how very painful! Kṛṣṇa now thinks we want such presents from him and deserve this kind of mercy.

Their statement is described in two verses (82-83). Now (samprati), he thinks that we desire these ornaments and that this giving or mercy is suitable for him. Otherwise he would not have sent them. Previously he did not think like this but now he does. How unfortunate for us. Samprati can also be connected to the next verse.

TEXT 83

tad asmaj-jīvanaṁ dhig dhik
tiṣṭhet kaṇṭhe 'dhunāpi yat
nanda-gopāṁś ca dhig dhig ye
taṁ tyaktvaitāny upānayan

"Damn our lives and the breath that still moves in our throats! And damn Nanda and the cowherd men! They left Kṛṣṇa and brought these ornaments."

Therefore our lives are most despicable since our lives are now in our throats. The people of Vraja live only by the air passing through their throats. The cowherds of Nanda are most despicable since they left Kṛṣṇa and brought these ornaments. This indicates that Nanda himself could not give up Kṛṣṇa (but the cowherds could). Or the plural is used out of respect to indicate Nanda. Or Nanda and the other cowherds are despicable since they left Kṛṣṇa and brought ornaments.

TEXT 84

tatas tvad-gamanāśāṁ ca
hitvā saha yaśodayā
mṛta-prāyā bhavan-mātrā-
rebhire 'naśanaṁ mahat

Thus the residents of Vraja, including your mother Yaśodā, have given up all hope of your return. Already dead, they now refuse to eat at all.

Because of what was described (tataḥ), giving up hope that you will come to Vraja, they are almost dead. Along with your mother, they are fasting till death, by giving up water, etc. Thus they do not desire the things you sent. They desire only you.

TEXTS 85–86

kṛtāparādha-van nando
vaktuṁ kiñcid dina-trayam
aśakto 'tyanta-śokārto
vraja-prāṇān avan gatān

bhavatas tatra yānoktiṁ
grāhayan śapathotkaraiḥ
darśayan yukti-cāturyam
amūn evam asāntvayat

Nanda felt like someone who has committed a great offense, and for three days he was so utterly miserable he couldn't say a thing. But then, to save the lives of the people of Vraja, he induced them to believe your departing words. With many ardent promises, Nanda used logic to prove your words true. In this way he placated the Vraja-vāsīs.

In two verses, Uddhava pacifies Kṛṣṇa by indicating that nothing unfortunate ultimately happened at that time. Nanda did not speak for three days, feeling as if he had committed some offense. To protect (avan) the lives of the people of Vraja which had left their bodies (gatān prāṇān), with plenty of oaths he made them accept your words (uktim) that you would return (yāna) to Vraja.

yāta yūyaṁ vrajaṁn tāta vayaṁ ca sneha-duḥkhitān
jñātīn vo draṣṭum eṣyāmo vidhāya suhṛdāṁ sukham

Now you should all return to Vraja, dear father. We shall come to see you, our dear relatives who suffer in separation from us, as soon as we have given some happiness to your well-wishing friends. SB 10.45.23

In this way he pacified them. Though overcome with lamentation, because of separation from Kṛṣṇa and because the people desired to die, he showed his great skill in logic or he revealed to them the best reasons for living.

TEXT 87

śrī-nanda uvāca
dravyāṇy ādau prema-cihnāni putra
etāny atra prāhiṇot satya-vākyaḥ
śīghraṁ paścād āgamiṣyaty avaśyaṁ
tatratyaṁ sva-prastutārthaṁ samāpya

Nanda said: Our son is an honest person who always speaks the truth. He has first sent us these things as a sign of prema. He is sure to come back to us quickly, as soon as he finishes what he has to do in Mathurā.

The gifts are signs of his love. He sent them with prema, not as his mercy, thinking that is what you wanted. He is our son. By this he emphasizes the affectionate relationship or rejects the idea that Kṛṣṇa is attached to his relationship with Vasudeva. Later he will quickly return, since he tells the truth. "Why does he not come now?When will he come?" He will finish matters of the moment concerning his devotees (sva) related to Mathurā and not other places, such as eliminating Jarāsandha.

TEXT 88

śrutvā te tatra viśvasya
sarve sarala-mānasāḥ
bhavat-prītiṁ samālocyā-
laṅkārān dadhur ātmasu

Hearing these words the simple-hearted residents of Vraja believed them. Thinking about your loving affection, they accepted the ornaments and put it on their bodies.

They had faith in Kṛṣṇa's words (tatra viśvasya) because their minds were devoid of crookedness (sarala-mānasāḥ). They all believed his words according to their hearts. They all thought, "Kṛṣṇa will be pleased if we wear the ornaments." They placed the ornaments on their bodies. But they did not experience happiness in their hearts.

TEXT 89

śrī-kṛṣṇo 'tra samāgatya
prasāda-dravya-saṅgrahāt
vīkṣyājñā-pālakān asmān
nitarāṁ kṛpayiṣyati

They thought, "When Kṛṣṇa returns, he will see how we have followed his order by accepting these remnants of his enjoyment. Then he will show us special mercy."

Their intention is described. By accepting their ornaments, his mercy, he will see that we followed his order and will thus show more mercy than previously. They felt joy in their actions by following his order, though the circumstances were most lamentable.

TEXT 90

bhavān svayam agatvā tu
yaṁ sandeśaṁ samarpya mām
prāhiṇot tena te sarve
babhūvur nihatā iva

But you never came. You sent me instead. And when they heard the message you had sent with me, they almost died from disappointment.

They acted in one way but you acted in another way. You sent a message saying that you were the antaryāmī everywhere and that they should see you everywhere through a vision of jñāna.

bhavatīnāṁ viyogo me na hi sarvātmanā kvacit
yathā bhūtāni bhūteṣu khaṁ vāyv-agnir jalaṁ mahī
tathāhaṁ ca manaḥ-prāṇa-bhūtendriya-guṇāśrayaḥ

You are never actually separated from me, for I am the Soul of all creation. Just as the elements of nature—ether, air, fire, water and earth—are present in every created thing, so I am present within everyone's mind, life air and senses, and also within the physical elements and the modes of material nature. SB 10.47.29

The meaning is this. You are not separate from me. "Why?" I am situated in all effects such as the mind, since I am the cause of all elements (sarvātmanā). An example is given. The elements (bhūtāni) such as ether, air, fire, water and earth, are present in all moving and non-moving beings. Similarly I am present as the shelter of all causes (guṇas) and effects (mind, life air, senses). By that message they almost died since that destroyed their hope that you would return. They were as if dead (iva) since their life was all that remained in their bodies.

TEXT 91

tathā dṛṣṭyā mayā tatra
bhavato gamanaṁ dhruvam
pratijñāya prayatnāt tān
jīvayitvā samāgatam

Seeing them so despondent, I made every effort to keep them alive by promising that you would certainly return. Then I returned here.

Experiencing directly their condition (tathā dṛṣṭyā), promising that you would certainly come to Vraja, promising that I would bring you, I returned here.

TEXT 92

tvat-prāptaye 'tha sannyasta-
samasta-viṣayāśrayāḥ
prāpur yādṛg-avasthāṁ te
tāṁ pṛcchaitaṁ nijāgrajam

To attain you, these devotees then renounced enjoyment of all objects. Please ask your elder brother here what state they are in.

However, you did not go personally. You sent your elder brother. It is not possible for me to describe what state they were in. It would produce a most sorrowful state in me. With this intention Uddhava speaks. After I came here (atha) they rejected enjoyment of all objects (viṣayāśrayāḥ) or they gave up their shelters or houses (āśrayāḥ) and all sense enjoyment (viṣaya). They lived in the forest gazing at the places of Kṛṣṇa's pastimes. When Balarāma went to Vraja there is the following description:

kṛṣṇe kamala-patrākṣe sannyastākhila-rādhasaḥ

They gave up all wealth for lotus-eyed Kṛṣṇa. SB 10.65.6

This means that they gave up everything to attain Kṛṣṇa.

When Uddhava had gone to Vraja he did not see Rādhā and other gopīs in this state of renunciation. He saw them apparently happy, wearing the ornaments sent by Kṛṣṇa since they had faith in the consoling words of Nanda.

tā dīpa-dīptair maṇibhir virejū
rajjūr vikarṣad-bhuja-kaṅkaṇa-srajaḥ
calan-nitamba-stana-hāra-kuṇḍala-
tviṣat-kapolāruṇa-kuṅkumānanāḥ

As they pulled on the churning ropes with their bangled arms, the women of Vraja shone with the splendor of their jewels, which reflected the lamps' light. Their hips, breasts and necklaces moved about, and their faces, anointed with reddish kuṁkuma, glowed radiantly with the luster of their earrings reflecting from their cheeks.

udgāyatīnām aravinda-locanaṁ
vrajāṅganānāṁ divam aspṛśad dhvaniḥ
dadhnaś ca nirmanthana-śabda-miśrito
nirasyate yena diśām amaṅgalam

As the ladies of Vraja loudly sang the glories of lotus-eyed Kṛṣṇa, their songs blended with the sound of their churning, ascended to the sky and dissipated all inauspiciousness in every direction. SB 10.46.45-46

It would be impossible for them to be in this condition if they were overcome with grief. Now, because Uddhava had destroyed their hopes by delivering Kṛṣṇa's message, they attained a more miserable state than previously.

Uddhava asks about their state in the presence of his elder brother since Balarāma had gone there and directly experienced their condition. Or you may not believe my words, but you should believe the words of your elder brother.

TEXTS 93–94

śrī-parīkṣid uvāca
tad-viccheda-mahā-duḥkhā-
śaṅkayā mlāpitāni saḥ
devakī-bhīṣmajādīnāṁ
mukhāny avanatāny adhaḥ

kṣarad-asrāṇi sa-snehaṁ
vilokya mṛdulāśayaḥ
masī-karpara-patrāṇi
vyagro 'yācata saṁjñayā

Parīkṣit continued: Anticipating suffering of separation from Kṛṣṇa, the faces of the ladies like Devakī and Rukmiṇī were pale, downcast, and full of tears. Looking at those women affectionately, gentle-hearted Kṛṣṇa quickly gestured for an inkpot and paper.

What did the Lord, dear to the cowherd people, do next? That is described in four verses (93-96).

Looking at the faces of Devakī and others with affection, by a gesture he asked for ink and paper. The two verses are connected. Their faces had wilted because they feared separation from Kṛṣṇa (if he went to Vraja). Their faces were bowed down and were flowing with tears. He used a signal for the request because he was in a state of agitation (vyagraḥ). Because of the extreme disturbance when he heard Uddhava's words, he was unable to request using words. He could only signal his request.

"Why did he not immediately go to Vraja?" He had a very tender heart (mṛdulaḥ). He could not suddenly give up Devakī and others who were wretched and personally present, because he could not tolerate their anguish.

TEXTS 95–96

prastutārthaṁ samādhāyā-
tratyān āśvāsya bāndhavān
eṣo 'ham āgata-prāya
iti jānīta mat-priyāḥ

evam āśvāsanaṁ prema-
patraṁ preṣayituṁ vraje
sva-hastenaiva likhitaṁ
tac ca gāḍha-pratītaye

In order strengthen the faith of his Vraja devotees, Kṛṣṇa wanted to send them a letter filled with loving sentiments and written by his own hand: "My dear residents of Vraja, please know that as soon as I settle the duties before me and satisfy my relatives here, I will return in no time. I will be there."

Why did he request the ink and paper? Two verses explain. He requested the ink and paper in order to send a love letter to Vraja, written by his own hand, in order strengthen their faith. What should the letter say?

"My dear residents of Vraja!" This indicates his great affection. "As soon as I have concluded necessary duties which have arisen, and having consoled the Yadus living in Dvārakā, have faith that I will come." The letter should console them in this manner (evam). Or in the manner stated he would console them (evam).

TEXT 97

tasyehitam abhipretya
prāpto 'tyantārtim uddhavaḥ
vraja-vāsi-mano-'bhijño
'bravīt sa-śapathaṁ rudan

Uddhava understood what Kṛṣṇa was about to do and was therefore greatly distressed. Knowing the inner hearts of the Vraja-vāsīs, he cried and begged Kṛṣṇa to reconsider his plans.

Understanding his intention to just send a letter, Uddhava became filled with pain. Crying, he spoke with some scolding (sa-śapatham).

TEXT 98

śrīmad-uddhava uvāca
prabho su-nirṇītam idaṁ pratīhi
tvadīya-pādābja-yugasya tatra
śubha-prayāṇaṁ na vināsya jīved
vrajaḥ kathañcin na ca kiñcid icchet

Uddhava said, O master, please turn your attention to this: Unless your two lotus feet make an auspiscious journey to Vraja, there is no way to assure that your people of Vraja will survive. Those people want nothing but your lotus feet.

Without the auspicious journey to Vraja of your sweet, attractive lotus feet, the people of Vraja will not live by any other means. They do not desire a letter sending messages of prema. Understand that I have discerned this. All other forms such as antaryāmī are rejected by his statement.

TEXT 99

śrī-parīkṣid uvāca
ku-matiḥ kaṁsa-mātāha
sa-hāsaṁ dhunvatī śiraḥ
hum hum devaki nirbuddhe
buddhaṁ buddhaṁ mayādhunā

Parīkṣit said: The befuddled Padmāvatī laughed at this, shook her head, and burst out: Aha! Aha, foolish Devakī, now I understand. I understand everything!

Padmāvatī laughed in order to make Uddhava's words appear insignificant. She laughed while shaking her head. Hum hum indicates her deep thinking or her great pain. O foolish Devakī! Budham is repeated to enforce the meaning: I understand very well.

TEXT 100

ciraṁ go-rasa-dānena
yantritasyoddhavasya te
sāhāyyāt tvat-sutaṁ gopā
nāyayitvā punar vane

With the help of Uddhava, whom the cowherds have brought under control by gifts of milk goods, those cowherds want to bring Kṛṣṇa back to the forest.

She speaks two verses (100-101). The cowherds headed by Nanda (te), bringing your son Kṛṣṇa back to the forest, desire him to herd the cows. Uddhava stayed for a long time in Vraja.

uvāsa katicin māsān gopīnāṁ vinudan śucaḥ
kṛṣṇa-līlā-kathāṁ gāyan ramayām āsa gokulam

Uddhava remained there for several months, dispelling the gopīs' sorrow by chanting the topics of Kṛṣṇa's pastimes. Thus he brought joy to all the people of Gokula. SB 10.47.54

Uddhava is controlled by their giving him buttermilk and other milk products.

TEXT 101

bhīṣaṇe durgame duṣṭa-
sattva-juṣṭe sa-kaṇṭake
saṁrakṣayitum icchanti
dhūrtāḥ paśu-gaṇān nijān

In that dangerous forest, hard to travel, full of thorns and vicious beasts, those frauds want to make him tend their cows.

"Why do they have to bring Kṛṣṇa? Can they not herd the cows themselves?" They fear tigers and other creatures. In the forest wicked animals like tigers and lions live. They want to bring Kṛṣṇa because they are crafty (dhūrtāḥ): they want to protect their own sons and send someone else's son to the forest.

TEXT 102

śrī-parīkṣid uvāca
tac chrutvā kutsitaṁ vākyam
aśaktā soḍhum añjasā
yaśodāyāḥ priya-sakhī
rāma-mātāha kopitā

Parīkṣit said: Balarāma's mother Rohiṇī, Yaśodā's dear friend, couldn't tolerate hearing these insults. Angrily, she replied.

Rohiṇī could not tolerate the vile words of Padmāvatī. Padmāvatī had spoken in this way because of her particular type of intense prema. Angered Rohiṇī spoke. Or she spoke, making Padmāvatī angry.

TEXT 103

śrī-rohiṇy uvāca
āḥ kaṁsa-mātaḥ kim ayaṁ
go-rakṣāyāṁ niyujyate
kṣaṇa-mātraṁ ca tatratyair
adṛṣṭe 'smin na jīvyate

Rohiṇī said: Indeed, O mother of Kaṁsa, will they just engage him in caring for cows? Unless the devotees there see him, they can't stay alive a single moment!

Ā expresses her anger. O mother of Kaṁsa! She hints that Padmāvatī has a wicked mind like Kaṁsa. Will Kṛṣṇa be engaged in herding cows only by the people of Vraja (tatratyaiḥ)? No. They cannot live for a moment not seeing Kṛṣṇa.

TEXT 104

vṛkṣādibhis tv antarite kadācid
asmin sati syāt saha-cāriṇāṁ bhṛśam
śrī-kṛṣṇa kṛṣṇeti mahā-pluta-svarair
āhvāna-bhaṅgyākulatā sa-rodanā

O chaste woman, if trees or other obstacles block Kṛṣṇa from sight even briefly, his companions at once shed tears and call in anxious, loud voices, "Kṛṣṇa! Kṛṣṇa!"

This is further explained in two verses (104-105). O chaste woman (sati)! This address in anger has the opposite meaning, since her chastity was broken by association with the demon Drumila. Sometimes when looking at the beauty of the Vṛndāvana forest, when the view of Kṛṣṇa becomes blocked by trees, his companions like Śrīdāma become disturbed with crying, with gestures indicating that they do not know where he is and with loud voices (mahāpluta-svaraiḥ).

TEXT 105

vraja-sthitānāṁ tv ahar eva kāla-
rātrir bhaved eka-lavo yugaṁ ca

raviṁ rajo-vartma ca paśyatāṁ muhur
daśā ca kācin muralīṁ ca śṛṇvatām

For those who live in Vraja, daytime is like the dark night of pralaya, and the blink of an eye a yuga. In such a state, they look at the sun and the trails of dust on the road again and again and listen for the sound of the flute.

For the people living in Vraja such as Rādhā, even the day is like the night of pralaya (kāla-ratriḥ). One moment is like four yugas. A short time seems like a long time. Causes of previous happiness become causes of suffering.

aṭati yad bhavān ahni kānanaṁ
truṭi yugāyate tvām apaśyatām
kuṭila-kuntalaṁ śrī-mukhaṁ ca te
jaḍa udīkṣatāṁ pakṣma-kṛd dṛśām

When you go off to the forest during the day, a tiny fraction of a second becomes like a millennium for us because we cannot see you. And even when we can eagerly look upon your beautiful face, so lovely with its adornment of curly locks, we think the creator was foolish in making eyelids. SB 10.31.15

They look at the sun, in order know when Kṛṣṇa is coming. Constantly they go outside the house and look at the path of dust raised by the cows. This is a sign that Kṛṣṇa is coming. They listen to the sound of his flute in the afternoon. They attain a state of madness because of most intense prema (daśā). The desire that he, instead of their sons, just go to the forest and herd cows does not occur to any of them, though this is Padmāvatī's accusation.

TEXT 106

ayaṁ hi tat-tad-vipineṣu kautukād
vihartu-kāmaḥ paśu-saṅgha-saṅgataḥ
vayasya-vargaiḥ saha sarvato 'ṭituṁ
prayāti nityaṁ svayam agrajānvitaḥ

Every day, Kṛṣṇa takes his older brother with him and goes out into the various forests, eager to enjoy with his herds of cows and wander about in the company of his many friends.

"Then how did he herd the cows there?" This is explained in five verses (106-110). Desiring to play in the most indescribable (tat tat) forests of

Vṛndāvana, he would go out daily with his friends to wander about (aṭitum) everywhere, since in herding the cows he would walk far away. He did this along with Balarāma, with great enthusiasm or with great wonder on seeing the forest (kautukāt).

TEXT 107

yatrāti-mattāmbu-vihaṅga-mālā-
kulī-kṛtāly-āvalī-vibhrameṇa
vicālitānāṁ kamalotpalānāṁ
sarāṁsi gandhair vilasaj-jalāni

In those forests are lakes with sparkling water, where kamala and utpala lotuses spread their fragrance. The lotuses tremble from the movements of swarms of agitated bees and flocks of excited water birds.

Because they took joy in the forests, the forests are described in four verses (107-110). In the forests (yatra) there are lakes, whose waters sport with the fragrance of kamalas and utpalas, which are moved about by the flocks of excited water birds like cranes and cakravākas and swarms of agitated bees.

TEXT 108

tathā mahāścarya-vicitratā-mayī
kalinda-jā sā vraja-bhūmi-saṅginī
tathā-vidhā vindhya-nagādi-sambhavāḥ
parāś ca nadyo vilasanti yatra ca

And in those forests flows the river Yamunā, the dearmost companion of the land of Vraja. The picturesque splendor of that river, the daughter of Kalinda, astonishes the mind. And besides her, Vraja-bhūmi glistens with other rivers, the offspring of hills like the Vindhyas.

In this manner (tathā) or "with all that has been said" Yamunā exists in the forests or plays in the forests. The number changes however from singular to plural (vilasanti). She causes astonishment with the great variety of her banks and other features. She is most indescribably beautiful (sā) because she is related to the land of Vraja. In the forests other rivers like Mānasa-gaṅgā play or radiate beauty (vilasanti), similar to the Yamunā (tathā-vidhāḥ).

TEXT 109

tat-tat-taṭaṁ komala-vālukācitaṁ
ramyaṁ sadā nūtana-śādvalāvṛtam
svābhāvika-dveṣa-visarjanollasan-
manojña-nānā-mṛga-pakṣi-saṅkulam

The beautiful shores of those rivers are always heaped with soft sand and covered by newly grown grass. To those shores come many different kinds of charming animals and birds, putting their natural enmity aside.

In the forest there exist the most indescribable (tat tat) shores (taṭam) or the shores of the lakes and rivers (tat tat). Or the shores are pleasant, not terrifying (ramyam). The shores are endowed with soft sand. Thus they are not inaccessible with thorns nor terrifying (as described by Padmāvatī). The word sadā (always) can be applied to all the descriptive elements of the banks. The banks are always covered with green grass. Thus there is no suffering in herding the cows. The shores are covered with various attractive birds and animals which play with each other, or are glorious to the highest degree (ullasan) because they give up natural enmity (such as mongoose and snake, or deer and tiger). This rejects Padmāvatī's claim that the forest is filled with wicked beasts. This description shows how the place causes happiness in Kṛṣṇa's playing.

TEXT 110

divya-puṣpa-phala-pallavāvalī-
bhāra-namrita-latā-taru-gulmaiḥ
bhūṣitaṁ mada-kalāpi-kokila-
śreṇi-nāditam aja-stuti-pātram

Trees, creepers, and shrubs further decorate the shores, bowing down with the weight of splendid flowers, fruits, and buds. The shores resound with the calls of maddened peacocks and cuckoos. And those shores receive praise even from Lord Brahmā.

The shores are decorated with trees, creepers and shrubs, bowing down with loads of clusters of flowers, fruits and buds and resounding with flocks of intoxicated peacocks and cuckoos. The shores are the object of praise of even Brahmā.

tad bhūri-bhāgyam iha janma kim apy aṭavyāṁ
yad gokule 'pi katamāṅghri-rajo-'bhiṣekam
yaj-jīvitaṁ tu nikhilaṁ bhagavān mukundas
tv adyāpi yat-pada-rajaḥ śruti-mṛgyam eva

My greatest possible good fortune would be to take any birth whatever in this forest of Gokula and have my head bathed by the dust falling from the lotus feet of any of its residents. Their entire life and soul is the Lord, Mukunda, the dust of whose lotus feet is sought even today by the Upaniṣads. SB 10.14.34

TEXT 111

vṛndāraṇye vraja-bhuvi gavāṁ tatra govardhane vā
nāste hiṁsā-haraṇa-rahite rakṣakasyāpy apekṣā
gāvo gatvoṣasi vipinatas tā mahiṣy-ādi-yuktāḥ
svairaṁ bhuktvā sa-jala-yavasaṁ sāyam āyānti vāsam

Vṛndāvana Forest, Govardhana Hill, and the whole area of Vraja are free from violence and theft. So one need not bother to watch one's cows. The cows simply go out into the forests in the morning with the buffaloes and other domestic animals, eat grass and drink water as they like, and then in the evening come home.

There is no suffering for Kṛṣṇa caused by his herding the cows. In Vṛndāvana, and in Nandīśvara and other places (vraja-bhuvi), or in Vṛndāvana in Vraja, and at Govardhana, one does not need to worry about protecting the cows. "Why?" There is absence of theft and violence from tigers etc. "How do the unintelligent animals maintain their lives then?" Those cows of Vraja or the indescribable cows (tāḥ), going to the forest in the early morning, eat juicy (sa-jalam) grass or grass with water freely, at their will, and in the evening go home to Vraja from the forest. Goats (ādayaḥ) also go along with the cows and buffalos.

ajā gāvo mahiṣyaś ca nirviśantyo vanād vanam
īṣīkāṭavīṁ nirviviśuḥ krandantyo dāva-tarṣitāḥ

Passing from one part of the great forest to another, the goats, cows and buffalo eventually entered an area overgrown with sharp canes. Thirsty because of the heat of the summer sun, they cried out in distress. SB 10.19.2

TEXT 112

vṛddhovāca
are bāle 'ti-vācāle
tat kathaṁ te gavādayaḥ
adhunā rakṣakābhāvān
naṣṭā iti niśamyate

Elderly Padmāvatī said: You child, you are too free with your words! If what you say is true, then why do we hear that the cows and other animals in Vraja are now in danger of dying because no one is taking care of them?

Why have the cows been destroyed without Kṛṣṇa taking care of them, since he is not there? It is not a lie. This is heard everywhere (iti). You said the cows do not need a herder to protect them. That is incorrect. Therefore you are ignorant and too talkative.

TEXT 113

śrī-parīkṣid uvāca
śrīmad-gopāla-devas tac
chrutvā sambhrānti-yantritaḥ
jātāntas-tāpataḥ śuṣyan-
mukhābjaḥ śaṅkayākulaḥ

Parīkṣit said: Having heard all this, the Lord Gopāla felt overwrought with worry for his devotees. Scorching anxiety dried up his lotus face. He was filled with dread.

TEXT 114

prathamāpara-kālīna-
vraja-vṛttānta-vedinaḥ
mukham ālokayām āsa
baladevasya sāśrukam

He glanced at the face of Baladeva, who knew all the tidings of Vraja, both past and present, and saw that it was covered with tears.

Hearing the words of the old woman Padmāvatī, and pained by agitation, he gazed at the face of Balarāma. Two verses (114-115) are connected. The reason is given. Balarāma should know the condition of Vraja in the past and present since coming to Mathurā. Kṛṣṇa's lotus face was dried up because of inner torment since he feared the dear devotees of Vraja would die. He glanced at Balarāma's tearful face. Or he glanced tearfully at his face.

TEXT 115

rohiṇī-nandano bhrātur
bhāvaṁ buddhvā smaran vrajam

sva-dhairya-rakṣaṇāśaktaḥ
prarudann abravīt sphuṭam

Baladeva, the son of Rohiṇī, was unable to keep his composure. Remembering Vraja and understanding his brother's intention, he began crying without control. But then he managed to speak distinctly.

Understanding the intention of his brother, by that remembering Vraja, he was unable to control himself. He cried loudly (prarudan) with an attractive voice and spoke clearly.

TEXT 116

śrī-baladeva uvāca
gavāṁ keva kathā kṛṣṇa
te te 'pi bhavataḥ priyāḥ
mṛgā vihaṅgā bhāṇḍīra-
kadambādyāś ca pādapāḥ

Baladeva said: Why speak only about the cows, dear Kṛṣṇa? All the animals in Vraja are your beloved friends, and so also are the birds, and the trees like the bhāṇḍīra and the kadamba.

Why speak (keva kathā) only of the cows and buffalos, etc. (gave)? Cows are mentioned because they are the chief of the village animals. When all the animals in the forest die, is it astonishing if the cows, who take you as their very life because you cared for them, die? The statement is kaimutya. Animals like kṛṣṇa-sāra deer and birds like peacocks are your dear friends.

TEXT 117

latāni kuñja-puñjāni
śādvalāny api jīvanam
bhavaty evārpayām āsuḥ
kṣīṇāś ca sarito 'drayaḥ

The grass, the creepers, the lush bushes have all dedicated their lives to you. Now they are all withering away, and so too are the rivers and mountains.

Rivers like the Yamunā and mountains like Govardhana have become thin.

TEXT 118

manuṣyāḥ katicid bhrātaḥ
paraṁ te satya-vākyataḥ
jātāśayaiva jīvanti
neccha śrotum ataḥ param

Some of the people, dear brother, live only on the hope that your promises were true. Better you not ask to hear more news than this.

That is the situation with the plants and animals. Some people live. This hints that many have died. At the time of leaving Gokula for Mathurā you said, "I will return." (SB 10.41.17) to Nanda you said, "I will come to see my relatives." (SB 10.45.23) Only (param) by the hope arising from those promises do they live. Do not desire to hear any other detailed news. A great problem would arise by hearing of the miserable condition of his dear devotees.

TEXT 119

kintv idānīm api bhavān
yadi tān nānukampate
yama eva tadā sarvān
vegenānugrahīṣyati

But if you don't show your kindness to them now, Yamarāja will soon show them his mercy.

If you do not show mercy to the remaining people of Vraja, Yama will show mercy: by dying, their misery and lamentation caused by separation from a friend will disappear.

TEXT 120

yat tatra ca tvayākāri
nirviṣaḥ kāliyo hradaḥ
śoko 'yaṁ vipulas teṣāṁ
śoke 'nyat kāraṇaṁ śṛṇu

That you rid Kāliya's lake of its poison has only increased their misery. And please hear of still other reasons for their sorrow.

If they have no means of dying quickly by their will, their lamentation will increase more. In regard to Yama's mercy (tatra), making Kāliya's lake free of poison is a cause of great sorrow, since it was impossible to die quickly without poison. They could not die by entering the water. That is explained: there is another reason for sorrow.

TEXT 121

tatratya-yamunā svalpa-
jalā śuṣkeva sājani
govardhano 'bhūn nīco 'sau
svaḥ-prāpto yo dhṛtas tvayā

There the river Yamunā has turned so dry that she has hardly any water. And Govardhana, which when you held him up touched Svarga, has now become short.

Thinness of everything was previously described. This is a cause of sorrow. The Yamunā, related to Vraja (tatratya), with huge waves, and great depth, the place of your pastimes (sā), has almost dried up, having very little water because of pain in separation from you. One cannot enter her waters to die. One cannot jump off a mountain to die. Govardhana, which you held in your hand, which reached Svarga, being very high, has become very low. It has entered the earth out of sorrow in separation from you. The peaks have fallen off.

śikharair ghūrṇamānaiś ca
sīdamānaiś ca pādapaiḥ
vidhṛtaś coddhataiḥ śṛṅgair
agamaḥ kha-gamo 'bhavat

When Kṛṣṇa lifted Govardhana, it reached the sky with high peaks and summits waving back and forth, and trembling trees.

āpluto 'yaṁ giriḥ pakṣair
iti vidyādharoragāḥ
gandharvāpsarasaś caiva
vāco muñcanti sarvaśaḥ

Vidyādharas, Uragas, Gandharvas, and Apsarās said that the mountain had risen up with wings. Hari-vaṁśa

TEXT 122

na yānty anaśanāt prāṇās
tvan-nāmāmṛta-sevinām
paraṁ śuṣka-mahāraṇya-
dāvāgnir bhavitā gatiḥ

The devotees who relish the nectar of your names cannot die of starvation; instead their end will be in a fire in a great dry forest.

Those who drink your name, which is sweet and auspicious like nectar will not leave their bodies by fasting. I guess something else (param) – a fire in the huge forest with trees like Bhāṇḍīra, which has dried up because of dying in separation from you, will be their recourse (gatiḥ).

TEXT 123

śrī-parīkṣid uvāca
śṛṇvann asau tat para-duḥkha-kātaraḥ
kaṇṭhe gṛhītvā mṛdula-svabhāvakaḥ
rāmaṁ mahā-dīna-vad aśru-dhārayā
dhautāṅga-rāgo 'rudad ucca-susvaram

Parīkṣit said: Having heard this, Kṛṣṇa, who is gentle by nature and tormented by the suffering of others, grasped Balarāma by the neck and shed a flood of tears, like a person whose life is in ruin. As he cried with loud sobs in his beautiful voice, the tears washed away the cosmetics from his body.

Hearing Balarāma's words (tat), the Lord (asau), who becomes faint-hearted by the grief of others (para-duḥkha-kātaraḥ), or by the grief of even enemies (para), because he had a soft nature, grasped the neck of Balarāma and cried loudly. His cosmetics were washed away by the flood of tears. This indicates that he wept profusely.

TEXT 124

paścād bhūmi-tale luloṭha sa-balo mātar mumoha kṣaṇāt
tādṛg-rodana-duḥsthatānubhavataś cāpūrva-vṛttāt tayoḥ
rohiṇy-uddhava-devakī-madanasū-śrī-satyabhāmādayaḥ
sarve 'ntaḥ-pura-vāsino vikalatāṁ bhejū rudanto muhuḥ

Dear mother, he and Balarāma then rolled on the ground and for a moment lost consciousness. Seeing the two Lords crying in this unprecedented, lamentable state, all the residents of the inner chambers lost control of themselves. Rohiṇī, Uddhava, Devakī, Rukmiṇī, Satyabhāmā, and all the rest — they all lost control and sobbed again and again.

After crying loudly, he rolled on the ground with Balarāma. From directly witnessing Kṛṣṇa and Balarāma crying in this manner and in a terrible condition, rolling on the ground, which had never occurred previously (apūrva-vṛttāt), all the residents of the palace cried constantly and became sorrowful. Madana-sū means Rukmiṇī, who was the mother of

Pradyumna (Cupid—madana). She mentioned in this way out of great respect for her, as the chief of all the queens.

TEXT 125

śrutvāntaḥ-purato 'purā-kalitam ākrandaṁ mahārta-svarair
dhāvanto yadavo javena vasudevenograsenādayaḥ
tatrāgatya tathā-vidhaṁ prabhu-varaṁ dṛṣṭvārudan vihvalā
viprā garga-mukhās tathā pura-janāś cāpūrva-dṛṣṭekṣayā

When the Yadus heard the sound of loud crying coming from the inner chambers — a sound never heard there before — they quickly came running, headed by Vasudeva and Ugrasena. The brāhmaṇas arrived, led by Garga, along with all the other people of the city. And when they saw their beloved master in this extraordinary state, as they never had before, they too began to cry, overwhelmed.

Hearing the loud crying (ākrandam) coming from the inner chambers or in the inner chambers, never before experienced (apurā-kalitam), the Yadus and Ugrasena came running, along with Vasudeva, who was always thinking of Kṛṣṇa since he was his father. Seeing the Lord who had loudly cried and fainted (tathāvidham), they cried. Garga, the priest, as well as other brāhmaṇas like Sāndīpani, came to pacify him, and also began crying. The residents of Dvārakā also cried since they directly experienced something never seem before—the Lord was crying.

Thus ends the sixth chapter of Canto One of Śrīla Sanātana Gosvāmī's Bṛhad-bhāgavatāmṛta, entitled "Priyatama: The Most Beloved."

Chapter Seven

Pūrṇa: The Complete Perfection

TEXT 1

śrī-parīkṣid uvāca
itthaṁ sa-parivārasya
mātas tasyārti-rodanaiḥ
brahmāṇḍaṁ vyāpya sañjāto
mahotpāta-cayaḥ kṣaṇāt

Parīkṣit said: Dear mother, as the sound of Kṛṣṇa lamenting with his family members filled the universe, a series of terrible omens quickly ensued.

In the Seventh Chapter, Brahmā relieves Kṛṣṇa of his confusion and Nārada becomes joyful on the glorification of the gopīs. Omens refers to earthquakes and meteors, etc.

TEXT 2

tatrānya-bodhakābhāvāt
svayam āgāc catur-mukhaḥ
vṛto veda-purāṇādyaiḥ
parivāraiḥ surair api

Because four-headed Brahmā could find no one else to explain the cause of these omens, he came to see for himself, accompanied by the Vedas, Purāṇas, his followers, and various devatās.

Since no one else could explain the omens, Brahmā came to Dvārakā. Gurus and priests were all bewildered. He was surrounded by the Vedas, Purāṇas and followers. This indicates that Brahmā had superior knowledge.

TEXTS 3–4

tam apūrva-daśā-bhājaṁ
preṣṭha-praṇaya-kātaram
nigūḍha-nija-māhātmya-
bhara-prakaṭanoddhatam

mahā-nārāyaṇaṁ brahmā
pitaraṁ gurum ātmanaḥ

sa-camatkāram ālokya
dhvasta-dhairyo 'rudat kṣaṇam

Brahmā found his own father and guru, the original Nārāyaṇa, in an unprecedented state, distressed by prema for his beloved devotees. Seeing the Lord thus boldly revealing his true glory, normally hidden, Brahmā was astonished. For a moment he too lost his gravity and began to cry.

Seeing with astonishment the Lord, Brahmā lost his self-control and for a moment cried. Two verses are connected. The Lord had attained a most astonishing state, not previously manifested, because he was overcome with prema for his dear devotees, since he now boldly revealed his great glory which was most secret. He had appeared on earth for that purpose. He was Mahā-nārāyaṇa, the great Nārāyaṇa, since such glories were not revealed even in Vaikuṇṭha (where the ordinary Nārāyaṇa resides). What was the cause of Brahmā crying, since, having great knowledge, he came to pacify the Lord? Kṛṣṇa was his father, his source, and his guru. He had taught him the Vedas. Thus it was possible for him to cry, losing self-control, because of the arousal of great prema, because of his special bhakti.

TEXT 5

saṁstabhya yatnād ātmānaṁ
svāsthyaṁ janayituṁ prabhoḥ
upāyaṁ cintayām āsa
prāpa cānantaraṁ hṛdi

With difficulty, Brahmā brought himself under control and started thinking of how to restore his Lord to normality. Soon an idea came into his heart.

Regaining his self-control, he thought. After thinking, a means (upāyam) manifested in his heart.

TEXT 6

tatraiva bhagavat-pārśve
rudantaṁ vinatā-sutam
uccaiḥ sambodhya yatnena
sabodhī-kṛtya so 'vadat

Crying at the Lord's side was Garuḍa, the son of Vinatā. Garuḍa's attention was hard to get, but after calling to him loudly for some time, Brahmā succeeded. Brahmā then spoke.

He made Garuḍa who was bewildered by the Lord's bewilderment, regain his consciousness (sabodhīkṛtya).

TEXTS 7–8

śrī-brahmovāca
yac chrī-vṛndāvanaṁ madhye
raivatādri-samudrayoḥ
śrīman-nanda-yaśodādi-
pratimālaṅkṛtāntaram

go-yūthais tādṛśair yuktaṁ
racitaṁ viśvakarmaṇā
rājate māthuraṁ sākṣād
vṛndāvanam ivāgatam

Brahmā said: There is another Vṛndāvana here (Nava-vṛndāvana), between Raivata Hill and the sea. And Nanda, Yaśodā, and others are present within it in replica images, with similar herds of cows. That Vṛndāvana, constructed by Viśvakarmā, appears just like the Vṛndāvana of Mathurā come here to Dvārakā.

TEXT 9

tatremaṁ sāgrajaṁ yatnād
yathāvasthaṁ śanair naya
kevalaṁ yātu tatraiṣā
rohiṇy anyo na kaścana

So carefully take Kṛṣṇa and his brother in their present state and gently carry them there. But only Rohiṇī should go with them — no one else.

There is a Vṛndāvana between Raivata Mountain and the salt ocean. Bring the Lord there with Balarāma in their present state of bewilderment on some pretext (yatnāt). Three verses (7-9) are connected. Inside that place are beautiful (śrī) statues of Nanda Yaśodā, Rādhā and other gopīs as well as cowherds like Śrīdāmā (ādi). Or there are forms of beautiful Nanda and others. There are also forms (tādṛśaiḥ) of cows or cows similar to those herded by the Lord in Vraja. How is this possible? They were made by Viśvakarmā. They will think that these statues are the real Nanda and residents of Vraja. It will be as if they are really coming to Vṛndāvana in Mathurā area. Forms of animals, birds and trees have also been made. Most intelligent Rohiṇī should go alone to that Vṛndāvana that has been made, since she previously lived in Vraja. No other person should go.

TEXT 10

śrī-parīkṣid uvāca
prayatnāt svasthatāṁ nīto
brahmaṇā sa khageśvaraḥ
viśārada-varaḥ pṛṣṭhe
mandaṁ mandaṁ nyadhatta tau

Parīkṣit said: Being brought back to normality by Brahmā, Garuḍa the most expert servant, very slowly placed the two Lords on his back.

Garuḍa was the best of the skillful (viśārada-varaḥ). This means he understood that they would recover from their bewilderment. Thus he very gently placed Kṛṣṇa and Balarāma on his back (pṛṣṭhe).

TEXT 11

sva-sthānaṁ bhejire sarve
catur-vaktreṇa bodhitāḥ
saṁjñām ivāpto rāmas tu
nīyamāno garutmatā

Advised by Brahmā, everyone else went back home. Meanwhile, as Kṛṣṇa and Balarāma were being carried by Garuḍa, Balarāma partially regained consciousness.

Vasudeva and others were brought back to normality by Brahmā and they went home. Balarāma partially (iva) regained consciousness.

TEXT 12

śrī-nanda-nandanas tatra
paryaṅke sthāpitaḥ śanaiḥ
sākṣād ivāvatiṣṭhante
yatra tad-gopa-gopikāḥ

Upon arriving at Nava-vṛndāvana, Garuḍa and Balarāma gently placed Kṛṣṇa on a bed. The gopas and gopīs (statues) of Nava-vṛndāvana stood around him, as if they were Kṛṣṇa's real cowherd men and women.

Kṛṣṇa was gently placed on a bed in the fabricated Vṛndāvana (tatra). The place is described. There the famous (tat) cowherds like Nanda and cowherd women like Yaśodā were standing.

TEXTS 13–14

uddhavena sahāgatya
devakī putra-vatsalā
rukmiṇī-satyabhāmādyā
devyaḥ padmāvatī ca sā

tādṛg-daśāgataṁ kṛṣṇam
aśaktās tyaktum añjasā
dūrād dṛṣṭi-pathe 'tiṣṭhan
nilīya brahma-yācñayā

Uddhava came there with Devakī, who dearly loved her son, and also with Rukmiṇī, Satyabhāmā, other queens, and Padmāvatī. They simply couldn't leave Kṛṣṇa in such a state. So at Brahmā's request they hid themselves and took up positions some distance away.

Others, like Devakī, who came along with Uddhava remained at a distance. Two verses are connected. Padmāvatī, the Lord's grandmother (sā) was also there. By Brahmā's request, they hid themselves among the trees from where they could see Kṛṣṇa.

TEXTS 15–16

nāradas tu kṛtāgaskam
ivātmānam amanyata
devānāṁ yādavānāṁ ca
saṅge 'gān na kutūhalāt

viyaty antarhito bhūtvā
baddhvaikaṁ yoga-paṭṭakam
niviṣṭo bhagavac-ceṣṭā-
mādhuryānubhavāya saḥ

Nārada, however, thinking he had committed an offense, did not accompany the devatās and the Yādavas. Instead, with great curiosity, he hid himself in the midst of the sky, arranging his cloth for meditation, to observe the sweetness of the Lord's acts.

Nārada thought he had committed an offense, since he had caused the Lord's bewilderment. However it was not actually so (iva). That will be explained by the Lord later. Thus he went neither with Brahmā and other devatās nor with Vasudeva and the Yadus. However out of curiosity he watched from the sky. He sat down to experience the sweetness of the Lord's activities.

TEXT 17

garuḍaś copari vyomnaḥ
sthitvāpratyakṣam ātmanaḥ
pakṣābhyām ācaraṁś chāyām
anvavartata taṁ prabhum

Garuḍa positioned himself even higher in the sky, unseen, following his master to provide shade with his wings.

Garuḍa situated himself invisibly high up in the sky so he could not be seen. But still he served (anuvavartata) his Lord or observed the Lord.

TEXT 18

atha kṛṣṇāgrajaḥ prāptaḥ
kṣaṇena svasthatām iva
taṁ sarvārtham abhipretya
vicakṣaṇa-śiromaṇiḥ

After a few minutes, Kṛṣṇa's brother came back almost to normal consciousness. That best of discerning thinkers understood the entire situation.

Balarāma did not fully recover (iva). He understood the plan initiated by Brahmā, to bring Kṛṣṇa to normal consciousness.

TEXTS 19–20

kṣipraṁ svasyānujasyāpi
sammārjya vadanāmbujam
vastrodarāntare vaṁśīṁ
śṛṅga-vetre ca hastayoḥ

kaṇṭhe kadamba-mālāṁ ca
barhāpīḍaṁ ca mūrdhani
navaṁ guñjāvataṁsaṁ ca
karṇayor nidadhe śanaiḥ

Balarāma quickly wiped his own lotus face and that of his younger brother. Then he gently placed a flute in the waist of Kṛṣṇa's waist cloth, a buffalo horn and stick in Kṛṣṇa's hands, a garland of kadamba flowers around his neck, a peacock-feather ornament on his head, and newly fashioned rings of guñjā berries on his ears.

He wipes his and Kṛṣṇa's face free of dust and gently placed a flute in Kṛṣṇa's waist cloth since Balarāma was the crest jewel of the intelligent. Navam (new) also modifies the garland and peacock feather.

TEXT 21

racayitvā vanya-veśaṁ
tvaṣṭṛ-kalpita-vastubhiḥ
balād utthāpayan dhṛtvā-
bravīd uccatara-svaraiḥ

Thus having arranged a forest dress for Kṛṣṇa with items made by Viśvakarmā, Balarāma with some effort raised Kṛṣṇa and then spoke to him loudly.

He arranged his forest dress. This includes a necklace of guñjā berries, though that is not mentioned. "How can the forest dress be complete if certain items are lacking?" The materials were made by Viśvakarmā. Flutes and other objects similar to those which were previously in Vṛndāvana were made by the special manufacturing powers of Viśvakarmā. Balarāma held Kṛṣṇa in his hands and raised him from the bed by his strength.

TEXT 22

śrī-baladeva uvāca
śrī-kṛṣṇa kṛṣṇa bho bhrātar
uttiṣṭhottiṣṭha jāgṛhi
paśyādya velātikrāntā
viśanti paśavo vanam

Baladeva said: Kṛṣṇa, Kṛṣṇa, My dear brother! Get up, get up! Wake up from your sleep! It is now getting late. The cows are already entering the forest. See!

The time of rising from bed or the time of waking the cows has passed. Thus the cows have gone on their own to the forest. See!

TEXT 23

śrīdāmādyā vayasyāś ca
sthitā bhavad-apekṣayā
snehena pitarau kiñcin
na śaktau bhāṣituṁ tvayi

Śrīdāmā and your other friends are here waiting for you. And your parents are so filled with love that they cannot even speak to you.

No cowherds have gone with the cows to protect them, since they are attracted to you in prema. "That may be true, but my mother and father should have woken me up and engaged me in herding the cows." Yaśodā and Nanda are not able to speak to you about waking up or about herding the cows, because of their affection.

TEXT 24

paśyantyas te mukhāmbhojam
imā gopyaḥ parasparam
karṇākarṇitayā kiñcid
vadantyas tvāṁ hasanti hi

These gopīs are watching your lotus face and laughing at you as they whisper something in one another's ears.

These gopīs who are directly present (imāḥ) are whispering, "Because he stayed awake all night he cannot give up sleep." They look at your face and laugh with certainty (hi) because they see there signs of last night's enjoyment.

TEXTS 25–26

śrī-parīkṣid uvāca
itthaṁ prajalpatābhīkṣṇaṁ
nāmabhiś ca sa-lālanam
āhūyamāno hastābhyāṁ
cālyamāno balena ca

rāmeṇotthāpyamāno 'sau
saṁjñām iva cirād gataḥ
vadan śiva śiveti drāg
udatiṣṭhat sa-vismayam

Parīkṣit said: In this way Balarāma filled the scene with talk. He called Kṛṣṇa by his various names, caressed him, and shook him with his arms

until Kṛṣṇa finally got up and came back to some sort of consciousness. Kṛṣṇa uttered the words "Śiva, Śiva!" and suddenly stood up, a look of surprise on his face.

Balarāma called his names such as Kṛṣṇa and Gopāla, along with sweet praises, and kissed his face (lālanam). Since Kṛṣṇa did not get up, Balarāma shook him with his strong hands and made him sit up. After a long time the Lord came back to consciousness and stood up suddenly in astonishment. His bewilderment was not completely vanquished (iva). That becomes clear later. He utters in astonishment, "Śiva! Śiva!"

TEXT 27

unmīlya netra-kamale
sampaśyan parito bhṛśam
smayamānaḥ puro nandaṁ
dṛṣṭvā hrīṇo nanāma tam

Kṛṣṇa opened his lotus eyes, smiled, and quickly looked around. Seeing Nanda in front of him, he felt embarrassed and bowed down to him.

He smiled slightly because he had been sleeping late. Seeing Nanda in front of him, he felt embarrassed and offered respects. It was his custom to greet his father on waking up in the morning.

TEXT 28

abravīt pārśvato vīkṣya
yaśodāṁ ca hasan mudā
snehāt tad-ānana-nyasta-
nirnimeṣekṣaṇām iva

Kṛṣṇa saw Mother Yaśodā also standing nearby, her eyes open wide and unblinking as if focused on his face. Laughing in joy, he lovingly spoke.

He saw Yaśodā whose unblinking eyes were as if focused on his face. Actually her eyes did not blink because they were eyes on a statue. But Kṛṣṇa thought that as previously she was not blinking out of affection. From this it is understood that Kṛṣṇa's bewilderment had not completely vanished.

TEXT 29

śrī-bhagavān uvāca
adya prabhāte bho mātar

asminn eva kṣaṇe mayā
citrāḥ kati kati svapnā
jāgrateva na vīkṣitāḥ

The Supreme Lord said: O mother, this morning during my sleep I saw many amazing things in just a short moment, as if I were awake!

As previously, I live in Vraja. That is true. Going to Mathurā is false. Thinking that going to Mathurā was an experience in a dream, he explains everything to his mother in three verses (29-31). I did not see a few dream objects, but I saw many objects, just as I experience objects in waking state.

TEXT 30

madhu-puryām ito gatvā
duṣṭāḥ kaṁsādayo hatāḥ
jarāsandhādayo bhūpā
nirjitāḥ sukhitāḥ surāḥ

I saw that I had gone from here to Madhupurī. There I saw wicked men like Kaṁsa slain, kings like Jarāsandha vanquished, and the devatās satisfied.

He summarizes what he saw in the dream. The devatās were satisfied by the killing of Naraka, etc.

TEXT 31

nirmitāmbho-nidhes tīre
dvārakākhyā mahā-purī
nānya-vṛttāni śakyante
'dhunā kathayituṁ javāt

A great city called Dvārakā was built on the shore of the ocean, and so many other things happened. But now there isn't time enough to tell you about them all.

Dvārakā was built on the shore of the salt ocean (ambho nidheḥ). "Tell all that happened in detail." Now it is time to go to the forest to gather the cows. I must hurry (javāt).

TEXT 32

anena svapna-vighnena
dīrgheṇa svānta-hāriṇā
anya-vāsara-vat kāle
śayanān notthitaṁ mayā

It's because this long dream distracted me that I didn't rise from bed on time like every other day.

Seeing Yaśodā staring at him with unblinking eyes for a long time, he though his mother must be worried that he was ill because of sleeping too long. He pacifies her in this verse. Because of this obstacle in the form of a dream, which distracted my mind I was not able to rise from bed at dawn (kāle).

TEXT 33

bho ārya tan-mahāścaryam
asambhāvyaṁ na manyate
bhavatā cet tadāraṇye
gatvā vakṣyāmi vistarāt

O respected brother, if you don't think this wonderful matter impossible, I'll explain it to you in detail when we go to the forest.

Baladeva may think that it is impossible that various events spread over a long time could be seen in a short dream in the morning. He speaks to Balarāma. "Do not think that the astonishing events that I saw in the dream (tat) are impossible."

TEXT 34

śrī-parīkṣid uvāca
evaṁ sambhāṣya jananīm
abhivandya sa sādaram
vana-bhogyepsur ālakṣya
rohiṇyokto 'ty-abhijñayā

Parīkṣit said: After speaking in this way, Kṛṣṇa offered his mother proper respects. Then the very expert Rohiṇī sensed that Kṛṣṇa wanted some food to take with him to the forest.

Rohiṇī, who was very intelligent, understood that the Lord desired to take some eatables like yogurt and rice to the forest, because he made gesture of extending his hands. She thought, "The statue Yaśodā cannot give anything and cannot answer by itself. If he does not get food from her and does not get answers, Kṛṣṇa will understand that it is a statue. He will fall into great disturbance as before." To prevent that she used her intelligence.

TEXT 35

śrī-rohiṇy uvāca
bho vatsa tava mātādya
tan-nidrādhikya-cintayā
tvad-eka-putrā duḥstheva
tad alaṁ bahu-vārtayā

Rohiṇī said: O child, your mother has no other son but you. She was so worried today by your excessive sleeping that now she feels a bit ill. So I think we have talked enough.

Thinking about your excessive sleep today, worried that you are ill, she seems to have (iva) fallen into a sad state (duḥsthā), since you are her only son. She uses the word iva (as if) to prevent Kṛṣṇa from developing mental anguish on thinking that his mother is ill, since he has great affection for her. Therefore it is not necessary to discuss a lot.

TEXT 36

agrato niḥsṛtā gās tvaṁ
gopāṁś cānusara drutam
mayopaskṛtya sad-bhogyaṁ
vana-madhye praheṣyate

The cows and the boys tending them have already gone ahead. You should quickly follow them. I will prepare some nice refreshments for you and send them to you in the forest.

"Therefore I will stay here. If I go to the forest, what will I eat?" Rohiṇī answers by revealing his childhood pastimes. I will prepare excellent food and send it quickly to the forest.

TEXTS 37–38

śrī-parīkṣid uvāca
tathā vadantīṁ su-snigdhāṁ
rohiṇīṁ cābhivādya saḥ
sthitaṁ kara-tale mātur
nava-nītaṁ śanair hasan

cauryeṇaiva samādāya
nija-jyeṣṭhaṁ samāhvayan
aprāpyāgre gavāṁ saṅge
gataṁ na bubhuje ghṛṇī

Parīkṣit said: Kṛṣṇa offered his respects to Rohiṇī, who had spoken to him with such affection. Then, with a smile on his face, like a thief he stealthily took from Mother Yaśodā's hand the butter she was holding. He then left to join his older brother, calling out his name. Generous Kṛṣṇa did not eat this butter before reaching the cows.

He trusted Rohiṇī's words since she was equal to Yaśodā, being very affectionate to him (susnigdhām). He offered respects by saying "I offer respect to your feet." Like a thief, he gently took, without Yaśodā's knowing, some butter situated in the palm of the hand of the statue. He called out to Balarāma who had gone ahead with the cows in order to eat with him. He did not eat before he caught up with Balarāma, because he was merciful (ghṛṇī). Viśvakarmā had made the statue of Yaśodā with butter in its hand, holding it for her son who loved butter. Balarāma had gone ahead noticing that Kṛṣṇa had somewhat returned to normal, previous to his desiring some food for taking to the forest. It was also the custom in Vraja previously that Balarāma went ahead so that Kṛṣṇa could speak to the gopīs freely without restriction.

TEXT 39

bhogyaṁ mādhyāhnikaṁ cāṭu-
pāṭavena sva-mātarau
samprārthya purato gatvā
gopīḥ sambhāṣya narmabhiḥ

In expertly pleasing words, Kṛṣṇa had asked his two mothers to make lunch for him. Then he had set off, and on the way he had met some of the gopīs and enjoyed some joking words.

Requesting food from Yaśodā and Rohiṇī, using humble words in order to satisfy his mother, he went ahead, talking to the gopīs such as Candrāvalī with joking words.

TEXT 40

rundhāno veṇu-nādair gā
vartamānāṁ sahālibhiḥ

rādhikām agrato labdhvā
sa-narma-smitam abravīt

As he continued walking, playing his flute to keep the cows from wandering off, he then came upon Rādhikā with her girlfriends and spoke to her with witty jokes and charming smiles.

Ahead, he met with Rādhikā and friends, and spoke to them with jokes and smiles. By the sound of his flute he stopped the cows which had spread out in front. The gopīs had left their houses in order to see the Lord who had departed for the forest and gone far away. They remained there in groups in various places.

prātar vrajād vrajata āviśataś ca sāyaṁ
gobhiḥ samaṁ kvaṇayato 'sya niśamya veṇum
nirgamya tūrṇam abalāḥ pathi bhūri-puṇyāḥ
paśyanti sa-smita-mukhaṁ sa-dayāvalokam

When the gopīs hear Kṛṣṇa playing his flute as he leaves Vraja in the morning with his cows or returns with them at sunset, the young girls quickly come out of their houses to see him. They must have performed many pious activities to be able to see him as he walks on the road, his smiling face mercifully glancing upon them. SB 10.44.16

TEXT 41

śrī-nanda-nandana uvāca
prāṇeśvari rahaḥ-prāptaṁ
bhaktam ekākinaṁ ca mām
sambhāṣase kathaṁ nādya
tat kiṁ vṛttāsi māninī

Nanda-nandana said: O mistress of my soul, why don't you speak to me, your devotee, whom you've now met in a secluded place? What are you so busy with, my proud lady?

Why do you not speak to me even though (ca) I am alone, though the place is secluded and though I am devoted to you.

TEXT 42

aparādhaṁ mayā kiṁ te
nūnaṁ jñātam aho tvayā
sarva-jñe 'dyatana-svapna-
vṛttaṁ tat tan mamākhilam

How did I offend you? O omniscient one, you probably know everything that happened today in my dream.

Not seeing any other visible cause for Rādhā's pride, he raises his dream as the cause. Nūnam indicates conjecture. Aho indicates astonishment. O all-knowing Rādhā! You know everything that happened in my dream today. Because of my offenses in the dream, you are angry. Since you know the contents of others' dreams, truly you are omniscient. He speaks these words to destroy her anger.

One should not think how the Lord could speak like this to statues, for previously in Vraja the gopīs became like statues from being stunned with intense, continuous prema. And sometimes, inspired by Kṛṣṇa's joking mood, they would act stunned as a joke. And now, having attained a special mood, seeing her silence he inferred she was angry at him. His words were thus appropriate.

TEXT 43

tvāṁ vihāyānyato gatvā
vivāhā bahavaḥ kṛtāḥ
tāsāṁ kṣitipa-putrīṇām
udyatānāṁ mṛtiṁ prati
putra-pautrādayas tatra
janitā dūra-vartinā

I left you and went elsewhere. In that distant place, I married many princesses, who had been preparing to end their lives, and I fathered sons, grandsons, and great-grandsons.

He describes the dream (in which he offended her). I went to Mathurā (anyataḥ) and I had many marriages far away in Dvārakā.

TEXT 44

astu tāvad idānīṁ tad
gamyate tvarayā vane
santoṣa-de pradoṣe 'dya
mayā tvaṁ modayiṣyase

Anyway, right now I have to go to the forest. Tonight at dusk, O delightful one, you will enjoy with me.

Now let that dream or your anger (tat) be, since I must now go to the forest quickly.

TEXT 45

śrī-parīkṣid uvāca
itthaṁ sa-puṣpa-vikṣepaṁ
vadan dṛṣṭvā diśo 'khilāḥ
tāṁ sa-cumbanam āliṅgya
go-gopaiḥ saṅgato 'grataḥ

Parīkṣit continued: Having said this, Kṛṣṇa threw a handful of flowers at Rādhā, looked all around, and then embraced and kissed her. He then went ahead to meet the cows and cowherd boys.

Talking to her in this way while throwing flowers at her, he went ahead to meet the cows and cowherd boys.

TEXT 46

adṛṣṭa-pūrvaṁ vraja-veśam adbhutaṁ
mahā-manojñaṁ muralī-ravānvitam
yadānvabhūt sneha-bhareṇa devakī
tadaiva vṛddhāpy ajani snuta-stanī

As Devakī saw for the first time how wonderfully and all-attractively Kṛṣṇa was dressed for Vraja and how he was playing his flute, milk started flowing from her breasts in great affection, even though she was no longer young.

Having described Kṛṣṇa's special love for the people of Vraja, after speaking of the actions of others in previous times, in four verses (46-49) he now describes the special love of Devakī and others that developed on experiencing Kṛṣṇa's forest dress, in order to show the special glory of the people of Vraja. Devakī was elderly and thus breast milk was not possible. But milk flowed from her breasts out of affection for Kṛṣṇa.

TEXT 47

rukmiṇī-jāmbavaty-ādyāḥ
purānutthena karhicit
mahā-premṇā gatā mohaṁ
dhairya-hānyāpatan kṣitau

Rukmiṇī, Jāmbavatī, and other queens, bewildered by an intensity of prema they had never felt before, lost their composure, fainted, and fell to the ground.

Though endowed with natural gravity and self-control, they became bewildered by special desire. Ādayaḥ indicates Mitravindā, Satyā, Bhadrā, Lakṣmaṇā and others. They were bewildered by great prema which had never manifested before in them, with loss of self-control. They thus fell to the ground.

TEXT 48

vṛddhā ca mattā saha satyabhāmayā
kāmasya vegād anukurvatī muhuḥ
āliṅganaṁ cumbanam apy adhāvad
dhartuṁ hariṁ bāhu-yugaṁ prasārya

Even old Padmāvatī became intoxicated. Driven by desire, she as well as Satyabhāmā acted out embracing and kissing Kṛṣṇa again and again and ran after him, arms extended, to try to catch Him.

Satyabhāmā and Padmāvatī developed great madness in love. They imitated embracing Kṛṣṇa, or acted it out by spreading their arms. They acted out kissing him, by moving their lips. They ran to catch him.

TEXT 49

purā tad-arthānubhavād ivāsau
kathañcid āditya-sutāvalambya
śamaṁ samaṁ prājña-varoddhavena
balād vikṛṣyāvarurodha te dve

Kālindī, the daughter of the sun god, had seen Kṛṣṇa like this before. Being very intelligent, she somehow calmed herself down. She and Uddhava grabbed Satyabhāmā and Padmāvatī and dragged them back.

Because she previously experienced Kṛṣṇa's forest dress in Vraja, Kālindī, fortunate to be related to the pastimes of Vraja (asau), was somewhat stable. Actually with great effort she remained calm, in order to maintain the method advised by Brahmā for destroying the bewilderment of Kṛṣṇa. She could remain calm because she was the best of the wise (prājña-varā). Kālindī stopped Satyabhāmā and Uddhava stopped Padmāvatī.

TEXT 50

govinda-devas tv anucārayan gā
gataḥ purastād udadhiṁ nirīkṣya

taṁ manyamāno yamunāṁ pramodāt
sakhīn vihārāya samājuhāva

Meanwhile Lord Govinda went ahead, tending his cows. When he saw the ocean before him, he thought it was the Yamunā, and with delight he called his friends to come play in the river.

Finishing the incidental occurrences, the activities of the Lord are described. Going ahead, seeing the ocean which surrounded Dvārakā, he thought it was the Yamunā River, having a similar dark color. Desiring to play in the water, he called out to his friends like Śrīdāmā by name in a sweet voice.

TEXT 51

gatāḥ kutra vayasyāḥ stha
śrīdāman subalārjuna
sarve bhavanto dhāvanto
vegenāyāntu harṣataḥ

"My dear friends, where have you gone? O Śrīdāmā, Subala, Arjuna! Happily come here, quickly!

Two verses (51-52) describe his calling out. O friends! Where have you gone?

TEXT 52

kṛṣṇāyāṁ pāyayitvā gā
viharāma yathā-sukham
madhurāmala-śītāmbu-
vāhinyām avagāhya ca

"We can let our cows drink water from this river Yamunā, and we can play as much as we want, swimming in her gently flowing clear cool water."

Come quickly so we can play in the Yamunā, submerging ourselves in its waters.

TEXT 53

evam agre saran gobhir
ambudher nikaṭaṁ gataḥ

mahā-kallola-mālābhiḥ
kolāhala-vato 'cyutaḥ

Thus Lord Acyuta went on further with the cows and neared the sea, where mighty roaring waves came one after another.

Going forward with the cows, he came close to the ocean, which was filled with huge waves making rumbling sounds. This was different from the Yamunā.

TEXT 54

sarvato vīkṣya tat-tīre
prakaṭāṁ svāṁ mahā-purīm
ālakṣya kim idaṁ kvāhaṁ
ko 'ham ity āha vismitaḥ

When Kṛṣṇa looked around the seacoast, he noticed his own great city visible in the distance. Kṛṣṇa was surprised and exclaimed, "What is this? Where am I? Who am I?"

Looking all around on the shore of the ocean he saw his own huge city (Dvārakā), very evident, since it was not hidden when he went outside the forest. Astonished, he spoke to himself. "Is this the ocean (kim idam)? Why is it in Vraja? This cannot be Vraja. Where am I? If I am in Dvārakā, it is not possible for me, the son of Nanda to function anywhere except in Vraja. Thus I must be someone else. Who am I? Or it is not possible to have this most different type of dress (forest costume) in Dvārakā, which is full of the highest ruling power. I cannot discern who I am."

TEXT 55

ity evaṁ sa-camatkāraṁ
muhur jalpan mahārṇavam
purīṁ cālocayan proktaḥ
śrīmat-saṅkarṣaṇena saḥ

Astonished, he spoke these words again and again as he gazed at the vast ocean and the city. Then Lord Balarāma told him something.

Bhagavān (saḥ) looked at the ocean constantly, or constantly considered "Is this true or false?" (avalokayan).

TEXT 56

śrī-baladeva uvāca
ātmānam anusandhehi
vaikuṇṭheśvara mat-prabho
avatīrṇo 'si bhū-bhāra-
hārāya jñāpito 'maraiḥ

Baladeva said: O my master, Lord of Vaikuṇṭha, please consider who you are. You were asked by the devatās to descend to remove the burden of the earth.

Recognize yourself as Bhagavān. How is that? O Lord of Vaikuṇṭha! Or master of me, Śeṣa (mat-prabho)! "But why am I here?" At the request of the devatās you have appeared to remove the burden of the earth. Recognize yourself as the Lord of Vaikuṇṭha. Or remember who you are. "I remember that I am the son of Nanda." You are the Lord of Vaikuṇṭha.

The meaning is this. True, you are the son of Nanda. However, please fulfill the purpose for which you have appeared with me from Vaikuṇṭha (for killing the demons). Though you have appeared from Goloka, that is largely non-different from Vaikuṇṭha. Or you have come from Vaikuṇṭha in the sense that all the Lords of Vaikuṇṭha in their forms have become one with you when you appear on earth.

Even though his main goal is spreading special prema at his lotus feet through the pastimes of Vṛndāvana, Balarāma did not reveal that here, since he feared Kṛṣṇa would again become bewildered and faint. Thus he did not say that Kṛṣṇa is the lord of Goloka. Or when the goal of relieving the earth of its burden by killing the demons and protecting the devotees was complete, the chief goal would gradually be achieved on its own without obstacles.

TEXT 57

duṣṭān saṁhara tac-chiṣṭān
pratipālaya samprati
yajñaṁ paitṛ-svaseyasya
dharma-rājasya santanu

Now please destroy the wicked and protect everyone else. Your cousin Dharmarāja, King Yudhiṣṭhira, has undertaken a sacrifice. Please see to getting it performed.

Therefore act for your dear devotees who are present. Arrange for the sacrifice of Yudhiṣṭhira at this time.

TEXT 58

pratiṣṭhitas tvayaivāsau
cakravartī yudhiṣṭhiraḥ
anuśālvādi-duṣṭānāṁ
bibheti vara-vikramāt

You have established Yudhiṣṭhira as emperor, but he is intimidated by Śālva's younger brother and by other exceedingly powerful villains.

Balarāma explains what is necessary to do. Yudhiṣṭhira is not capable of performing the sacrifice without you, since you have established him. He fears the great (vara) strength of Śālva's younger brother.

TEXT 59

tat tatra gatvā tān hantuṁ
yatasva yadubhiḥ saha
tavaiva vairatas te hi
tāvakān pīḍayanti tān

Please, therefore, go to Yudhiṣṭhira and with the help of the Yadus try to kill his enemies, who are persecuting your devotees out of hatred for you.

He speaks so that Kṛṣṇa will give up the great rasa of the sweetest, tender prema and become inspired with its opponents, the rasa of anger. Endeavor with the Yadus. It is impossible to slay them easily alone. He speaks this to instill anger in Kṛṣṇa. To instill anger, he also mentions that the demons harass the devotees out of hatred for Kṛṣṇa (vairataḥ), since Kṛṣṇa had killed Śālva. They hated Kṛṣṇa not Yudhiṣṭhira, since he hated no one (ajāta-śatruḥ). The demons like Anuśālva (te) persecute the devotees like Yudhiṣṭhira (tān).

TEXT 60

śrī-parīkṣid uvāca
evaṁ rasāntaraṁ nītvā-
nujaṁ svasthayituṁ vacaḥ
yad uktaṁ balarāmeṇa
śrutvā bhāvāntaraṁ gataḥ

Parīkṣit said: Balarāma spoke these words to change his younger brother's ecstatic mood and bring him back to normal. Indeed, upon hearing what Balarāma said, Kṛṣṇa did change his mood.

Balarāma spoke in order to change Kṛṣṇa's rasa. Hearing those words, Kṛṣṇa adopted another mood (bhāva). Previously, he was inundated with tasting prema arising from the essence of unlimited rasas. Now however he took up vīra-rasa. The subject is bhagavān, mentioned in the next verse. The two verses may be linked together as one statement.

TEXT 61

jagāda bhagavān kruddho
bhrātaḥ śālvānujādayaḥ
ke te varākā hantavyā
gatvaikena mayādhunā

The Lord grew angry and said, "Brother, who are those useless creatures — Śālva's younger brother and those like him? I will go by myself and kill them at once!

Thus, becoming angry, Kṛṣṇa speaks in five lines (verses 61-62). Who are these people? Nothing at all. None among them should even be considered because they are most insignificant (varākāḥ). Or are they low? They cannot be considered even among the low, since they are most fallen. I will go alone and kill them.

TEXT 62

bhavān pratyetu satyaṁ me
sa-pratijñam idaṁ vacaḥ
itthaṁ prasaṅga-saṅgatyā
mugdha-bhāvaṁ jahau prabhuḥ

"Trust these words of mine as true. They give my firm promise." In this way the circumstances of the moment made Lord Kṛṣṇa gave up his beautiful state.

Please believe these words. The Lord gave up his beautiful state (mugdha-bhāvam) of absorption in the rasa of prema. Or he gave up the activities (bhāvam) of bewilderment (mugdha). He became complete aware, as previously.

TEXT 63

parito muhur ālokya
śrīmad-dvāravatīśvaram

śrī-yādavendram ātmānaṁ
pratyabhijñātavāṁs tadā

Looking around again, Kṛṣṇa remembered that he was the master of Śrī Dvārakā, the divine king of the Yādavas.

Looking around (ālokya), he remembered that he was king of Dvārakā.

TEXT 64

prāsādābhyantare suptaṁ
sasmārātha kare sthitām
vaṁśīṁ svasyāgrajasyāpi
vanya-veśaṁ ca dṛṣṭavān

He remembered he had been sleeping inside the palace. Then he saw the flute in his hand, and he and his older brother dressed in forest garments.

He remembered that he was sleeping in the palace room. After that memory, he saw the flute in his hand.

TEXT 65

puryā bahiḥ-prayāṇenu
go-pālanam avekṣya ca
vismayaṁ saṁśayaṁ cāpto
jahāsa hṛdi bhāvayan

Kṛṣṇa perceived he had gone out of the city to tend cows, and this filled him with surprise and doubt. He laughed as he pondered it.

He saw that he had gone out of Dvārakā to the shore of the ocean and was herding cows. He was surprised. When or how did I get the forest ornaments? He had a doubt. Is this true or a false like a dream? He pondered in his heart the cause and laughed since he could not understand at that moment, or since he was investigating his experience of long lasting mental confusion.

TEXT 66

tato haladharaḥ smitvā
tadīya-hṛdayaṅ-gamaḥ
sarvaṁ brahma-kṛtaṁ tasyā-
kathayat tat sa-hetukam

His brother Balarāma understood what Kṛṣṇa was thinking. Smiling, Balarāma explained that this was all Brahmā's arrangement and told Kṛṣṇa the reasons why it had been done.

After Kṛṣṇa laughed, Balarāma explained. By Kṛṣṇa's laugh, Balarāma understood that Kṛṣṇa was happy. He told Kṛṣṇa everything—how Brahmā made a plan, how they transported him outside the palace on Garuḍa, etc.—to gain his trust, along with the reason – Kṛṣṇa's bewilderment in prema.

TEXT 67

tato hrīṇa iva jyeṣṭha-
mukhaṁ paśyan smitaṁ śritaḥ
rāmeṇodvartya tatrābdhau
snāpito dhūli-dhūsaraḥ

Seeming embarrassed, Kṛṣṇa then looked at his brother's face and smiled. And since Kṛṣṇa's body was covered with dust, Balarāma wiped him clean and bathed him in the sea.

Kṛṣṇa seemed embarrassed. However, he had no cause of embarrassment (hrīṇaḥ) since he was engaged in most praiseworthy actions.

bhago ma aiśvaro bhāvo lābho mad-bhaktir uttamaḥ
vidyātmani bhidā-bādho jugupsā hrīr akarmasu

Lordship means my controlling power. Gain means gaining bhakti. Knowledge is nullifying what is not ātmā in the jīva. Real modesty is dislike of sinful activities. SB 11.19.40

Hrī means dislike of sinful activities, not just shame. Looking at Balarāma's face, he smiled slightly and constantly. He was covered with dust because he had rolled on the ground in the palace, or was covered with the dust raised by the cows while herding them in the manufactured Vṛndāvana. Wiping off the dust, Balarāma bathed him in the ocean.

TEXT 68

tadānīm eva samprāptaṁ
bhagavad-bhāva-kovidam
āruhyālakṣitas tārkṣyaṁ
nija-prāsādam āgataḥ

At that moment Garuḍa arrived, because he understood the Lord's moods perfectly well. Kṛṣṇa mounted him and returned unseen to the palace.

While he was bathing, Garuḍa arrived, since Garuḍa knows the mental state of the Lord, such as his desire to return to the palace. He entered the palace unseen by anyone else.

TEXT 69

sarva-jñenoddhavenātha
devakī-rukmiṇī-mukhāḥ
prabodhyāntaḥ-pure devyo
bhagavat-pārśvam āpitāḥ

The all-knowing Uddhava informed Devakī, Rukmiṇī, and the others what was happening. He brought all the queens back to the palace, to Lord Kṛṣṇa's side.

Uddhava knew everything about the dissipation of the Lord's bewilderment and returning to the palace (sarva-jñena). He brought them all to normal consciousness (prabodhya) or informed them accurately about the Lord's return. He brought the queens to the Lord's side. But he sent Padmāvatī, the gossip monger somewhere else, since she was unqualified for the discussions which follow.

TEXT 70

mātā ca devakī putram
āśīrbhir abhinandya tam
bhoga-sampādanāyāsya
kālābhijñā drutaṁ gatā

Mother Devakī greeted her son with blessings. Well aware of what time it was, she quickly went to prepare his meal.

Devakī left the place with respect, since she should not hear what the Lord would describe without restriction to the queens—the topmost excellence of the gopīs, which is the conclusion of the story. Greeting her son who had returned to normal (tam), knowing it was time for her son to eat (kāla abhijñā) she went away quickly. Or knowing it was not proper to stay at that time Devakī left.

TEXT 71

stambhādy-antaritāḥ satyo
devyo 'tiṣṭhan prabhu-priyāḥ
satyabhāmā na tatrāgāt
tāṁ kṛṣṇo 'pṛcchad uddhavam

The beloved queens of the Lord stayed hidden behind objects such as columns, not approaching him. But Satyabhāmā had not come there with the others, so Kṛṣṇa asked about her from Uddhava.

All the queens such as Rukmiṇī remained there but hidden behind columns because they were dear to the Lord or he was dear to them (prabhu-priyāḥ). Satyabhāmā had not come to his side (tatra). He asked, "Where is she?"

TEXTS 72–73

śrī-hari-dāsa uvāca
vṛndāvane yadā jāto
vijayo raivatārcite
prabhos tadātanaṁ bhāvam
abudha-bhrāmakaṁ param

kam apy ālokya devībhiḥ
saha tatraiva dūrataḥ
sthitā nilīya durbuddhir
ūce padmāvatī khalā

The Lord's servant Uddhava replied: When you took your glorious excursion to Nava-vṛndāvana, which is embraced by Raivata Hill, your special mood might have bewildered the unintelligent, but your queens were able to perceive it. They therefore hid themselves, watching from a distance. Then the spiteful, weak-minded Padmāvatī addressed them.

Haridāsa is Uddhava.

sarid-vana-giri-droṇīr vīkṣan kusumitān drumān
kṛṣṇaṁ saṁsmārayan reme hari-dāso vrajaukasām

Seeing the rivers, forests, mountains, valleys and flowering trees of Vraja that servant of Kṛṣṇa was satisfied by giving them direct association with Kṛṣṇa through remembrance. SB 10.47.56

When you made your auspicious journey (vijayaḥ) to Vṛndāvana served (arcite) by Raivata Mountain, seeing the indescribable (kam api) special prema (bhāvam) directed to the statues of Nanda and others, which was incomprehensible (bhramakam) only (param) to those who do not know about the rasa of prema, then Padmāvatī spoke. Two verses are connected. Param can also mean "most excellent prema" directed to the statues. Padmāvatī along with the queens was situated far away, hidden in that Vṛndāvana. Padmāvatī had wicked intelligence (durbuddhiḥ) since she created dissension. Thus she was treacherous (khalā).

TEXTS 74–75

devaky are puṇya-hīne
re re rukmiṇi durbhage
satyabhāme 'vare hanta
jāmbavaty-ādayo 'varāḥ

paśyatedam ito 'rvāk svam
abhimānaṁ vimuñcata
ābhīrīṇāṁ hi dāsyāya
tapasyāṁ kurutottamām

"O Devakī, devoid of pious credits! O unfortunate Rukmiṇī! Wretched Satyabhāmā! Jāmbavatī and you other miserable women! Look here! From now on, you should give up your pride and undergo the greatest penances to become servants of those Ābhīra nomad women."

Two verses describe what she said to the queens. Hanta expresses lamentation. O low women (avarāḥ)! Look at Kṛṣṇa's activities (idam). From now on (itaḥ arvāk), you should give up your pride in being married to him since he has been shown to have love for the cowherd people. Do austerities to attain positions as servants of the cowherd ābhīras like Yaśodā. Nanda and his companions are actually twice born, excellent persons born as vaiśyas with the profession of cow herding. Ābhīras are outcastes.

kirāta-hūṇāndhra-pulinda-pulkaśā
ābhīra-śumbhā yavanāḥ khasādayaḥ
ye 'nye ca pāpā yad-upāśrayāśrayāḥ
śudhyanti tasmai prabhaviṣṇave namaḥ

I offer respects to the Lord of inconceivable power. The Kirātas, Hūṇas, Andhras, Pulindas, Pulkaśas, Abhīras, Śumbhas, Yavanas, Khasas and others of low birth, and those sinful by actions, by taking shelter of the devotees who take shelter of the powerful Lord, become purified of their prārabdha-karmas. SB 2.4.18

But because they herded cows like the Ābhīra tribe, they are called Ābhīras. Or Padmāvatī says they are outcastes because of her bad intelligence and wicked nature.

TEXTS 76–78

tad-durvaco niśamyādau
devakyoktam abhijñayā
samasta-jagad-ādhāra-
bhavad-ādhāra-bhūtayā

āścaryam atra kiṁ mūrkhe
pūrva-janmani yat tapaḥ
samaṁ śrī-vasudevena
mayākāri sutāya tat

ato 'yam āvayoḥ prāptaḥ
putratāṁ vara-deśvaraḥ
asmin nanda-yaśodābhyāṁ
bhaktiḥ samprārthitā vidhim

[Uddhava told Kṛṣṇa:] The wise Devakī shelters you, who shelter the entire world. When she heard those wicked words, she said, "Foolish woman, what is unusual here? Vasudeva and I, in our previous lives, underwent austerities to get the Lord as our son, and therefore the Lord, the bestower of all boons, accepted that role. But Nanda and Yaśodā prayed to Lord Brahmā for pure bhakti.

Hearing Padmāvatī's bad words, Devakī had spoken with great intelligence. She was most learned. The Lord who is the shelter of the universe, appeared from her. She had spoken in four verses (77-80). What is astonishing about Kṛṣṇa's special prema for Nanda and other cowherds? Nothing at all. The reason is given.

They did austerities for a son who would be like the Lord.

tadā vāṁ parituṣṭo 'ham amunā vapuṣānaghe
tapasā śraddhayā nityaṁ bhaktyā ca hṛdi bhāvitaḥ
prādurāsaṁ varada-rāḍ yuvayoḥ kāma-ditsayā
vriyatāṁ vara ity ukte mādṛśo vāṁ vṛtaḥ sutaḥ

O Devakī, free of offenses! After twelve thousand celestial years, I was completely satisfied and became fixed constantly in your hearts by austerity, which produced faith, which produced bhakti, which then produced prema. I, the king of benedictors, then appeared before you with a desire to give you benedictions. I said, "Please request a boon." You asked for a son like me. SB 10.3.37-38

The Lord is the best of those who bestow benedictions (vara-deśvaraḥ). Thus by his bestowing one benediction, they again and again got the Lord as their son, each time being better and better.

Nanda and Yaśodā prayed to Brahmā (vidhim) for prema (bhaktiḥ) to Kṛṣṇa,

jātayor nau mahādeve bhuvi viśveśvare harau
bhaktiḥ syāt paramā loke yayāñjo durgatiṁ taret

Born on earth, may we two develop prema-bhakti to the attractive Lord, engaged in sweet pastimes, though he is the Lord of the universe. By this bhakti others in this world will easily cross material existence. SB 10.8.49

By this bhakti, by hearing, etc. others will easily cross saṁsāra.

TEXT 79

tasyaitad-bhakta-varyasya
tādṛśena vareṇa tau
āvābhyām api māhātmyaṁ
prāptau sa-parivārakau

"By the blessings of that foremost devotee of the Lord, Nanda and Yaśodā along with their whole household became greater than us.

By the blessings of Brahmā (who was the best among the devotees) which were according to their prayer, Yaśodā and Nanda attained a greater glory than us, Devakī and Vasudeva. That included all people of Vraja. Jagatām paro guru: Brahmā was the best of the devotees. (SB 2.9.5)

By praying to the best devotee for bhakti, the fulfilment of the benediction given by his devotee became greater than what could be given by the Lord himself, since he has such affection for his devotee. Thus Yaśodā and Nanda obtained a greater benediction from Brahmā, his devotee, than we did from the Lord.

TEXT 80

tābhyāṁ sneha-bhareṇāsya
pālanaṁ tat-tad-īhitam
ato 'syaitādṛśo bhāvas
tayor yukto hi me priyaḥ

"Because of their exceptional love, they were allowed to raise the Lord as their child and cherish his many wonderful activities. Therefore his special attitude toward them is fitting, and very much pleasing to me."

The characteristics of their greatness are very evident. What was done in raising Kṛṣṇa by Nanda and Yaśodā (tābhyām) is very famous or of great variety, or is indescribable (tat tat). Because of what I have described, Kṛṣṇa's (asya) love (bhāvaḥ) for them which was directly experienced was appropriate (yuktaḥ) and is pleasing to me also. Otherwise he would be accused of being ungrateful.

TEXT 81

atha śrī-rukmiṇī devī
sa-harṣam idam abravīt
yad-vākya-śravaṇāt sarva-
bhaktānāṁ prema vardhate

[Uddhava continued:] Then Rukmiṇī-devī joyfully spoke. By hearing her words, all the devotees' prema for Kṛṣṇa increases.

Her words (idam) are in the next verse. From hearing those words all the devotees develop prema for the Lord since they hear the greatest glories of the devotees with special prema.

TEXT 82

yā bhartṛ-putrādi vihāya sarvaṁ
loka-dvayārthān anapekṣamāṇāḥ
rāsādibhis tādṛśa-vibhramais tad-
rītyābhajaṁs tatra tam enam ārtāḥ

[Rukmiṇī had said:] "Those women gave up everything — their husbands, sons, and all else they had — disregarding their own fortune in this world and the next. Enduring distress, they worshiped the Lord in their own way, enchanting him in the rāsa dance and other pastimes.

The gopīs (yā) giving up husbands and sons, worshipped him by indescribable (tādṛśaiḥ) pastimes (vibhramaiḥ) like the rāsa dance, with indescribable glory (tan-rityā), or in a way unsuitable to be revealed since it was most confidential (tan-rītyā). They had special sweet love similar to that with a paramour. Thirsty for the Lord (enam ārtāḥ), dressed in special clothing in Vṛndāvana's bowers, they served (abhajan) him. That special prema of the Lord for them, greater than his prema for us, is appropriate. These gopīs were indifferent to the practices and goals of this world and the next.

TEXT 83

ato hi yā no bahu-sādhanottamaiḥ
sādhyasya cintyasya ca bhāva-yogataḥ
mahā-prabhoḥ prema-viśeṣa-pālibhiḥ
sat-sādhana-dhyāna-padatvam āgatāḥ

"We can hope to achieve the Lord only by following many rigorous sādhanas, and we can meditate upon him only by strictly training the attention of our hearts. But those gopīs cherished such exceptional prema for him that they easily attained the success of the most advanced stages of meditation.

Because of such worship, produced by heaps of outstanding prema for Kṛṣṇa. They completely attained (āgatāḥ) the results (padatvam) of the best sādhana and meditation—the highest object of worship and the highest attainment of any sādhana.

Uddhava said to the gopīs:

viyoginīnām api paddhatiṁ vo
na yogino gantum api kṣamante
yad dhyeya-rūpasya parasya puṁso
yūyaṁ gatā dhyeya-padaṁ durāpam

Since in your mood of separation, you have traversed a path on which even great yogīs cannot go, you have achieved the Lord, the object of your meditation, though other seekers can focus their attention on Him only with great travail. Padyāvalī

The gopīs attained the highest results because of such worship produced by heaps of outstanding prema for Kṛṣṇa (mahāprabhoḥ), who is achieved by us (naḥ) by many excellent sādhana of services, though not easily, and who is concentrated on or meditated on with great prema (bhava-yogataḥ cintyasya), but not directly attained.

TEXT 84

tāsv etasya hi dharma-karma-suta-pautrāgāra-kṛtyādiṣu
vyagrābhyo 'smad athādaraiḥ patitayā sevā-karībhyo 'dhikaḥ
yukto bhāva-varo na matsara-padaṁ codvāha-bhāgbhyo bhavet
saṁślāghyo 'tha ca yat prabhoḥ priya-janādhīnatva-māhātmya-kṛt

"It is befitting, therefore, that Kṛṣṇa loves them more than us, for we are obsessed with our religious duties, children, grandchildren, homes, household affairs, and so on. We are but his maidservants, worshiping him with reverence like fallen conditioned souls. We married wives should not envy his exceptional love for the gopīs. Rather, we should always glorify that love, for it proves how very subservient he becomes to his beloved devotees."

We are attached (vyagrābhyaḥ) to the activities of dharma (dharma-karma). We serve him with reverence as the master, being fallen (patitayā), since we are married to him. This is the opposite of the gopīs. The gopīs do not depend on unlimited actions for achieving goals in this life or the next, whereas we are attached to these actions. They participate in the indescribable pastimes of the rāsa dance, whereas we simply serve, with great respect, seeing ourselves as fallen, and not with special pure, intense prema. Going to a solitary place in the house, hearing some sounds as messages coming from Kṛṣṇa hiding himself, rising from bed softly because of worry about mothers-in-law, carefully undoing the door bolt, leaving the house, meeting him face to face, they enjoy with him by tight embraces and kisses.

Sometimes in the day time, Kṛṣṇa makes a bed of soft flowers and buds within an appointed bower on the Yamunā, and looks at the path on which the gopīs will come, imagining their coming by the sound of falling leaves. On the pretext of fetching water from the Yamunā, they go to him and enjoy with him.

Sometimes in the evening, maddened by the signals from his flute, with their hair and clothing undone, with ornaments put on the opposite limb, running quickly, they become pained when he shows indifference and speaks deceptive words. Requesting clearly what they desire in humble words, they become overjoyed when he gives up his indifference understanding that it was a joke. Seizing his yellow cloth with force, they pull him to the bower, and satisfy him. In various ways, they serve him spontaneously as a paramour.

We however, marrying him according to the rules, depend on popular dharma, and serve him according to household dharma. Thus their love is not the object of envy for us, since it is improper for the most inferior to be rivals with the greatest persons, just as servant girls do not envy legitimate wives of their master. Rather that love is most worthy of praise, since that love in which the Lord is controlled by his dearest devotees should be especially glorified. It is the best bhāva. That being so, we also desire to be like them. That is the deep intention of her words.

Though actually the queens do not have attachment to dharma and karma, even if it were to exist in them it would not be a fault since it is all for serving the Lord. Rather it becomes a good quality since it causes variety in their service. However, they speak in this way out of natural humility since they lack the auspiciousness of the service of the gopīs. This is understood in other cases also.

TEXT 85

tato 'nyābhiś ca devībhir
etad evānumoditam
sātrājitī paraṁ māna-
gehaṁ tad-asahāviśat

[Uddhava said:] The other queens all agreed. Only Sātrājitī (Satyabhāmā), unable to tolerate those words, entered her chamber of anger.

Jāmbavatī and other queens agreed with Rukmiṇī. They said, "This is correct." Only Satyabhāmā (param) could not tolerate Kṛṣṇa's special affection for the people of Vraja. She became angry and went into her room.

TEXT 86

śrī-parīkṣid uvāca
śrīmad-gopī-jana-prāṇa-
nāthaḥ sa-krodham ādiśat
sā samānīyatām atra
mūrkha-rāja-sutā drutam

Parīkṣit said: The blessed Lord of the life of the gopīs then ordered angrily, "Bring here at once that daughter of the foolish king!"

He whose life is controlled by the gopīs or the master of the gopīs like Rādhā, who were endowed the greatest prema or with all beauty (śrīmat) ordered in anger, because he could not tolerate envy for the gopīs. Satrājit, her father, was the king of fools because he gossiped falsely that Kṛṣṇa had stolen the Syamantaka jewel. Satyabhāmā was his daughter. By his anger he removed that foolish nature in her.

TEXT 87

śreṣṭhā vidagdhāsv abhimāna-sevā-
cāturyato nandayituṁ pravṛttā
gopāla-nārī-rati-lampaṭaṁ taṁ
bhartāram atyanta-vidagdhatāḍhyam

Satyabhāmā, most expert in the arts of amorous love, was always ready to serve her husband in the mood of jealous pride, knowing him also to be fully conversant with the skills of love and eager to enjoy with the cowherd women.

"She was his dearest queen. Why did he act to disturb her mind?" Being the king of lovers, he was preparing to break the anger of a proud woman or acted in this way in order to produce great happiness by the descriptions of the great excellence of his devotees. She was the best of women and was prepared (pravṛttāḥ) to give pleasure to her husband by the skillful service of being proud. The actions of breaking women's pride is a cause of joy for the person most skillful in the arts of love.

TEXT 88

dāsībhyas tādṛśīm ājñāṁ
tasyākarṇya vicakṣaṇā
utthāya mārjayanty aṅgaṁ
tvarayā tatra sāgatā

Upon hearing this order from her maidservants, the intelligent Satyabhāmā got up, bathed, and quickly came before Kṛṣṇa.

Hearing from servant girls the order of her husband (tasya) made in anger (tādṛśīm) "Bring her here", she went to him quickly. Pravṛttāḥ can also be taken as an active verb. She began to give him pleasure by her show of pride.

"Breaking women's pride will decrease respect for the Lord. Why would he become joyful?" He is endowed (āḍhyam) with unlimited (atyanta) skill in the arts of love (vidagdhatā) since he relishes (lampaṭam) amorous relations (rati) with the gopīs like Candrāvalī. He who is most skillful in the arts of love derives great happiness by breaking the pride of the women who are the most skillful in the arts of love. She was knowledgeable about the time to show pride (viśakṣaṇā). She rose from lying on the earth and removed the dust stuck to her limbs from lying on the ground.

TEXT 89

stambhe 'ntardhāpya dehaṁ svaṁ
sthitā lajjā-bhayānvitā
saṁlakṣya prabhuṇā proktā
saṁrambhāveśataḥ sphuṭam

She hid herself behind a pillar and stood there, filled with shame and fear. Kṛṣṇa noticed her and, still angry, spoke to her in a clear voice.

Hiding her body behind a pillar, she remained there. She was noticed by Kṛṣṇa by her special fragrance. Still influenced by anger, he spoke to her clearly. She was filled with shame, because of showing pride at the wrong time (though suppposedly knowledgeable of when to show pride), and was fearful of the Lord's anger.

TEXTS 90–91

śrī-bhagavān uvāca
are sātrājiti kṣīṇa-
citte māno yathā tvayā
kriyate rukmiṇī-prāpta-
pārijātādi-hetukaḥ

tatha vraja-janeṣv asman-
nirbhara-praṇayād api
avare kiṁ na jānāsi
māṁ tad-icchānusāriṇam

The Supreme Lord said: O weak-minded Sātrājitī, just as you grew angry when Rukmiṇī obtained special favors like the pārijāta flower, now you are angry at our intense love for the people of Vraja. Silly woman, don't you know that I am ruled by their desires?

O daughter of foolish Satrājit! He addresses her in anger. O small minded one (kṣīna-citte)! Just as you became angry because Rukmiṇī obtained a pārijāta flower from me, which was brought by Nārada from Svarga, so you become angry because of the great prema I have for the people of Vraja such as Rādhikā. Kṛṣṇa speaks in the plural (asmad) to indicate the similar prema of Balarāma, Rohiṇī and others, or out of respect for himself since he has such great prema for the people of Vraja. Out of anger he addresses Satyabhāmā, "O inferior person!" Do you not know that I follow the desires of the people of Vraja?

TEXT 92

kṛte sarva-parityāge
tair bhadraṁ yadi manyate
śape te 'smin kṣaṇe satyaṁ
tathaiva kriyate mayā

If the people of Vraja thought it good that I renounce everything, I promise you that in a moment I would do just that.

He illustrates how he follows them. If they thought it was good that I give up my wives and children—everything, I would do that immediately. I would give up everything. That is the truth. I swear this to you. By this, he indicates special prema for her, since in the world one makes oaths only to one's dearest.

TEXT 93

stuvatā brahmaṇoktaṁ yad
vṛddha-vākyaṁ na tan mṛṣā
teṣāṁ pratyupakāre 'ham
aśakto 'to mahā-ṛṇī

The praise offered by the venerable Brahmā was not spoken in vain: I can never fully repay these devotees, and so I am utterly indebted to them.

"Why do you not do something to please them? By your powers, anything can be accomplished." What was said by Brahmā in praise of me is not useless since they are statements of an authority (vṛddha).

What did he say? I, the Supreme Lord, am incapable of repaying the people of Vraja. Because of that, I am controlled by them completely like a complete debtor. I am always most anxious because I desire to repay them somehow or other. The praise mentioned are the excellent praises of Brahmā in the Tenth Canto:

eṣāṁ ghoṣa-nivāsinām uta bhavān kiṁ deva rāteti naś
ceto viśva-phalāt phalaṁ tvad-aparaṁ kutrāpy ayan muhyati
sad-veṣād iva pūtanāpi sa-kulā tvām eva devāpitā
yad-dhāmārtha-suhṛt-priyātma-tanaya-prāṇāśayās tvat-kṛte

O Lord! What can you give to the people of Vraja whose houses, possessions, friends, dear ones, bodies, sons, life airs and hearts are dedicated only to you, since there is nothing superior to you or Vraja (which you have already given)? Thinking of this, my mind becomes bewildered. You awarded yourself even to Pūtanā and her family members because she wore the disguise of a nurse. SB 10.14.35

The meaning of the Bhāgavatam verse will be explained later (Bṛhad-bhāgavatāmṛta 1.7.101 onwards).

TEXT 94

yadi ca prītaye teṣāṁ
tatra yāmi vasāmi ca
tathāpi kim api svāsthyaṁ
bhāvyaṁ nālocayāmy aham

But even if for their pleasure I were to return to live with them, I don't see how that would benefit.

"Would they not be satisfied if you went there?" That is not so. This is explained in five verses (94-98). Just going there will not produce happiness. I do not understand how this will cause happiness (svāsthyam), how it will remove the suffering arising from separation from me. Or I do not understand how I will be able to produce (bhāvayam) happiness

TEXT 95

mad-īkṣaṇād eva vigāḍha-bhāvo-
dayena labdhā vikalā vimoham
na daihikaṁ kiñcana te na dehaṁ
vidur na cātmānam aho kim anyat

Just by seeing me they become so dazed and bewildered by ecstasies from deep within that they fail to recognize their own bodies and everything that has to do with their bodies, what to speak of the rest of the world.

The reason why going would not solve the problem is explained. With the appearance of firm or very deep prema just from seeing me, first they will become disfigured (vikalāḥ) with sāttvika-bhāvas like perspiration and shaking of the body, and then because of the Lord appearing there with his associates, they will become completely bewildered (vimoham). This will not be like samādhi. It is inferior since there will be complete emptiness in their consciousness. Or because they will become unhealthy, the people of Vraja, or the cowherds and the gopīs (te) will faint. Or te can refer to the gopīs as gopijanāḥ, without using the feminine form tā. In this way, the gopīs are kept secret. In this state they do not know at all activities related to their bodies or their husbands or sons.

Aho indicates astonishment or lamentation. They do not even know their own selves (ca) or anything related to themselves such as goals in this world and the next. What can be said? Since they are not aware of anything, it is impossible for me to bring them to a normal state of consciousness. Rather, by my glance, they faint because of a manifestation of the highest prema. From seeing their miserable condition, it is better that I do not go there.

TEXT 96

dṛṣṭe 'pi śāmyen mayi tan na duḥkhaṁ
viccheda-cintākulitātmanāṁ vai
harṣāya teṣāṁ kriyate vidhir yo
duḥkhaṁ sa sadyo dvī-guṇī-karoti

So their pain won't be relieved even if they see me. Their hearts will be so disturbed by thoughts of separation from me that whatever measures I take for their happiness will only double their grief.

"In the state of moha why should they not be aware of other things? When you appear with your associates internally, they should also see you externally since that is the nature of deep prema. Since Dhruva did not have such deep prema, though he was absorbed in meditation on the Lord, he did not see the Lord externally. Only by the mercy of the Lord did the Lord make his internal form disappear and let Dhruva see him externally.

sa vai dhiyā yoga-vipāka-tīvrayā
hṛt-padma-kośe sphuritaṁ taḍit-prabham
tirohitaṁ sahasaivopalakṣya
bahiḥ-sthitaṁ tad-avasthaṁ dadarśa

Seeing that the Lord – brilliant as lightning, manifested in the lotus of his heart by intense meditation of advanced yoga, had disappeared suddenly, Dhruva then saw that form situated externally. SB 4.9.2

Thus on seeing you externally, which is the highest result, they will return to normal."

That is true. However, since they have intense grief, even if they see me, they will not immediately return to normal condition. Or because they will worry that there will be future separation, they will again become unconscious.

Even if they see me (mayi dṛṣṭe), their sorrow (duḥkham) produced by separation from me (tat) will not disappear because their bodies, minds or natures (ātmānām) are disturbed (ākulita) by lamentation (cinta) from separation (vicchedena).

The word ākulita is used with the following intention. Because the dhātus become wasted away by fasting for a long time, a person pained by hunger cannot become healthy by obtaining food. He must eat the food, but he will not recover immediately. It will take a long time, using the proper method. Similarly just by seeing me they cannot recover. But if I perform pastimes, this recovery will take place. But it will take a long time by the correct manner as they experience joy. But this cannot be done by me now since I am busy with many activities that must be done elsewhere. How can they become healthy?

Or they are completely disturbed (akulitātmanām) by thinking that in the future, another separation will occur. Since it is their nature to think like that, seeing me directly will not bring them to a normal state. Vai indicates "what has been experienced about this should be remembered by me (Kṛṣṇa)." Or it means "you queens should remember this."

kurari vilapasi tvaṁ vīta-nidrā na śeṣe
svapiti jagati rātryām īśvaro gupta-bodhaḥ
vayam iva sakhi kaccid gāḍha-nirviddha-cetā
nalina-nayana-hāsodāra-līlekṣitena

O kurarī bird, you are lamenting. Now it is night, and somewhere in this world our husband is asleep in a hidden place. But you are wide awake, O friend, unable to fall asleep. Is it that, like us, you have had your heart pierced to the core by the lotus-eyed Lord's munificent, playful smiling glances? SB 10.90.15

The queens uttered ten verses. This however is not at a time of real separation since the verses mentions that the Lord is sleeping at night. However it is actually daytime, during their pastime of playing in the water. Śukadeva says:

ūcur mukundaika-dhiyo gira unmatta-vaj jaḍam
cintayantyo 'ravindākṣaṁ tāni me gadataḥ śṛṇu

The queens would become stunned in ecstatic trance, their minds absorbed in Kṛṣṇa alone. Then, thinking that their lotus-eyed Lord was absent, they would talk as if insane. Please hear these words from me as I relate them. SB 10.90.14

The meaning of this verses is as follows. The queens were absorbed in Mukunda completely and for a moment could not speak (agiraḥ). Again thinking of their lotus-eyed Lord, they spoke as if stunned. Please hear those words from me as I speak.

"Since you are the most skillful lover and full of all powers, you should give them enjoyment, so that they can live happily even if there is sometime separation." Whatever arrangements (sweet pastimes) I made for the happiness of the people of Vraja, or the gopīs (teṣām), immediately upon being made doubled their grief. An example may be given. In order to reduce the heat, if one sprinkles water on hot oil, fire bursts forth.

The meaning is this. They say, "How can we tolerate separation from Kṛṣṇa?" However even if I remain for a long time, they will think, "Being of fickle nature, now he is about to go somewhere else." Because their grief has been aroused, if I perform very sweet pastimes, their suffering will simply increase. I have imparted the quatlity of heat to fire. How can I take away that quality from fire? Similarly I have given to them this special nature by my extraordinary mercy. How can I take away that nature from them, since this is the special perfection of their outstanding greatness?

Kṛṣṇa is the form of condensed sweet bliss. Though great bliss, which corresponds to his bliss, sometimes manifests in the gopīs by his direct embraces, etc., the special prema arising from separation from him, is generally manifested in the gopīs, who are recipients of special great mercy, since that form of prema is composed of the highest pinnacle of happiness, the greatest state.

Though separation arises generally in all devotees when they do not have the Lord, the happiness experienced by the gopīs does not arise in them, since they do not have similar prema, and consequently the similar pain of separation does not arise. That type of prema is achieved only by Kṛṣṇa's special great mercy, usually by meeting him face to face. I cannot at all directly witness their manifestation of disturbance from the highest prema. Thus I do not live there or go there.

TEXT 97

adṛśyamāne ca mayi pradīpta-
viyoga-vahner vikalāḥ kadācit
mṛtā ivonmāda-hatāḥ kadācid
vicitra-bhāvaṁ madhuraṁ bhajante

And when they cannot see me they become so torn that the fire of separation leaves them sometimes as though dead and sometimes as though insane. Thus they partake of the nectar of wonderful activities.

"But it is not proper to reject them. This would give you the fault of ingratitude." This is answered in two verses (97-98). Becoming confused because of the fire-like pain from separation, they sometimes appear dead since they are devoid of external activities, by the spread of extreme bewilderment. Sometimes becoming overcome by insanity, the people of Vraja (te) take shelter of a variety of activities (bhāvam).

TEXT 98

tamisra-puñjādi yad eva kiñcin
madīya-varṇopamam īkṣyate taiḥ
sa-cumbanaṁ tat parirabhyate mad-
dhiyā paraṁ tat kva nu varṇanīyam

If they see a patch of darkness resembling my complexion, they embrace and kiss it, mistaking it for me. What more can I describe?

If some dark object, having a complexion similar to mine is seen by the people of Vraja or the gopīs, thinking it is me, they embrace it while kissing it. "That is amazing! Describe more." To what person (kva) can imitating my pastimes be described? It cannot be described to anyone since no one is qualified. Or on hearing, they will also develop similar lamentation.

Thus, even being there I cannot remove their suffering of thinking of future separation or cannot give them any happiness. Even in separation from me, they sometimes experience the happiness of meeting me and seeing me. I cannot repay that at all. I am a great debtor. Ingratitude is negated since he is incapable of doing anything.

TEXT 99

ata eva mayā svasya
sthitim apy asthiteḥ samām

dṛṣṭvā na gamyate tatra
śṛṇv arthaṁ yuṣmad-udvahe

Therefore my staying with them would be equal to my absence. Realizing this, I have not returned there. Now hear the real reason I married you.

For this reason I do not stay personally in Vraja. Understanding that it is the same as my being absent, I do not go there. The meaning is this. Seeing their disturbance by seeing me, I disappear. And when I have disappeared seeing their disturbance, I directly appear. I cannot bring them to a normal healthy state by any means. Thus I am always in anxiety. I am in an unhealthy state. Thus it was properly said that I cannot see how going there will bring them to a normal condition. So I am their debtor. Whatever arrangements I make for their happiness, such as going there, living there and having pastimes there, doubles their grief.

The Lord indicates that he did go to Vraja, stay there and perform pastimes there. The people of Ānarta praise the Lord as follows:

yarhy ambujākṣāpasasāra bho bhavān
kurūn madhūn vātha suhṛd-didṛkṣayā
tatrābda-koṭi-pratimaḥ kṣaṇo bhaved
raviṁ vinākṣṇor iva nas tavācyuta

O lotus-eyed Lord! When you go to Hastināpura or Vraja to see your friends, one moment becomes like a trillion years for us, who belong to you, and who become like eyes without the sun. SB 1.11.9

The women of Mathurā speak:

aho alaṁ ślāghyatamaṁ yadoḥ kulam
aho alaṁ puṇyatamaṁ madhor vanam
yad eṣa puṁsām ṛṣabhaḥ śriyaḥ patiḥ
sva-janmanā caṅkramaṇena cāñcati

Oh! Most praiseworthy is the family of Yadu! Most purifying is Mathurā-maṇḍala which Kṛṣṇa, the best of men, the Lord of auspiciousness, respects by taking birth there, moving about and performing pastimes. SB 1.10.26

puṇyā bata vraja-bhuvo yad ayaṁ nṛ-liṅga
gūḍhaḥ purāṇa-puruṣo vana-citra-mālyaḥ
gāḥ pālayan saha-balaḥ kvaṇayaṁś ca veṇuṁ
vikrīdayāñcati giritra-ramārcitāṅghriḥ

How pious are the tracts of land in Vraja, for there the oldest person, disguising himself with human traits, wanders about, enacting his many pastimes! Adorned with wonderfully variegated forest garlands, he whose feet are worshiped by Śiva and Lakṣmī vibrates his flute as he tends the cows in the company of Balarāma. SB 10.44.13

Particularly in Padma Purāṇa, Uttara-khāṇda, Śiva in speaking to Pārvatī indicates that Kṛṣṇa returned to Vraja. In this work, in the second part, in the glorification of Goloka, his many continual pastimes there are described. The Lord does not clearly indicate his going to Gokula to the queens like Satyabhāmā, since he could not tolerate anyone's great pain. He was worried about their mental anguish.

"Why did you marry us?" Hear the cause (artham) of those marriages in six verses (100-105).

TEXT 100

tāsām abhāve pūrvaṁ me
vasato mathurā-pure
vivāha-karaṇe kācid
icchāpy āsīn na mānini

My dear proud lady, when living in Mathurā-purī without the gopīs I at first had no desire to marry.

Being separated from the gopīs like Rādhā, I did not desire to marry. Now, in this verse Kṛṣṇa uses the feminine form (tāsām), whereas previously he used a masculine form to indicate the gopīs indirectly, since the queens became absorbed in them by the discussions or it is suitable to the present discussion.

TEXT 101

mad-anāptyā tu rukmiṇyā
vāñchantyāḥ prāṇa-mocanam
śrutvāsyā vipra-vadanād
ārti-vijñapti-patrikām

But from the mouth of a brāhmaṇa I heard Rukmiṇī's letter, which told of her distress and her intention to give up her life if she could not obtain me.

"Being most confused, how did you take Rukmiṇī at the svayaṁvara ceremony and marry her?" That is explained in two verses (101-102).

Mad-anāptyā can mean "by not attaining me" or as a pun, "by attaining someone other than me as a lover." Not attaining me she desired to give up her life.

yasyāṅghri-paṅkaja-rajaḥ-snapanaṁ mahānto
vāñchanty umā-patir ivātma-tamo-'pahatyai
yarhy ambujākṣa na labheya bhavat-prasādaṁ
jahyām asūn vrata-kṛśān śata-janmabhiḥ syāt

O lotus-eyed one, great souls like Śiva hanker to bathe in the dust of your lotus feet and thereby destroy their ignorance. If I cannot obtain your mercy, I shall simply give up my vital force, which will have become weak from the severe penances I will perform. Then, after hundreds of lifetimes of endeavor, I may obtain your mercy. SB 10.52.43

She reveals her pain and misery:

śrutvā guṇān bhuvana-sundara śṛṇvatāṁ te
nirviśya karṇa-vivarair harato 'ṅga-tāpam
rūpaṁ dṛśāṁ dṛśimatām akhilārtha-lābhaṁ
tvayy acyutāviśati cittam apatrapaṁ me

O beauty of the worlds, having heard of your qualities, which enter the ears of those who hear and remove their bodily distress, and having also heard of your beauty, which fulfills all desires of those who see, I have fixed my shameless mind upon you, O Kṛṣṇa. SB 10.52.37

In this way she made her request in seven verses. I heard of her pain through a letter coming from the mouth of a brāhmaṇa, the son of a priest she had sent. Kṛṣṇa ordered the brāhmaṇa to read the letter. The word āsyaḥ (of her) indicates that Rukmiṇī was present as Kṛṣṇa spoke, so there was nothing false in what he said.

TEXT 102

mahā-duṣṭa-nṛpa-śreṇi-
darpaṁ saṁharatā mayā
pāṇir gṛhītaḥ saṅgrāme
hṛtvā rājñāṁ prapaśyatām

So I destroyed the pride of a host of wicked kings in battle, took her hand, and carried her off as all the kings watched.

In order to destroy the pride of a host of evil kings like Jarāsandha and Śiśupāla, I took her away forcibly in the midst of battle, while the kings watched (helplessly), bringing her from Kuṇḍina to Dvārakā, and married her. I married her out of necessity, not out of affection in my mind.

TEXT 103

asyāḥ sandarśanāt tāsām
ādhikyena smṛter bhavāt
mahā-śokārti-janakāt
paramākulatām agām

But the sight of Rukmiṇī made me remember the gopīs all the more. And the sorrow and distress this caused me made me very much disturbed.

"Why did you marry other queen like me?" Three verses (103-105) answer. Because of arousal of memory even more of the gopīs from seeing Rukmiṇī, which produced lamentation, I became more disturbed. Because of some resemblance of Rukmiṇī to the gopīs he began to remember the gopīs even more. The great sorrow and lamentation from separation which had somehow disappeared now increased, and created a great disturbance.

TEXTS 104–105

ṣoḍaśānāṁ sahasrāṇāṁ
sa-śatānāṁ mad-āptaye
kṛta-kātyāyanī-pūjā-
vratānāṁ gopa-yoṣitām

nidarśanād iva svīyaṁ
kiñcit svasthayituṁ manaḥ
tāvatya eva yūyaṁ vai
mayātraitā vivāhitāḥ

Some 16,100 gopīs had with vows worshiped Kātyāyanī to obtain me. To bring my mind somewhat to peace by seeing a likeness of them, I married the same number of you queens here in Dvārakā.

16,100 unmarried gopīs worshipped Kātyāyanī to marry Kṛṣṇa. Concerning gopī-tīrtha, Mathurā-māhātmya says gopyo gayanti nṛtyanti sahasrāni ca ṣoḍaṣa: sixteen thousand gopīs sang and danced. The word ca indicates that a hundred extra gopīs were there, though not mentioned. All the young gopīs were in love with Kṛṣṇa. Thus there were many more not mentioned.

kātyāyani mahā-māye mahā-yoginy adhīśvari
nanda-gopa-sutaṁ devi patiṁ me kuru te namaḥ

"O goddess Kātyāyanī, O great potency of the Lord, O possessor of great mystic power and mighty controller of all, please make the son of Nanda Mahārāja my husband. I offer my obeisances unto you." SB 10.22.4

Uttering this mantra while making their vow, undertaking this vow with thirst in great prema, praying that Kṛṣṇa be their husband, these unmarried gopīs showed great attraction to Kṛṣṇa. These gopīs are particularly praised here. They worshipped Kātyāyanī in order to attain him as their husband.

Because it was somewhat like seeing them directly with their distinctive features, though exact likeness was lacking, I married sixteen thousand one hundred and eight queens, a similar number. In mentioning large numbers smaller numbers (like eight) are not mentioned, but are included in the large number. Vai indicate that it is well known.

TEXT 106

aho bhāmini jānīhi
tat tan mama mahā-sukham
mahimāpi sa māṁ hitvā
tasthau tatrocitāspade

Ah, willful woman, please understand. All that I relished in Vraja gave me the highest pleasure. And though the glory of those times has now abandoned me, it still resides in that most worthy place.

However, here I do not have that same happiness. Such great happiness has gone by separation from them. That indescribable (saḥ) great happiness has given me up. It remains in Vraja (tatra), the suitable place (ucita āspade) for it.

TEXT 107

citrāti-citrai rucirair vihārair
ānanda-pāthodhi-taraṅga-magnaḥ
nājñāsiṣaṁ rātri-dināni tāni
tat-tan-mahā-mohana-loka-saṅgāt

When submerged in the waves of that ocean of ecstasy, enjoying the ever-fresh charming pastimes of Vraja, I was so attracted to each of the

all-enchanting residents that I was never aware of the passing of the nights and days.

Six verses (107-112) explain this. First three verses (107-109) describe the great happiness he experienced in Vraja. By attractive pastimes, more astonishing than the astonishing—what astonishes the hearts of everyone in the universe, I was immersed in the waves of an ocean of bliss. I was not aware of the days at that time or the days related to Vraja (tāni) because of association of the most indescribable (tat tat), enchanting residents of Vraja. I was also immersed in waves of bliss because of their association.

TEXT 108

bālya-krīḍā-kautukenaiva te te
daitya-śreṣṭhā māritāḥ kāliyo 'pi
duṣṭo nirdamyāśu niḥsārito 'sau
pāṇau savye 'dhāri govardhanaḥ saḥ

In the joy of my childhood sports, I killed various eminent demons. I quickly subdued the evil Kāliya and sent him into exile. And on my left hand I held Govardhana Hill.

"But there would be sorrow due to exertion in killing the wicked demons." No, they were killed as child's play. They were like dolls. They were many (te te), like Pūtanā who had a hard stone-like body extending six krośas. They were the best of demons, showing their powers by manifesting shapes at will. They were not human forms like Śālva.

Most frightening Kāliya, (asau), was completely subdued (nirdamya) in the joy of childhood pastimes. Because of the punishment of dancing on his thousand hoods, he was exiled from the Yamunā lake. The most high (saḥ) Govardhana was held on my left hand with joy as child's play. It was not suffering or fearful at all. Rather it produced great joy.

TEXT 109

tādṛk-santoṣārṇave 'haṁ nimagno
yena stotraṁ kurvatāṁ vandanaṁ ca
brahmādīnāṁ bhāṣaṇe darśane ca
manvāno 'ghaṁ vyasmaraṁ deva-kṛtyam

I was so absorbed in that ocean of contentment that having to talk to such devatās as Brahmā and watch them offer me prayers and homage

seemed a painful disturbance. I forgot the work I had to do for the devatās.

What was that happiness? By being immersed in the ocean of happiness, I consider speaking to and seeing Brahmā and even Indra and Nārada (ādīnām) to be suffering (agham) when they offered respects and praises to me. I forgot the work I had to do for the devatās, such as killing Kaṁsa.

TEXT 110

rūpeṇa veṣeṇa ravāmṛtena
vaṁśyāś ca pūrvānuditena viśvam
sammohitaṁ prema-bhareṇa kṛtsnaṁ
tiṣṭhantu dūre vraja-vāsinas te

My beautiful form, my dress, and the nectarean sound of my flute, never heard before, enchanted the whole universe with overwhelming prema. So what to speak of how these affected the residents of Vraja.

The unparalleled greatness of the people of Vraja is described in three verses (110-112). The universe was enchanted with his beauty while he was in Vraja. Of course, he speaks in this way out of regret, since he is still beautiful after leaving Vraja. His beauty never changes. He is ornamented with peacock feather and guñja berries in his crown. The sound of his flute produces the sweetest bliss (amṛtena). The beauty, dress and flute sound had not previously manifested (pūrvānuditena) in this world. The whole universe was bewildered by my beauty, dress and flute sound. Why? Because it was all filled with great prema (prema-bhareṇa), with rasa greater than the bliss of Brahman, and not with the happiness of māyā or of samādhi. The cowherds and gopīs of Vraja, who taste the rasa of affection for me constantly, are thus far beyond the general public in this regard. It is fitting that they are completely bewildered because of the great prema caused by my beauty, dress and flute. Or how can the response of the people of Vraja be described?

TEXTS 111–112

ākāśa-yānā vidhi-rudra-śakrāḥ
siddhāḥ śaśī deva-gaṇās tathānye
gāvo vṛṣā vatsa-gaṇā mṛgāś ca
vṛkṣāḥ khagā gulma-latās tṛṇāni

nadyo 'tha meghāḥ sa-carāḥ sthirāś ca
sacetanācetanakāḥ prapañcāḥ

prema-pravāhottha-vikāra-ruddhāḥ
sva-sva-svabhāvāt parivṛttim āpuḥ

Brahmā, Rudra, Indra, Candra, the Siddhas, and other devatās moving in the sky were overcome by changes aroused in them by the current of prema. So too were the cows, bulls, calves, and wild beasts, the trees, birds, bushes, creepers, and grass. The rivers were overcome, and the clouds, and all other beings, both moving and nonmoving, alive and inert. Each of them underwent a transformation by which their own nature changed into a nature just the opposite.

This is explained in two verses. Besides those in the list, the sages, Gandharvas, and Vidyādharas developed transformations such as perspiration, trembling and hairs standing on end which arose because of full taste of prema and also experienced changes from their normal natures. Those who flew in the air touched the earth. The cows and other animals, moving entities, went into samādhi, a state of the highest jñāna. Trees and shrubs, immovable entities, starting moving about with trembling, etc. The unconscious rivers which flow downwards sometimes stopped their flow and sometimes flowed backwards. What to speak of the entities in Vraja, things in the sky such as the fast moving clouds became motionless and became umbrellas.

vividha-gopa-caraṇeṣu vidagdho
veṇu-vādya urudhā nija-śikṣāḥ
tava sutaḥ sati yadādhara-bimbe
datta-veṇur anayat svara-jātīḥ
savanaśas tad upadhārya sureśāḥ
śakra-śarva-parameṣṭhi-purogāḥ
kavaya ānata-kandhara-cittāḥ
kaśmalaṁ yayur aniścita-tattvāḥ

O pious mother Yaśodā, your son, who is expert in all the arts of herding cows, has invented many new styles of flute-playing. When he takes his flute to his bimba-red lips and sends forth the tones of the harmonic scale in variegated melodies, Brahmā, Śiva, Indra and other chief devatās listen repeatedly to the sound. Although they are the most learned authorities, with hearts in submission, they cannot ascertain the meaning and forget everything. SB 10.35.14-15

These verses will be explained later.

TEXT 113

etat satyam asatyaṁ vā
kālindī pṛcchyatām iyam
yā tu vraja-jana-svaira-
vihārānanda-sākṣiṇī

You can ask Kālindī whether or not this is true. She witnessed the blissful pastimes freely enjoyed by the people of Vraja.

Do not think that I am praising just become I am full of prema. The sister of Yamarāja, the most pious Yamunā, is the witness. Ask her about all that I said. She is the witness to the bliss of my independent pastimes performed with the people of Vraja or caused by them. Or she is the witness to the bliss of the independent pastimes of the people of Vraja with me.

TEXT 114

adhunā tu sa evāhaṁ
sva-jñātīn yādavān api
netuṁ nārhāmi taṁ bhāvaṁ
narma-krīḍā-kutūhalaiḥ

But I cannot arouse the same emotions now in my relatives the Yādavas, either with joking or with entertaining pastimes.

"Being separated from your people and those pastimes, why can you not still have such happiness of pastimes? Since your greatness is unchanging at all times, it must exist here in Dvārakā also."

No that is not possible. I, being unchanging by nature (saḥ), cannot arouse that prema previously described (tam) in my relatives, even though they are related to me (sva-jñātīn). Or I am not able to produce prema like that of the people of Vraja (tam) in them even if I joke, have water pastimes in the ocean or have festive marriages (kutūhalaiḥ) with them.

TEXT 115

duṣkaraṁ me babhūvātra
tvādṛśāṁ māna-bhañjanam
ato 'tra muralī tyaktā
lajjayaiva mayā priyā

Here in Dvārakā I have found it difficult to break the jealous pride of queens like you. Embarrassed, I have therefore put aside my dear flute.

Here it is difficult for me to break the pride of queens like you. Actually it is not difficult but easy for him to break their pride since pride is unfavorable to the heart of the Lord. "Even hear you should take up your flute, which enchants the whole world." Because I cannot break their pride I have given up the dear flute, as if (iva) out of embarrassment. The lord of lords would be embarrassed in front of people by accepting pastimes of a cowherd. Actually he covered up the glories of his skillful flute playing in Dvārakā.

Or iva is just an ornament, and because he could not play the flute in the same manner here, he gave up trying out of embarrassment. My glories manifest in the appropriate place (not in Dvārakā).

TEXT 116

aho bata mayā tatra
kṛtaṁ yādṛk sthitaṁ yathā
tad astu kila dūre 'tra
nirvaktuṁ ca na śakyate

Alas, what I did and how I lived in Vraja seem here so far away that with you I cannot even speak of those things.

"You are always full of all powers. If you desire to do anything or establish anything, will it not immediately happen just as you wish, even here in Dvārakā?"

That is true. That desire arises in my particular place. Thus the same pastimes do not appear elsewhere. Aho bata indicates great lamentation. I performed pastimes as a child and by some means I remained there with the happiness as the enjoyer of the gopīs. What to speak of performing those actions or remaining in such happiness in Dvārakā, I cannot even describe those pastimes here. If the queens hear those pastimes, they will faint in prema.

TEXT 117

ekaḥ sa me tad-vraja-loka-vat priyas
tādṛṅ-mahā-prema-bhara-prabhāvataḥ
vakṣyaty adaḥ kiñcana bādarāyaṇir
maj-jīvite śiṣya-vare sva-sannibhe

Just one person, almost as dear to me as the devotees of Vraja, will be able to describe those topics — Śukadeva, the son of Badarāyaṇa Vyāsa.

By the power of his great prema in the mood of the Vraja-vāsīs, he will speak something of those matters to his excellent disciple who resembles him in spiritual qualities and whom I once brought back to life.

"Without speaking and without hearing about those pastimes, how will the main goal of your avatāra—spreading the rasa of prema—take place in Kali-yuga?" One person, most famous (saḥ), dear to me like the cowherds and gopīs of Vraja, Śukadeva, will speak by the power of great prema, which is similar to that of the people of Vraja, a little of my childhood pastimes (adaḥ) to his disciple Parīkṣit, who was brought to life by me.

Kṛṣṇa prevented the brahmāstra sent by Aśvatthāma from burning Parīkṣit up in the womb. Or according to Mahābhārata, Parīkṣit was born dead but was brought back to life by Kṛṣṇa. Or Parīkṣit's very life was Kṛṣṇa. Without bhakti to Kṛṣṇa, nothing could take place in his life. He could not live for a moment without Kṛṣṇa. He was similar to Śukadeva (sva-sannibhe). He was the best disciple or the incomparable disciple. Thus Śukadeva would reveal to him the highest secret. Because of the power of such a speaker and listener, the knowledge could be spread anywhere in Kali-yuga.

TEXT 118

śrī-parīkṣid uvāca
etādṛśaṁ tad-vraja-bhāgya-vaibhavaṁ
saṁrambhataḥ kīrtayato mahā-prabhoḥ
punas tathā-bhāva-niveśa-śaṅkayā
tāḥ preritā mantri-vareṇa saṁjñayā

Parīkṣit said: As the Supreme Lord continued ardently praising the splendor of the good fortune of Vraja, the expert counselor Uddhava grew anxious, for the special ecstasies of Vraja might again draw the Lord into a trance. With a gesture, therefore, he prompted the ladies to do something.

The Lord praised the good fortune of the people of Vraja in anger (at Satyabhāmā) or with absorption (samrambhataḥ). Worried that Kṛṣṇa would again enter into great pain and start crying (tathā-bhava), Uddhava, the best counsellor, made a signal to all the queens.

TEXT 119

sarvā mahiṣyaḥ saha satyabhāmayā
bhaiṣmy-ādayo drāg abhisṛtya mūrdhabhiḥ
pādau gṛhītvā ruditārdra-kākubhiḥ
saṁstutya bhartāram aśīśamaṁś chanaiḥ

Satyabhāmā, Rukmiṇī, and the other queens at once surrounded their husband, touching his feet with their heads. By offering prayers with plaintive voices wet with sobs, they gradually calmed him down.

All the queens along with Satyabhāmā quickly approached their husband Kṛṣṇa, and gradually calmed him of his anger or absorption. It was not possible for him to quickly give up that mood. They touched his two lotus feet with their heads and praised him with plaintive impassioned (ārdra) voices while crying.

TEXT 120

bhojanārthaṁ ca tenaiva
devakī rohiṇī tathā
anna-pānādi-sahite
tatra śīghraṁ praveśite

Uddhava also urged Devakī and Rohiṇī to come in quickly with the food and drink for Kṛṣṇa's meal.

How could Kṛṣṇa give up the topics? It was the skill of the great devotee Uddhava. Two verses (120-121) explain this. Rohiṇī entered at this time. She was the best of the clever. Previously she had gone to the kitchen to prepare a meal. Now she came to the Lord. Balarāma, the best of the wise, had gone to his room on the pretext of taking a bath. (Thus they did not hear the confidential topics).

TEXT 121

baladevaṁ kṛta-snānaṁ
praveśya kṛtinā tadā
dvārānte nāradas tiṣṭhed
iti vijñāpito vibhuḥ

The expert Uddhava had Baladeva come in after finishing his bath. Uddhava then informed Lord Kṛṣṇa that Nārada was standing in the doorway.

Kṛṣṇa (vibhuḥ) was informed by Uddhava, the clever (kṛtinā), that Nārada was standing at the door.

TEXT 122

sarvāntar-ātma-dṛk prāha
sa-smitaṁ nanda-nandanaḥ
adya kena niruddho 'sau
yan nāyāty atra pūrva-vat

Kṛṣṇa is the all-knowing seer of everyone's heart, but he asked with a smile, "Why is he being kept standing there? Why doesn't he come in as usual?"

As antaryāmī, Kṛṣṇa knew what was happening. Thus he spoke with a smile, understanding why Nārada had come. "Why did he not become angry with Nārada's actions, which caused great problems?" Nārada was there in order to reveal the glories of the people of Nanda's Vraja. Kṛṣṇa as Nanda-nandana did not disagree with this.

Or though Kṛṣṇa knows everyone's heart, he asked why Nārada did not come in, as if he did not know. "Why does he not come in?" He acted in this way because he is the crest jewel of all rasikas (nanda-nandanaḥ). Has he been stopped since (yat) he does not come to my side (atra) as previously. Just as at all times he is unobstructed, and by himself comes here, why he does not come today?

TEXT 123

pratyuvācoddhavaḥ smitvā
prabho bhītyāpi lajjayā
tato brahmaṇya-devena
svayam uktaḥ praveśya saḥ

Uddhava smiled and answered, "My Lord, because he is afraid and embarrassed." Then the Lord, who always favors the brāhmaṇas, himself brought Nārada inside and spoke to him.

Uddhava also smiled, remembering Nārada's actions. Uddhava then answered. Nārada did not enter the room because he feared committing an offence. "But he is never afraid of me." He is also embarrassed. Great devotees are naturally embarrassed by their ecstatic transformations arising from deep prema. Or he is embarrassed at causing a great disturbance in the universe. For that reason (tataḥ) the Lord, attracted to brāhmaṇas, got up, approached Nārada, offered him respect with reverence, took him by the hand and brought him into his excellent room.

After worshipping him he spoke to him. All this is understood from the words brahmaṇya-devena, respectful to brāhmaṇas.

TEXT 124

śrī-bhagavān uvāca
mat-prīty-utpādana-vyagra
śrī-nārada suhṛt-tama
hitam evākṛtātyantaṁ
bhavān me rasikottama

The Supreme Lord said: Nārada, my dearest friend, you are always eager to please me, and you are the best of those who relish transcendental emotions. You have now done me a great favor.

O Nārada always anxious to please me! O best friend, acting for my benefit in the best way (suhṛttama)! Or best helper, with no conditions! You have helped in the best way. You did not commit any offense. O best of those greedy for my lotus feet (rasika uttama)! Those actions are the very nature of my rasikas. There is nothing to be ashamed of.

TEXT 125

prāg yady api prema-kṛtāt priyāṇāṁ
viccheda-dāvānala-vegato 'ntaḥ
santāpa-jātena duranta-śokā-
veśena gāḍhaṁ bhavatīva duḥkham

It is true that, when one is parted from those one loves, prema makes one suffer within, as if from a blazing forest fire. The burning pain creates a remorse that further deepens into irrepressible sorrow. Thus one at first seems wretched.

"I am not ashamed of trembling with bhakti for you. But by causing great suffering to you by producing bewilderment, how does that benefit you?" Kṛṣṇa answers in two verses (125-126).

Because of the force of great pain internally and externally like a forest fire, caused by separation from dear ones, in the beginning there is deep sorrow because of entering into or being conquered by unlimited lamentation arising from the internal pain. That force of intense pain in separation arises from prema (prema-kṛṭāt). According to the intensity of prema, there is intensity of sorrow in separation.

The word iva is used to indicate that the sorrow transforms, with manifestation of happiness in the end. Or it only resembles sorrow, but is internally a type of happiness. It has an appearance of sorrow—being disturbed like an ordinary miserable person. Or iva is uttered as common practice with no particular meaning.

TEXT 126

tathāpi sambhoga-sukhād api stutaḥ
sa ko 'py anirvācya-tamo mano-ramaḥ
pramoda-rāśiḥ pariṇāmato dhruvaṁ
tatra sphuret tad-rasikaika-vedyaḥ

This sorrow always transforms at last into an abundance of pleasure, which is praised as greater than the happiness of meeting, which is most indescribable, and which is pleasing to the mind. Only a person greedy for prema can understand this.

Though there is such sorrow, from a transformation, later great joy (pramoda-rāśiḥ) certainly will appear. That joy is praised more than the happiness at the time of meeting (sambhoga). That joy is greater than the joy of meeting. How is it described? The bliss of worship is more indescribable that the indescribable bliss of Brahman. The bliss of prema is more indescribable than that. But the bliss arising through pain of separation is even more indescribable, because that joy reaches the highest limits (anirvācyatamaḥ). Though that joy arises from sorrow, it is not displeasing. It is very pleasing (manoramaḥ). "How is it possible to experience happiness in sorrow?" It can be known only by the person who is greedy for prema (rasika ekena).

TEXT 127

tac-choka-duḥkhoparamasya paścāc
cittaṁ yataḥ pūrṇatayā prasannam
samprāpta-sambhoga-mahā-sukhena
sampanna-vat tiṣṭhati sarvadaiva

After the pain of despair is relieved, one's heart feels fully satisfied, delighting constantly as one enjoys the great pleasure of meeting with one's beloved.

"From intense sorrow at its height, bewilderment filled with that intense sorrow or death may occur. How does great joy arise from that? After happiness there is sorrow. After sorrow there is happiness. One follows the other. In that sense, one causes the other. But how can one recognize that joy arises from a transformation of sorrow?"

The proof is one's own experience, because of a manifestation of happiness at this time. One sees no other cause (other than the sorrow). After the cessation of lamentation and sorrow caused by separation, or after the sorrow caused by lamentation arising from separation, because of that (yataḥ), the minds of those suffering and lamenting from separation becomes happy at all times, and remains with fullness, with no lacking. That mind is as if endowed with the great happiness of having achieved perfect union. "As if" is used to express the fact that actually the happiness arises from the sorrow of separation, not from the union. For this reason, one can believe that joy arises from a transformation of sorrow.

The meaning is this. Just as when performing actions with dear friends, the mind becomes full of great happiness, one must infer that, when the lamentation subsides, there is a manifestation of joy (cause), because of the happiness of the mind (effect inferred). There can be no happiness in the mind without the manifestation of special happiness. Because there is no other cause for the manifestation of happiness, one must infer that it manifests from the sorrow of separation.

TEXT 128

icchet punas tādṛśam eva bhāvaṁ
kliṣṭaṁ kathañcit tad-abhāvataḥ syāt
yeṣāṁ na bhātīti mate 'pi teṣāṁ
gāḍhopakārī smṛti-daḥ priyāṇām

One may want to feel that separation again, and may indeed feel distressed if one cannot. Thus a person who can remind one of a beloved not present is considered the most sincere and helpful friend.

"It is said that after happiness comes suffering and after suffering comes happiness. So after suffering there is happiness. At the time of lamentation, however, there is only suffering. To have a manifestation of happiness at that time is illogical. The happiness of worship is greater than the bliss of Brahman. And the bliss of prema is greater than the bliss of worship. If there is pain and lamentation of suffering within that prema, that bliss of prema would be contradicted."

That is not so since on considering such suffering, it is a form of happiness. That is explained in this verse. One may desire such a condition—the heart of the person in separation, in great lamentation, pain and weeping. This condition is never absent in the beloved gopīs. If that were to happen for some reason, they would feel the greatest suffering. Since no one desires sorrow, the lack of sorrow in separation should normally be considered happiness. Though it appears like sorrow it is actually the highest level of happiness. When ice is applied to the limbs of the body, one may feel it to be like the touch of fiery coals, because of the lack of sensitivity that has arisen. Just as the perception of hot coals is false, and the numb sensation is true, the perception of sorrow in separation is false, and happiness is true. The suffering due to separation is of this nature (bliss) for some of the devotees of the Lord, and not for all. Thus there is no contradiction.

Though this is stated by the Lord concerning himself, it also applies to his devotees suffering in separation. It applies to the devotees other than the gopīs since the gopīs are never free of the pain of separation. Even in union they are worried about separation and this means suffering. That was previously explained.

They also never desire the pain in separation since it feels like a million forest fires. The gopīs speak to Uddhava:

saric-chaila-vanoddeśā gāvo veṇu-ravā ime
saṅkarṣaṇa-sahāyena kṛṣṇenācaritāḥ prabho

Dear Uddhava, when Kṛṣṇa was here in the company of Balarāma, he served all these rivers, hills, forests, cows and flute sounds.

punaḥ punaḥ smārayanti nanda-gopa-sutaṁ bata
śrī-niketais tat-padakair vismartuṁ naiva śaknumaḥ

All these remind us constantly of Nanda's son. Because we see Kṛṣṇa's footprints, which are marked with fine symbols, we can never forget him. SB 10.47.49-50

The meaning is this. Kṛṣṇa served the rivers and hills (ācaritāḥ). The unhappiness of forgetting Kṛṣṇa does not take place. Because of the increased pain of separation by remembering him, they desire to forget him. How could they desire the fire of separation?

Thus the gopīs will always experience the greatest happiness from the manifestation of sorrow in separation with great force at all times. Because such happiness is produced in this way and takes this form, the gopīs are thus considered greater than all the other devotees. That was said by me and is hereby proven.

In the opinion of those who do not have this manifestation of pain, the person who can give the dear devotees remembrance is considered to be the best benefactor. It should be considered that such persons think like this.

TEXT 129

kathañcana smāraṇam eva teṣām
avehi taj-jīvana-dānam eva
teṣāṁ yato vismaraṇaṁ kadācit
prāṇādhikānāṁ maraṇāc ca nindyam

Please understand: When somehow reminded of those one loves, one is given back one's life. Forgetting those more dear than one's own breath is more painful than dying.

This can be understood by stating the opposite. Understand that remembrance somehow or other of the beloved gives life. For that reason (yataḥ), forgetting those who are dearer than life is always more detestable than death since that condition produces suffering worse than death. Or death is preferable to forgetting them, since that is most subject to condemnation.

TEXT 130

na sambhaved asmaraṇaṁ kadāpi
sva-jīvanānāṁ yad api priyāṇām
tathāpi kenāpi viśeṣaṇena
smṛtiḥ praharṣāya yathā su-jīvitam

One can never forget those dear as life, but when reminded of them in a special way one feels happy, like one who has lived a life of good fortune.

"Since they do not forget at any time their lover, who would be the benefactor of persons who always remember, to make them remember?" Such assistance could take place because the person could invoke memories which were especially attractive. Just as people never forget their own life (sva-jīvanānām), they do not forget the dear ones. Even though loss of memory of dear ones never takes place, memory with particulars gives the highest happiness, just as life becomes happy by a continual variety of festivities. It is also hinted that, just as life by itself, devoid of the happiness of festivals, does not give happiness, but rather gives the greatest lamentation by suffering from poverty[19], etc., so without prema, remembrance of dear ones does not give happiness.

TEXT 131

ity evam upakāro 'dya
bhavatākāri me mahān
tat te 'smi parama-prīto
nijābhīṣṭān varān vṛṇu

So today you have favored me greatly, and therefore I am delighted with you. Please choose whatever benedictions you would like.

Today you have made me remember the gopīs, by the most excellent means. You have rendered the best benefit to me. You have benefited me in the manner stated. Therefore I am most pleased with you (te).

TEXT 132

śrī-parīkṣid uvāca
munir jaya-jayodghoṣaiḥ
sa-vīṇā-gītam aiḍata
vraja-krīḍottha-nāmāḍhyaiḥ
kīrtanaiś ca vara-pradam

Parīkṣit said: The sage began singing Kṛṣṇa's glories. Playing on his vīṇā and shouting "Jaya! Jaya!" he praised Lord Kṛṣṇa, the giver of benedictions, with songs filled with names arising from his pastimes in Vraja.

Nārada first praised the Lord in order to attain the highest benediction, dear to him, and most rare. Loudly shouting "Jaya jaya!" while chanting along with tunes on his vīṇā, using names which arose from the pastimes of the Lord in Vraja, he praised (aiḍata) the Lord, who gives benedictions excellently (vara-pradam). He chanted names like Gokula-mahotsava, Yaśodā-nandana, Nanda-kumāra, Gopa-gopījana-priya, Gopi-gaṇa-mahohara, Pūtanā-mocana, etc.

TEXTS 133–134

svayaṁ prayāgasya daśāśvamedha-
tīrthādike dvāravatī-parānte

---

[19] Poverty, sickness and death of family create suffering and lamentation.

sambhāṣitānāṁ viṣaye bhramitvā
pūrṇārthatāṁ śrīmad-anugraheṇa

viprādīnāṁ śrotu-kāmo munīndro
harṣāt kṛṣṇasyānanād eva sākṣāt
evaṁ mātaḥ prārthayām āsa hṛdyaṁ
tasmin ramyodāra-siṁhe varaṁ prāk

From Daśāśvamedha-tīrtha in Prayāga to Dvārakā, Nārada had wandered. And he had spoken with devotees — the brāhmaṇa at Prayāga and all the others — who by the Lord's divine grace had each achieved perfection. Feeling great pleasure, Nārada, the king of sages, now wanted to hear of this perfection directly from Lord Kṛṣṇa's own mouth. O mother, Lord Kṛṣṇa is the all-attractive lion among generous benefactors. Now, therefore, Nārada begged from him the first blessing he wished to receive.

In two verses is explained the reason for Nārada's request that devotees should be unsatisfied with the Lord's mercy. Nārada wandered in places starting with Daśāśvamedha-tīrtha in Prayāga up to Dvārakā, talking to the brāhmaṇa and others. Nārada first saw a brāhmaṇa engaged in worshipping the Lord and who had come to feed brāhmaṇas. He talked to others as well (viprādīnām), starting with the King of the southern states, and ending with Uddhava. These devotees had attained all objects (pūrnārthatām)—dharma, artha, kāma, mokṣa and worship of the Lord, by the mercy of the shining Lord or he who possesses all śrī—Bhagavān, or Kṛṣṇa (śrīmat), who was standing there.

Though he already knew, because of joy, he desired to hear from the mouth of Kṛṣṇa directly first a benediction, which will be described. O mother! He prayed to Kṛṣṇa, the best (siṁhe) among generous (udara) and excellent persons (ramya). The benediction was dear to him or existed in his heart for a long time (hṛdyam).

TEXT 135

śrī-kṛṣṇa-candra kasyāpi
tṛptir astu kadāpi na
bhavato 'nugrahe bhaktau
premṇi cānanda-bhājane

[Nārada said:] Kṛṣṇacandra, please grant that no one will ever feel he has enough of your mercy, your bhakti, or prema for you, the reservoir of ecstasy.

May no person ever be satisfied with the Lord's mercy. That was Nārada's request. You may give the highest levels of mercy, but the devotee should not think, "I have attained full mercy." Even though from mercy bhakti arises, and from bhakti prema arises, they do not occur completely at once. There will be some mercy to some person. There will arise some bhakti in some person. (Similarly with prema). That is why they are mentioned separately. Why should he not be satisfied? The mercy (anugraha), bhakti and prema are shelters of bliss (ānānda-bhājane). Atmārāmās, those fixed in monistic jñāna, are satisfied with the insignificant happiness of realizing their svarūpa. But devotees are not satisfied at all with the Lord's mercy, bhakti and prema. Otherwise the realization of special bliss in these items would not be perfect.

TEXT 136

śrī-bhagavān uvāca
vidagdha-nikarācārya
ko nāmāyaṁ varo mataḥ
svabhāvo mat-kṛpā-bhakti-
premṇāṁ vyakto 'yam eva yat

The Supreme Lord said: O preceptor of all clever scholars, what kind of benediction is this? My mercy, my bhakti, and prema for me all have this nature. That should be simply obvious.

O guru of all clever people! This must be a joke. Otherwise, the benediction is meaningless, since the very nature of these items is dissatisfaction. Or, you know all this, and directly experiences all this now. You ask for this benediction out of cleverness, actually with some hidden intention. Though the intention was already indicated, he desired to hear directly from Kṛṣṇa's mouth. This is the obvious or famous (vyaktaḥ) nature of mercy (kṛpa), bhakti and prema.

TEXTS 137–138

prayāga-tīrtham ārabhya
bhrāmaṁ bhrāmam itas tataḥ
atrāgatya ca ye dṛṣṭāḥ
śrutāś ca bhavatā mune

sarve samāpta-sarvārthā
jagan-nistārakāś ca te

mat-kṛpā-viṣayāḥ kiñcit
tāratamyaṁ śritāḥ param

O sage, each of the devotees you saw and heard about in your wanderings here and there, from Prayāga-tīrtha to Dvārakā, is perfect in all respects. Each of them can deliver the entire world, and each has truly received my mercy. There exist between them only degrees of perfection.

You have realized all this now. You wandered here and there inside and outside the universe and came here to Dvārakā (atra). You saw some of these persons and heard about others—the inhabitants of Vaikuṇṭha and Vraja. All of those persons deliver the world. They are capable of giving others all objects as well as attaining everything themselves (samapta-sarvārthāḥ), since they are the objects of my mercy.

"If that is so, they would all be one in form. But I have seen many types of devotees." That is true. That is because of the nature of bhakti. They, more or less (tāratamyam), take shelter of only (param) a small amount (kīñcit) bhāva. The previous persons are lesser and the later ones are superior. The supreme devotees are Rādhā and her group. Though there are degrees of devotion, all the devotees have attained perfection with the highest wealth of happiness in their individual varieties of rasa. This will be explained later in the glorification of Goloka.

TEXT 139

tathāpi teṣām eko 'pi
na tṛpyati kathañcana
tad gṛhāṇa varān anyān
matto 'bhīṣṭa-tarān varān

Yet none of these devotees is ever satisfied. Please, therefore, ask from me some other, more satisfying benedictions.

None of these persons, though along with their followers have attained my great mercy, are satisfied, since they all feel that they are not fortunate, placing themselves in low positions. Therefore please accept from me the best benedictions, objects worthy of giving, and also what are dear to you.

TEXT 140

śrī-parīkṣid uvāca
nartitvā nārado harṣād
bhaikṣya-vat sad-vara-dvayam
yācamāno jagādedaṁ
taṁ vadānya-śiromaṇim

Parīkṣit said: Nārada danced in sheer joy. And like a mendicant asking alms, he begged from Kṛṣṇa two excellent boons. Speaking to the Lord, the crest jewel of charitable persons, this is what Nārada said.

Nārada danced in joy because he heard from the Lord's mouth that the brāhmaṇa and all others were not satisfied with the Lord's mercy by their natures as devotees or that they had attained everything. He danced for a few moments. Like a beggar asking for food, extending his cloth or folding his hands, he asked for two excellent (sat) benedictions. Or he asked just as a beggar asks with insistence for food for maintaining his life. Asking for two excellent benedictions, he first spoke to the Lord. He praised the Lord to the highest degree to attain these benedictions.

TEXT 141

śrī-nārada uvāca
sva-dānātṛpta vṛtto 'ham
idānīṁ sa-phala-śramaḥ
tvan-mahā-karuṇā-pātra-
jana-vijñānam āptavān

Nārada said: O Lord never satisfied with your own charity, I have now achieved my goal. My labors have borne fruit, for I now understand in a practical way who the objects of your greatest mercy are.

O Lord who is unsatisfied with whatever he gives! My labors – studying or wandering to Prayāga and other places—having been successful, my task is complete (vṛttaḥ), because I have attained understanding of who are the recipients of your great mercy. I have directly realized now that the gopīs are the greatest recipients of your mercy.

TEXT 142

ayam eva varaḥ prāpto
'nugrahaś cottamo mataḥ
yāce tathāpy udārendra
hārdaṁ kiñcic cirantanam

This is the only benediction I need obtain, and for me it is the greatest mercy. But still, O king among those who give charity, I have one long-cherished desire.

I have attained a benediction of getting knowledge about the devotees' mercy. I consider this to be the best mercy you give. Though that is so, I ask for something I have long desired, since you are the king of benedictors. If you do not give, you would be dissatisfied. Or this has been in my heart as something I have desired for a long time. "That is most rare to attain." You are the best of the generous. There is nothing you will not give.

TEXT 143

pāyaṁ pāyaṁ vraja-jana-gaṇa-prema-vāpī-marāla
śrīman-nāmāmṛtam aviratam gokulābdhy-utthitaṁ te
tat-tad-veśācarita-nikarojjṛmbhitaṁ miṣṭa-miṣṭaṁ
sarvāl lokān jagati ramayan matta-ceṣṭo bhramāṇi

O swan gliding in the lakes of the Vraja-vāsīs' prema, I wish that I may wander everywhere always chanting, drinking the nectar of your names. Those most sweet names arise from the ocean of Gokula and spread the glories of your infinitely varied dress and ways of acting. As I wander, behaving like a madman, may I distribute joy to everyone in all the worlds.

Having praised the Lord, he makes his request in two verses (143-144). O swan in the lakes of prema of the people of Vraja! You are like a swan, always playing happily. Constantly drinking (pāyam pāyam) the nectar of your names endowed with your beauty (śrīmat), which have manifested from the milk ocean of Gokula, giving joy (ramayan) to all people by spreading the rasa of your kīrtana, having activities like those of madmen such as dancing, laughing and weeping all at the same time because of constant prema, or forgetting my body and all related activities (matta-ceṣṭaḥ), may I wander everythere in the universe. He expresses his desire for a benediction using the imperative form of the verb (bhramāṇi).

Those names are sweeter than the sweet names of Viṣṇu, Nārāyaṇa, Narasiṁha, Rāmacandra, Mathurā-nātha, Yādavendra, since those names reveal (ujjṛmbhitam) a divine treasure (nikara) of most indescribable (tat tat) ornaments (veśa) and activities (ācarita). The ornaments are his peacock feather crown, his guñja earrings and kadamba ornaments. His activities are killing Pūtanā, breaking the cart, etc. The sweet names are Nanda-nandana, Yāśodā-vatsala, Gopikā-manohara, Vraja-janānanda, etc.

TEXT 144

tvadīyās tāḥ krīḍāḥ sakṛd api bhuvo vāpi vacasā
hṛdā śrutyāṅgair vā spṛśati kṛta-dhīḥ kaścid api yaḥ
sa nityaṁ śrī-gopī-kuca-kalasa-kāśmīra-vilasat-
tvadīyāṅghri-dvandve kalayatu-tarāṁ prema-bhajanam

Whether by words, mind, ear or limbs, if any person in this world comes in touch even once with these pastimes of yours and is convinced of their importance, may he be endowed eternally with the power to worship your feet in pure love, feet resplendent with the saffron dust from the pitcherlike breasts of the blessed gopīs.

May the person who contacts even once (sakṛt) the pastimes related to Vraja (tāḥ krīḍāḥ) or the places in Vraja such as Vṛndāvana, be endowed with prema. Just by contacting the land of Vraja, spontaneously the pastimes and kīrtana become manifest, since the nature of those places is to give remembrance of Kṛṣṇa.

saric-chaila-vanoddeśā gāvo veṇu-ravā ime
saṅkarṣaṇa-sahāyena kṛṣṇenācaritāḥ prabho

Dear Uddhava, when Kṛṣṇa was here in the company of Balarāma, he served all these rivers, hills, forests, cows and flute sounds. SB 10.47.49

One can contact the pastimes by listening even with only one ear (śrutyā). By this contact the person develops faith, or has a convinced mind (kṛta-dhīḥ). Anyone who contacts develops this faith. It is not depend on caste or other considerations.

One can contact the pastimes by the limbs (aṅgaiḥ). This means touching the Bhāgavatam which reveals those pastimes. One can contact the pastimes and places by words. That means glorifying the pastimes and places. One can also use the limbs to touch the dust of Vraja.

May that person who contacts the pastimes or places and develops faith attain (kalayatu) bhakti in the form of prema (prema-bhajanam) every day or permanently (nityam), completely (tarām), at your two lotus feet (vilasat) shining with kuṁkuma (kāśmīra) from the pot-like breasts of Rādhā and other gopīs. This is his second request.

TEXT 145

śrī-parīkṣid uvāca
tataḥ śrī-hasta-kamalaṁ
prasārya paramādarāt
evam astv iti sānandaṁ
gopī-nāthena bhāṣitam

Parīkṣit said: Lord Gopīnātha then extended his divine lotus hand and with great respect for Nārada blissfully said, "So be it."

Kṛṣṇa extended his right hand since he was giving him a blessing. Spreading his hand indicates that the Lord directly fulfilled the two benedictions according to what Nārada had requested. Kṛṣṇa is the master of the gopīs (gopī-nāthena). The use of this name indicates that he was pleased with giving these two benedictions (since they involved realizing the love of his dear gopīs.) Thus he spoke with bliss.

TEXT 146

tato mahā-parānandā-
rṇave magno munir bhṛśam
gāyan nṛtyan bahu-vidhaṁ
kṛṣṇaṁ cakre su-nirvṛtam

The sage was suddenly plunged into a vast ocean of supreme bliss. He sang and danced in various ways, thus delighting Lord Kṛṣṇa.

Because of Kṛṣṇa's words (tataḥ), he sang and danced. He gave the greatest happiness to Kṛṣṇa, even though he by nature is full of the highest bliss. This shows the greatness of Nārada's bhakti and kīrtana.

TEXT 147

bubhuje bhagavadbhyāṁ sa
paramānnaṁ sa-pānakam
devakī-rohiṇī-dṛṣṭaṁ
rukmiṇyā pariveṣitam

Nārada then partook of excellent food and drink with the two Lords, as Devakī and Rohiṇī supervised and Rukmiṇī served.

With Kṛṣṇa and Balarāma, Nārada ate excellent food such as sweet rice accompanied by various drinks, inspected by Devakī and Rohiṇī, and then served by the best of the queens, Rukmiṇī, in proper order, putting a little of each item on his plate.

TEXT 148

uddhavena smāryamāṇaṁ
vījitaṁ satyabhāmayā
anyābhir mahiṣībhiś ca
rañjitaṁ tat-tad-īhayā

Uddhava suggested to Nārada what was best to eat, Satyabhāmā fanned him, and the other queens pleased him with various kinds of service.

Uddhava said, "Don't eat this. This is dear to you. Eat this. Eat this." In this way Nārada was made to remember what to eat (smāryamāṇam). He was fanned by Satyabhāmā, the dearest queen, to dispel the heat. He was made the object of affection (rañjitam) by others such as Jāmbavatī, who performed actions necessary during eating (īhayā) such as offering cups filled with cool water, praising the various foods, fanning all the limbs and offering aguru incense.

TEXT 149

ācānto lepito gandhair
mālābhir maṇḍito muniḥ
alaṅkārair bahu-vidhair
arcitaś ca murāriṇā

After the sage finished eating and washed his mouth, Lord Kṛṣṇa worshiped him, anointing him with fragrant oils and adorning him with flower garlands and varied ornaments. He performed ācamana and was respected with various ornaments by Kṛṣṇa.

TEXT 150

atha prayāge gatvā tān
mad-apekṣā-vilambitān
munīn kṛtārthayānīti
samanujñāpya mādhavam

Nārada then took leave of Mādhava, Lord Kṛṣṇa, and went to Prayāga, thinking, "Let me bestow perfection on the sages who have waited so long for me to return."

After that (atha) the best of sages Nārada, taking permission to leave from the Lord, the moon in the ocean of the Madhu dynasty (mādhavam), went to Prayāga (yayau in next verse). Why did he go? Going to the sages who bathed early in the morning in the river during Māgha month and who were waiting a long time for him, he should fulfil their desires (kṛtārthayāni). He took permission, since without the order of the Lord it would be improper to cause the same bewilderment in them by revealing the confidential topics.

The sages had taken shelter of Kṛṣṇa, since they served Prayāga, whose presiding deity is Mādhava.

TEXT 151

svayaṁ yad-bhakti-māhātmyam
anubhūtam itas tataḥ
sānandaṁ vīṇayā gāyan
sa yayau bhakti-lampaṭaḥ

Thus Nārada started on his journey to Prayāga, intoxicated with eagerness for bhakti. Wherever he passed he vibrated his vīṇā and blissfully sang the glories of the kṛṣṇa-bhakti he had seen with his own eyes.

What did he do? He sang what he had experienced in going from Prayāga to Dvārakā (itas tataḥ) since he was a rasika of bhakti to the Lord (bhakti-lampaṭaḥ).

TEXT 152

te 'pi tan-mukhataḥ sarvaṁ
śrutvā tat tan mahādbhutam
sāra-saṅgrāhiṇo 'śeṣam
anyat sadyo jahur dṛḍham

When the sages at Prayāga heard the whole wonderful account from the mouth of Nārada, they once and for all gave up all interest in everything other than Kṛṣṇa's service, for they were able to grasp the essence of what is of value.

The sages (te), hearing everything that Nārada had experienced from his mouth, immediately gave up everything else—jñāna, karma, etc. since they were able to completely grasp the truth or best portion (sāra-saṁgrāhinaḥ).

TEXT 153

kevalaṁ paramaṁ dainyam
avalambyāsya śikṣayā
śrīman-madana-gopāla-
caraṇābjam upāsata

Entering a mood of great and single-minded humility, they began worshiping the lotus feet of Madana-gopāla according to Nārada's instructions.

"By giving up everything insubstantial, what is accepted as the essence?" By the instructions of Nārada, they worshipped the lotus feet of the Lord with humility—understanding they were unsuccessful, they thought themselves devoid of bhakti for the Lord. By this attitude the Lord gives his great mercy.

TEXTS 154–155

mātar gopa-kiśoraṁ taṁ
tvaṁ ca rāsa-rasāmbudhim
tat-prema-mohitābhiḥ śrī-
gopībhir abhito vṛtam

amūṣāṁ dāsyam icchantī
tādṛśa-prema-bhaṅgibhiḥ
nityaṁ bhajasva tan-nāma-
saṅkīrtana-parāyaṇā

O mother, you as well should always worship. Desiring to be a servant of these gopīs, dedicating yourself to the saṅkīrtana of his names, you should constantly worship in prema as the gopīs did this young cowherd boy, an ocean that yields the nectar of the rāsa dance, in which divine gopīs fully surround him, entranced by prema.

Having concluded the story, he teaches his mother. O mother! You should worship the cowherd boy whose glories were described (tat) with successions or methods of prema (prema-bhaṅgibhiḥ) similar to that the gopīs (tādṛśa). Kṛṣṇa is a steady continuous shelter (abdhim) of pastimes (rasa) in the rāsa dance (rāsa) or is the shelter of attraction (rasa) to the rāsa dance or is the shelter of the highest bliss (rasa) of the rāsa dance. He is surrounded by a circle of gopīs who are bewildered with prema for Kṛṣṇa in the rāsa dance.

"Since I am the wife of Kṛṣṇa's nephew, it is contrary for me to worship him in the mood of the gopīs." You should desire to be the servant of the gopīs. What is the main quality of the worship? You should be absorbed in kīrtana, loud singing of the names of Kṛṣṇa, or simply the famous name Kṛṣṇa. That is the characteristic of worship in prema and the characteristic of the wealth of prema.

TEXT 156

gopīnāṁ mahimā kaścit
tāsām eko 'pi śakyate
na mayā sva-mukhe kartuṁ
merur makṣikayā yathā

I cannot describe with my own words even one of the glories of the gopīs, any more than a fly can swallow Mount Meru.

You should widely glorify the gopīs. It is impossible for me to pronounce with my mouth even one glory of the gopīs whose greatness has been described (tāsām) since I am unqualified. An example is given. A fly cannot swallow in its mouth the best of mountains, Meru.

TEXT 157

aho kṛṣṇa-rasāviṣṭaḥ
sadā nāmāni kīrtayet
kṛṣṇasya tat-priyāṇāṁ ca
bhaiṣmy-ādīnāṁ gurur mama

Oh, but my guru is fully absorbed in the loving moods of serving Kṛṣṇa. He can constantly glorify Kṛṣṇa's names and those of Rukmiṇī and Kṛṣṇa's other beloved devotees.

What to speak of glorifying the gopīs, I am unable to even chanting their names properly. He fears that he will lose control by the prema that manifests, and this will stop his kīrtana which is the cause of his very life. This is expressed in two verses (157-158).

Śukadeva, my guru at all times, is able to chant the names of Kṛṣṇa and his dear devotees like Rukmiṇī since he is overcome (āviṣṭaḥ) with attraction to Kṛṣṇa (kṛṣṇa-rasa) or is overcome with the highest bliss related to Kṛṣṇa's form.

TEXT 158

gopīnāṁ vitatādbhuta-sphuṭatara-premānalārciś-chaṭā-
dagdhānāṁ kila nāma-kīrtana-kṛtāt tāsāṁ viśeṣāt smṛteḥ

tat-tīkṣṇa-jvalanocchikhāgra-kaṇikā-sparśena sadyo mahā-
vaikalyaṁ sa bhajan kadāpi na mukhe nāmāni kartuṁ prabhuḥ

The gopīs were consumed by the expansive flames of the wondrous blazing fire of prema for Kṛṣṇa. If my guru chants the names of these gopīs and recalls a gopī's distinguishing qualities, he too is touched by sparks shooting forth from the flames of this intense fire, and he at once becomes greatly agitated. Therefore he had to avoid pronouncing the gopīs' names.

He cannot chant the names of the gopīs like Rādhā and Candrāvalī. Why? From chanting the names of the gopīs who are burnt by the spreading flames from the fire of most astonishing and full manifested (spuṭatara) prema (whose nature is to reveal everything and burn as well) because of intense remembrance of the gopīs or remembrance in detail about the gopīs, he immediately develops great agitation by the touch of the sparks from the tips of the intense high flames. For this reason Śukadeva does not mention specific names of the gopīs in Bhāgavatam.

duhantyo 'bhiyayuḥ kāścid dohaṁ hitvā samutsukāḥ
payo 'dhiśritya saṁyāvam anudvāsyāparā yayuḥ

Some of the gopīs were milking cows when they heard Kṛṣṇa's flute. They stopped milking and went off to meet him. Some left milk curdling on the stove, and others left cakes burning in the oven. SB 10.29.5

kasyācit pūtanāyantyāḥ kṛṣṇāyanty apibat stanam
tokayitvā rudaty anyā padāhan śakaṭāyatīm

One gopī imitated Pūtanā, while another acted like infant Kṛṣṇa and pretended to suck her breast. Another gopī, crying in imitation of infant Kṛṣṇa, kicked a gopī who was taking the role of the cart demon, Śakaṭāsura. SB 10.30.15

tais taiḥ padais tat-padavīm anvicchantyo 'grato'balāḥ
vadhvāḥ padaiḥ su-pṛktāni vilokyārtāḥ samabruvan

The gopīs began following Kṛṣṇa's path, as shown by his many footprints, but when they saw that these prints were thoroughly intermixed with those of his dearest consort, they became perturbed and spoke as follows. SB 10.30.26

ity evaṁ darśayantyas tāś cerur gopyo vicetasaḥ
yāṁ gopīm anayat kṛṣṇo vihāyānyāḥ striyo vane
sā ca mene tadātmānaṁ variṣṭhaṁ sarva-yoṣitām
hitvā gopīḥ kāma-yānā mām asau bhajate priyaḥ

As the gopīs wandered about, their minds completely bewildered, they pointed out various signs of Kṛṣṇa's pastimes. The particular gopī whom Kṛṣṇa had led into a secluded forest when he had abandoned all the other young girls began to think herself the best of women. She thought, "My beloved has rejected all the other gopīs, even though they are driven by Cupid himself. He has chosen to reciprocate with me alone. SB 10.30.35-36

kācit karāmbujaṁ śaurer jagṛhe 'ñjalinā mudā

kācid dadhāra tad-bāhum aṁse candana-bhūṣitam

One gopī joyfully took Kṛṣṇa's hand between her folded palms, and another placed his arm, anointed with sandalwood paste, on her shoulder. SB 10.32.4

kācit samaṁ mukundena svara-jātīr amiśritāḥ
unninye pūjitā tena prīyatā sādhu sādhv iti
tad eva dhruvam unninye tasyai mānaṁ ca bahv adāt

One gopī, joining Mukunda in his singing, sang pure melodious tones that rose harmoniously above his voice. Kṛṣṇa was pleased and showed great appreciation for her performance, saying "Excellent! Excellent!" When another gopī sang in the dhruva style, Kṛṣṇa praised her even more. SB 10.33.9

kāścit tat-kṛta-hṛt-tāpa śvāsa-mlāna-mukha-śriyaḥ
sraṁsad-dukūla-valaya keśa-granthyaś ca kāścana

Some gopīs felt so pained at heart that their faces turned pale from their heavy breathing. Others were so anguished that their dresses, bracelets and braids became loose. SB 10.39.14

kācin madhukaraṁ dṛṣṭvā dhyāyantī kṛṣṇa-saṅgamam
priya-prasthāpitaṁ dūtaṁ kalpayitvedam abravīt

One of the gopīs, while meditating on her previous association with Kṛṣṇa, saw a honeybee before her and imagined it to be a messenger sent by her beloved. Thus she spoke as follows. SB 10.47.11

One should not think that he did not mention the gopīs' names simply out of great respect since the verse gives the reason: Śukadeva became overcome with attraction for Kṛṣṇa and lost control (mahā-vaiklavyam).

TEXT 159

tāsāṁ nāthaṁ ballavīnāṁ sametaṁ
tābhiḥ premṇā saṁśrayantī yathoktam
mātaḥ satyaṁ tat-prasādān mahattvaṁ
tāsāṁ jñātuṁ śakṣyasi tvaṁ ca kiñcit

If you follow my advice and with prema take shelter of the gopīs and their master, Lord Kṛṣṇa, then, O mother, I promise that by Kṛṣṇa's mercy you will be able to understand something of the gopīs' greatness.

"Without knowledge of the gopīs' greatness, how will I be able to worship in prema like them, with a desire to be their servant?"

You should take shelter of Kṛṣṇa, following the scriptures describing Kṛṣṇa worship, not going beyond that (yathoktam), or following what I said (verses 154-155). Take shelter of, serving with prema, the master of the gopīs who gathered with the gopīs in the rāsa dance. By the mercy of Kṛṣṇa and the gopīs even you will be able to know a little of the glories of the gopīs or the indescribable glories of the gopīs.

It is impossible to describe everything with the mouth. It is impossible for you to grasp everything described. You should understand something of this in your mind through the actions of worship described. Then the complete worship will be achieved. And then the details will be understood. And then prema-bhakti will be achieved. The cause and effect relationship between knowledge of the worship of the Lord and the glories of the gopīs has been shown.

Though it is said everywhere that from knowledge of the great glories of the Lord and his devotee prema-bhakti arises, where there is knowledge of the greatness of the gopīs, the chief of all devotees, the special greatness of bhakti and the Lord will be completely known.

TEXT 160

etan mahākhyāna-varaṁ mahā-hareḥ
kāruṇya-sārālaya-niścayārthakam
yaḥ śraddhayā saṁśrayate kathañcana
prāpnoti tat-prema tathaiva so 'py aram

With the help of this most excellent narration about the Supreme Lord, which shows who has received the essence of the Lord's mercy, one can understand him for certain. Anyone who for any reason takes shelter, with faith, of this narration will quickly attain prema for Lord Kṛṣṇa.

What to speak of attaining prema for the Lord with a wealth of special worship, from knowing the special glories of the gopīs, by taking shelter as described, even by hearing this scripture which explains it, one can attain a similar type (tathā) of prema.

Even if one nicely with faith serves this great excellent story whose goal (arthakam) is to determine (niścaya) the greatest (sāra) recipient (ālaya) of Kṛṣṇa's mercy (mahā-hareḥ karuṇya), by hearing and chanting, what to speak of the person who shares this work with others, he attains prema for Kṛṣṇa quickly (aram).

May kṛṣṇa-bhakti be pleased with me, who am similar to a stone, trembling with dancing ink.

Thus ends the seventh chapter of Canto One of Śrīla Sanātana Gosvāmī's Bṛhad-bhāgavatāmṛta, entitled "Pūrṇa: The Complete Perfection."

Thus ends Canto One.

ABOUT THE AUTHOR-TRANSLATOR

His Holiness Bhanu Swami maharaja was born in Canada on the 26th December 1948 to the most fortunate Japanese parents. HH Bhanu Swami Maharaja is one of the senior disciples of His Divine Grace A.C Bhaktivedanta Swami Srila Prabhupada, founder acharya of ISKCON, the International Society for Krishna Consciousness. He holds a BA Degree in Oriental fine arts history from the University of British Colombia. He joined the Hare Krishna movement in India in 1970. Initiated in 1971 by Srila Prabhupada, he took sannyasa vows in 1984. Bhanu Swami was personally instructed in the art of Deity worship by Srila Prabhupada, and within ISKCON he has become an authority on the topic. He is a great inspiration for many devotees around the world and he preaches Krishna consciousness in Australia, Japan, Malaysia, Russia and India.

HH Bhanu Swami Maharaja met the disciples of His Divine Grace A.C. Bhaktivedanta Swami Srila Prabhupada in 1971 in Tokyo, just after his graduation in history. Srila Prabhupada was about to set on his India tour with his Western disciples and Bhanu Maharaja joined with them.

By 1972, His Holiness Bhanu Swami maharaja already earned credit from Srila Prabhupada for his exact Sanskrit pronunciation, expertise in cooking and excellence in deity worship. He also began to translate Srila Prabhupada's books into Japanese.

He continues with this translation service to this day, giving us the nectar from the Bengali and Sanskrit works of the previous Vaishnava acharyas to enhance our understanding of the Gaudiya Vaishnava philosophy. He is also a member of the Governing Body Commission of ISKCON.

His other works are listed here - https://www.amazon.com/author/hhbhanuswami

Made in the USA
Coppell, TX
06 September 2023